Volume 2: International

International Film Stars
Series Editor: Homer B. Pettey and R. Barton Palmer

This series is devoted to the artistic and commercial influence of performers who shaped major genres and movements in international film history. Books in the series will:

- Reveal performative features that defined signature cinematic styles
- Demonstrate how the global market relied upon performers' generic contributions
- Analyse specific film productions as case studies that transformed cinema acting
- Construct models for redefining international star studies that emphasise materialist approaches
- Provide accounts of stars' influences in the international cinema marketplace

Titles available:

Close-Up: Great Cinematic Performances Volume 1: America
edited by Murray Pomerance and Kyle Stevens

Close-Up: Great Cinematic Performances Volume 2: International
edited by Murray Pomerance and Kyle Stevens

www.euppublishing.com/series/ifs

Close-Up

Great Cinematic Performances

Volume 2: International

Edited by Murray Pomerance and Kyle Stevens

EDINBURGH
University Press

Edinburgh University Press is one of the leading university presses in the UK. We publish academic books and journals in our selected subject areas across the humanities and social sciences, combining cutting-edge scholarship with high editorial and production values to produce academic works of lasting importance. For more information visit our website: edinburghuniversitypress.com

Edinburgh University Press Ltd
The Tun—Holyrood Road
12 (2f) Jackson's Entry
Edinburgh EH8 8PJ

First published in hardback by Edinburgh University Press 2018

Typeset in 12/14 Arno and Myriad by
IDSUK (Dataconnection) Ltd,
and printed and bound by CPI Group (UK) Ltd, Croydon, CR0 4YY

A CIP record for this book is available from the British Library

ISBN 978 1 4744 1703 7 (hardback)
ISBN 978 1 4744 3180 4 (paperback)
ISBN 978 1 4744 1704 4 (webready PDF)
ISBN 978 1 4744 1705 1 (epub)

Images (all digital frame enlargements)
Viktor Sjöström in *Wild Strawberries [Smultronstället]* (Ingmar Bergman, Svensk Filmindustri, 1957)
Emil Jannings in *Blonde Venus* (Josef von Sternberg, Paramount, 1932)
Charles Laughton in *Hobson's Choice* (David Lean, London Film Productions/British Lion, 1954)
Nikolai Cherkasov in *Ivan the Terrible* (Sergei Eisenstein, Mosfilm, 1945, 1946)
Peter Lorre in *M* (Fritz Lang, Nero-Film AG, 1931)
Anna Magnani in *The Golden Coach [Le carrosse d'or]* (Jean Renoir, Delphinus/Hoche, 1952)
Alec Guinness in *Last Holiday* (Henry Cass, Associated British Picture Corporation, 1950)
Ingrid Bergman in *Stromboli* (Roberto Rossellini, Berit/RKO, 1950)
Toshirô Mifune in *Throne of Blood [Kumonosu-jô]* (Akira Kurosawa, Toho, 1957)
Setsuko Hara in *Tokyo Story [Tôkyô monogatari]* (Yasujirô Ozu, Shôchiku Eiga, 1953)
Marcello Mastroianni in *8½* (Federico Fellini, Cineriz, 1963)
Jeanne Moreau in *The Bride Wore Black [La mariée était en noir]* (François Truffaut, Les Films du Carrosse/Les Productions Artistes Associés/Dino de Laurentiis Cinematografica, 1968)
Michel Serrault in *La cage aux folles* (Édouard Molinaro, Da Ma Produzione/Les Productions Artistes Associés, 1978)
Madhubala in *Mughal-e-Azam [The Emperor of the Mughals]* (K. Asif, Sterling Investment Corp., 1960)
Michael Caine in *Alfie* (Lewis Gilbert, Lewis Gilbert/Seldrake Films, 1966)
Amitabh Bachchan in *Deewaar [The Wall]* (Yash Chopra, Trimurti Films Pvt. Ltd., 1975)
Catherine Deneuve in *The Umbrellas of Cherbourg [Les parapluies de Cherbourg]* (Jacques Demy, Parc Film/Madeleine Films, 1964)
Jean-Pierre Léaud in *Stolen Kisses [Baisers volés]* (François Truffaut, Les Films du Carrosse/Les Productions Artistes Associés, 1968)
Isabelle Huppert in *The Piano Teacher [La pianiste]* (Michael Haneke, Arte France Cinéma, 2001)
Emma Thompson in *The Remains of the Day* (James Ivory, Columbia/Merchant Ivory, 1993)
Tilda Swinton in *I Am Love [Io sono l'amore]* (Luca Guadagnino, First Sun/Mikado, 2009)
Denis Lavant in *Holy Motors* (Leos Carax, Pierre Grise Productions/Théo Films, 2012)
Choi Min-sik in *Oldboy [Oldeuboi]* (Chan-wook Park, Egg Films/Show East, 2003)
Maggie Cheung in *In the Mood for Love [Faa yeung nin wa]* (Kar-Wai Wong, Block 2 Pictures, 2000)
Omotola Jalade-Ekeinde in *Mortal Inheritance* (Andy Amenechi, Silverscreen Studios, 1996)
Gael García Bernal in *The Motorcycle Diaries [Diarios de motocicleta]* (Walter Salles, FilmFour/Wildwood, 2004)

Contents

Acknowledgments

We wish to express gratitude to our friends and collaborators at Edinburgh University Press—Eddie Clark, Gillian Leslie, Rebecca Mackenzie, Emma Rees, and Richard Strachan—as well as to Barton Palmer and Homer Pettey for welcoming this volume into their series, "International Film Stars"; also to Sarah Burnett for copy-editing and Steve Flemming for cover design.

Further assistance along the way has come from Matt Bell, Başak Candar, Alex Clayton, Nick Davis, Mark Kermode, Chris Meade, David Orvis, Bob Rubin, Dan Sacco, Jonathan Soja, Rick Warner, and Evan Williams.

Our families have sheltered us in the storms of production, such as any endeavor involving the art of performance inevitably endures. We dedicate these volumes to James Pearson, Nellie Perret, and Ariel Pomerance.

True realism consists in revealing the surprising things which habit keeps covered and prevents us from seeing.

(Jean Cocteau)

The audience have no interest in what you might be feeling. You're supposed to give the appearance of feeling something, like you did when you were a kid.

(Bill Nighy)

Close-up: great international performances

Kyle Stevens and Murray Pomerance

Humans are storytelling creatures, and as, in the last century, the dominant medium for public narratives shifted from theater to cinema, cinema placed the fruits of performative labor before the eyes of the world in an unprecedented way. What actors do in front of the camera remains central to the attraction of cinema for audiences, and influences—even marks the standard for—performance styles in other audiovisual media. Indeed, one could go further: many of the figures discussed in the pages that follow became cultural and mythical icons in the global consciousness of their time. Audiences care about actors, the characters they create, and the responses they engender. Performances are even the reason some films are preserved. But beyond vague assertions about which performances are ineffably great, profoundly moving, hopelessly terrible, or cringe-worthy, relatively little discussion of what actors *really do* exists, either in popular or academic film criticism. Movements within the discipline of Film Studies (semiotics, psychoanalysis, cognitive psychology, and so forth) tend to look first to the sciences, and thus outside films themselves, for legitimate—meaning objective—means of verifying claims about movies.

This poses a problem for the analysis of performance, as we respond to and love the displays of feelings, desires, and intentions at a personal level, if also collectively. We might thus wish to grapple with questions of what makes a performance meaningful, how we can share this sense, and, in sharing, possibly come to agreement. How do we journey experientially and thoughtfully from the obvious to the ineffable, from a jitter to a movement to a gesture? Or from the perception of a seemingly ordinary gesture to the more meaningful revelation of the significance that such gestures are ordinary? Why does this often feel like an epiphany? How many others experience it as significant in the same way? Why do we feel such a distinctive fellowship when another person responds to a performance just as we do? Answering such questions helps us to better grasp the aesthetics and politics of cinematic performance, and, in turn, the relevance of particular performances to the styles of individual directors, even the development of national cinemas and the cultures those cinemas shape.

In our introductory chapter to Volume 1, we expound on the treatment of acting within the history of Cinema Studies, detailing the field's general anti-performance critical stance. What we did not point out there is that if this negative stance lends a deliciously indulgent flavor to analyzing the pleasures of cinematic acting, and such indulgence certainly need not be opposed to scholarly rigor. Our aim is to situate performance as an element worthy of attention *as cinematic*. Doing so could include considering the composition of the shot—the "body in space" strategy of appreciating actorly presence that has been in vogue for the past few years—but the authors of the following chapters do not limit themselves to this approach, one that reduces the complexity of performance and relies on an ontology of film that is strictly visual. The authors here are not afraid of the psychological, and discounting that in the name of "the cinematic," or out of a commitment to critical ideology that avoids the individual psyche, is to misunderstand a key aspect of most audience members' experience. Besides, performed expressions must be an expression *of* something: exteriority requires interiority.

We do not intend that the performances herein designated "great" should seem singled out simply because they are achieved by some of the most famous screen actors or because they appear in films that have been dubbed canonical at some point in cinematic history. "Great" is meant as a capacious term, not one that solidifies a canon of objectively *best* performances. Authors offer up perspectives on single performances because they are especially moving, unique, or interesting. A great performance may overtake the film, or the film may be unimaginable without it, inspiring us to reflect on the (as Roland Barthes would have it) *puncta* around which we build our ideas of filmic worlds, which may be achieved in different ways in different nations, periods, and cultures.

Performance around the world

The division between American and International cinema risks implying that the US is not part of the world; or worse, reinforcing its power as globally dominant. It also risks implying that a clean division is possible, delineated so clearly by side-by-side volumes. There are certainly a few tricky instances, particularly when demarcating US and UK productions. For example, James Ivory's *The Remains of the Day* (1993) was produced by Merchant Ivory, a company that made films in both the United States and the United Kingdom, and distributed them through the Hollywood-based Columbia Pictures. James Ivory is himself American, while Indian-born Ismail Merchant became a British citizen, and lead actress Emma Thompson is British. There is a case to be made for the film as American, yet we felt we could not deny its reputation as a British heritage film, nor the richly British inflection and construction of Thompson's performance. Similar ambiguities surround pinpointing the national identity of other films in this volume, such as Roberto Rossellini's *Stromboli* (1950), Lewis Gilbert's *Alfie* (1966), and Michael Haneke's *The Piano Teacher* (2001). There is a further danger in including performances from a wide array of cinematic histories from different nations, namely, that single performances or performers may be understood to stand in metonymically for complex, robust aesthetic legacies. At the same time, one must not avoid situating performances within their national and transnational contexts, and several chapters do this. Two examples are the chapters by Corey Creekmur and Dolores Tierney. Creekmur teaches us that in order to understand Madhubala's achievement in her role in K. Asif's *Mughal-e-Azam* (1960), we have to understand the performance codes unique to popular Hindi cinema. Indeed, what might seem histrionic to Western eyes and ears is vitally central to the style that Madhubala harnesses in order to look back at the audience in self-awareness, commenting upon her character's erotic allure and tragic fate. *The Motorcycle Diaries* is, as Tierney explains, a multinational co-production, and involved funding from, among other countries, Chile, Peru, Argentina, and France, as well as from the American independent sector. It is partly through these intersections of contexts that Tierney considers Gael García Bernal's depiction of the young Ernesto "Che" Guevara as both fetching and radical.

Even in light of these taxonomical complications, we believe that the division between American and International cinema is a helpful one. Mainstream American cinema rooted itself in performance more than other national cinematic traditions, and has wielded enormous influence on the development of global cinemas at the level of production and distribution models. In this respect, the two volumes of this set inform each other and comprise a whole. Patterns and flows of gesture and style emerge, yet we make no claim to offer the global geography of film performance. Surely it will be evident, as well, that there are omissions.

We made the attempt to collect, in an arbitrary way, performances that struck us as eminently notable and important, rather than offering a representative picture of the cinematic global scene to date. Finnish, Israeli, Argentinian, Belgian, Moroccan, and numerous other cinemas and performers will not, sadly, be found here; but neither will legion other stunning performances from cinematic cultures already well represented, such as those of England and France. As international cinephiles, when we experience a performance from a national culture with which we are unfamiliar—a possibility continually diminishing in the age of globalization—we may feel not just that the world is being reflected but that *our* world is expanding. Indeed, there is no denying that we can fall in love with a performance in part because it is foreign to us; it presents us with all the excitement that the unknown affords (even as we refuse to exoticize or Other the sights and sounds we encounter). We may be moved by a performance that makes the foreign familiar, encouraging us to feel that we intuitively understand something about life in another culture or historical epoch. Or unfamiliar performances and performance styles may simply let us practice our language skills.

Beyond stardom

When approaching performance as cinematic, as a formal element, one may naturally be tempted to think in terms of stardom. And, as we discussed in depth in the introduction to Volume 1, the phenomenon of the movie star is so pronounced that it has been regarded as intrinsic to the medium's specificity, regardless of national aesthetic differences. Accordingly, stardom has received much attention in the history of film criticism, both academic and otherwise. The art of performance, however, has received less attention. Although within Film Studies "the actor" has often served as an ideological category opposed to "the star," the work of screen actors is still usually regarded merely as an element among elements, or as a craft, a *techne*. But being a star has no necessary connection to being an excellent performer. Star studies, as Wojcik puts it, is not "inclined to deal extensively with acting *per se*" and tends "to extract particular mannerisms or gestures that are repeated across a body of films as a feature of the star's persona" (7). We can anticipate further studies in significant cinematic performances given at the character-player level.

This is not to say that this volume ignores stardom and star power. On the contrary, many remarkable performers *use* the star persona they created across multiple appearances. Performances can be forged in dialogue with personae, blurring the lines between the creation of a character and a star turn, in ways that invite audience reflection and symphonic registers of meaning. Jerry Mosher argues that Emil Jannings's training and fame as a silent actor affects his work in the talkie Josef von Sternberg's *The Blue Angel* (1930). With the medium's newfound ability to be silent, *The Blue Angel* takes advantage of Jannings's pantomimic talents while building to the jouissance of the character finding his voice in the release of a bestial bellow. Ulka Anjaria situates Amitabh Bachchan's performance in Yash Chopra's *Deewaar* (1975) in relation to other performances by the star, and by other actors in the film. In examining this constellation, and how Bachchan acts a façade that crumbles, Anjaria reveals that the character types that scholars write into history are often too coarse, and that finer things are really going on, as, in this case, lessons about the limits of masculinity and anger. Adrienne McLean illuminates how, in *8½* (1963), Marcello Mastroianni manages to play both himself and director Federico Fellini at the same time. His star persona and the director's exist together, and the mystery that results from the fact that we may never be able to distinguish their boundaries is integral to the lure and legacy of the film. Or, to take a more recent case, Noah Tsika reads Andy Amenechi's *Mortal Inheritance* (1996) as hinging upon Omotola Jalade-Ekeinde's unique ability to show equanimity in the face of adversity. The film itself thus becomes a testimony to the actor's talent and relentless stoicism.

But stardom does not always simply animate a performance. It is sometimes easy to forget that star personae are *predicated upon* performances, not just effulgences that shine down from the screen upon us. Janet Bergstrom works systematically through each of Peter Lorre's scenes as the tragic murderer in Fritz Lang's *M* (1931), a performance so indelible that it did more than inflect his star persona; it haunted his career (and, in a way, film itself). She also chronicles Lorre's history as one of Bertolt Brecht's favorite actors, and what the actor brought to the screen from that past. Similarly, Victoria Duckett inverts the common impulse to read a performance in light of the star's biography, instead illuminating how Ingrid Bergman brings the maturity, integrity, and fierceness she demonstrated in her personal life to the role of Karin in *Stromboli* (1950). Duckett discovers precisely how Bergman creates the effect of a perceptive, thinking agent, particularly in so-called quiet moments.

David Desser argues that Setsuko Hara's enigmatic stardom is a result of her enigmatic performances. A star so glamorous and mysterious that she was likened to Greta Garbo, Desser attends closely to Hara in Yasujiro Ozu's *Tokyo Story* (1953) to reveal that she deliberately crafts ambiguity, drawing us into the intoxicating secrecy of her character. Adrian Danks writes on another actor known for her mysterious charisma, Jeanne Moreau. With François Truffaut's *The Bride Wore Black* (1968) as case study, Danks helps us to understand how Moreau's persona functioned within European modernist cinema and concomitant notions of *modern* performance style, one committed to the "inner rhythms of the movie," to quotidian immediacy, and to sustaining a tension between the sensual and cerebral.

Explicating ways that actors attempt the high-wire act of deliberately deploying the impression of illegibility, or modulating registers of convincingness, emerges as another theme across chapters. A performance can be made deliberately inert, not pointing to the historical world or to the truth of an actor's body (like neorealism) but to storytelling itself, thereby challenging the myth of authenticity upon which traditional film stardom relies. Homer Pettey contends that in Ingmar Bergman's *Wild Strawberries* (1957), Victor Sjöström conjures an effect of distance and contemplativeness. In turn, these minimalist choices afford a range of responses and interpretations and even inspire Bergman to make directorial choices. But not all actorly restraint distances us. Alexia Kannas argues that Catherine Deneuve's restraint—she cannot, unlike other characters, smile a smile that is "all teeth and gums" in Jacques Demy's *The Umbrellas of Cherbourg* (1964)—echoes the film's aching refusal of catharsis. Deneuve's expression of not-expressing paradoxically encourages us to invest in Demy's romance even as the character's desire wanes. In a chapter as prismatic as Luca Guadagnino's *I Am Love* (2009) itself, Murray Pomerance analyzes the absence of articulateness and explanatory gestures in Tilda Swinton's performance in the film, uncovering the sophistication of her choice to allow context its force. Yet ultimately he leaves its mystery intact, admitting—enjoying—critical loss in the face of the ineffable.

While subtlety and restraint are values often ascribed as honorifics to performances in film criticism, grandness and theatricality—the baroque—can also be vital. Anna Magnani, for example, is famously one of the deftest and most convincing actors in film history. Yet gone are the virtuoso speeches and ferocious depth in Jean Renoir's *The Golden Coach*

(1952), a fact that Sergio Rigoletto believes should invite us to consider the very conscious theatricality in her performance, and even in her stardom. Karla Oeler teaches us that actor Nikolai Cherkasov becomes a screen himself in Sergei Eisenstein's *Ivan the Terrible* (1945), fulfilling the director's minutest desires by balancing the need for painfully achieved but graphically necessary poses with precariously poised emotional accuracy. Cherkasov demonstrates exemplary Stanislavskian technique in order to manifest an aesthetic of the eccentric, a difficult impression to achieve without falseness. Marcia Landy considers how the very theatricality of Charles Laughton's personality inflects the comic, the melodramatic, even the surreal in David Lean's *Hobson's Choice* (1954). In Landy's view, Laughton's acting style comports with Lean's vision for his genre-blending adaptation.

The description and the described

When describing a character's performed action, we often resist acknowledging the fact that we are already interpreting. It may seem obvious that the actor is sad or afraid or happy, and so, describing a particular aspect of a film may not feel scholarly in the way that pointing out a long take or camera movement might do. However, indicating a long take or camera movement implies that the editing or cinematography could have been otherwise, and critics go on to make something of this choice. Describing an actor's gesture or expression functions similarly: an actor showing his character feeling happy has made precise and articulate choices of posture, gesture, intonation, quality of movement, and so on. The "happiness" doesn't simply happen.

One reason that screen performance receives so little scholarly consideration is that many scholars presume that observing it and writing about it constitute a less rigorous undertaking than, say, noting complicated editing schemes. In order to write about screen performance, the story goes, one need not trouble to acquire more expertise than a typical audience member unthinkingly brings to the screen. There is some truth in this, to the extent that the impulse to mimic being perfectly ordinary, audiences the world over *can* be experts in mimetic performance without additional training. However, it is also true that describing precisely what is to be seen onscreen at a given performative moment is not easy. It is difficult work. The contributors to this volume expose the level of energy required to appreciate the intricacies of performances, and to thereby create and disseminate the vocabulary necessary for reporting and conversing about the richness of our experiences at the cinema with others. Regardless of the particular style of the actor under scrutiny, there is a notable emphasis throughout this volume on careful attention.

The following chapters do more than insist that actorly gestures matter. By isolating a single performance, authors are able to show how powerful a weapon specificity can be in the attempt to grasp the complex. All gazes are not the same. Playing despair *that* way, without losing all resolve, or playing anger *that* way, so close to tears, invoking a kind of nexus where aesthetics and politics merge. In Isabelle Huppert's work in *The Piano Teacher*, Alison Taylor finds a performance that exceeds what is pointed to by the screenplay. Taylor tackles the difficulty of pitching our critical awareness of Huppert's style, in which impassiveness squares with bald expressivity, sometimes, it seems, at the same time. Timotheus Vermeulen innovates an approach to reading Emma Thompson's performance in *The Remains of the Day* (1993) that demonstrates a method of interpreting a performance that is inherently sketchy, drawn from emotionally gripping, seemingly montaged, moments. Vermeulen argues that changes in rhythm or posture do not signal an inconsistent character or thoughtless choices by the actor, but rather exhibit different ways of being that are not contradictory but very human, and central to the meaning of the film. Aaron Taylor presents an account of Jean-Pierre Léaud in Truffaut's *Stolen Kisses* (1968) that suggests a performer can work in an essayistic register. At a meta-level, Léaud presents an idea of acting as a dangerous, demanding love; rehearsal can seem like an incantation and the craft can create self-delusions.

Actors playing roles in realist fictions in some way cover another way of being in the world. However, writing about performance—the contributors' challenge here—entails balancing one's own real voice with one's imaginative, intellectual, affective engagement with the character, as well as distinguishing the impression of the character's psychology from that of the actor—regardless of whether we wish to believe, or are told, that the actor *really* felt or thought what the character felt or thought during a particular moment. It is easier, of course, to make such distinctions when writing about stars, as the performative choices onscreen become more apparent in contradistinction to the star's other (very often well-known) characters. But the subject of any screen performance is agency, a subject that is blood-close to our hearts. We want to know that we do something, and (at the risk of stating the obvious) screen performances cultivate concepts of subjectivity. These concepts, in turn, configure ideas of inter-subjectivity. The absorption of screen performances is thus fundamental to the creation of conceptual schemes for thinking about others, for envisaging the social and political spheres in which we see them. Who are these people? Where do they come from and why do they react this way? In short, how do we proceed along the path of life?

Several chapters divulge ways that performances support or subvert socio-political ideologies. For example, Jason Jacobs uncovers how Michael Caine used his voice to soften the provocative (class-based) content of *Alfie*. In turn, the verbal intimacy Caine creates negotiates, even commodifies, a 1960s crisis of masculinity and incidentally changed the picture of the "leading man" in film history. In examining Michel Serrault's work in Édouard Molinaro's *La cage aux folles*, Kyle Stevens also shows that an actor's formal choices can make a political case. In *La cage*, Serrault not only plays an androgynous figure but also creates one formally, by balancing the so-called masculine aggressive-ness of satire with actorly choices that foreground the so-called feminine virtues of nurture and care. Gina Marchetti argues that Maggie Cheung's impeccable turn in Wong Kar-Wai's *In the Mood for Love* (2000) offers an idea of what it meant to be a Shanghai expatriate in the 1960s. Cheung's performance, Marchetti writes, brings coherence to the narrative by "concretizing the contradictions" between 1960s Shanghai-Hong Kong society and millennial fin-de-siècle sensibilities associated with global arthouse cinema. Douglas McFarland also argues for the importance of the ways that a performance can embody ideological tensions present in the film at large. He analyzes Toshirô Mifune in Akira Kurosawa's *Throne of Blood* (1957), and how Mifune leads his character to function as a dialectical center so as to echo the story's difficult questions about selfhood, freedom, and tradition.

R. Barton Palmer extols the virtues of Alec Guinness, as evinced most clearly in Henry Cass's *Last Holiday* (1950). Guinness plays the Everyman type, confronting mortality (there's nothing more quotidian than that) with a peculiar calm, an "almost joyful" acquiescence to "existential randomness." Out of such observations, Palmer concludes that an actor can create and embody an aesthetics of poignancy, giving dullness, even pain an appealing, amusing ache. This topic pushes him beyond the text to reflect upon the significance of casting and to relate how a film's production history can contextualize what appears onscreen in an illuminating way. Hye Seung Chung and David Scott Diffrient also look at an actor's work through the lens of performance history. Their chapter tells us that Choi Min-sik not only clashed violently with director Chan-wook Park during the filming of *Oldboy* (2003), but Min-sik went to extremes that crucially shaped the film: he should be seen as an author of the film through and beyond his performance.

All the world's a screen

The international scope of this project evades narrow notions of realist performances. However, we elected not to include nonrealist or arealist performances, however accomplished, such as the famously and intentionally anemic ones found in Robert Bresson's oeuvre. Nevertheless, a diversity of styles is represented in the following chapters, and across this array emerges the durability of psychological realism in global cinema history. Appreciating that there may simply be a human instinct for mimetic play, one that manifests in the way that people typically enjoy acting out little stories or putting on little voices every day—that we have a sense of performance that is second nature—is not at odds with appreciating screen acting as a serious form of iconic representation. We want to ask how, *exactly,* an actor creates a poetic "I," a position from which to awe, amuse, or berate us. This is rarely simple, of course. Nick Davis considers the counterintuitive quality of Denis Lavant's "surrealist mosaic" of twelve different personae in Leos Carax's *Holy Motors* (2012). Although one might assume that the exposure of Lavant's shape-shifting is alienating, Davis argues that this is not the case. Rather, Lavant and Carax use the display of virtuosity to reflect on the actorly methods that subtend Lavant's career, and to lure the audience into the film's mysteries: mysteries that concern subjectivity, even as the film belongs to a contemporary post-human moment.

Presenting a comprehensible progression of thoughts, desires, and feelings is not limited to a particular register of performance or genre of storytelling. Over the course of the careful readings included here, and through their variety of critical approaches, the fact surfaces that actors do not simply populate our beloved onscreen diegetic worlds; they can play a vital role in the affective and moral intensities of those worlds. They can bestow guilt or redemption, sympathy or repulsion, relief or judgment on characters that may be missing from, or even denied them, by the script. A movie can hang on the unstated tensions between a character's search for happiness and her own self-destructive impulses. A great performance is thus not just about actorly movement, not just about the visual geometry of figures onscreen, not just about the fact of recorded persons. Effective performances can innovate new subjectivities and generate new levels of compassion for persons, or kinds of persons. On the other hand, performances can also explain something about people, and kinds of people, that we did not know we already knew.

Works cited

Barthes, Roland. *Camera Lucida: Reflections on Photography.* New York: Hill and Wang, 1982.

Wojcik, Pamela Robertson, ed. *Movie Acting: The Film Reader.* New York: Routledge, 2004.

Chapter 1

Victor Sjöström in *Wild Strawberries*

Homer B. Pettey

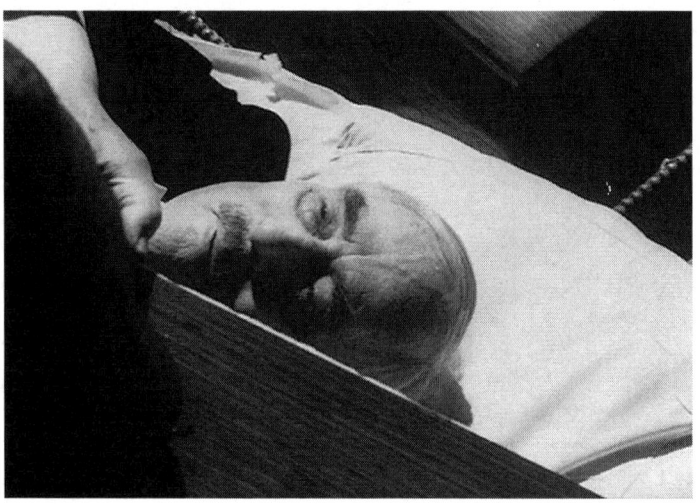

Ingmar Bergman's *Wild Strawberries* (*Smultronstället*, 1957) uses the
frame narrative of a journey story to relate elderly, alienated, and
egocentric Isak Borg's (Victor Sjöström) coming to self-awareness. Told
with interspersed voiceover, flashbacks, and dream sequences, the film
chronicles Borg's progressive self-accusation, guilt, and judgment of his
death-in-life existence. Relying upon his training as a silent-film actor and
director, Sjöström employs controlled facial movements to convey Borg's
confusion, shame, and revelations about his failings with his first love and
family. Sjöström negotiates Borg's memories, dreams, and nightmares as
both an anguished observer of his mental images and a bewildered actor
trapped within his subconscious symbolic world. Like the film's audience,
Borg must interpret as he experiences, especially three major dream
sequences: Isak confronting his own corpse; Isak being forced to look at
himself in a mirror and the successive self-examinations he endures; and

Isak experiencing nostalgia in seeing his parents. Sjöström plays Isak as both spectator and spectacle with subtle facial gestures that convey, as they conceal, his reactions. In the end, the two Borgs appear to merge as Isak comes to his own reckoning, which Sjöström plays with a simple, yet enigmatic smile.

A withdrawn, self-satisfied professor of bacteriology, Isak will drive from Stockholm to Lund University to receive a Jubilee Award, accompanied by his daughter-in-law Marianne (Ingrid Thulin), pregnant and planning to divorce Isak's son Evald (Gunnar Björnstrand). The film begins with a complicated nightmare of Isak discovering his own coffin on the night before the road trip. Significantly, this nightmare establishes Sjöström's choices for the character of Isak and becomes the paradigm for his reactions (more than his actions) throughout the film. For most of the film, in fact, rather than acting Isak is acted upon and then reacts.

Along their way, Isak and Marianne pick up two sets of hitchhikers. First is a shifting love triangle of two young men, Anders and Viktor (Folke Sundquist, Björn Bjelfvenstam), and Sara (Bibi Andersson), a young woman who reminds Isak of his lost love, who gathered wild strawberries with him but eventually married his cousin Sigfrid (Per Sjöstrand). Then comes a middle-aged bickering couple, the Almans, Berit (Gunnel Broström) and Sten (Gunnar Sjöberg), who remind Isak of his own failed marriage. Marianne and Isak visit his extremely elderly and lonely mother (Naima Wifstrand), who shows them artifacts of past family moments, and as they leave she offers Isak a pocketwatch that lacks any hands, calling up a prominent image from the coffin nightmare that opened the film. Isak then experiences a complex dream in which after meeting Sara, who confronts him with his mirror image and discusses the nature of love, he enters a house to find her and his cousin Sigfrid kissing. Again, this second dream focuses upon Isak's reactions, not his actions. The dream continues with Isak cutting his palm on a nail as a kind of stigma, then meeting Sten Alman, who leads him to a lecture hall where he must undergo a surreal examination. The examiner leads Isak to a burnt-out house where he observes his wife, Karin (Gertrud Fridh), with her lover (Åke Fridell), after she has condemned Isak for his aloofness. Isak awakes in the passenger seat and they arrive at his son Evald's house.

They attend the august ceremony. As Isak prepares for sleep that night, he interacts with his antagonistic son and with his daughter-in-law. A final dream sequence concludes the film, with Sara returning to explain that there are no more wild strawberries before a vision of Isak's parents in a tranquil, natural setting at a river's edge. The final shot of Isak's expression as he lies in bed remains Bergman's ambiguous, multivalent interpretative moment.

Interpretations of *Wild Strawberries* are numerous, not just because of the symbolic dreams but primarily because of Sjöström's performance. Bergman structured the film, as Marc Gervais contends, as "a journey through place, time, and the psyche," in particular "a classical demonstration of the Freudian journey to sublimation and fulfillment" (58). Isak's encounters with his own nightmares, with various neurotics, with alienated and self-involved family members, and with bittersweet reminiscences present "a coherent system of incorporating dreams and dreamlike flashback" that creates a new cinematic time by merging external and internal reality (Hubner 96). To navigate this iconographic journey of confrontations—psychological (Freudian dream symbolism), mythological (the Fall allegory, the lost pastoral), Christian (sin and redemption), and metaphysical (transcendent imagery of time and death)—requires Sjöström both to observe and to react, but in a manner of subdued, contemplative distance. In fact, distance characterizes both the film's plot and Sjöström's performative choices. Spatial distance can be observed between Isak and family members; temporal distance between Isak's past and the present; psychological distance between Isak's egocentrism (seen in his isolation in his study, early in the film) and moments of affection (toward his beloved Sara); and theological distance between Isak the cold, alienated scientist and Isak the receptive, not necessarily repentant, man. To express these various distances requires not emotive performance, but understated, even withheld physical movements. Sjöström's acting relies more on complex facial expressions than on bodily gesture. As a veteran actor of the stage and silent film, his minimalist choices, effected mostly through restrained, yet multi-layered facial expressions, allow for interpretations on symbolic, allegorical, and religious levels. To some degree, *Wild Strawberries* sustains interpretive distance as well between Isak's conscious acceptance of his life and the audience's evaluation of his existence.

After Ingmar Bergman, Victor Sjöström remains the most celebrated and best known of Swedish directors. In fact, Bergman himself viewed his cinematic work "as some kind of continuation" of Sjöström's, having made extensive, analytic study of the other artist's films, which, he discovered, employed "multi-dimensional" acting by "using actors to project several things at once" and producing an "intimacy of expression" (quoted in Forslund 261). Those impressive screen performances were primarily Sjöström's own, since he acted in most of the Swedish films that he directed. Sjöström also appealed to Bergman because of both men's fondness for working in the legitimate theater. Between 1896 and just before the First World War, Sjöström was a working actor with various theatrical companies, first in a traveling troupe in Finland, then throughout Sweden, finally landing at established theatres in Gothenberg and Stockholm. His theatrical roles during this pre-cinema period included parts in naturalist works, Hermann Sudermann's one-act *Fritz* and August Strindberg's *Gustav Wasa*, as well as a very successful staging of Shakespeare's *A Midsummer Night's Dream* (Forslund 23–31 *passim*).

At the beginning of the 1912 theatrical season, Sjöström began contemplating his career in film, as both a director and an actor. In the summer, he began at the newly-built studio of Svenska Biografteatern, which was founded in 1907 as Sweden's response to the overwhelming success, the year before, of Denmark's Nordisk Films Kompagni. By the next year, Sjöström secured his position not only as a director but also as a principal actor, in *Livets konflikter* (*The Conflicts of Life*). Sjöström's screen presence astounded audiences and critics in his adaptation of Henrik Ibsen's poem *Brand, Terje Vigen* (*A Man There Was*, 1917), in which he directed himself as the lead in the most lavish and expensive Swedish film of its time. One reviewer extolled Sjöström for his poetic acting abilities:

> The real poet is the director—in this instance, Victor Sjöström, who furthermore plays the lead and is all that matters in the play. He has his powerful head with its massive, sculpted features, and at the same time the simplified and expressive mimicry that is required, the weight of the character as the Nordic archetype. (Forslund 59)

This simplified mimicry, particularly in facial expressions, would be Sjöström's signature throughout his career. His directing and acting gained international success with *Berg-Ejvind och hans hustru* (*The Outlaw and His Wife*, 1918). He contributed to Swedish filmmaking not only a national style for the 1910s but also a style of acting, a "lyrical intimacy, created through downplayed acting" (Florin 20). Sjöström's intimate performance dominates *Wild Strawberries*, as Bergman was forced to acknowledge:

> He took my text, made it his own, invested it with his own experiences, loneliness, coldness, warmth, harshness, and ennui . . .

> Borrowing my father's form, he occupied my soul and made it all his own—there wasn't even a crumb left over for me! He did so with the sovereign power of a gargantuan personality. I had nothing to add, not even a sensible or irrational comment. *Wild Strawberries* was no longer my film: it was Victor Sjöström's! (quoted in Macnab 102)[1]

Because of his training in both direction and acting in silent film, Sjöström's choices reveal a dual understanding of performance. The opening voiceover scene of Isak Borg writing in his study establishes his familial, household, and professional relationships to the world, with Sjöström exhibiting little facial expression, mostly blank contemplation or a slight frown, as we learn that he has a son, a mother still living, a deceased wife, and a housekeeper. The matter-of-fact recounting of his life Sjöström delivers in a flat, banal, and detached voice. Yet, Isak's egotism and his detachment from others come through in Sjöström's ability to reveal the internal life of the character through even the slightest movements of eyes and mouth. Sjöström chooses these minor facial movements in order to convey Isak's pride in himself as well as his alienation from and displeasure with others.

Dream I

After the credits, as he lies in his bed, a spot of light illuminates only his face as the voiceover proceeds to recount "a weird and very unpleasant dream." Here, with only slight tension and head movement, Sjöström conveys the uncomfortable sensation of his nightmare, surely cinema's best-known dream. "I lost my way among empty streets with ruined houses," he recalls, maintaining a placid, enigmatic expression. He has arrived at a street corner, which begins his labyrinthine progression through this dreamscape. He turns from the camera and walks down the empty sidewalk, pausing to look up at a large pocketwatch—without hands—suspended above a storefront, with a pair of pince-nez spectacles and eyes attached below. The steady thumping of a heartbeat can be heard, as Sjöström pulls out his own pocketwatch and discovers that it, too, is a face without hands.

He removes his hat, looking up again at the hanging pocketwatch and bespectacled eyes, his face over-illuminated by Bergman's use of high-contrast lighting. The slightly open mouth expresses his disconcerted state. He wipes his brow and moves out of the glaring sunlight in order to perceive the watch sign better. He turns away in a moment of quiet resignation, then moves down the sidewalk again, seen in a long tracking shot. Distant from the camera, Isak's movements seem desperate and confused, notably as he returns back up the sidewalk at a quickened pace, the camera re-tracking along with him. Now he goes past the hanging pocketwatch, but stops. In a medium close-up, his bare head fully illuminated, Sjöström maintains a tense yet almost blank expression as he surveys the empty street. His choice for this subtle mien invites the audience to become spectator to the bizarre, surreal dreamscape.

Just beyond the suspended pince-nez Isak sees a figure dressed exactly as he was, in hat and overcoat, and with his back turned, so that the face is occluded. He approaches, raises his hand to touch the left shoulder, and then, in the first significant reaction shot of the film, with Sjöström flinching and startled, Bergman cuts to the figure turning. The face is a grotesque of squashed features. His hand still suspended, Isak moves his head forward as if to see the figure better, a look of curiosity on his face. The figure collapses to the ground, prostrate. Isak bends his head to examine the figure, who is now headless and handless with what appears to be blood flowing out onto the street. We can hear the sound of bells, a lamenting death toll to whose clanging Isak reacts, again out of curiosity. The choices that Sjöström has made correspond exactly to Isak the scientist-observer, not exactly Isak the participant in the world.

Now, in medium close-up, the camera tracks Isak as he reaches another corner. Cut to a facial close-up, the eyes narrowed slightly as though trying to see down another empty street. Around the corner at the far end appears a hearse drawn by two horses. In a long shot, the camera frames the pocketwatch and pince-nez in the middle distance and Isak in the background near the approaching hearse, which now turns the corner. Isak turns his head to follow the hearse's movement and Sjöström expresses a mixture of curiosity and contempt. Cut to the hearse moving diagonally through the left side of the frame as Isak stands in the background staring at it. The hearse knocks into a lamppost, dislodging the glass lantern atop it. With its left rear wheel on one side and its frame on the other, the hearse continues to knock into the lamppost until the wheel comes off, rolling directly at Isak who shifts quickly away before the thing crashes into the wall next to him, smashing to pieces.

Now, the three-wheeled, unsteady hearse creaks and rocks, which Bergman conveys in an eight-shot, fifteen-second montage: low-angle of struggling horses with the unstable hearse; close-up of the missing wheel axle and more rocking; Isak looking up from where the wheel crashed, the creaking sound, like the bells, attracting his attention; the cherub-decorated top of the back of the hearse and the crucifix swaying in its center; Isak looking on, his blank expression corresponding to his own uncertainty; a coffin inside the hearse as it rocks almost cradle-like; close-up of Isak's face, his mouth frowning deeply in a kind of annoyed bewilderment; the swaying back-and-forth of the hearse causing the coffin to fall out the back; and, as the coffin hits the pavement, the horses galloping off diagonally on the right side of the frame.

The final montage sequence of this first nightmare employs cinematic techniques usually observed in dialogue sequences. Isak, his back to the wall, looks down on the coffin. Cut to an over-the-shoulder shot of him with the now-open coffin before him in the street, a hand and arm protruding from it. A reverse shot captures the tight, frowning face of Isak. Back to the coffin, then back to Isak's same frown. A silent dialogue seems to be forming. Cut to the coffin in the foreground with the hand outstretched upward as Isak approaches with tentative steps. Cut to the hand whose fingers open up and move toward the approaching Isak. Cut to Isak's wincing and then back to the hand as it reaches for Isak's hand, which it grabs at the wrist. Isak recoils in disgust, but cannot free himself. Cut to the coffin as a figure, bracing on Isak's arm, pulls itself up. Cut to Isak now afraid, and thence to revelation of the figure's identity—Isak himself emerging from the coffin. The dreaming/observing Isak moves backward in disgust and terror, but cannot break the grip. Cut to the placid face of coffined Isak, impassively observing dreamer-Isak, back to dreamer-Isak's fear, then to a close-up of that blank, yet judging face of coffined-Isak, then to a half-muttering dreamer-Isak in extreme canted-angle close-up, and zoom to an extreme close-up of coffined-Isak, whose lips part slightly as though prepared to speak. Two zooms to extreme close-ups complete the nightmare, before a sudden cut to a closed-eyelid Isak in bed, struggling as he returns to consciousness. Bergman's choice of a dialogue shot/reverse-shot approach afforded Sjöström the opportunity to play out the spectator-spectacle roles.

Dream II

Later, Isak is dozing off, but "haunted by vivid and humiliating dreams." As he watches the young Sara in a two-shot, his face is illuminated with a circle of light produced by a mirror she is holding up to him. She describes his visage: "You're a worried old man who's soon going to die, but I have all my life before me."

Sjöström chooses to add a slight shaking of his left hand to indicate his anxiety, even as he denies her accusations. When she forces the mirror before him again, he recoils the way he did before his image in the coffin in the first dream. She informs him that she is going to marry his brother Sigfrid. Bergman cuts to her holding the mirror that captures a slightly distorted image of Isak, his mouth tightened. "Now, try to smile," she commands, and Sjöström shifts his lips almost imperceptibly upward from his usual frown, before returning to resignation, his eyes searching and despondent: "But it hurts so." Sara runs off to comfort a baby, whom she removes from a bassinette outside and carries into a brightly lit interior. Isak approaches the empty bassinette, his face implacably still, then turns toward the house. Bergman emphasizes Isak's death-in-life existence as the camera tilts upward to reveal the black limbs of a dead tree. In a medium close-up, the camera follows Isak as he approaches the house, his mouth in a deeper frown yet his eyes searching. He hears the sound of a piano playing and peers through a pane door to discover Sara, dressed in an evening gown, seated at a candelabra-lit piano, with a tuxedoed Sigfrid standing next to her. Sigfrid bends down and kisses the back of Sara's neck, then her lips, and she takes his hands as he leads her to a table where they clink wine glasses in celebration.

Bergman cuts to the dark, dead forest night, then to the emergence of a full moon in the sky, as Isak, now in bright illumination, stares upward. He returns to the pane door, with the room now darkened, his back to the camera, and bangs on the glass. His right hand reaches to the doorjamb and he receives the cut on his palm, that foreshadows the personal suffering to follow. The figure of the examiner now appears in the pane door; he opens it and invites the professor in. They move through an empty house to a locked door, before which Isak removes his overcoat, almost as though it were a habitual gesture. The examiner unlocks the door and leads Isak down a narrow hallway to another locked door, which he unlocks as well. The opening of locked doors obviously points to personal revelations to come. Isak enters a seven-tiered, double-aisled narrow lecture hall, with ten students in attendance. Commanded to sit, his back to the observing audience, Isak tentatively takes a chair before a laboratory table, behind which the examiner is already riffling through papers. On the table are a binocular microscope, its slide light, and a set of test tubes. Next to Isak's chair is a small table with a tray, a glass bottle of water, and several small glasses. After asking for and receiving Isak's grade book, the examiner tells Isak to "identify the bacterial specimen under the microscope," but looking in and adjusting the magnification Isak can see only one large eye, its pupil partially illuminated by the slide lamp. Of course, this moment symbolizes Isak's blindness due to his egotism. Disconcerted, his face drawn in disbelief, he claims that "There must be something wrong," to which the examiner mockingly rejoins by peering into the microscope and correcting him.

The examiner demands that Isak read some text on the blackboard. He pronounces the syllables in an almost childlike rendering. Asked their meaning, Isak, mouth agape, cannot answer. "I'm a doctor, not a linguist!" The examiner points to the words as "a doctor's first duty" and asks Isak what that is. A baffled and ruffled Isak requests time to think. He tries to repeat the words, but seems incapable of completing the sentence. The examiner says the first duty of a doctor is "to ask for forgiveness." More expressively than at any other point in the film, Sjöström erupts into nervous laughter—a pitiable, pathetic laugh—broadly gesturing as he turns to the students to seek their approval. Only stoic faces meet him. He turns back to the examiner bewildered, his eyes widely open in panic.

"You have been accused of guilt," pronounces the examiner, the academic test now transformed into a judicial proceeding. In disbelief, Isak leans forward not understanding this charge against him. "Is it serious?" Unfortunately, it is. Now, angrily pouring himself a glass of water with shaky hands, his lips in a deep frown, he proffers a series of outraged excuses:

> I have a weak heart!
> I'm an old man!
> You must be lenient with me. It's only fair!

The examiner asks Isak if he wishes to halt the test. "No, no, for God's sake," Isak responds before gulping water down.

The examiner asks Isak, "Please diagnose the patient." The Inquisition has now become an autopsy. As physician Isak enters the frame and bends down for a close inspection, he lifts a seated woman's head to see her face and pronounces, "The patient is dead." From her deathlike passive face the woman looks up at Izak, smiles, and laughs loudly, almost hysterically, to which he rises, mouth agape in confusion, backs away, and rejoins the examiner, who is writing his verdict in Isak's grade book: "You are incompetent." Almost imploring, Isak repeats "Incompetent," but only finds himself guilty of more offenses: "Callousness, selfishness, ruthlessness. Your wife has made the charge." To each word, Isak shakes his head and disagrees. Told that he will be confronted by his wife, the disoriented Isak explains that she has been dead for years, but the examiner demands again that he follow him. Isak turns and moves toward the hallway, now consumed with the shadows of dead branches.

Bergman dissolves to a pond that reflects the examiner leading Isak through the woods. They reach the remains of a house destroyed by fire. Through the charred frames of a ladder, which resembles frames of film, Isak looks out to a distant glade and hears a woman's laughter, as his wife appears accompanied by a man. The man kisses her ear, she mockingly and lightly slaps him. Cut to Isak's bemused look. As his wife pulls out a hand mirror, her lover pulls away her hairpins, for which she slaps him away. The man grabs her and she struggles violently, slapping him with both hands. Cut to a concerned Isak, who raises his left hand to the ladder, in the same gesture he used with Sara when she held the mirror before him. Isak's wife falls to the ground and crying sounds can be heard. Her lover approaches and they make love. Cut to Isak, framed by the ladder, as the examiner explains that this is the image that Isak retains again and again of his marriage, from this very spot when he first observed his wife's infidelity: "Tuesday, May 1, 1917." Ironically, May Day represents the birth of spring, a day of renewal and of sexuality. Cut back to his seated wife pulling her gown back over her spread legs, as she tells her lover that she will inform Isak, "Just as if he were God." Readjusting her hair, she dismisses Isak, "because he's cold as ice." When the lovers depart in opposite directions, Isak, no longer merely the spectator, moves quickly from behind the ladder as though trying to stop his wife from leaving, but then stops, somewhat breathless and confused by her disappearance. He turns to his examiner and wonders where she is. The examiner responds:

> Gone. All are gone.
> Removed by an operation, Professor.
> A surgical masterpiece. No pain.
> Nothing that bleeds or trembles.

When Isak asks about his punishment, the examiner informs him that it is the usual, "Loneliness." Isak repeats the word and Sjöström chooses to convey his pain through a simple gesture of closing his eyes. The result is Isak the blind, Isak the dormant, Isak the cold—Isak as a death mask. Cut to him awakening in the passenger seat.

Dream III

The final dream sequence concludes *Wild Strawberries*. Bergman returns to a similar overhead medium close-up of Isak in bed, his head the central object of the lighting, as he begins his fantasy: "If I have been worried or sad during the day, it often calms me to recall childhood memories. I did so on this evening, too." In bright sunlight, Sara comes running from a crowd of people before a country house and states, "Isak, there are no wild strawberries left." Her prophetic words invite numerous interpretations of the film's meaning: lost innocence, the pain of lost moments, the inability to return to one's past. When he says that he cannot find his father and mother, Sara rushes to his aid. She leads him through a meadow and up to a rocky prominence among healthy pine trees, then departs. In the distance, Isak's father and mother wave to him. His father is fishing in the river and his mother lies on a blanket on the riverbank. Sjöström, for the first time in the film, allows his face to express a kind of pleasure, a nostalgic reflection in his eyes, as Bergman moves in for a close-up of what appears to be a smile moving along his lips. Cut to Isak in bed, with Sjöström having the same expression: his eyes open and a smile seeming to emerge on his face. He gives a sigh or a cough as he turns his head slightly, then fade to black.

Sjöström's subtle portrayal leaves open several readings for the symbol-laden film. Bergman's screenplay hardly provides a specific meaning in its final words:

> I dreamt that I stood by the water and shouted toward the bay, but the warm summer breeze carried away my cries and they did not reach their destination. Yet I wasn't sorry about that; I felt, on the contrary, rather lighthearted. (Bergman 239)

This final ambiguous moment could be an affirmation, Isak's awareness of a world still offering hope and renewal and the "culmination and fulfillment of the Christian side of Bergman," as Robin Wood suggests (96). That faint smile could reflect Isak's nostalgia for a world that never was, his retreating "from the world of real needs and cares before he dies" (Kalin 85). Still, it could represent a trace of an ironic smile that may be Isak's dismissal of those previous nightmares. The power of Sjöström's performance lies in the subtlety of Isak's reactions, which, deciphered by the audience, tell much more about our desires and needs than this old man's.

Note

1. Bergman's father was a Lutheran minister, who was quite distant emotionally and strict toward Ingmar.

Works cited

Bergman, Ingmar. *Four Screenplays of Ingmar Bergman*. New York: Simon and Schuster, 1960.

Florin, Bo. *Transition and Transformation: Victor Sjöström in Hollywood 1923–1930*. Amsterdam: Amsterdam University Press, 2013.

Forslund, Bengt. *Victor Sjöström: His Life and Work*. New York: Zoetrope, 1988.

Gervais, Marc. *Ingmar Bergman: Magician and Prophet*. Montreal: McGill-Queen's University Press, 1999.

Hubner, Laura. *The Films of Ingmar Bergman: Illusions of Light and Darkness*. New York: Palgrave Macmillan, 2007

Kalin, Jesse. *The Films of Ingmar Bergman*. Cambridge: Cambridge University Press, 2003.

Macnab, Geoffrey. *Ingmar Bergman: The Life and Films of the Last Great European Director*. London: I. B. Tauris, 2009.

Wood, Robin. *Ingmar Bergman, New Edition*. Ed. Barry Keith Grant. Detroit: Wayne State University Press, 2013.

Chapter 2

Emil Jannings in *The Blue Angel*

Jerry Mosher

"I had told him in plain language that I would not do another film with him were he the last remaining actor on earth" (Liebmann 9). Two years after director Josef von Sternberg leveled that parting shot at Emil Jannings—after they had completed the silent drama *The Last Command* at Paramount in 1927—Sternberg was on his way to Berlin, summoned by the world-renowned actor to direct his debut in sound cinema. The result would be *The Blue Angel (Der blaue Engel*, 1930), one of Germany's first feature-length talkies, with Jannings's name featured prominently above the title. The film would showcase what is now considered to be the most iconic performance of the late Weimar Republic, encapsulating the decadence, creativity, and despair of its last few years before the rise of the Third Reich; a performance not by Jannings, to his everlasting anguish, but by his co-star, a relatively unknown German actress and singer named Marlene Dietrich.

Dietrich's performance as seductive cabaret singer Lola-Lola is undoubtedly brilliant; groundbreaking in its cool modernity, it would bring her international stardom and a long-term contract at Paramount, where she would star in five more films with Sternberg. But can the same be said for that of Jannings, playing the more chastened role of Professor Immanuel Rath, the film's humiliated protagonist? While it cannot compare with Jannings's groundbreaking silent portrayal of a disgraced hotel doorman in F.W. Murnau's *The Last Laugh* (1924)—a role that had brought him his own share of international acclaim as the world's greatest purveyor of pantomimic art—Jannings's fussy, anxious performance in *The Blue Angel* can be appreciated like a finely crafted but temperamental antique instrument. The actor's sounds and gesticulations are occasionally vacillating and high-strung, but Sternberg modulates Jannings's archaic, pantomimic excesses to painstakingly express an aging gentleman's struggle to maintain his sense of honor in a corrupt modern world.

Everything, it seems, worked against Jannings's chances of making a triumphant debut in the talkies. Fearful of working with sound (it was his stated reason for leaving Hollywood after starring in six silent films at Paramount), Jannings was now expected to star in a new sound film for producer Erich Pommer at the Ufa studios in Babelsberg. The actor asked for Sternberg because he respected the director's talent and discipline; because the director had knowledge of the German language (Sternberg was born in Austria and raised in New York City); and, most importantly, because Sternberg had recently directed a sound feature at Paramount (the disappointing crime drama *Thunderbolt* (1929)).[1] Jannings knew full well that Sternberg detested him but summoned him anyway, thereby demonstrating the masochist's repetition compulsion that seemingly motivated the actor to engage in a series of screen portrayals of humiliated characters throughout the 1920s. Working together on *The Last Command*—in which Jannings plays a Russian Tsarist general who is reduced to working as a Hollywood extra—Sternberg had found Jannings to be an enormous talent with a body and ego to match. A shy and petulant actor who could not bear any attention given to others, Jannings had undermined the director's intentions at every turn (Sternberg 128–33). And nothing at Babelsberg would change Sternberg's opinion of Jannings; the director would resist facilitating Jannings's German comeback, and relished the chance to thwart the anticipated triumph of an "Emil Jannings sound film" (Wieland 158). He would enact several directorial strategies calculated to contain Jannings and thereby render a superior performance.

For Sternberg to make his own imprint on the production, he would need a star vehicle for a charismatic German actress. After rejecting a proposed Rasputin biopic, Sternberg decided to adapt Heinrich Mann's 1905 novel *Professor Unrat*, about a troubled university professor who is ruined by the seductive charms of a cabaret singer. "In converting the novel into a film which would meet my standards of visual poetry," Sternberg recalled, "I introduced the figure of the clown as well as all the episodes and details that led the professor to be confined in a strait-jacket" (Sternberg 136–7). Physical containment and humiliation of Jannings's character would be total. And Jannings approved; here was a familiar story of ruin into which he could really sink his teeth. But then Sternberg had the audacity to cast the little-known Dietrich (supported by Pommer but opposed by many at Ufa) and add several songs for her to sing throughout the film. In contrast to Jannings, Dietrich was comfortable working with a microphone. She had trained in music and, while acting in a handful of supporting roles in silent films, had for the most part worked with her voice as a stage singer and performer. To make matters worse for Jannings, after production began Dietrich was soon bringing lunch for the director, who was spending more and more time in her dressing room, to Jannings's infuriation. How, Jannings wondered, could he plausibly enact an onscreen romance with this woman under these circumstances? Dietrich was a nobody, getting paid a mere one-tenth of Jannings's record-setting salary (Kreimeier 190). And unlike Jannings, she "had never been a silent film star and had no reputation to defend" (Wieland 162).

Between silence and sound

Overcoming Jannings's reputation as the greatest actor in silent film proved to be Sternberg's biggest challenge. To contain the actor's outsized screen persona in *The Blue Angel*, the director planned to use silence to his advantage. Recording techniques at Ufa in late 1929 were even more primitive than in Hollywood; sound and vision had to be recorded together, without the use of multitracking or overdubs, and camera noise was stifled by boxing the device within a huge crate. But Sternberg, S.S. Prawer notes, "was thrilled by the idea that sound would open up new possibilities of effective silences in the same way as every light brought with it its own shade" (31). From his experience on *Thunderbolt*, Sternberg had developed a sophisticated technique of counterpoint in which "sound had to bring to the image a quality other than what the lens included, a quality out of the range of the image ... Sound was realistic, the camera was not" (Sternberg 219). Extended silent passages would not only offer the opportunity for more camera mobility; they would also limit Jannings's spoken performance and take advantage of his expressive pantomime, suggesting the deep turmoil of Rath's inner life in a way that sound could not. Sternberg's success in containing Jannings's performance would be confirmed by German theatre director Max Reinhardt, who observed after seeing *The Blue Angel* in 1930, "It is not altogether a talker nor yet a silent. It's an in-between situation. Jannings does nothing, says nothing, but expresses much" (Abel Green, "Germans Slam Hollywood: Reinhardt with Molnar-Pommer," *Variety*, 7 May 1930).

The film's quieter moments would occur in the professor's apartment and classroom, giving them the intimacy of the silent Weimar *kammerspiel* films in which Jannings had made his artistic reputation. The film's bravura sound passages would occur at the Blue Angel nightclub, during Dietrich's musical numbers and amid the commotion of its raucous audiences and hustling performers, giving them the vitality of a Hollywood backstage musical. In between those spaces, when the professor wanders down a dark street lined with prostitutes on his way to the nightclub, *The Blue Angel* demonstrates an affinity with the "street film," a Weimar genre that, Prawer notes, "dealt typically with the dangers that the streets outside ... held for buttoned-up bourgeois men lured out of their stuffy homes and secure professions by desires of the flesh" (18). As Reinhardt and many scholars have noted, it is this quality of "between-ness"—between the silents and the talkies, Hollywood and Ufa, the Old World and the New World, high culture and low culture—that reflects the volatility of the period and gives *The Blue Angel* its lasting, transformative power.

In the film's opening scene, Jannings's first utterance in a sound film is not a word, but a whistle. Entering his study, Professor Rath enacts a series of gestures with costume and props: he searches his frock coat pockets and desktop for his notebook; fishes a watch from his waistcoat pocket and checks the time; fastens the top button of his frock coat; and finally sits down at a table and meticulously pours his morning cup of coffee. The professor then breaks the silence with a whistle to his caged bird, which he thinks will want a sugar cube. Hearing no response, he gets up and extracts the dead bird from its cage, holding it close to his face to examine it. "Anyway, he stopped singing long ago," his housemaid tells him as she snatches the bird from his hands and tosses it into the fire. The professor's whistle, and the death of this caged animal, will foreshadow his tragic fate. He sits down again and resignedly drops the sugar cube into his coffee. The scene fades to black, without Jannings speaking a word. The actor's silent, pantomimic gestures establish Rath as a fussy, fastidious man who needs his daily routine; his audible whistle and the morbid discovery that follows it suggest this day will be different.

In his next scene, entering the classroom as debauched adolescent schoolboys scramble to their desks to stand at attention, Jannings speaks his first words, authoritatively ordering the boys to "Sit down." The gestures and words that follow reveal a pompous man desperate to maintain his authority. Before speaking again, the professor takes his seat and performs a series of nervous gestures, tucking his waistcoat under his seat, taking out a handkerchief and blowing his nose, and squinting to examine the boys' graffiti on his notebook, which has altered his name to "Prof. Unrath" ("Prof. Garbage"). When he finally begins to teach the class (Rath and a student recite "To be or not to be, that is the question," from *Hamlet* III.1), the professor continues to neurotically adjust his eyeglasses, fidget with a pencil, and blow his nose. The class's insubordination and the professor's insistence on repetition and drilling (harping on a student's mispronunciation of the article "the"), followed by his vindictive assignment of an in-class essay (inexplicably switching to *Julius Caesar*), reveal Rath's failure as a teacher. He is nothing but a stuffed shirt, clinging to the ostentatious title "Prof. Dr. Rath" that hangs on his door. The professor's confiscation of a student's postcard depicting Lola-Lola, like finding the dead bird in the preceding scene, signifies a break in his routine that will foreshadow his personal tragedy. By closing a window in exasperation, to silence the song of schoolgirls outside, Rath affirms Lola's seductive lure, to which the professor and these insolent schoolboys—whom Siegfried Kracauer would later characterize as "born Hitler youths" (218)—are not immune.

Jannings's palsy-like head movements, arching eyebrows, squinting eyes, craning neck, and fluttering hands in these opening scenes are immediately recognizable from the pantomimic repertoire he had honed in numerous silent *kammerspiel* films and Hollywood dramas. In 1924 the actor's finely hewn gesticulations to depict a proud hotel doorman's downfall had been a revelation in *The Last Laugh*, as captured in the expressionist light and shadow of Murnau's "unchained camera." After arriving in Hollywood, Jannings won the first Academy Award for Best Actor in 1928 for his portrayals of tragic figures in Victor Fleming's *The Way of All Flesh* and Sternberg's *The Last Command*. But after four similar, increasingly disappointing films at Paramount, Jannings's familiar mannerisms and downward spirals were being ridiculed by some American critics as formulaic shtick (Gemünden 194). *The Nation's* critic noted in 1928 that "this very serious, inquiring, and gifted actor is succumbing to the slick efficiency of the rubber stamp" (Alexander Bakshy, "Moving Pictures: Character and Drama," *The Nation* 126: 3276, 18 April 1928, 463). In a 1929 article in *Theatre Magazine* titled "Jannings—The Moan-Maker," critic Rex Smith observed, "On the screen a heavy, moon-faced man shuffles through the motions of a very sad pantomime." Writing in 1927, budding filmmaker Luis Buñuel put some of the blame on directors who indulged Jannings's excesses: "Filmmakers overdo it with Jannings, multiplying his slightest facial contractions to the nth degree. For him, suffering is a prism cut into a hundred facets. That's why he's capable of acting in a close-up from 150 feet" (Buñuel 110).

In *The Blue Angel*, Jannings's exaggerated gestures and nervous tics could have continued his slide into self-parody. Under Sternberg's direction, however, they reinforce the professor's psychology, making the character legible as a tragic figure whose need to assert his title and prestige leave him vulnerable to humiliation. Sternberg shrewdly capitalized on Jannings's artistic decline by pairing him with the rising star of Dietrich, who displays a thoroughly modern sensibility that features restrained acting and a calculating sexuality. Jannings's theatricality, in contrast, appears fussy and anachronistic, further enriching his characterization of the aging professor. Jannings often seems to be trying too hard; his acting calls attention to his sacrifice for his craft, which is perhaps why he garnered so many awards. Dietrich's performance, on the other hand, appears effortless and ambivalent. Jannings unwittingly highlighted his own obsolescence by insisting on speaking what he considered to be perfect German, which Sternberg noted "was embellished with archaic inflections that had not been heard since the Middle Ages" (141). While Jannings's speech is brusque and overly formal, Dietrich flirts and sings with a wry detachment suffused with irony.

Dietrich's Lola breaks from her smirking detachment into full-blown theatricality only when Rath asks for her hand in marriage. Confirming that he's serious, Lola claps her hands and laughs uncontrollably. This crack in the performer's streetwise façade suggests that Lola might "truly desire a relationship that promises moral elevation" (Zucker 89). Indeed, her laughter is stifled when the old-fashioned gentleman soberly cautions, "I hope, my child, that you are aware of the gravity of this moment." Stunned, Lola will accept Rath's proposal, for she has long considered herself "beyond the pale of monogamy and normality" (89). And of course, Lola will prove to be beyond the pale. The moment will instead mark the accelerated downfall of Rath, who has forsaken his profession for a singer and her life in the clubs. Lola will not break from her ironic detachment again until her cuckolded husband tries to strangle her.

Corporeal containment

Jannings's massive size (six feet tall and 300 pounds) often dwarfed his fellow actors in his Hollywood films, including Sternberg's *The Last Command*. Praising the actor's "stylized monumentality," critic Rudolf Arnheim noted, "His physical structure is such a center of energy, his look is so horribly fascinating because it is that of a maturely built, ponderously sound man, so that not everything that contributes to this actor's merit is his own artistic accomplishment" (116). Seeking to contain Jannings's outsized corporeal presence in *The Blue Angel*, Prawer notes, Sternberg

> counteracted the physical bulk Jannings used to dominate his films, in which even his broad back had been celebrated for its expressive power, by casting as many fat actors around him as Ufa could turn up—including an array of enormous women sitting on the Blue Angel stage in early sequences who seemed to have stepped out of paintings by George Grosz or Otto Dix. (21)

Jannings's male counterparts—the stage magician and troupe manager Kiepert (German cabaret star Kurt Gerron) and the Blue Angel's proprietor (Hungarian actor Karl Huszar-Puffy)—are so fat that when they run into each other again late in the film, they almost touch bellies while comparing their corpulence; indeed, they make Jannings appear merely stout in comparison. Nevertheless, Jannings distinguishes himself by wearing multiple layers of formal clothing and accessories consistent with Rath's professional status (overcoat, waistcoat, vest, top hat, cane), and he continues to explore the expressive possibilities of his broad back.

When Professor Rath first encounters Lola at the Blue Angel, for example, his back is turned to her. He has entered the club during her performance of "They Call Me Naughty Lola" and, in his excitement and confusion, has become entangled in fishing nets that decorate the room, presaging his entanglement in the singer's web of seduction. The professor then backs into the room toward the stage, from which Lola shines a spotlight on his massive back. Draped in his overcoat and hat, Jannings cranes his neck around to squint into the glare of the spotlight, caught like the proverbial "moth around the flame" that Lola will sing about in "Falling in Love Again." He then glimpses one of his students at the bar and chases after him, losing his bearings as he hastens through several backstage rooms. Lola concludes her song and retreats to her dressing room, which the professor inadvertently enters by backing down a circular staircase, to her amusement. Backing into Lola's public and private spaces, the professor physically reveals the awkwardness and embarrassment that result from his compulsive curiosity and desire.

By backing Jannings into the Blue Angel and Lola's world, Sternberg was also exploiting Jannings's reputation for "acting with his back." It had started with Ewald Dupont's *Variety* (1925), in whose opening scene Jannings's face is never revealed as the camera follows his character Boss Huller trudging down a prison hallway and into the governor's office to tell his tragic story. Several more scenes focused on the actor's back, as Dupont and cinematographer Karl Freund deliberately portrayed Heller's story with many unusual camera angles, culminating in a bravura circus acrobat sequence. The results were often breathtaking, and Jannings, who the year before had been followed through revolving doors and narrow corridors by Freund's camera in *The Last Laugh*, became globally renowned as the film actor most associated with artistic innovation. The extensive focus on Jannings's back was indeed startling, for it violated a longstanding rule of the stage. Acting manuals from the late nineteenth century advised that an actor should avoid turning his back to the audience, except for rare instances of prayer, grief, humiliation, retirement, or concealment, or "to allow proper action to a superior character" (Shaftesbury 201). In *The Blue Angel*, Jannings's acting with his back emphasizes his inwardness and humiliation, and contrasts with Dietrich's frontality as an entertainer and seductress. She is always a "showgirl" in various stages of undress, both onstage and off.

Disrobement

Much of *The Blue Angel* takes place in dressing rooms, and the frequent depictions of Lola dressing and undressing are mirrored by the robing and disrobing of Professor Rath. Again, Sternberg here creatively exploits and builds upon Jannings's reputation; in addition to his pantomime and acting with his back, the actor had been celebrated for roles in which he is disrobed to enact humiliation. Most famous were the hotel doorman in *The Last Laugh* and the general in *The Last Command* (1928), both of whom are stripped of rank and uniform and then recover the uniform in an attempt to save face. *The Blue Angel*'s opening scene reveals the professor's orderly morning ritual to prepare for work, which culminates in donning his hat as he heads out the door to campus. Later, after his first evening at the Blue Angel, Rath wakes up in his bed disheveled and still partially clothed (and with Lola's underwear in hand). Leaving for work, the professor and his housemaid search unsuccessfully for his hat, which he has left at the nightclub; he is thus forced to wear a more formal top hat to school. After his next evening at the Blue Angel, which includes heavy drinking and fighting with a sea captain to gallantly defend Lola's "honor," the professor again awakes in bed disheveled and partially clothed—but this time, it is Lola's bed. And it is Lola, serving morning coffee and feigning domestic bliss, who helps the professor put on his overcoat as he scurries out the door, late for school. The professor continues to don impeccable formal wear for his engagement, wedding reception, and afterward when he proclaims to Lola that she will not have to sell her racy postcards "as long as I have a penny to my name."

Soon, however, we are presented with a much scruffier Rath on the nightclub circuit, who struggles to sell these same postcards after Lola's show. Rath blames the "ignorant bunch," prompting an outburst from Kiepert: "You need a shave! Just look at you! Who'd buy a postcard from you? . . . You're not at the college anymore." Rath's decline into shabbiness reveals not only the loss of his professional prestige, but also his loss of status among these working-class entertainers. Lola the showgirl may project questionable morals, but she is a trouper who maintains the show-business discipline to respect the audience in order to earn a living from it (Prawer 25). Rath's shame is incited not by his wife but by the economics of the troupe. Now *he* must feign domestic bliss, for he is useful only as Lola's housemaid, helping her put on her stockings and curl her hair. To continue earning his keep, he will be forced into a final act of disrobement. After an interval of four years, we find Rath sitting at a backstage mirror, not in professorial coat and tie but in the costume and makeup of the Auguste clown. Kiepert informs Rath and Lola that the troupe will be returning to the Blue Angel to feature Rath's cockcrowing act. Wearily, Rath says he will never do it, but Lola knows he will; not simply to undergo more disgrace, but to maintain a sense of worth in her eyes and in the judgment of the troupe. In Rath's mind, humiliation is a pathway, however torturous, to honor.

Jannings's silent acting tics marked the professor as an anachronistic presence amid the earthy naturalism of Dietrich and the Blue Angel club, but in his final scenes as the clown the film comes full circle to reveal where his pantomimic excesses will lead. As Kenneth S. Calhoon notes, "certain of Jannings's roles make explicit his affinity to the gestural and pantomimic practices that grew out of mystery cycles, street theater, and the carnival" (89). These roles included the trapeze artist in *Variety* and the devil-trickster in *Faust* (1926). But Jannings's clown in *The Blue Angel* is no trickster; he is utterly strange and ridiculous, enacting the mute passion of a caged animal. Moving with the slow, heavy rhythm recognizable from his silent films, Rath trudges to the stage for his "ecce homo" moment, when Kiepert will present him to the hostile crowd. For his rooster act Rath wears a top hat, the only vestige from his days as a distinguished professor. Warily keeping an eye on Lola as she flirts offstage with Mazeppa the strongman, a stuporous Rath teeters onstage and fails to perform his part of the act. Frustrated, Kiepert complains aloud, "You were once a professor!" eliciting jeers from the audience. Kiepert produces an egg and breaks it on Rath's head, but the clown still refuses to do his "kikiriki" crowing, even after Kiepert threatens to kill him. Not until Rath gets another glimpse of Lola in the clutches of Mazeppa does he let loose with his crowing. It is a howl for the ages, audibly expressing all of the humiliations Jannings's characters—and Jannings himself—had silently endured during more than a decade of pictures. Rath continues to shriek as he attempts to strangle Lola backstage and is finally subdued offscreen. He will not utter another word. The professor's initial whistle to his caged bird culminates in the clown's animal scream.

Rath's trajectory demonstrates Walter Benjamin's observation that "the horror that stirs deep in man is an obscure awareness that in him something lives so akin to the animal that it might be recognized" (448). Rath recovers some dignity by robing himself with a hat and overcoat after Keipert sets him free from his straitjacket, and he escapes the tawdry world of the Blue Angel while Lola croons "Falling in Love Again." As a night watchman's flashlight illuminates his massive back, Rath lurches down a hallway towards his former classroom, where he will die at his desk. In Rath's mind, it is the only honorable thing to do and the only honorable place to do it. Rath and Jannings have come full circle. Like his first scene, Jannings's last scene in *The Blue Angel* is performed without dialogue. Having found his voice, the actor has now gained the wisdom to relinquish it.

Note

1. Paramount's distribution agreement required both German- and English-language versions of *The Blue Angel*. Sternberg shot each version with the same cast, who spoke passable English or remained silent where the German version had dialogue. The English version premiered in the US in New York City on 5 December 1930. Jannings demonstrated proficient usage of English, which raised doubts about whether the language barrier—his stated reason for leaving Hollywood to return to Germany—was really the issue. This chapter is based on the German version, to which Sternberg always referred in interviews.

Works cited

Arnheim, Rudolf. *Film Essays and Criticism*. Trans. Brenda Benthien. Madison: University of Wisconsin Press, 1997.

Benjamin, Walter. *Selected Writings, Volume 1: 1913–1926*. Ed. Marcus Bullock and Michael W. Jennings. Cambridge, MA: Harvard University Press, 2004.

Buñuel, Luis. *An Unspeakable Betrayal: Selected Writings of Luis Bunuel*. Trans. Garrett White. Berkeley: University of California Press, 2000.

Calhoon, Kenneth S. "Emil Jannings, Falstaff, and the Spectacle of the Body Natural," *Modern Language Quarterly* 58: 1 (March 1997), 83–109.

Gemünden, Gerd. "Emil Jannings: Translating the Star," in Patrice Petro, ed., *Idols of Modernity: Movie Stars of the 1920s*, New Brunswick, NJ: Rutgers University Press, 2010, 182–201.

Kracauer, Sigfried. *From Caligari to Hitler: A Psychological History of the German Film*. Princeton, NJ: Princeton University Press, 1947.

Kreimeier, Klaus. *The Ufa Story: A History of Germany's Greatest Film Company, 1918–1945*. Trans. Robert and Rita Kimber. Berkeley: University of California Press, 1999.

Liebmann, Robert, ed. *The Blue Angel, A Film by Josef von Sternberg: An Authorized Translation of the German Continuity*. New York: Simon and Schuster, 1968.

Prawer, S. S. *The Blue Angel*. London: BFI, 2002.

Shaftesbury, Edmund. *Lessons in the Art of Acting: A Thorough Course*. Washington, DC: The Martyn College Press, 1889.

Smith, Rex. "Jannings—The Moan-Maker," *Theatre Magazine* 49: 1 (January 1929), 24+.

Von Sternberg, Josef. *Fun in a Chinese Laundry*. New York: Macmillan, 1965.

Wieland, Karin. *Dietrich & Riefenstahl: Hollywood, Berlin, and a Century in Two Lives*. Trans. Shelley Frisch. New York: Liveright, 2011.

Zucker, Carol. *The Idea of the Image: Josef von Sternberg's Dietrich Films*. Rutherford, NJ: Fairleigh Dickinson University Press, 1988.

Chapter 3

Charles Laughton in *Hobson's Choice*

Marcia Landy

> Laughton was very capable of being funny, but he was not at all comic. (Simon Callow, *Charles Laughton: A Difficult Actor*)

Charles Laughton was renowned for his acting in the role of the monarch in Alexander Korda's London Films production of *The Private Life of Henry VIII* (1933), for which he was given an Academy Award for Best Actor, along with Korda, the producer-director who was nominated for Best Picture (Lanchester 128–9). Laughton had also won two Academy nominations for *Mutiny on the Bounty* (1935) and *Witness for the Prosecution* (1957). *Hobson's Choice* (1954) won awards for director David Lean, Brenda de Banzie as Best British Actress, and John Mills as Best British Actor; and a BAFTA award for David Lean, Norman Spencer, and Wynyard Browne for Best British Screenplay—but surprisingly none for Laughton who acted the title role.

A RADA trained, British-born actor, and star of theater, cinema, and television, Charles Laughton (1899–1962) was a leading, though at times controversial, figure in Hollywood, British, and European theater and cinema. He was described as an actor who often tried to reflect on and understand a role: "what it was to be an actor" (Callow 22, 88), immersing himself in such difficult roles as Quasimodo, the hunchback of Notre Dame (1939), to express the non-verbal, gestural character of acting. In the case of certain other roles, Laughton often settled for directorial or technical accommodation to the character he was playing (Callow 22, 88). According to actor, director, and critical biographer Simon Callow, Laughton is a difficult actor and *Hobson's Choice* does not reveal his acting to advantage. Indeed, critical response to his characterization of Hobson has been mixed (Anderegg 84; Callow 222).

My chapter claims that this Lean comedy is an exemplary text for discussing the quality of Laughton's acting. His uses of his countenance, described by some as childlike; his bodily appearance, girth, carriage, and quality; and the range of his voice were keys to the success of his performances from Henry VIII, to Captain Bligh, the Hunchback, and Henry Horatio Hobson. The theatricality of his personality lends itself to the comic, melodramatic, and, at times, horrific and surreal. Laughton's relationship to film directors with whom he worked was a contribution to the success or failure of his performances, for example in his work for Alexander Korda, Billy Wilder (Bosley Crowther, "Hobson's Choice," *New York Times*, 15 June 1954, online at www.nytimes.com; see as well Peck 464–78), and Bertolt Brecht in *Galileo*. David Lean's mode of directing played a large role in Laughton's performance in *Hobson*. Laughton' s character is dependent on the uses of sound (music, natural sounds, and special effects), the romance, and the grotesque. My discussion of Laughton's acting is based on a consideration of these elements, identified with his acting, that distinguishes this adaptation from theater to cinema and entails a reconsideration of comic form to account for and revise the divergent critical responses to his work in *Hobson's Choice* specifically, if not more generally.

The critical literature on David Lean presents a formidable persona who began his career with his father's begrudging help by registering his son in the film industry at Gaumont Studios, where David learned about the phases of industrial film production, including being wardrobe master, and making contact with and learning from film technicians, actors, writers, and directors to become a respected film editor. His work with Noël Coward gradually altered his reluctance to becoming a director, but the films they made together (*In Which We Serve* (1942), *This Happy*

Breed (1943), and *Blithe Spirit* (1945)) were propaganda entertainments focusing on the war and starring a range of British actor types he would use in his production of *Brief Encounter* (1945), particularly Celia Johnson and Trevor Howard. *Brief Encounter* became a popular success, a British and transnational classic (Brownlow 203), and was followed by *Great Expectations* (1946), a significant instance of Lean's innovations in transposing the novel to cinema as a "rare example of pure cinema" (209), and still a guide to understanding Lean's conception of adapting narrative *and* theatrical texts.

After *Oliver Twist* (1948) and *The Sound Barrier* (1952), Alexander Korda intervened in the creative lives of both David Lean and Charles Laughton, in his suggestion of *Hobson's Choice* for Lean to direct and Laughton to act. In *Hobson's Choice*, Lean "achieved something in the costume genre which no-one else managed in the 1950s; he used it to interrogate aspects" of feminism, and "to provide a rueful critique of patriarchy" (Harper and Porter 102). Lean's film with Laughton's acting does provide a critique of patriarchy, but rather than being rueful it is a dark comedy in probing Hobson's misogyny, alcoholic verbal abuse, and self-aggrandizement.

Hobson's Choice is Lean's adaptation of Harold Brighouse's regional Manchester comedy that appeared in 1915. Its subsequent popularity was established in two film versions, in 1920 and 1931. Differently visualized by Lean and reminiscent of his Dickensian works, the film opens in an obscurely lit scene with the sounds of a raging stormy wind blowing a squeaky shop sign bearing the image of a boot, as if introducing an imminent horror. The camera insinuates itself into the showroom of a boot shop, panning the items for sale. Abruptly, the wind blows in a rotund, staggering, and drunken Hobson (Laughton), chased upstairs to bed (minus dialogue) by a woman, his daughter Maggie (Brenda de Banzie). This dramatic opening introduces a dilemma: how capable is an alcoholic father of controlling the lives of three daughters, Maggie, Vicky (Prunella Scales), and Alice (Daphne Anderson). Thwarting marriages of the younger women in miserly fashion by refusing to pay their dowries, and conspiring to keep the eldest, Maggie, as spinster, Hobson remains master of his domain through insult, bluster, and threat.

Awakening from his drunken night, and ready to depart as is his custom to meet his drinking cronies at the Moonraker tavern, Hobson enacts his proprietorial paternalistic stance, eyes bulging, index fingers in vest pockets, his substantial girth thrust forward, and his mouth open issuing orders. The wealthy customer Mrs. Hepworth (Helen Kay) arrives to order more boots, based on her admiration for the high quality of the ones she has bought from Hobson before. Hobson kneels before her, fawning and unaware that seated before him is the future liberator of Maggie. Here the film prefigures and offers a twist on the folk elements inherent in the Cinderella myth in its play between fantasy and the everyday, with Mrs. Hepworth a pragmatic, worldly godmother, and Maggie an older and experienced housekeeper and businesswoman. At the proper time, Mrs. Hepworth becomes a key figure in financially aiding Maggie and her protégé Will Mossop (John Mills) to create their own boot-making shop, an enterprise that will compete with and finally overtake Hobson's, forcing him to merge with them and placing them in charge of the business.

As soon as Hobson leaves for the Moonraker, after roundly insulting his daughters, Maggie, determined now to reject spinsterhood and a life of subjection under her father's tyranny and taunts, selects Will as her future husband. Sequestered in the basement where he makes the shoes they sell, Will is the embodiment of the subjected worker. Once he has become the proper mate for Maggie, she will groom and free him from his lower social status, setting up the confrontation with her father that frees her sisters in the process. A fusion between Cinderella fable and social realist regional comedy, the film has its roots in popular fiction and drama as well as cinema. While Lean has been described as having turned the film into what might be termed "a gothic comedy or baroque farce" (Anderegg 81), a significant aspect of the visual and aural design that contributes to the characterizations of the actors exists in a tension between its expressionist and regional mise-en-scène. This tension is inherent to the acting styles of de Banzie, Mills, and Laughton.

In critical analyses of the film's form, Laughton's acting has been the main source of contention. In one conception, "Laughton turns Henry Hobson, drawn by Brighouse as a vivid but conventionally 'heavy' father, into an incredible grotesque. Frequently resembling a beached whale, Laughton acts like an intruder from an entirely different story" (Anderegg 84). This view is contradicted by the director's own view, one that bears on a different conception of the film. Lean was tremendously impressed with Laughton's talent and Laughton in awe of Lean's directorial ability. Lean left Laughton free to be "inventive": Charlie "was so entertaining to watch. I just sat there applauding him going through his part and giving various versions of it. He went over the top every now and then—my fault for not holding him back—but I just sat there on a ninepenny seat in the stalls, just watching" (Brownlow 300).

If the grotesque or "gothic" is Laughton's comic medium, it is necessary to test how it functions within the film and within comic forms. The film is not Hobson's but Laughton's "choice." He is the block to his daughter's life in the everyday world and to its transformation. The style provides clues to the conflict between Hobson and his daughters through the physical character of the domestic and street settings of the town of Salford, and through actions generated by Maggie on behalf of her courtship largely enacted outside the shop. The spatial parameters involve narrative movement into the streets, the park, and outside the church where Maggie acts on her marriage to save Will from "the wrath to come," prefigured humorously by a sign displayed by a Salvation Army band marching past on a narrow street. That "wrath to come" is embodied in the Dickensian appearance of Will's large, sloppy, and proprietary landlady Mrs. Figgins (Madge Brindley), who, in her rage to maintain him as both her tenant and a future son-in-law for her straggly daughter Ada (Dorothy Gordon), attacks Will with a dustpan, occasioning a brief contretemps between the women that culminates with Will being told by Maggie that he need never come back to that place, as the couple marches off with his smiling face and blissful (reflexive) comment, "It's like a dream!"

Maggie's actions on behalf of her conquest of Will can be charted by the rhythm of her actions with and for him and against her father. Her movements are goal-driven, and vertical. Her assertive forward movement is often checked as Will hesitates before acknowledging that a different world is at hand, until by stages he assumes partnership with Maggie and an ultimate dominance over Hobson. After being menaced with a whipping by Hobson, Will leaves the shop with Maggie and the pair goes to Mrs. Hepworth, who agrees to give them a loan of £100 to begin their boot-making establishment.

As he becomes physically and socially removed from the Hobson basement, Will's appearance gradually changes as he is groomed for his inevitable confrontation with Henry Horatio Hobson. His hair grows out from its bowl shape, his pants get longer, he begins to wear suits that fit, he becomes well groomed, and more. Thus, the film can be identified as a romance comedy, involving courtship, overcoming obstacles to marriage, and financial support to achieve independence. The narrative adheres to the Brighouse text when it comes to the relationship between Maggie and Will, her progressive wooing of him and his succumbing to a new sense of his personhood. The romance elements involve inverting predictable conventions. The couple is not young; mutual erotic desire is muted, and the ending, given the antagonism between Hobson and Will and Maggie's subjection, compromises a happy ever after.

Aligned with Maggie, if Will's movement is upward and purposive, Hobson's is downward and horizontal, revealing another, and significant, aspect of the film's comedy and Laughton's acting. Bergson in his description of the comic distinguishes between gesture and action relevant to an understanding of this film: "By *gestures* we mean the attitudes, the movements and even the language by which a mental state expresses itself outwardly . . . from no other cause than a kind of inner itching" (153).

In the case of *Hobson's Choice* as romance, the viewer is in the realm of action; in other words, action is intentional or at any rate conscious, while gesture, rigid and automatic, is a source of the comic. Unwittingly Hobson exposes his rigidity, becoming a character falling (literally) "into a ready-made category . . . in which some aspect of his person of which he is unaware crystallise[s] into a stock character" (Bergson 157). This occurs after his decisive and violent attempt to threaten Maggie and Will into submission, followed by another disappointing encounter with his cohorts at the Moonraker. After insulting his cronies, he gets totally drunk and storms out of the tavern onto the street.

This most commented-upon episode of *Hobson's Choice* is visually comparable to the noir treatment of the film's opening. Hobson's staggering from the tavern places him on dark slick cobblestones where, staggering, he vainly tries to step on the moon's image and ultimately falls into the cellar of his competitor Beenstock, who has regularly been observing Hobson's pantomime of dominance from a window above the street. This fall precedes the critical wedding day where Will declares that he will "toe the line" with Maggie. Hobson's inebriated loss of control over his body is a critical stage in his struggle to maintain a now-fragile dominance over his daughters in the face of a status reduction tied to Maggie and Will's growing power.

As a performative tour de force, this episode vies with Laughton's memorable and oft-cited episode characterizing Henry VIII's defiantly rejecting gustatory ritual, when the monarch tears his chicken apart without recourse to eating utensils and throws the bones over his shoulder onto the floor behind him. The oft-quoted nocturnal street scene in *Hobson's Choice* is dark, illuminated by spotlights; the bricks on the street shine, the camera glides to Beenstock's sign, to a poster advertising against the evil tempter drink, and to a window above the scene. A puddle clearly reflects an image of the moon as well as Hobson's face in close-up. Then in medium shot he steps into other puddles until he finally slides into the basement of Beenstock's establishment, where he is found asleep the following morning.

Hobson finds himself in a predicament over which he can no longer exercise control. His present physical impasse, connected to Maggie's impending wedding, foreshadows his loss of control over his life. As he vainly attempts to grasp the reflection of the moon that disappears with each step, he falls lower and lower until he lands flat on his back in the basement of Beenstock's. That fall will be quite costly. It will become financial for Hobson when, at the wedding party for Maggie and Will, he is threatened by the lawyer Albert Prosser (Richard Wattis) with damages of £500 for transgressing on Beenstock's property. Hobson is enraged, bewailing his loss of choice, his reputation, and his penuriousness. But as the major conspirator in this plan to curb him, Maggie informs her father that his reputation can be saved by paying the marriage settlement of £250 for each daughter, to which he sullenly agrees.

If the romance comedy between Maggie and Will can be charted in its upward movement, Hobson's grotesque comedy relies on falling deeper into Maggie's plan. What was required of Laughton, as associate producer and scenarist Norma Spencer claimed, was that he be able to handle the physical performative requirements of this scene that required he slide down a chute into the cellar. Spencer suggested to Lean and Laughton that when it came to falling down, the fall should be accompanied by the sort of music "you get in a music hall or circus where there's someone left on the high wire" (Brownlow 304). Worried about this stunt, Laughton asked to for help and Billy Russell, a music hall clown, was hired. Though fearful, Laughton attended to and followed the "business invented by the old tumbler" (305).

The attempt at comedy here, described as "a tour-de-force of comic surrealism" (Silver and Ursini 120), does indeed connect to the film's opening, which promises a cruel, if not horrific narrative and turns the tables somewhat on the spectator. Laughton as Hobson is in a different world in which automatism prevails. His facial expressions and choreographed movements in this moon-mad scene convey a dreamlike state, in which he is unaware of what is happening. Bergson accounts for this lack of self-consciousness as inherent to the comical, because the character cannot be comical "unless there be some aspect of his person of which he is unaware, one side of his nature which he overlooks" (155).

The charges, by Simon Callow and Michael Anderegg, that Laughton fails to be comic are riddled with clichés about comedy, about its necessity to be funny and to produce audience identification with the comic figure. According to Anderegg, "Neither Lean nor Laughton allows Hobson to be merely funny." Although "the situations Hobson finds himself in may be comic, he is not a figure of fun: we laugh at but seldom with him" (84). Similarly, and borrowing from Anderegg, Callow regards Laughton—if not Lean as well—as having handled the humor simply as "comic business," adding that Laughton's Hobson does not "convince us—neither as a father, nor as a tyrant, as a shoemaker, even as an alcoholic; nor does he offer any other reality" (223). As I have been suggesting, contrary to Callow and to Anderegg, Laughton's acting as Hobson is indeed an example of the effective role Lean's permissiveness played in the determination of this comic character.

Callow confronts us with a naïve conception of comedy, categorizing it as moral and pedagogical, and necessarily convincing the viewer of some vague "other reality." The nocturnal street segment and the penultimate one of the delirium tremens both reveal the fragility, repetitiveness, and loss of status of the marginalized and angry paternal figure who rejects compromise. Comparing Laughton to Chaplin and Keaton rather than asking if there were other forms of comedy, Callow opines that "Laughton actually lacked a gift for the balletic, one might say the choreographic side of comedy—the side in which Chaplin and Keaton, for example, excelled," referring to his [Laughton's] "dismaying ponderousness" and "lack of self- knowledge" (88).

According to Callow, Laughton was most at home when immersed in a role, and especially one that released the misshapen and marginalized "mockery of nature" that inspired his "grotesque comic acting" as an attempt to "[come] to terms with his strangeness by displaying it" (295). What is comic (and commented upon by critics both receptive and ill disposed toward the film) are the episodes such as the drunken and later delirium episodes where the focus is on flailing bodily movement, lack of control, and regaining control only to fall inebriated, not too far from the sign about the evils of drink, into the Beenstock basement (a setting that parallels Will's workshop in the Hobson store basement).

If Laughton is indeed injecting himself as himself, this is not a refutation of the comic role he enacts; indeed through his gestures Laughton awakens the viewer to his "lack of self-knowledge." His comic obsessions proceeding from his inebriation have exposed his mental rigidity as physical. A character is generally comic in proportion to his ignorance of himself, a trait here intensively demonstrated to the viewer. According to one biographer, in making the film Laughton was unhappy: with his sexual life, his marriage, and his discomfort with the part (Higham 180), yet according to Lean, "Charlie was a fascinating man . . . Charlie knew it all in some strange way" (180).

The singularity of the drunken episode resides in its fusing multiple elements of the film that exceed the narrative. It sheds light on a type of cinematic acting that eludes conventional descriptions, through involving a focus on Laughton's expressions of bemusement, confusion, surprise, and horror. In Lean's description of an actor's performance, he states, "Most of the time, directing actors is a matter of gentle suppression and gentle encouragement. This was certainly true of Laughton, a remarkable actor" (Pratley 122). Yet there is more to be said about Lean's "gentle encouragement." The puddle sequence, acknowledged as the most remembered from the film (Maxford 84), is usually praised for its cinematic quality. Indicative of Lean's modes of transformation of the theater play into cinema, the sequence offers a visual account of how Lean and his production team created an innovative role in the performance of this actor which they found admirable. This scene is also revealing of Laughton's dilemma, conveying as it does another dimension to Hobson's alcoholic character as angry, petulant, and childlike in his antics. He exposes the paternal figure rather than merely relying on its conventional pomposity, rendering Hobson grotesque rather than trite, thus leaving open analytic and affective potential. Teddy Darvas, an editorial assistant for this film and on *The Bridge on the River Kwai* (1957), reports that "David took advantage of Laughton's overacting" in that he "encouraged Laughton to be larger than life so that Maggie and Mossop would be more realistic by contrast" (Brownlow 300).

The other grotesque episode frequently characterized as "over the top" takes place on New Year's Day when Hobson is awakened from his drunken sleep by an image of a swarm of insects. Lean's camera conveys his facial and bodily responses to horror at the delirium tremens he is trying to shake off in the images that refuse to disappear. He closes his eyes, then opens them again thinking the images will disappear, but a large mouse with big ears is superimposed on the foot of his bed. His facial expressions convey fright, confusion, and hopeless attempts to eradicate what he is seeing.

The doctor arrives. Hobson is told he needs a wife, that he has drunk himself within six months of the grave, and that he must practice abstinence. After the doctor's diagnosis, Maggie informs Hobson that he must be taken care of now and abjure drink, pronouncing and eradicating the last vestige of his power. The family gathering entails a meeting among Hobson, the two daughters, and Will to address the issue of caring for Hobson but, in the vein of realist and folk art, the narrative returns to the fairy-tale motif, as the daughters refuse to be civil to Will, as well as refusing to care for the old man, both flouncing out arrogantly. Now the question of Maggie and Will's relation to Hobson is negotiated as Hobson smugly assumes his former self-importance and dictates terms, offering Will his old job at the same salary with Maggie looking on while he returns to his customary stance in pronouncing these terms. In response, however, Will mirrors Hobson's stance, fingers in his waistcoat, chest puffed out as he offers his father-in-law a share of a "silent partnership." The contest is not over between them until proprietorship is settled. A quarrel wages about the firm's name, "Hobson and Mossop," but Will makes his own terms by insisting on "Mossop and Hobson."

Looking at Will in a new light, Maggie acquiesces. "He's the old master, and you're the new." Hobson then concedes to the couple, "I will fence you in the law by agreeing to have Prosser draw up a deed of partnership." Surveying his shop, Will runs to join Hobson and Maggie on the street. The last shot is the sign of the hanging boot, a reminder of the film's opening and a suggestion of repetition, perhaps with a difference. Although Hobson has no choice but to conform, the mirroring and circularity suggest that the new master may be the old master refashioned.

The Lean film adheres to the Brighouse play when it comes to the relationship between Maggie and Will, her progressive wooing of him, and his succumbing to a new sense of his personhood, while Laughton's Hobson diverges from this upwardly mobile scenario. *Hobson's Choice* signified Lean's movement into an epic and transatlantic style. Lean's treatment of colliding styles is exemplary of stylistic and ambivalent conflicts between authority and desire in his later films. Despite his claims of his disaffection at having to play in a film with so many drunken scenes (Higham 177), Laughton's performance situated Hobson in the comedic gallery of his other cinematic figures and, moreover, validated that the film deserved consideration for its nuanced, if surreal, sense of comedic form.

Works cited

Anderegg, Michael. *David Lean*. Boston: Twayne Publishers, 1984.

Bergson, Henri. "Laughter: An Essay on the Meaning of the Comic," in Wylie Sypher, ed., *Comedy*, Garden City, NY: Doubleday, 1956.

Brownlow, Kevin. *David Lean: A Biography*. New York: St. Martin's Press, 1996.

Callow, Simon. *Charles Laughton: A Difficult Actor*. London: Methuen, 1987.

Harper, Sue, and Vincent Porter. *British Cinema of the 1950s: The Decline of Deference*. Oxford: Oxford University Press, 2003.

Higham, Charles. *Charles Laughton: An Intimate Biography*. New York: Doubleday and Company, 1976.

Lanchester, Elsa. *Charles Laughton and I*. London: Faber and Faber, 1938.

Maxford, Howard. *David Lean*. London: B. T. Batsford, 2000.

Peck, Russell A. "Working Girl, Cinderella, and the New Jerusalem," *Christianity and Literature* 42: 3 (Spring 1993): 464–78.

Pratley, Gerlad. *The Cinema of David Lean*. South Brunswick: The Tantivy Press, 1974.

Silver, Alain, and James Ursini. *David Lean and His Films*. Los Angeles: Silman-James Press, 1992.

Chapter 4

Nikolai Cherkasov in *Ivan the Terrible*

Karla Oeler

The difficulty of describing Nikolai Cherkasov's performance in Sergei Eisenstein's *Ivan the Terrible Parts I* (1945) and *II* (1946, released 1958) lies in disentangling the actor's creative contributions from those of the makeup artist Vasilii Goriunov, the cinematographer Andrei Moskvin, and most of all, Eisenstein, whose precise vision for, and control over, every mise-en-scène is well documented and analyzed. Important scholarship on the film tends to emphasize the actor's passivity before Eisenstein's directorial will. In his 2001 multi-media essay "Eisenstein's Visual Vocabulary," for instance, Yuri Tsivian states, "Eisenstein treats the face of Cherkasov as if it were a screen upon which to project a kaleidoscope of conflicting identities." Anne Nesbet emphasizes Eisenstein's molding of Cherkasov's middle-aged body as if it had the flexibility of Mickey Mouse (191–2). And in his autobiography, *Notes of a Soviet Actor*, Cherkasov himself acknowledges Eisenstein's controlling dominance in several sometimes self-effacing passages. He writes, "I have always placed faith in the director. This, in my opinion, is the professional duty of the actor" (88). He reminisces about playing Alexander Nevsky:

> Eisenstein was ... a man of inflexible will-power and very exacting ... He not only helped me to portray epic characters, but also taught me a good deal about spacing, the use of gestures and movements. Under his guidance I was able to perfect my acting technique before the cameras. It was he, too, who taught me to be exacting to all aspects of artistic creation. There is no doubt that my association with Eisenstein has helped me to develop greatly as an artist. (103)

Of his work on *Ivan* in particular, he underlines his obedience despite the difficulty of forcing his body into the uncomfortable positions demanded by Eisenstein:

> In some of his mises-en-scène, extremely graphic in idea and composition, an actor's strained muscles often belied his inner feelings. In such cases, the actor found it difficult indeed to mould the image demanded of him. Eisenstein insisted that his ideas be carried out. This insistence infected us. We had great confidence in him and often followed him blindly, fired by enthusiasm. (105)

While we have much information concerning Eisenstein's direction of Cherkasov, there is also evidence that Eisenstein thought Cherkasov's creative contribution went beyond his flexible body, technical training (at the Russian State Institute of Performing Arts), wide range of experience, and a face that lent itself to inscription by makeup and lighting. Mikhail Kuznetsov, who played Fyodor Basmanov, states that Eisenstein told his actors, "Watch Cherkasov. He can do everything. He's the ideal film actor (quoted in Parfenov 112; my translation).

Cherkasov suggests that Eisenstein's demands presented him with an acute manifestation of a classic problem, "whether in portraying a character the actor should proceed from inner content to outer form, or vice versa" (133). Cherkasov defines "inner content" as "what to play" and "outer form" as "how to play." In James Naremore's formulation: "At one extreme, the actor develops the body as an instrument, learning a kinesics, or movement vocabulary [Cherkasov's "outer form"]; at the other, he or she is encouraged to behave more or less normally, letting gesture or facial expression rise 'naturally' out of deeply felt emotion [Cherkasov's "inner content"]" (51). Cherkasov writes, "I am convinced that whatever may be the method the actor uses, it is in his character and nature to think in images, and for that reason outer form with him is inevitably linked with inner content . . . I personally think that both ways are constructive." He adds that in theater, the question of "what to play" or "inner content" often takes precedence whereas with film, "the question 'how' is the more important, blending with 'what' as the actor prepares to act before the cameras . . . Penetration of inner content is impossible without a search for outer form. That is why a stage actor seeks for concrete outer forms in inner content, and, conversely, a film actor discovers inner content in the process of his search for outer form" (133).

In *Ivan*, the tension between "inner content" and "outer form" is spectacularly heightened. Eisenstein's (and sometimes Moskvin's) dicta on "how to play" are often felt by the actors to confound the "what to play." They experience the "outward form" as alienating them from the "inner content" they think it should convey. In short, they feel "form" as it seems to resist "content." This resistance is the precondition of *Ivan*'s, and Cherkasov's, art. What distinguishes Cherkasov's performance is the fluidity with which he plays the contradictions—both the Hamlet-like contradictions *in* his character's psychology that scramble the clear motivations of classical narrative logic, and the contradictions between what his body must perform and what his character must think and feel.

To tease out Cherkasov's responses to this problem of trying to "discover" an "inner content" commensurate with an "outer form" that threatens to subsume it requires attending to Eisenstein's precise visual imagination of Ivan, Cherkasov's recollections about the difficulty of performing within the lines drawn for him by Eisenstein, and qualities and details specific to Cherkasov's performance.

Eisenstein eschewed making the image of Ivan mundane by saddling it with ordinary human detail: everything was to be played at a heightened pitch. Drawing on Cherkasov's reminiscences, Parfenov writes that he "demanded from the actors deep psychological comprehension" of the characters and their actions, but he wanted them to express this not on the level of everyday verisimilitude, "but on the level of Shakespearean passion and emotion" (111; my translation). According to Parfenov, Eisenstein typically thought out and sketched in advance the composition of the frame and the position of the actors within it. He required his performers to bring emotional credibility to body positions that sometimes seemed to them overly stylized and improbable. Cherkasov was well trained in both eccentric and Stanislavskian methods. (Eccentric acting, unlike Stanislavsky's method, downplays—even disregards—"inner content," emphasizing instead a highly stylized "outer form" "made up," as Naremore has written, "of peculiar movements and an interesting combination of expressive codes" (235).) The role of Ivan required Cherkasov to draw on Stanislavskian technique to ground eccentric poses and movements so that his performance, despite its heightened stylization, would also seem emotionally real.

Eisenstein visualized Ivan through a palimpsest of images. Some of these were local to a specific scene. In the scene in Part I where Ivan lies ill, for instance, he resembles Christ in Hans Holbein's *The Body of the Dead Christ in the Tomb* (1520–2) (see Tsivian, *Ivan* 40–1). Other images served as guidelines for creating the "outer form" of the tsar throughout the film: Ivan as phallus, Ivan as bird of prey, and even Ivan as Mickey Mouse. Eisenstein writes:

> Even in the very first idle steps working on Ivan he always figured in my caricatures as … a phallus. Young and powerfully erect in speech at Uspensky and further, through various phases, becoming drooping and bent with old age. A full collection of these drawings was done for Cherkasov and he held onto them—we call this "working on a role." (*Disney* 78)

Eisenstein, Cherkasov, Moskvin, Goriunov, and costume designer Leonid Naumov, working from Eisenstein's sketches, collaborated to create this phallic Ivan. Eisenstein writes about working on this image with his cinematographer:

> Moskvin asks me what the general feeling of the scene of Vladimir's murder should be. How to understand the cathedral in this scene.
>
> I tell him "with an image"—the cathedral is like a womb. Ivan steps into it like the father entering the mother.
>
> That is exactly how I build things in regard to color and scenic concerns.
>
> *Two little walls of oprichniki* [secret police] move apart and along this *narrow path* Ivan enters. (*78)*

Of costume design he writes, "Ivan in a skull cap—he is conic-phallic" (78). In addition to the skull cap, Ivan also wears a Phrygian cap, which suggests the drooping phallus Eisenstein associates with Ivan's advancing age. (The Phrygian cap calls to mind figures who famously wore it, ranging from Louis XVI to Disney's seven dwarfs from the 1937 animated film that was inspirational for *Ivan*.)

To show the aging of Ivan across decades of his reign required more than making him appear increasingly bent. Cherkasov writes:

> Much effort was exerted both by V. Goryunov, the make-up artist, and Eisenstein before I was made to resemble Ivan the Terrible. Experiments with make-up stretched for six weeks. Our chief difficulty was in showing Ivan the Terrible growing older. At the beginning of the picture he is seventeen and at the end fifty-three. (161)

Famously shot in Alma-Ata (now Almaty), Kazakhstan, where the Soviet film industry decamped during the war, Ivan was filmed at night since the city could not spare electricity during the day. Cherkasov typically began the makeup process at around 9 p.m. and removed the makeup at 10 a.m. (Parfenov 110). Particularly in the coronation scene, where Cherkasov's Ivan is at his youngest, the makeup, while it helped create the "outer form," impeded the actor's ability to move his face. Goriunov used adhesive to pull back the looser, more creased flesh of middle age, transforming the forty-year-old actor into a smooth-cheeked teen. In this scene, the locus of the performance is in the movement of the eyes—they widen, they shift—and movements of the entire head. The actor speaks and his voice is expressive, now stern, now soft, but the lower half of his face moves very little.

Instead of using his jaw for expression, expression is inscribed on his jaw when his staff casts the shadow of the double-headed eagle onto his lower cheek, inaugurating the imagery of what Eisenstein considered Ivan's totem animal, a bird of prey. This avian image literally overshadows the image of the upright, phallic Ivan, and foreshadows his future predatory profile. Meanwhile, Cherkasov makes a virtue out of the necessity of the coronation scene's restricted facial movement. Sharply turning his head and shifting his eyes instead of using his whole face, he establishes in this scene the abrupt, birdlike head movements and surveying glances that correspond so well to his aquiline makeup and postures later in the film. Future scenes involve additional birdlike movements: he will crane his neck and spread his resting fingers like talons, or thrust his face forward, his shoulders and arms back, like wings. It is an eccentric stance. Cherkasov writes, "When we use the word eccentric in relation to human behavior, we mean a departure from the normal, an absence of logic in our actions, and asymmetry in our movements." He continues, "When it pursues the definite aim of . . . stressing idiosyncrasies, [eccentric acting] is extremely useful," and notes that it is a technique particularly well suited to "showing madness or other forms of mental derangement," "historical plays," and "tragic roles" (137–8). All of this describes Eisenstein's Ivan. Cherkasov developed eccentric technique at school and early in his career while performing pantomime acting at the Mariinsky Theater of Opera and Ballet. When he joined the Pushkin Theater, he writes, "My technique was becoming more and more firmly rooted in the Stanislavsky method—thanks to my association in the making of films with producers and actors of the Moscow Art Theatre" (139). The role of Ivan demands this combination of eccentric and Stanislavskian training.

In addition to Ivan-as-phallus and Ivan-as-eagle, Eisenstein took inspiration from Disney, drawing, for instance, on *Snow White* (1937) and "The Sorcerer's Apprentice" from *Fantasia* (1940) in his creation of Ivan's shadows and postural lines. He wanted his cast to strive for the impossible "plasmaticity" of Disney's characters, where limbs elongate and figures morph from one kind of creature into another. Thus, when Ivan cranes his neck to look like a bird of prey, it is also a Disneyesque move. Human bodies cannot match the plasmaticity of Disney's creations just as human limbs cannot match the seemingly weightless appendages of marionettes, which follow the movement of their central point, obviating the need for a million threads. In *Method (Metod)*, Eisenstein opposes the preference for marionettes over human dancers expressed in Heinrich von Kleist's 1810 essay, "On the Marionette Theater." He emphasizes the human element of performance in the body's resistance to the aimed-at movement (*Metod* 174–6). It's not just the leap going up and up, but also the body's response to gravity's call that interested Eisenstein, who consistently stood by the principle of reverse movement, or the idea that an actor's movement draws attention, and is thus meaningful, only through its difference from a contiguous, opposing movement (200–5). The strain, physical and mental, that he placed on his actors was deliberate in that he wanted to achieve certain graphic contours and expected the actors to reach the point of failure, and to perform at it. For instance, an actor's pose might cause his limbs to tremble involuntarily; or physical discomfort might distract him, making him feel unable adequately to sustain the emotional register of the performance. With this in mind let's consider Cherkasov's resistance, body and mind, to the aimed-at look of Ivan.

Cherkasov notes several hindrances to his performance. We have already seen how heavy makeup restricted his facial movements in the coronation scene. Another scene he found frustrating comes toward the end of Part I:

> In close-ups the actor often has to take up a very uncomfortable position and remain in it for some time. This happened when we were shooting the scene from *Ivan the Terrible* showing the tsar at the coffin of his dead wife. Eisenstein and cameraman Andrei Moskvin suggested that I get behind the coffin in which the tsarina lay, look at her and speak the line, "Am I right?" Getting no answer, I was to lower my head and touch the edge of the oak coffin with my forehead. I thought their suggestion of how the scene should be played interesting and began working on it at once. But we were so cramped for space after I had changed my position to the back of the coffin that the settings were in my way. To move or reconstruct them would have meant spending extra time and money which we could not afford. And so I had to rehearse the scene over and over again and act before the camera with my body in a most uncomfortable position. This, of course, interfered with my acting and made it difficult for me to keep in the emotional state of my character. (174)

Cherkasov complains about this scene not once, but twice:

> In the scene in which Ivan the Terrible stands before the coffin of Tsarina Anastasya [Lyudmila Tselikovskaya]—a deeply psychological scene—he not only demanded highly emotional acting, but sharply defined outer plastic form, often shackling me by the rigid line of his graphic and artistic thought. (105)

Cherkasov's sense of restriction by elements of the set and "the rigid line" of Eisenstein's "graphic and artistic thought" leads him to question his performance. The uncertainty his character expresses on the level of the story, "Am I right?" seems to infiltrate his feelings about his acting: "Am I right in the way I'm performing Ivan's emotional state?" In this scene, Ivan also rests the back of his head along the coffin's edge so that he faces directly upward, his beard jutting out horizontally to form a cross with the candle behind it. Orson Welles found this symbolism gratuitous (Tsivian, *Ivan* 43–4) and Cherkasov levels a similar criticism:

> Carried away by his enthusiasm for pictorial composition, Eisenstein moulded expressive, monumental mises-en-scène, but it was often difficult to justify the content of the form he was striving to achieve … Absorbed in his tasks as director and designer, Eisenstein began to sacrifice the story to their fulfillment … succeeding as a designer, Eisenstein failed as a director … he did not effectively control the length of each sequence or ensure cohesion. The result was

a film that was at times slow and tedious. Some of the scenes—for instance the poisoning of Anastasya by Boyarina Staritskaya [Serafima Birman]—were monotonously long. Minor episodes and sometimes mere details were given too much prominence. (105)

Cherkasov felt "the form" Eisenstein "was striving to achieve" bore a "difficult to justify" content. The Ivan whom Cherkasov was "living" did not match the Ivan whom Eisenstein was "authoring." What the actor thought unimportant had significance for the auteur. This mismatch of the director's and actor's understanding speaks to a principle Cherkasov considers fundamental to acting: one must act as if one does not know what will happen to the character one plays. He writes:

An actor should not play up the result of action and anticipate the climax from the very first scene. On the contrary, if he is fully to live the role, if he is to develop it logically, he must not think of what is to take place or of how the play is to end, but go through the experiences and action as if he did not know what was ahead. (123)

Cherkasov means the actor shouldn't perform as if he knows what's going to happen to his character later in the story, but in the case of *Ivan*, he also had to cope with his ignorance of, and resistance to, what would happen to his character in the final version of the filmic discourse. His technical performance of not knowing what happens to his character in the story draws on his actual inability to foresee the final "gestalt" of his performance onscreen. Cherkasov writes:

After watching scenes of the second part run through I criticized some episodes, but Eisenstein brushed my criticism aside, and in the end stopped showing me ready bits altogether. In films, it is the director who has the last word. Soon Eisenstein revived my interest in the role by setting me complex tasks of predominantly plastic character. Thus, in the scene with Metropolitan Philip, I had to run up to the camera for a close-up to within twenty inches of the lens, taking good care to have my chin, nose and forehead well within the camera's eye, then look wrathfully and speak lines that were supposed to terrify not only the metropolitan, but the spectators too. (106)

Attending to the specific movements required in a particular scene, Cherkasov could lose his concern with the look of the whole. But his uneasy sense of misalignment between "inner content" and "outer form" is important: it complements the self-doubt, duplicity, and conflictedness of his character. Cherkasov's not knowing how to act corresponds with

Ivan's not knowing how to act. It's an apt role for an actor's not-knowing to make itself felt, just as Ivan is a role where it makes sense for acting to fail, for palpable artifice to cause discomfort.

Inspired by Nikolai Evreinov's invention of the monodrama—a play that takes place within the mind of a single character—Eisenstein creates with his mise-en-scène the world as Ivan sees it. Thus, within this mise-en-scène Ivan is his own conflicted self-reflection, and he moves in the frame in ways that are incommensurate with what we might extrapolate to be his actual being in the world. Consider the scene where, seemingly felled by illness, he begs the boyars to recognize his son Dmitri as lawful heir to the Russian throne. At the heart of this scene lies a question: is Ivan as weak as he seems, or is he playing up his illness to test the loyalty of the boyars? On one level, he genuinely sees himself as weak: this scene rhymes with the flashback to his childhood, in Part II, where young Ivan (Erik Pyriev) appears similarly dressed in white and shrinking from boyar threat. The boy's fear persists in the man. Ivan in this scene is particularly Disneyesque even as Cherkasov's very human body is also on display—his white smock sometimes exposes his nipple. Ivan is on the floor at the boyars' knees. Reversing a pattern that dominates most of the film, it is he who strives to make eye contact with other characters, and they who look away from him. Kneeling, after begging a recalcitrant boyar to recognize Dmitri, he leans remarkably far back, up against the robe of another unmoved nobleman. He plants both hands behind his heels for support and his robe stretches taut, cleanly marking his torso's unusual 45-degree angle with the floor. With the elasticity of an animated character, Cherkasov performs Ivan not as being himself but as seeing himself being—here, being weak and afraid. His sudden recovery and chiding of the boyars underlines the illusive quality of this performance of abjection, but where the illusion lies remains unclear even to Ivan, who swings between abject weakness and crafty power.

Playing Ivan's oscillation between seeing himself as victim and as scourge, Cherkasov nimbly skips from absentmindedness to realization, to feigned playfulness hiding vengeful intent—all on the repetition of a single word, *beri* ("take"). "Take the crown," he mechanically parrots his drunken cousin Vladimir (Pavel Kadochnikov), who is parroting—and thus revealing—Efrosinia's treasonous instructions. (Efrosinia Staritskaya, also referred to above as Boyarina Staritskaya by Cherkasov, is Vladimir's mother, Ivan's aunt, and a staunch defender of boyar privilege.) Backlit and in close-up, Cherkasov turns to the camera. With most of his face in shadow and the white corner of his eye glinting, "take" becomes a shocked interrogative, and, in the next shot, a disingenuous exhortation: Vladimir must "take" the crown, dress as tsar (and be murdered in Ivan's stead).

Let's return to the scene at the coffin where Cherkasov thought his acting suffered. Ivan's response to the news that the boyars are trying to turn the people against him morphs from pure suffering into suspicion. His forehead rests against the coffin, still in the posture of debilitating grief, but his eye swivels toward Archbishop Pimen (Alexander Mgebrov), who officiates at Anastasia's funeral and is reading from Psalm 69. Cherkasov's lowered head turns to follow his eye, forehead peeling away from the wood. He gazes out suspiciously from under his brow and his movement becomes more abrupt. A cut to a close-up shows his head thrusting forward as he shouts at Pimen, "You lie!" With this turn of eye and head, Cherkasov's Ivan pivots from feeling threatened to issuing a threat. No middle ground unites and mitigates these opposing extremes. If discomfort or uncertainty as to the right emotion plagues Cherkasov, it plays right into his portrayal of Ivan as an unstable, unmediated alternation of opposites.

The performance similarly opposes vision to blindness, as in the "monotonously long" scene of Anastasia's poisoning. At the heart of this scene lies a strange, dreamlike misalignment between doing and seeing. At one extreme, Ivan moves through the world in an unseeing way, as if his inner vision, fixated on the strong Russian state that has yet to come into being, displaces his ordinary sense of sight. His mind filled with statecraft (he has just sent a message to England to circumvent his enemies via the White Sea), Ivan heads toward bedridden Anastasia and passes Efrosinia on the stairs without seeming to see her. Then he swiftly turns and even more swiftly casts his arm around his aunt's shoulders and peers closely into her face, tilting his head as if to question her. She drops her eyes. Their pantomimed interaction has double meaning. On one hand, anxious about his wife's health Ivan looks to Efrosinia for news about her condition. She drops her eyes, signaling that the news isn't good. On the other hand, this wordless interaction dramatizes the origins of Ivan's well founded suspicion of his murderous aunt: Efrosinia drops her eyes not because Anastasia's health isn't good but because she's guilty of plotting to poison her.

Anastasia swoons, Ivan reaches for her bedside cup and finds it empty. He hastens out of her chamber to seek a drink. Malyuta Skuratov (Mikhail Zharov), who spies on the boyars for Ivan, stands in the foreground, moving his eyes right and left. In the middle ground in soft focus, Ivan swings left and right with outstretched fingers, looking for a cup. Shots intervene of Anastasia, Efrosinia, and Efrosinia's hand placing the poisoned cup on the ledge above the stairs. With expert reverse movement (moving slightly back before hastening forward), Cherkasov heads to the cup and, seizing it, leans over the ledge so that, were he to glance downward, he could easily see Efrosinia standing beneath him. He takes the cup without indicating that he has seen her.

His blindness here sets the scene for his belatedly "seeing" Efrosinia in his mind's eye when Fyodor Basmanov, the first member of his secret police, or *oprichniki*, tells him she poisoned his wife. These paired scenes of the actual, but unseen poisoning, and Ivan's belatedly seeing it as he physically re-enacts it in Part II, offer one heightened instance of the systematically pronounced contrast between Ivan's visionary blindness to the world around him and key, punctuating moments of eye contact. Cherkasov follows a pattern of not looking directly at other characters except to explicitly seek their confirmation and as he suspects and accuses them (as when he rolls his forehead away from the coffin to turn his suspicious eye on Pimen). The marked moments of threatening eye contact and speech inflate the drama of very small parts of his face—the whites of his eyes, his teeth—small, but forcefully expressive, features that in turn contrast with the exaggerated movements of Ivan's pleading with the boyars to recognize his son, his athletic pleading with Philip to support his reign, his excessive gestures of humility at the mock coronation of Vladimir. When Ivan moves most, he threatens least; it's the cocking of a brow that kills.

This deft interplay between exaggerated movement and the slight, but meaningful shifting of an eye demonstrates Cherkasov's utter fluency in even the most extreme manifestations of eccentric and Stanislavskian technique. Perhaps the most powerful eruption of the eccentric in Cherkasov's performance of a conflicted tsar comes in Part II, when Malyuta, with his permission, has carried out the first executions. Ivan walks toward the corpses in the bowed posture of solemnity and regret. He removes his hat and begins to make the sign of the cross: forehead, heart, right breast . . . but instead of completing the sign by touching his left breast, he points at the corpses, flings his head back in defiance, and exclaims, "Too few!" Ivan is unpredictable not just for those around him, but for himself: uncertainty defines him. That Cherkasov, in reflecting on playing the tsar, acknowledges his own uncertainty regarding various scenes attests, paradoxically, to his Stanislavskian immersion in this properly eccentric role.

Works cited

Cherkasov, Nikolai. *Notes of a Soviet Actor*. Trans. G. Ivanov-Mumjiev and S. Rosenberg. Honolulu: University Press of the Pacific, 2004.

Eisenstein, Sergei M. *Disney*. Ed. Oksana Bulgakowa and Dietmar Hochmuth. Trans. Dustin Condren. Berlin: Potemkin Press, 2011.

Eisenstein, Sergei M. *Metod*. Ed. Naum Kleiman. Moscow: Muzei Kino, 2002.

Naremore, James. *Acting in the Cinema*. Berkeley: University of California Press, 1988.

Nesbet, Anne. *Savage Junctures: Sergei Eisenstein and the Shape of Thinking*. London: I. B. Tauris, 2003.

Parfenov, Lev. *Nikolai Cherkasov*. Moscow: Materik, 2003.

Tsivian, Yuri. "Eisenstein's Visual Vocabulary," on *Ivan the Terrible* DVD, Criterion Collection, 2001.

Tsivian, Yuri. *Ivan the Terrible*. London: BFI, 2002.

Chapter 5

Peter Lorre in *M*

Janet Bergstrom

Fritz Lang's best film, *M* (1931), is unthinkable without Peter Lorre as the child murderer, compelled to kill yet hoping to be stopped even as he is drawn to new victims. *M* was theater actor Lorre's first real film role and Lang's first sound film.[1] Lorre used his face, body, and voice as instruments evoking depths of horror. In his unforgettable final scene, he pleads with passionate helplessness for sympathy, moaning and shrieking for protection against the inner voices he hears that torment him and drive him on.

The film's working title was "Murderer (or Murderers) among Us," shortened to *M* for murderer (Kaes 15). A serial killer of children is at large in Berlin. The police have no suspects: the murderer must seem ordinary, like a neighbor or someone on the bus. Accusations break out wildly as terror overtakes the city. Newspapers publish the image of a hand-written note from the killer saying he is not finished. Politicians pressure the police, who race against time to prevent another murder, using their full personnel and the latest methods of crime detection. Nightly raids on the underworld fail to turn up clues, but they disrupt a parallel organization of city life: the underworld is as hierarchically organized as the official guardians of peace. Their leaders decide they must find the murderer themselves to stop the police from interrupting their business. The underworld elite enlist the beggars' organization—as well-ordered and classified by type as the crime world or the police—to stand watch over the city street by street, corner by corner. A beggar recognizes the murderer from the song he whistles. Another slaps the chalked letter "M" onto the back of his coat. The murderer is followed by a relay of whistled signals. He realizes what is happening and disappears into an office building. The criminal elite break in, find him, and take him to an abandoned factory where they hold a trial, including a defense lawyer. The murderer pleads that he is compelled to kill his victims, he has no choice. Before his punishment can be decided (death or a mental institution), the police arrive. A hand comes down on the accused man's shoulder as we hear: "In the name of the law." Ellipsis. Judges take their seats behind a courtroom bench (nothing else is visible, not even the accused man). The first words of the verdict are read: "In the name of the people . . ." Ellipsis. Three women dressed in black are seated, grieving, perhaps outside the courtroom. One says, "This will not bring our children back to life. We have to keep closer watch over them."[2]

When Fritz Lang made *M*, he was the top director in Germany and had established a strong international following.[3] Known for films that combined new aesthetic ideas with technical and stylistic innovations, he had thought long and hard about how to use sound in an unusual way; he did not simply want to add dialogue and sound effects or music. In fact, his use of silence in *M* is as remarkable as his use of sound: during the production of the film, seventeen days were shot silent, thirty-five days with sound (Eisenschitz, *Travail* 88). Sound in *M* is never casual or unthinking. Stretches in which ambient sound is absent may go unnoticed, however the few sounds admitted must be carefully orchestrated to add bits of external "realism" if they do not serve a dramatic purpose.

Withholding or using sound for dramatic purpose went hand in hand with Lang's strategy for hiding or showing his main character, the centripetal force of the film. We must wait fifty minutes until we can really see his face: before that, it was visible only for brief moments or veiled by shrubbery, distorted by "making faces" in a mirror, or was at too great a distance. Finally we see the murderer clearly—we can even study him—through the plate-glass window from inside Henkel's store as he stands outside looking at the array of cutlery and other wares on sale, casually eating an apple: reflected in the glass, we see his head framed by a display of knives. The street noises have disappeared when we see that configuration, heightening our opportunity to concentrate on his changing expressions. Suddenly he freezes and stares fixedly down into the window: a young girl nearby is now perfectly framed by the knives. Still staring, he wipes his hand back and forth across his mouth distractedly. His eyes close and he begins to fall forward as if about to faint. His fast, deep breathing is palpable. Then his eyes widen, the girl's reflected image begins to disappear, and now we see him from outside the store on the sidewalk: the sounds of traffic return. His head in profile, he tilts it forward so that his eyes are shadowed by the brim of his hat, and begins to walk in her direction whistling Edvard Grieg's "In the Hall of the Mountain King," just as he had done when at the beginning of the film he was with the child who would soon become his victim. But this girl is joined by her mother. The murderer half-hides at the corner of a building, looking in the direction of the girl who aroused him. Within minutes of screen time, he will find another little girl who is alone on the street; this time, his whistled murder theme will be overheard by the blind beggar who remembers hearing it when he sold him the balloon shaped like a child before Elsie Beckmann was murdered.

As the film moves toward the capture of the child killer, we see more and more of the man whom the police learn is named Hans Beckert. Two exceptional scenes near the end continue the strategy of hiding or revealing the protagonist, coordinated with the prominence of silence or dialogue. The first is almost wordless and at times absolutely silent as Beckert hides in a storage room, but his thoughts and emotions are exposed to the audience at close range through his expressive body and face. The second scene follows directly after the first: Beckert's nine-minute near-monologue in the trial scene—after more than ninety minutes without us hearing him say more than a few words—describing how he was forced to kill by voices inside him, and how he fought against them, using his entire body and a powerful vocal range. It is the murderer's longest scene (over thirteen minutes) and the last time we will see him. Lorre's performance in that final scene is so persuasive that the film is impossible to remember without it and without him.

Born László Loewenstein, Lorre grew up around Vienna. Obeying his father, he graduated from a Viennese business school in July 1921 and took a supervisory position in a bank, a job he hated (Youngkin 10).[4] Acting in the theater was presented as an alternative and he began in small roles using his new stage name Peter Lorre. His first official production premiered in November 1924 in Breslau, Germany. He appeared in theater productions continuously, working his way from small roles to significant parts, moving back and forth from the classical canon to experimental plays with controversial, often politically charged subjects that were socially unacceptable for the mainstream but that had their own following.

Lorre was an experienced actor by the time he appeared on the stage in Berlin. He had already acted in sixty-five productions, moving from Breslau to Zurich to Vienna. Even when he played small parts or when a production drew bad reviews, Lorre was singled out for praise. In Berlin he had important roles in controversial plays that drew the intelligentsia, artists, and the city's best theater critics. He also became addicted to morphine after it was administered for medical reasons, and he would undergo many attempts at a cure. He came close to joining Max Reinhardt's Berlin theater group, like so many other actors and directors who went on to fame in the cinema, but instead he chose Brecht, with whom he established an immediate rapport. According to Lorre, Brecht "cast me in one of the plays because I did not look like an actor." Lotte Lenya said that Brecht was immediately interested in Lorre: "Anything a little off-beat appealed to him." Marta Feuchtwanger observed, "So many actors were good-looking. Peter's physical appearance was a new thing to Brecht, who looked for the exception. He wanted characteristics, not beauty, and sought the unique, the distinctive" (see Youngkin 26).

In August 1928, the night before he was to begin his role as Peachum, head of the beggars in Brecht's *The Threepenny Opera*, he had an internal hemorrhage from pulmonary tuberculosis and left the city to recover in a sanitarium. Lorre's first appearance on a Berlin stage was in Marieluise Fleisser's scandalous *Engineers in Ingolstadt* on 30 March 1929. She had written and rewritten the play under the guidance or supervision of Brecht. Frank Wedekind's *Spring's Awakening* had been staged by Max Reinhardt in 1909 and immediately censored, then toned down in the face of public outrage at the indecency of explicit youthful sex and suicide. Karl Heinz Martin updated the production in October 1929, reviving sex and suicide among adolescents as well as public scandal. Lorre played a leading role: after his character's suicide, he appears in a cemetery carrying his own head. Such productions did not last long, but made a big impression.

Lang saw Lorre in *Spring's Awakening* and decided he was the person to play the lead in *M*. Lorre needed convincing that, with his looks, he could be successful in films, but Lang was certain, without a screen test, and made Lorre promise not to appear in another film before *M*.

Lorre didn't stop working with Brecht. In February 1931, during the last weeks of shooting *M*, Lorre was also rehearsing a major role in Brecht's newly politicized restaging of his play *Mann ist Mann (Man Equals Man*, or *Man Is Man)* which premiered on 6 February.[5] This was a time when the director was working through his ideas for what he called Epic Theater (Eisenschitz, "Production" 33). In early March, Brecht published a long letter in the *Berliner Börsen-Courier* about Lorre's contribution to the advancement of his theatrical staging. During the rehearsals for *Man Is Man*, the changes that Lorre gradually introduced into his depiction of the main character, Galy Gay, and their discussions of his rationale, led Brecht to change his text and staging, and his political view of his main character.[6]

Working with Brecht toward a controlled, non-naturalistic style transferred well to Lang's split-personality protagonist in *M*, although his role as Beckert may seem far from his characterizations in Brecht's or Brecht-influenced plays. Lorre had been interested in psychology for many years. Given the shot-by-shot precision of Lang's scene development and narrative progression, the coherence of Lorre's performance came from his ability to draw on diverse strains of character embodiment in view of the demands of specific shots and whole scenes: his character would be presented visually in different ways throughout the film, with greater complexity as momentum builds toward its ending. Although the narrative strategy designed by Lang and his collaborator Thea von Harbou parceled out Lorre's onscreen moments bit by bit until late in the film, when his scenes would be longer, the actor had the task—along with the director—of building up a consistent character who represented the opposite of the exactitude of the police hierarchy or the mirror world of the highly organized criminals, yet not so far from the norm as to appear suspicious on the street. Lorre was not someone who looked like everyone else, but he was filmed in such a way, and held his head and body in such positions, so as not to reveal his unusual eyes and his astonishing range of physical and vocal expressiveness until his climactic scenes.

Lorre did not conform to the image of the usual screen murderer, as Lang could appreciate after watching him in *Spring's Awakening*. Moreover he didn't resemble any of the actual serial killers who had haunted Germany's recent past: Georg Karl Grossmann, Karl Denke, Fritz Haarmann, and especially Peter Kürten, whose sensational case was in the news as the script was being written, and throughout production and pre-release publicity, and whose trial ended with a death penalty at almost the same time that *M* was submitted to the Censorship Board. As Anton Kaes pointed out, *M* premiered soon after Kürten's trial ended and eight weeks before his execution (Kaes 30).[7] Some reviewers referred to *M* as Lang's "Kürten-Film."

In *M*'s 107 minutes, Beckert appears only nine times, and the last two count for most of his screen time: in the storage room of the office building—about twelve minutes (almost wordless); the trial scene—over thirteen minutes (he speaks for about nine minutes).

1. At about 4 and a half minutes: He appears first as a shadow seen against a reward poster for the murderer of two children, bending down toward a little girl bouncing her ball against it. We only hear him speak these words: "What a pretty ball you have. What's your name?" She replies, "Elsie Beckmann." In the next shot, we see him from behind as he buys her a balloon from a blind street vendor, while whistling "In the Hall of the Mountain King." He says nothing, and we don't see his face. Then we see Elsie's ball roll out from behind a bush and her balloon float up to the telephone wires.

2. At about 8 and a half minutes: The murderer, seen from behind, is hunched over a broad window ledge writing a note to the newspapers. His pudgy hand is prominent; we can't see his face. He doesn't speak.

3. At about 17 minutes: We get a fleeting glimpse of the murderer walking out of his lodging onto the street, momentarily facing forward but at a distance. He almost crosses paths with a detective investigating him as one of a long list of those released as harmless or cured from a mental clinic. He doesn't speak.

4. At about 14:51 for less than a minute: As we hear the Police Commissioner on the telephone with a political figure about the situation, we see the murderer and his mirror image as he looks at himself grimacing. His face is fully visible, but unrevealing. An oblique angle shows unnatural expressions, making his eyes like slits or bulging, pulling his mouth back and down as if practicing a frightening or childlike mask. He doesn't speak.

5. At about 49 minutes: This is the scene described earlier, in front of Henkel's store with the knife display. The murderer's facial expressions and body movements keep changing, and repeated cutaway shots to the little girl nearby leave no doubt that she has aroused him and

caused his reactions. He begins to whistle as he turns toward her at about 51 and a half minutes, then stops after her mother appears. He doesn't speak. The scene takes about four minutes of screen time.

6. At about 53 minutes, lasting about one minute: A direct cut shows him entering a leafy alcove where a waiter appears and he orders coffee—no, vermouth—no, cognac, and when that arrives, a second one. The camera moves in, showing his face briefly after he begins to whistle his theme, but as he moves, the branches veil him. He drinks, whistles very fast, then drops his head to his hands. The camera pulls back again to a distance as he stands to pay. He speaks only to give his orders to the waiter.

7. At about 55 minutes: We hear him whistling his murder theme, but we don't see him. The blind balloon vendor recognizes him from the sound and calls another beggar, Heinrich, who sees him and follows him. He is inside a candy store with another little girl, buying her something—we see them talk but cannot hear them. Heinrich chalks a big letter "M" on the palm of his hand and manages to imprint the mark on the back shoulder of the murderer's coat. The man and girl walk along, followed. His arm is around the girl's shoulder and he is smiling. When the girl sees the M mark, the murderer looks around into a mirror on a shop wall and becomes frightened. Leaving the girl behind, he tries to vanish, but realizes that he is being watched. His pursuers whistle to alert each other. Caught because of his own whistling, now he is trapped by those around him who whistle every time he starts to go in a different direction. He runs into a large office building. In this scene, he speaks only a few words to the girl. The street scenes are mostly—and now strangely—silent except for the whistled signals.

8. At about 66 to 78 minutes, hiding in the storage room, almost twelve minutes to watch Beckert constantly: as the night watchman checks the storage room with a flashlight because the door was open, Beckert, in a darkened, wood-slatted storage unit, is hiding, backed up against the wall, his face expressing fear but not panic. He is not found, but the watchman locks the door and Beckert cannot get out, breaking his knife trying to force the lock. He pounds nails to straighten them to attack the lock, but these noises reveal his location to the criminal elite, now searching the building for him. Beckert hears them coming, looks terrified through and through, turns out the light and runs full speed to hide again. Once they are inside and nearing his hiding place, shots of Berkert show him in a state of panic, standing stiffly,

eyes wide, mouth open, every fiber at attention, waiting helplessly, then dropping to the floor to try to hide. At the last minute before the police will arrive, he is caught: he bolts upright, eyes bulging, nostrils flaring, lit up by his pursuers' flashlights in a low-angle shot. He has not uttered a word during this long scene when he has been exposed to our view constantly, except to curse his knife for breaking. Lorre has shown himself to be a gifted physical actor who can communicate his desires, frustrations, and fears with every part of his body, wordlessly. Sometimes, his body positions and expressions recall published photographs from his earlier plays, where only the costumes and makeup were more extreme.

9. At about 92 to 106 minutes, the trial scene: Beckert finally speaks— for an astonishing nine minutes with little interruption. After that, cutaway shots to his spent, cringing, crumpled body, holding onto itself on the ground to reduce his exposed surface, include him in the rest of the testimonies of this trial scene, including his defense lawyer's. Considering how Lang and von Harbou structured the film to withhold the child murderer from view except for small moments now and then, and considering how precisely Lang controlled his mise-en-scène, it is no surprise that when Beckert finally has his long dialogue scene, he would vary not only his physical acting but would phase in, so to speak, different kinds of objections or defenses as he could muster them. This could be explained in terms of maintaining audience interest in such a long scene with little physical movement, but it is even more compelling as a demonstration of the murderer's double personality: rational and calculating, aware of society's norms on the one hand, and out of control on the other.

As he is pushed and pulled up and down stairs to the trial room, his suit jacket over his head, Beckert screams furiously at the men bringing him in, demanding to know what is going on. Once inside, able to stand up and see, he turns and stops silent as he (and we) see what is behind him: the reverse field is revealed as the camera pans slowly across a huge room full of silent, motionless, seated people: the underworld and beggars involved in capturing him. The heads of the criminal elite, Schränker in charge at the center, sit at a table in front as the judges.

As the interrogation goes on, Beckert's inner defenses come undone, as enacted brilliantly by Lorre. At first indignantly shouting about the injustice being done to him, denying wrongdoing, making polite supplications (this must be a mistake), his demeanor changes entirely as deep fears emerge when he sees the balloon like the one he bought for Elsie Beckmann and the pictures of the children he murdered. He backs away more each time from those images until he tries to run up the stairs out of the room again. After he is punched and beaten all over, his hands pounded to make them let go of the door handle, and when he is thrown down the stairs, he still has the strength to demand his rights as a citizen in this most unlikely of places: he insists on being turned over to the police for a real trial. Harsh objections and derision, calls for his death, heartfelt testimony from a mother and his exhaustion send him into an inward state. He tries to gain sympathy by describing what happens to him. His phrases become shorter and louder. He twists his body around, holding his ears, not wanting to hear those voices that drive him on, no matter how he fights them. He has no choice. Then he becomes quiet as he says that he reads what he has done but he does not remember. In the end, of course, the police arrive, although we don't see anything but a hand on his shoulder.

How did Lang exact such a performance from Lorre? Or was Lorre, with the theatrical background that he had, able to bring much of the physical, mental, and emotional energy to create such a lost character, particularly in two scenes so restricted in space and themes? Lang was a physical, hands-on director. Countless photographs show him demonstrating to an actor exactly how he wanted that actor's body to be positioned or to move. Some actors complained about this bitterly, seeing it as interference with their acting skill. To my knowledge, Lorre was not one of them but he didn't like countless re-takes during the trial scene that left him bruised and exhausted, probably helping the final phase of his multi-stage, virtuoso performance in that scene, when he is reduced to a whimpering, cowering mass, no longer with the will or strength to speak or scream.

The role Peter Lorre played in *M* followed him all his life. He left Germany because of the Nazi takeover: although he may have had other compelling reasons, as a Jew it was impossible for him to remain there. After that, aside from a number of good and sometimes excellent parts in significant films, among them Hitchcock's British version of *The Man Who Knew Too Much* (1934) and *Secret Agent* (1936), Sternberg's unjustly maligned *Crime and Punishment* (1935), Karl Freund's *Mad Love* (1935), John Huston's *The Maltese Falcon* (1941), and Michael Curtiz's *Casablanca* (1942), Lorre acted continuously, in films—including as the lead in a slew of popular Mr. Moto movies (1937–9)—and later on television. But he never felt he was working at the level he had achieved in *M*. In 1950–1, he made his first film as a director, not in Hollywood but in postwar Berlin, *The Lost One*. Only twenty years after *M*, and owing a lot to it, it feels a lifetime older, with the dark look of film noir. With his haunted, sad, weary yet elegant appearance, Lorre was a commanding screen presence. He plays a doctor who realizes he has a compulsion to kill women and a political reason for murdering a man hiding from an ugly Gestapo past in this film committed to remembering, although Lorre's character ends in suicide. Unfortunately that kind of film was destined to fail with a German audience, and Peter Lorre's striking image destined to fade, so soon after the war when people wanted nothing more than to forget.[8]

Notes

1. Lorre repeated throughout his life that *M* was his first film, although he had appeared on-screen once before, uncredited, as a patient waiting to see a dentist in *The Missing Wife* (1929), one of Austria's last silent films (Youngkin 37–8).
2. This three-part ending corresponds to the release version of the film. Other versions still in circulation omit one or both of the last two shots, among other things. I am basing my observations on the 2011 film restoration, on the German Universum Film DVD.
3. Lang always affirmed that he worked closely with his wife, Thea von Harbou, one of Germany's most successful screenwriters, from conception through scripting and shooting from 1920 (*Das wanderne Bild*) until *The Testament of Dr. Mabuse*, after which, the film banned, he left for France and exile in 1933. Von Harbou remained in Germany and joined the Nazi Party. They had separated as a couple by the time *M* was made. Of course, Lang had other important collaborators, especially his cinematographers and art directors.
4. Biographical information is drawn mainly from Youngkin's book, which includes a substantive appendix of credits for Lorre's theater, film, and radio productions. See also Omasta et al.
5. Shooting for *M* finished on 16 February.
6. On 8 March 1931, Brecht published a letter in the *Berliner Börsen-Courier* titled "The Question of Criteria for Judging Acting," reprinted as "Notes to *Man Is Man*" and later as "The Question of Criteria for Judging Actors," in Willett 53–7.
7. See also the excellent documentary "The Hunt for *M*" by Torsten Kaiser (2003, 68 min. with English subtitles) on the German Universum Film DVD.
8. An excellent German DVD of *Der Verlorene* was issued by ArtHaus which unfortunately does not have English subtitles; however Robert Fischer's documentary on the film, "Displaced Person," is available on YouTube with English subtitles.

Works cited

Eisenschitz, Bernard. *Fritz Lang au travail*. Paris: Cahiers du Cinéma, 2011.

Eisenschitz, Bernard. "La production, le film," in Noël Simsolo, ed., *M, le Maudit*, Paris: Editions Plume et Cinémathèque Française, 1990.

Kaes, Anton. *M.* London: British Film Institute, 2000.

Omasta, Michael, Brigitte Mayr, and Elisabeth Streit, eds., *Peter Lorre, ein Fremder im Paradies,* Vienna: Paul Azolnay Verlag/Österreichisches Filmmuseum/Synema, 2004.

Willett, John, ed. and trans. *Brecht on Theatre.* New York: Hill and Wang, 1964.

Youngkin, Stephen D. *The Lost One: A Life of Peter Lorre.* Lexington: University Press of Kentucky, 2005.

Chapter 6

Anna Magnani in *The Golden Coach*

Sergio Rigoletto

During the postwar period, film audiences around the world came to know Anna Magnani in a number of Italian films made soon after the end of fascism, including *Rome Open City* (1946), *Angelina MP* (1947) and *Bellissima* (1951). American critics were especially struck by the naturalistic quality and intense emotionality of Magnani's acting. Writing for *The New York Times*, Bosley Crowther commends her performance in *Rome Open City* for its "humility and *sincerity*" ("How Italy Resisted," *New York Times*, 26 February 1946, 32; emphasis added). Touching on another aspect of Magnani's performance style, another *Times* critic lauds the Italian actress for the fierce passion and emotional power of her acting by comparing her to a tigress (Jane Cianfarra, "Tigress of Italy's Screen," 16 October 1949, 28).

Released in 1952, Jean Renoir's *The Golden Coach* (*Le Carrosse d'or*) presents Magnani in a seemingly unfamiliar light. Here, she gives the impression that she is not trying to come across as sincere or believable. Lacking the visceral emotional power and ebullient physicality for which the actress had become famous, her acting in this film strikes one as ironic. Magnani's verbal delivery, normally rapid and animated, appears slower and under careful control here. In the first half of the film especially, the lines that she delivers are strikingly short. Magnani's most famous film performances feature very long monologues during which the camera often appears deferential to her onscreen presence, "taking its cues from her as it 'trails' the actress in a variation of the neorealist technique of *pedinamento*" (Marcus, *After Fellini* 43). These are moments in which Magnani's body makes its expressive potential fully manifest, making the camera completely subservient to her movements. By contrast, in *The Golden Coach* the camera frequently cuts away from Magnani halfway through her delivery. She is rarely given enough time in front of the camera to warm up and showcase her virtuoso acting; the editing slows down the tempo of her performance and contains her expressive movements at the same time. Magnani's scenes often look like staged poses, the camera taking the position of an ideal theater audience. Especially at the beginning of the film, framed mainly in frontal medium shot, Magnani sits as she delivers her lines, carefully enunciating each word. She also appears frequently within windows and balconies, which cause her presence in front of the camera to appear stagey.

Calling attention to its own status as a performance, Magnani's acting in *The Golden Coach* reveals a distinctive theatricality. In discussions of film acting, theatricality normally carries negative connotations involving some degree of indulgence in ostentatious gestures and behavior too large for film, connotations that arguably stem from the assumption that film acting should look effortless and casual. Thus, it has become common to dismiss film performances that look stagey or overstated. This common view inevitably clashes with the undeniable theatrical quality of much of film acting (Naremore 9–33). Exploring the significance of theatricality in film may be, as André Loiselle and James Maron have argued, "a means to fracture the impression of reality and transparency that cinema projects" and for cinema to reflect upon itself "through the eyes of its older sibling, theater" (5). One may also suggest that theatrical performances probe the presumption of transparency within naturalistic film acting, a transparency often predicated on the medium's assumed intrinsic closeness to the physical world and on a critical discourse that has both emphasized and exaggerated cinema's ontological distance from the theater (for example, that of André Bazin).

This critical discourse was especially central to neorealism. Karl Schoonover has shown how neorealist films worked to present the body "as a site of spontaneity, immediacy and truth" within the cinematic image (97). Magnani's star image was heavily shaped by the aesthetic, political, and ethical concerns of neorealism, within the institutional discourse of which she was the embodied cinematic sign of a historical reality that cinema was now called on to rediscover, after years of fascist obscurantism (see also Wagstaff). The echoes of this institutional discourse appear clear in Millicent Marcus's discussion of Magnani's performance in *Rome Open City*. For Marcus, this performance transcends its narrative context. She refers to Pier Paolo Pasolini's famous poem on Magnani, in which he describes the experience of watching *Rome Open City* and the feeling of being "kidnapped" by Magnani's performance and led through the streets of Rome ("Pina's Pregnancy" 428).

Magnani's compelling performance in *The Golden Coach* invites us to reconsider the significance of theatricality in the consolidation of her star image. The film presents a theatrical space in which her performance does not point to a historical reality beyond the film but remains confined, self-contained, within the boundaries of its diegetic world. I read the theatrical gestures, postures, and facial expressions comprising Magnani's acting in *The Golden Coach* "as a gestic critique of the notion that the cinematic image provides privileged access to history by way of its depiction of the human body" (Schoonover 94). I argue that Magnani's performance in *The Golden Coach* goes even further. As the quintessential icon of neorealism, and in relation to the "body" as privileged historical referent in cinema, she has been understood to have a central function. Magnani's performance in *The Golden Coach*, reconfiguring film acting within the sphere of production, articulates a critique of the discourse of authenticity within the star phenomenon. Such a critique, I argue, sheds light on the constructedness of the myth of the essential self on which much of the appeal of film stardom is predicated.

*

By contrast with relatively low-budget Italian films shot mainly on location, in which Magnani starred, *The Golden Coach* was a lavish international co-production filmed almost entirely at the Cinecittà studios in Rome. With a budget of over 600 million lire, it was one of the biggest productions of 1952 and the first feature film ever produced in Continental Europe (without American participation) in Technicolor (Bergstrom).

Adapted freely from Prosper Mérimée's play *Le Carosse du Saint Sacrément, The Golden Coach* is a tribute to the theater and an exploration of the pleasures of theatricality. The engagement with the world of theater appears explicitly *narrativized* at the beginning and at the end of the film with the rise and fall of a theater curtain. The film explores the intimate relation between acting on stage and in real life. The character played by Magnani, an Italian actress called Camilla, is torn between two worlds: one is the theater, in which she performs in front of an audience by playing the *commedia dell'arte* character Columbine; the other is the everyday, a world of mundane passions and romantic adventures.

Renoir declared that while working with Magnani he tried "to deviate from the naturalist style, the so-called realist style, which had been the style of most of Magnani's films until that point" by turning her into a *commedia dell'arte* actress" (243). Emerging in sixteenth-century Italy, *commedia dell'arte* was a form of popular theater[1] that well suited Magnani, whose star persona maintained strong ties with popular culture. She had extensive experience acting in the variety theater and in her films often played working-class characters. *Commedia dell'arte* provided a natural link to her star persona since it was by definition an "actor's theatre" heavily reliant on witty improvisation and expressive gesturing. The actors generally worked with prefabricated scenarios and archetypal characters that were developed onstage through improvisation. For an actress such as Magnani, who was known for her improvisational skills and expressive physicality, the film's diegetic use of *commedia dell'arte* provided an opportunity to develop a different acting style without straying too far from her established star image. In *The Golden Coach*, Magnani worked not in her native language but in English, a significant obstacle to her improvisational talents. A close look at the final version of the script alongside her actual performance shows that Magnani's inventive additions mainly consist of emphatic sounds (like "Oh!" or "Eh?") and repetitions of single words ("It's wonderful, [wonderful!]"). Magnani certainly appears more at ease when she improvises in Italian: moments in which the actress was presumably asked by Renoir to come up with creative solutions in her native language for sections of the script that simply read "CAMILLA: invective." Here Magnani produced long tirades punctuated by abuses and screams, partly consistent with her typical demotic style.

Matthew Buckley notes that for *commedia dell'arte* actors, the body served as a crucial instrument of expression to overcome linguistic barriers, as they traveled across Europe and an as yet linguistically fragmented Italy (251). To overcome these linguistic barriers, the actors made use of emphatic postures and exaggerated gestures. While providing the model for the kind of non-naturalistic acting that Renoir wanted from Magnani, *commedia dell'arte* also offered a playful solution to Magnani's difficulties with acting in English. At one point Magnani/Camilla sits on the floor next to one of her lovers, Felipe (Paul Campbell), looking down as she mends a costume for the show. She looks up, as if struck by a sudden thought. This impression of a spontaneous reaction on Magnani's part is annulled, however, by the following mid-shot of the actress appearing merely to rehearse a line. "Within my heart love struggles to wake," says she slowly, carefully enunciating each syllable. But Magnani here mispronounces "struggle," uttering the word as an Italian would: "struggle" to rhyme with "frugal" rather than with "juggle." Felipe repeats the word correctly for her. Magnani's face shows a hint of frustration. She tries again, this time looking into Felipe's eyes. Now her pronunciation is even more strained, to the point that she cannot even complete the sentence: the "struggle" is literally too much of a struggle for her. Frustratedly, she complains to Felipe that she won't be able to perform in front of the audience in another language. The irony, of course, is that up to this point she has already been acting in English; and later, onstage, she will have no trouble delivering this line.

This moment playfully highlights what has already appeared obvious to viewers: Magnani's shaky command of English. In preparation for *The Golden Coach*, she allegedly memorized the script by learning her lines phonetically (Bergstrom 277). The producer's initial plan was to film with direct sound in both English and French, hoping to find success in English-language and European markets. Renoir had originally accepted to direct *The Golden Coach* because he was looking forward to the opportunity of making a French-language film with Magnani, whose masterful command of that language was well known. Eventually, because of financial problems, the film was shot with direct sound only in English.[2] According to the producer Francesco Alliata, conscious of Magnani's problems with the English language Renoir tried to "Italianize" the script, transforming the Peruvian actress of the Mérimée play into an Italian (283). However, an early version of the film's script in French, held at the UCLA special collections, shows several lines in Italian already assigned to Magnani's character. Thus, it is reasonable to assume that the later decision to shoot the film in English only led to an increase in the number of lines the actress would deliver in her native language. The moment in which Magnani rehearses next to Campbell reveals an undeniable degree of self-consciousness about her own difficulties in performing in a language she hardly knows. It dramatizes the struggle of the actress who, out of her comfort zone, has to work hard with the challenges that have been placed in front of her. But, most importantly, this moment sheds light on the film's own concern with the labor involved in film acting.

Magnani was a quintessential example of the "actor-star," namely a star for whom acting featured as a major aspect of her public image (Shingler and Gledhill). A common motif that accompanied Magnani's rise to film stardom was the idea that she was different from the glamorous female stars promoted by Hollywood: here was an actress with extraordinary acting talents and a work ethic, not just a personality but "the sort of performer who overwhelms whatever part she is given and makes it her own" (Murray). As the quintessential icon of neorealism, she has been understood to epitomize the idea of the "body" as privileged historical referent in cinema. At a time in which non-professional actors were simply cast for their physical type and valued above all for their authentic looks and behavior in front of the camera, directors such as Vittorio De Sica and Roberto Rossellini were said to be able "to lure even a sack of potatoes into acting" (Kracauer 24). The master critical narrative of neorealism did not exactly ignore the contribution and the craft of professional actors, but it did emphasize their improvisational talents and the naturalness of their acting. Rossellini's often-cited remark, that the true origins of neorealist cinema should be traced back to the "spontaneous creations" of popular stage and film actors such as Aldo Fabrizi and Anna Magnani, is just one example of a pervasive tendency to describe Magnani as a natural, instinctive performer—one of the implicit effects of this tendency being the inevitable downplaying of the labor and craft involved in her acting (Verdone).

Danae Clark has suggested that the discourse of realism works to naturalize actors' labor. According to this discourse, film stars do not work; they simply *are*. Clark has shown that, during the Hollywood Golden Age, the studios were involved in the task of turning stars' acting into commodity form, masking the process of labor and the source of the stars' value. As their images were being disassociated from the sphere of production, stars were encouraged by the studios to conduct their private lives as if there was an essential connection between their person and their image. The crucial point made by Clark is that, while the star phenomenon promises "the mystery" of the star's essential being, to draw attention to a star's acting as a form of labor is to reveal the constructedness both of the star image and of the myth of her essential being that the star phenomenon promotes (18–36). Despite frequently declaring in interviews that in her films she did not really act but simply "lived" the emotions of her characters, Magnani was also often keen to highlight the challenges of the acting profession, the long training she had undertaken and the importance of paying one's dues before becoming a star (Hochkofler 122). Before reaching film stardom, Magnani worked for many years in the theatre, becoming one of the most popular stage actresses of her generation. Despite marrying one of the most prolific and influential Italian filmmakers of the fascist period, Goffredo Alessandrini, through the 1930s and early 1940s Magnani was cast only in minor acting roles. She became a film star only in the mid-1940s, after having impressed Italian critics and audiences with her performances in popular comedies such as *Doctor, Beware* (1941), *The Peddler and the Lady* (1943) and *The Last Wagon* (1943).

By emphasizing the significance of acting as a form of labor, *The Golden Coach* directs our attention to a crucial component of Magnani's star persona that postwar concerns about realism with regard to film acting have partly obfuscated. Fittingly, the character played by Magnani in *The Golden Coach* is a stage actress and the monetary return of her work onstage becomes a significant aspect of the plot. When invited to perform at court by the Viceroy, her character anxiously asks the emissary, "Does he pay?" Later, she excitedly counts the golden coins that have been paid for the troupe's performance at court. In *The Golden Coach*, acting is neither effortless nor natural. It requires effort and hard work, and as such is compensated. By showing the troupe's exhaustive rehearsals and preparations for their shows, *The Golden Coach* unequivocally reveals acting as a form of labor, the product of "doing" rather than simply "being." Onstage, performing as Columbine, Magnani deftly exploits her background in the theater to sing, dance, mime, and play instruments. At one moment, the Viceroy explains why he paid such an extravagant price for a golden coach: "It is the crafts-manship that counts," says he, as if commenting on Magnani's presence in the film, and on the significance of her artistry. But these words also suggest how *The Golden Coach* invites us to indulge in an aesthetic of the artifice, the spectacular play of surfaces and masks in the film, its layers of performance ultimately more important than the representational quality of the actress's performance.

In *The Golden Coach* Magnani's acting seems to lack another familiar modulation that has been so frequently described in the literature on the Italian actress: the image of Magnani as a volcano of emotion. In 1952, *The Herald Reporter*, for example, published an article entitled "Volcanic Magnani" (11 November 1952, n.p.). Two years earlier, another British newspaper published "Volcano erupts" (*Sunday Express*, 28 November 1950, n.p.). Often conjured up to describe Magnani's full-blooded, feisty personality—both off- and onscreen—the image of the volcano seems most apt, however, to describe the kind of acting that made her famous. The image suitably describes the frequent outbursts that punctuate most of her famous film performances: from the hysterical bursts of laughter interrupting her singing in *Volcano* (1950) and in *Mamma Roma* (1962) to her heartbreaking screams in *Rome Open City* and *The Human Voice* (1948). Seemingly uncontainable, these outbursts are usually preceded by moments in which the ebullient surface of her body attempts to contain the threat of an emotional eruption until containment is no longer possible and the emotion bursts through the surface. In *The Golden Coach*, on the other hand, no hidden emotion threatens to erupt from beneath the surface. The surface remains intact. Magnani's acting relies on a vigorous use of her body, as in her squabbles with her lovers backstage. But this is the pantomime-like, overstated physicality that is typical of *commedia dell'arte*, one that is based on unrealistically exaggerated gestures and emphatic bodily movements and verbal delivery. There's no fire underneath that threatens to burst forth.

In displaying the visible signs of its labor, Magnani's is a body that appears engaged in a "doing." Rather than for what it may promise or hide, her performing body offers itself to spectators as a canvas, as pure exteriority. Let us consider a scene in which Magnani has just left the royal palace. We are given one long take, mostly an extended close-up of Magnani lasting over fifty seconds. Wearing a black dress and a typical Spanish mantilla, she does not appear engaged in any significant diegetic action, other than watching. The object of her gaze appears unclear. The camera remains steadily close to Magnani's face for most of the long take. Particularly in the absence of verbalization, the close-up tends to have the objective of externalizing feelings and thoughts through the actor's facial expression. But what is interesting here is that this externalization seems to have no obvious referent: the absence of any cuts or reaction shots does not really allow us to make sense of what Magnani's character may feel or think in relation to the diegesis, and why. This segment is remarkable for the challenge faced by Magnani. During this extended close-up, she has to convey an assorted range of emotions using only her face and the upper part of her body. What seems to matter here is not the cause of her emotions (the representational quality of the performance) but first and foremost their expression. Everything seems to take place at the level of surface, that surface being Magnani's face, which is here internally re-framed and focalized by Magnani's black dress and mantilla.

The subtle, gradual modulation of emotions Magnani accomplishes is striking. The scene begins with Magnani looking down to her right, and then, with a swift movement of her head, to the left, her gaze inquisitive, as if she is trying to locate something. She looks apprehensive, her hand frantically moving the fan below her face. Her face slowly lifts, as if finally locating the object of her search. Her eyes move rapidly to the left and then to the right, as if pondering the significance of what she has seen. At this point, Magnani has stopped moving her fan: the search for the object has now become absorption into it. But absorption soon gives way to hesitation, inquisitiveness. Her head moves slowly back to the left, now facing the camera. The movement of her eyes precedes the movement of her head, thus creating a sense of anticipation. A slight, oblique head movement seems to suggest a gratified acknowledgment of the object she is looking at. As the fan goes up again, just beneath her mouth, Magnani hints at a smile. The fan starts moving very slowly and Magnani's smile fades. Her mouth opens, hinting at another smile, together with another slight oblique movement of her head. Approval? Contentment? Her mouth immediately closes. Frowning, she appears increasingly worried, the movement of the fan broader, her breathing more vigorous. Magnani closes the fan, looking increasingly alarmed. She keeps staring. The muscles of her neck swiftly contract. She gasps. Her arms move alarmingly, as if confronted with real danger. It is at this point that the performative tour de force is over. Magnani finally unleashes a liberating smile. As the smile turns into laughter—hers and the other actors' of the troupe and the crowd's—she starts applauding. Magnani appears to direct her applause straight ahead to the camera, whereas the bullfighter appears significantly below her eyeline. It is as if Magnani, supported by the audience around her, is really applauding herself, the camera functioning as a kind of reflecting mirror through which we are invited to appreciate the craftsmanship and strenuous labor required for such a skillful modulation of emotions.

The facial close-up has often been described as a moment of truth within the cinematic image. As Béla Balázs suggested, the face speaks much more truthfully than words could ever do, allowing spectators access to the hidden essence of things: "In close-ups every wrinkle becomes a crucial element of the character and every twitch of a muscle testifies to a pathos that signals greater inner events" (37). But Magnani's gradual modulation of emotions promises no privileged access to a truth behind the surface. In this long take, her performance seems to reject the logic of the inner/outer, the close-up magnifying the subtleties of her expressive modulation but hinting at no inner experience. This moment thus encapsulates the film's idiosyncratic engagement with the discourse of authenticity that frequently informs discussions of film acting and stardom. This is a discourse that points to an inward movement through all the role playing and masks "to some place where all movement ends and begins": the organic self (Trilling 12).

At the end of *The Golden Coach*, Don Antonio (Odoardo Spadaro), the leader of the *commedia dell'arte* troupe, addresses an imaginary theater audience. The curtain has been drawn and he has moved to the edge of the stage. In addressing this imaginary theater audience, Don Antonio is also implicitly addressing us, the film viewers. The drawing of the curtain suggests now the closing of the narrative frame, and the inclusion of a kind of afterword. Here, as well as the audience, Don Antonio directly addresses Magnani's Camilla: "Don't waste your time in the so-called real life. You belong to us: the actors, acrobats, mimes, clowns, mountebanks. Your only way to find happiness is on any stage, any platform, any public place, during those two little hours when you become another person, your true self."

Don Antonio's words are puzzling. The notion of the "true self" conjures up the idea of an original core, of an essence to be found under all role playing and pretensions that society forces us to embrace. Yet, he seems actually to suggest that the true self is outside oneself: far from being an inner, essential quality of the subject, Camilla's true self is to be located in the acting roles she plays on stage ("when you become another person"). Don Antonio's statement should be considered to be implicitly addressing also the perceived authenticity of Anna Magnani's star persona. In addressing Magnani, Antonio suggests that far from being an essence waiting to be uncovered and embraced once all of its external layers have been removed, the "true self" actually comes into existence through these layers, namely through the task of acting. The notion of the true self being articulated here is the result of a process—a making—and relies on the very performances and role-playing procedures which are convention-ally dismissed as antithetical to the notion of authenticity. The view that *The Golden Coach* seems to endorse is that the Magnani we have come to recognize as authentic is somehow an outgrowth of her performances, of the gestures, vocal modulations, costumes, and mannerisms that the actress displayed through her career.

Notes

1. In his production notes, Renoir highlighted this important connection between *commedia dell'arte* and the vaudeville.
2. This was to be Magnani's first film to be shot with direct sound, post-synchronization being the most common practice in Italy up to that point.

Works cited

Balázs, Béla. *Béla Balázs: Early Film Theory. Visible Man and The Spirit of Film*. Ed. Erica Carter and trans. Rodney Livingstone. New York: Berghahn, 2010.

Bazin, André. *What is Cinema? Vol. 1 & 2*. Berkeley: University of California Press, 2005.

Bergstrom, Janet "Genealogy of 'The Golden Coach,'" *Film History* 21: 3 (2009), 276–94.

Buckley, Matthew. "Eloquent Action: The Body and Meaning in Early Commedia dell'Arte," *Theatre Survey* 50: 2 (2009), 251–315.

Clark, Danae. *Negotiating Hollywood: The Cultural Politics of Actors' Labor*. Minneapolis: University of Minnesota Press, 1995.

Crowther, Bosley, "'The Golden Coach' Rolls into the Normandie with Stunning Color and Anna Magnani," *The New York Times*, 22 January 1954.

Dyer, Richard. "A Star is Born and the Construction of Authenticity," in Christine Gledhill, ed., *Stardom: Industry of Desire*, New York: Routledge, 1991, 136–44.

Hochkofler, Matilde. *Anna Magnani*. Rome: Gremese Editore, 2005.

King, Barry. "Stardom as an Occupation," in Paul Kerr, ed., *The Hollywood Film Industry: A Reader*, New York: Routledge, 1986, 154–84.

Kracauer, Siegfried. "Remarks on the Actor," in Pamela Robertson Wojcik, ed., *Movie Acting. The Film Reader*, New York: Routledge, 2004, 19–28.

Loiselle, André, and Jeremy Maron, eds. *Stages of Reality: Theatricality in the Cinema*. Toronto: Toronto University Press, 2012.

Marcus, Millicent. *After Fellini: National Cinema in the Postmodern Age*. Baltimore: Johns Hopkins University Press, 2002.

Marcus, Millicent. "Pina's Pregnancy, Traumatic Realism and the After-Life of Rome Open City," *Italica* 85: 4 (2008), 426–38.

Murray, William. "Anna Magnani, An Obituary," *The New Yorker*, 18 April 1974.

Naremore, James. *Acting in the Cinema*. Berkeley: University of California Press, 1988.

Nowell-Smith, Geoffrey. "Anna Who?," *The Guardian*, 13 June 1978.

Renoir, Jean. *Renoir on Renoir*. Trans. Carol Volk. Cambridge: Cambridge University Press, 1988.

Schoonover, Karl. "Histrionic Gestures and Historical Representation: Masina's Cabiria, Bazin's Chaplin and Fellini's Neorealism," *Cinema Journal* 53: 2 (2014), 93–116.

Shingler, Martin and Christine Gledhill. "Bette Davis: actor/star," *Screen* 49: 1 (2008), 67–76.

Trilling, Lionel. *Sincerity and Authenticity*. Cambridge, MA: Harvard University Press, 1971.

Verdone, Mario. "Colloquio sul neorealismo (interview with Roberto Rossellini)," *Bianco e nero* (February 1952), 7–16.

Wagstaff, Christopher. *Italian Neorealist Cinema: An Aesthetic Approach*. Toronto: University of Toronto Press, 2007.

Chapter 7

Alec Guinness in *Last Holiday*

R. Barton Palmer

Anti-bravura bravura

David Lean's *Great Expectations* (1946) impresses with its extraordinary tableaux and outsized characters, with its unabashed literariness and National Heritage tone, as well as its faithfulness to a Dickensian display of bold colors. Ordinary life as such would seem to claim little place in such a sprawling production. And yet memorable for critic John Russell Taylor is Alec Guinness's brief performance as Herbert Pocket, the self-possessed young man whose principal function in the drama is to offer the naïve Pip (John Mills) friendship and (in an unforgettable scene whose Englishness is laid on thick) advice about table manners. "It is not necessary to fill the mouth to its utmost capacity," Pocket admonishes the famished Pip. This carefully calculated litotes, uttered with absolute insouciance, indelibly marks the class difference between them. The slight part was Guinness's first film role, and it remained memorable for Taylor, as he surveyed an extraordinary career in the cinema, because of the "intensity and singlemindedness of the actor's absorption in his role" (7). "It was a memorable performance," Taylor remembers, "because it seemed not to be a performance at all" (7–8).

On one level, this is of course simply a banal comment about credibility. A fundamental goal of naturalistic acting is to ease the viewer's limited investment of belief in character as "real," a schizophrenic mode of awareness that, as Baxter's comment exemplifies, is simultaneously cognizant of the talented work that goes into the confection of the illusion and its self-effacement. One might praise Mills's performance in the film on the same grounds. It would not be the last time that the two actors discovered a complex, appealing synergy in the characters they created. Ronald Neame's *Tunes of Glory* (1960) offered them the opportunity to portray disastrously conflicting forms of insecurity in a penetrating critique of British military culture. That drama eventually erupts into a series of spectacular performance moments in which emotional breakdown (that Actors Studio specialty) is the inevitable conclusion. In contrast, the more restrained connection between Mills and Guinness in *Great Expectations* resonates with a quiet everydayness, an anti-bravura bravura.

Guinness's embodiment of Herbert Pocket, so Taylor thinks, reveals something quite particular about him as an actor, a quality of which he was himself quite conscious. In character (especially on screen) and in his private life, he was characteristically less on display and "actorly" than fellow Shakespeareans John Gielgud and Laurence Olivier (with whom he otherwise shared much in common), never—so says biographer Gary O'Connor—embodying the cultural stereotype of "the great stage actor," though he could claim this status (279). Guinness always seemed "a sphinx without a secret, someone whose extraordinary quality resided in his very ordinariness, his lack of distinguishing features" (8). His late-career incarnation of John Le Carré's unassuming and quietly tragic George Smiley in two acclaimed BBC miniseries adaptations confirms, in the view of Russell Davies, that in fact "dullness is his specialty" (quoted in Taylor 9).

However, Guinness's is a dullness that is most poignantly appealing, the expression of what the actor confessed was a "certain uncomfortable void" at his center, a place whose pain he found eminently exploitable (quoted in O'Connor 122). That pain, subtly accessed, provides his more substantial characterizations with a note of wistful sadness; this is especially true of his early, and unappreciated, screen performance in Henry Cass's *Last Holiday* (1950) as an ordinary man, selected by an unusual destiny, who, as the story begins, is provided with a pain he can only after much suffering even dare to express. If modernity means disconnected solitariness for many, then George Bird is living that life. He has no family, friends, or romantic attachments and spends his days working at a job that provides little pay or satisfaction. But then his doctor tells him he has contracted "Lampington's disease," which is always rapidly fatal. Having no cure to offer, he tells Bird to empty his bank account and spend his last days in relative luxury at a "deluxe" seaside hotel, a middlebrow version of all the best that life has to offer. There, so the doctor seems to think, Bird might give himself over to a self-indulgence meant to compensate for a life cut short.

With no ideas of his own, except quitting the job he no longer needs, Bird takes this advice, making a reservation at an establishment that the travel agent suggests, by way of discouraging him, is "selective." "This time," Bird says defiantly, "they can select me." Setting out, he dons a disguise that will ease his way. A second-hand clothes peddler persuades him to purchase a wardrobe belonging to a recently deceased nobleman that, magically enough, fits him perfectly. At "The Regal," Bird finds himself uncomfortable among the upper middle-class permanent residents, but his bespoke tailoring and a pair of used suitcases plastered with travel stickers make him seem, as the receptionist puts it, a "man of the world." At first cowed into silent withdrawal, he decides to abandon his accustomed reticence among people who are in one way or another movers and shakers: politicians, successful businessmen, and a noted inventor. Being open and friendly brings unexpected success with those in a position to appreciate and reward his intelligence, sharp instincts about people, and accommodating benignity. In a matter of a few days, he becomes involved with almost everyone in the household, including the manager and chief housekeeper, even as his luck seems remarkably changed. Playing croquet for the first time, he makes an impossible shot; in his first ever round of poker he draws to a royal flush, winning a small fortune; one of the businessmen gives him a long-shot tip on a horse, who wins and pays off handsomely; and at one point he expresses a desire for rain only to see the heavens immediately fill with dark clouds.

Offers of interesting and well-remunerated employment come his way, as for the first time fortune dangles before him the prospect of a useful and satisfying life, at least as the middle class defines it. Even a government minister finds himself duly impressed by the opinions Bird provides on business-friendly economic policy. Now supplied with a substantial sum he will not live to spend, Bird gives most of it to a couple, down on their luck, who are determined to abandon a life of petty crime and incessant mooching. The irony of his (he thinks pointless) success drives him toward despair, but then it turns out, in yet another stroke of remarkably good luck, that the diagnosis was incorrect. Dr. Lampington himself checks into the hotel and, presented with Bird's case, tells him that he is not suffering from any disease, including the one to which he gave his name. Now Bird can make plans for a life that seems to hold out enormous promise, including, it should be pointed out, a significant change in his social class affiliation. His new friends are overjoyed to learn that Bird will in fact live, and they plan a dinner to celebrate his good luck. Indignant as well as pleased at his deliverance, Bird borrows a car so that he can drive home and upbraid the doctor, who discovers that his X-rays were mixed up with those of another patient. It is that man who is doomed to an early demise, not our Bird, and this, of course, as J.B. Priestley felt obligated to point out, smacks of a self-deception experience will correct.

On the return trip, Bird swerves to avoid hitting a dog and is fatally injured in the resulting crash. Still conscious as he lies dying, he is amused by the irony of how death has come for him. Eschewing regret, he reconciles to this strange destiny, which he pronounces "good," perhaps grateful for the brief moment of promised fulfillment that misdiagnosis has allowed him. Informed of his passing, the assembled guests at The Regal find themselves deeply chagrined. They had already begun disavowing any interest in or affection for Bird when he failed to return as promised. Only the housekeeper, horrified at the easy betrayal of those who had offered the newcomer friendship, feels any real sense of loss, which she thinks inappropriate to communicate to anyone else, as the hotel community, constructed by Bird's goodwill and charisma, falls apart. The film ends, as it began, with a tableau of bewildered sadness and a silent indictment of human frailty. "It's a bit thick, you know," Bird had said to the doctor after hearing the news of his imminent demise, "It's going to be all over before I've properly begun." Like the doctor's prognosis, this prediction turns out to be both right and wrong. There is no deliverance from life's sentence of death, but the reprieve can be all, or so Bird's calm, almost joyful acceptance of existential randomness suggests.

The death scene (which Cass shoots as a close-up of his disembodied face) provides Guinness with an acting moment in which his character-ization finalizes the anger Bird felt upon receiving the grim prognosis has been transformed into acceptance in this de-dramatized moment of recognition. To put this another way, Guinness's performative use of self here differs absolutely from the *dépiautage*, the peeling away, energized by recovered memory, that is at the Ibsenian heart of most celebrated Method performances. In this allegorical fable, Bird is an everyman, a cipher demanding infusion with the foundational truths of human experience. He is not a character in whom "character" in the ordinary sense is even a minimal value, and yet, with subtle changes in manner, he moves through a complex developmental arc. This role called upon Guinness more to be rather than to project, and it is an appealing ordinariness that makes his performance so memorable. It is impossible to imagine any other actor of his generation managing to portray with such affective grace a character who, lacking any strong intentions of his own, becomes the center of interest for others. We could say much the same for filmgoers, especially those in the US, many of whom, like *New York Times* reviewer Bosley Crowther, found Guinness's "doomed man ... pitiable in his misery ... funny in his bourgeois attempts at fun, but, above all ... touchingly noble in his serene and wistful despair" ("Last Holiday," 14 November 1950, online at nytimes.com). *Last Holiday* invites a metafictional reading in which the drama of Bird introducing himself to a hotel full of strangers reflects the way in which this project, offering the highly experienced stage actor his first screen starring role, asked filmgoers to find a similar appeal in his ordinariness.

Little men

Screen careers owe much to the uncontrollable vagaries of production trends, and during the first decade of his film career Guinness was fortunate to be associated with producer Michael Balcon's Ealing Studio. As Charles Barr (among others) has suggested, Ealing produced a series of comedies of manners and mores whose general theme was "the celebration of the little man," a conventional character whose screen embodiment would seem eminently suited to an actor who had projected an intriguing dullness in his first starring role (Barr 6; see as well Rawlings). Guinness is featured in some seven or eight of these films (depending on how one counts productions such as Neame's *The Card* and *Father Brown* (1954, 1956)). His Ealing productions display, as O'Connor enthuses, Guinness's "extraordinary capacity for ordinariness" (126). More than the other performers who constituted a kind of stock company at the studio (Stanley Holloway, Joan Greenwood, John Gregson, Jack Warner, and Katie Johnson), Guinness is associated with the Ealing period of cinematic excellence and cultural prominence, its resolute embodiment of the virtues and vices of a middle-class (mostly) English culture not previously a focus of the national cinema. Guinness's performance of littleness for Priestley, however, speaks, with more affecting seriousness to the underlying modern problematic of unexceptionality and aspirational mobility, of which more below.

O'Connor makes an uncharacteristic error when he signals *Last Holiday* as an Ealing production (126). Actually, Frederick Gotfurt produced the film for one of Ealing's rivals, the Associated British Picture Corporation. Gotfurt was a left-wing German émigré whose three productions for the studio all concern, as Sue Harper and Vincent Porter write, "the troubled relationship between an outsider . . . and a smug inward-looking middle-class English community," which in *Last Holiday* is the far from happy long-term residents of a seaside hotel, once "deluxe," but now fallen on hard times (77). This film is certainly "more prophetic of Guinness's future development and more revealing of the human condition" than his initial appearance for Ealing in Robert Hamer's *Kind Hearts and Coronets* (1948), where in brief sketches he played eight members of the D'Ascoyne family. In *Last Holiday*, O'Connor goes on, Guinness "played the first of his little men," and, also for the first time, managed "to turn the screen into an intimate, private form of communication" (126–7). This relationship with the spectator was not one that Guinness was able to recreate in his work for Ealing, whose projects required a different kind of performance.

That said, O'Connor's mistake about the film's production history seems more symptomatic than careless. It speaks to how deeply on some levels *Last Holiday* resonates with Guinness's subsequent work for Ealing and with what Balcon had established as the studio's artistic project, in his words: "the projection of the true Britain to the rest of the world" (quoted in Barr 7). *Last Holiday*'s engagement with values both national and universal is hardly surprising. Postwar Britain's best-known public intellectual and resolutely middlebrow author, J. B. Priestley, wrote the original script, and, for the first and only time in his distinguished career as an author and media pundit was directly involved in the film's making, with journeyman Henry Cass officially serving as director. Priestley was a fiery socialist, with views that resonated with those of Gotfurt, who contributed substantially to the final script. As *Last Holiday* exemplifies, Priestley saw life as an irremediable solitude always yearning for community, with fortune good and bad producing unexpected vicissitudes; this is certainly an Ealing theme as well and is central of some of Ealing's Guinness films, including most notably perhaps Alexander Mackendrick's *The Man in the White Suit* (1951).

In addition to its philosophical themes, *Last Holiday* spoke uncomfortable truths about a class system dependent on dubious symbols (such as Bird's second-hand Savile Row suits) and institutions, while avoiding the energetic zaniness that made the Guinness Ealing films so popular. This seriousness seems to have harmed its commercial prospects in the UK. In contrast, the film's defense of a human spirit limited by universal existential truths was more appreciated in the US, where it established Guinness as a rising star, capable of sustaining audience interest as a main character. The Ealing myth is powerful, in large measure because of Guinness's substantial contributions to the studio's golden era. However, his performances in those much-celebrated films do not sketch the full picture of his early screen career. Guinness's achievement in Priestley's film asks, at least in part, to be understood comparatively—as connected to but distinct from the work done subsequently for Ealing, to one of whose best-known Guinness "little man" productions we must briefly turn.

"When I was merely a nonentity"

In Charles Crichton's *The Lavender Hill Mob* (1951), made for Ealing the year after *Last Holiday*, Guinness portrays a mild-mannered and punctilious London *fonctionnaire*, a character who, superficially at least, resembles Bird in his deferential manner and subaltern position in the social order. Dressed in a three-piece black suit, wearing a bowler hat, and habitually carrying an umbrella, Holland seems no different in appearance or manner from the horde of his similarly-equipped fellows, whom the film shows swarming over Waterloo Bridge on their way to work. Yet the job that the middle-aged Henry Holland performs is unusual, to say the least. He oversees shipments of bullion from the mint where the gold bars are cast, riding along in the back of an armored car in order to keep a look-out for trouble. The shy, retiring Holland takes home a weekly salary whose meagerness (barely eight pounds) seems appropriate in a drab metropolis still scarred by rubble-strewn bombsites and in a country officially embracing "austerity." As far as the bank is concerned, Holland appears perfectly suited to the Sisyphean repetition of an act that mocks without hope of change his servile insignificance. Interrupted in a conversation with one of the managers, he beats a hasty retreat when another executive enters the office, folding in on himself and covering his face with one hand. Who should think that Holland was no loyal employee, but an *eiron* biding his time until he could pull off the most outrageous robbery of the public goods with which he is entrusted?

To be ordinary is to be engaged meaningfully in the social order, but it also is to live out subordination in gestures of compliance and inferiority, which, of course, is the fate, at least initially, of George Bird as well. For both characters, ordinariness and low status initially seem natural conditions. But then narrative energy is directed against apparently unshakable hierarchies, complicating, if not challenging, the notion of "littleness," and revealing it as a condition whose inhabiting incites a depression played out in scenarios of transcendence, real or imagined.

It is in a flashback (which constitutes the bulk of the film) that Holland draws a portrait of his long-term service, compliance with the rule of law, and acceptance of socio-economic marginalization. However in voiceover he quickly undercuts the truth value of this succession of images, which reflect the time, so he says, "when I was merely a nonentity," and which he proclaims would soon be marked by the most daring and unexpected of transgressions, the caper he delights in re-living. Holland endured ordinariness, but only by suppressing his *ressentiment*. He plotted robbing one of the gold shipments, a crime that, after assembling a "mob," he proved able to pull off, eventually absconding with his share of the loot to Brazil. In the film's present frame, the erstwhile clerk, become spectacularly rich, tells his story to another Englishman in a Rio de Janeiro café that seems to serve him as a kind of informal office.

Holland's ill-gotten wealth manifests itself in a certain self-indulgence, but it is also dispensed generously to the social circle that, being well-financed, he has been able to assemble around him—yet another mob of sorts. The emotionally stunted loner, trapped by the drudgery of unrewarding labor, has become an engaged, joyful, and generous member of a community in which, and, evidently with good reason, he finds himself well loved. Holland has found a life worth living in the vein of hail fellow, well met. Sharing out his good fortune from a regularly renewed pile of banknotes (the proprietor cashes his checks when he runs low), he has thoroughly shed the low-church reticence and dislike of "show" that seemed central elements of his Englishness. The film's never raucous humor depends on a nuanced exploration of the qualities of "personal restraint and concern for others, of duty and service," what Jeffrey Richards suggests became in the course of the nineteenth century the most important elements of "the national character" through their promotion by Evangelical Protestantism (12).

A heavy mindset

Holland's actions and mannerisms in *Lavender Hill* ask to be read as a presentation designed to create a certain impression, avoiding any "tells" that might disrupt the elaborate plot in which Holland's "innocence" is key. Ordinariness is both a condition to escape from and a useful lie. His tale at an end, he stands up revealing that handcuffs link him to his table companion, who is thus identified as an agent of British justice. Of course, such a banal gesture toward the coercive power of the state sidesteps rather than resolves the cultural issue at the heart of the narrative, which *Last Holiday* takes up in depth.

Holland's ordinariness, unlike Bird's, is relieved of the poignancy or moralism with which it might otherwise resonate as the film's energies are displaced onto the complex caper. Clearly both little men suffer from that most characteristic of modern discontents: the "weariness of the self" that results from the depression famously described by psychologist Alain Ehrenberg as a "pathology of grandeur." It is a drive upward in the social order that manifests itself both in Holland's seemingly unrealizable dreams of financial transcendence and also Bird's desire to finish out his life in a British version of self-indulgent luxury (166; see also 167–229). Holland is forbidden any sense of *ressentiment*, as the darker energies that the story engages, both individual and collective, remain only barely perceptible. Guinness could hardly be faulted therefore if, as O'Connor opines, "his performance [was] not revealing of his deeper self in any way" (128). And yet his portrayal of Holland *is* characterized by a kind of depth, by, as O'Connor suggests, "the commanding absence he sometimes managed to place at the centre of his best film performances" (128).

This absence is a known, or rather sensed, unknown that, as theorist Andrew Klevan suggests, constitutes a feature of film acting at its best. We are called upon to appreciate this absence meta-dramatically, not within the illusion of character, but, as Klevan suggests, within "the *performer's* capacities for revealing *and* withholding aspects of the character's sensibility" (Klevan 9, emphasis mine). Encouraging such meta-dramatic readings constituted an essential element of Guinness's approach to acting, and it has been noticed consistently by his critics and biographers. Consider Taylor's comment that the actor's characters always seem to be façades "from behind which a caring, involved, and probably very complex person is unconsciously *signaling*" (9, emphasis mine).

Sometimes the message to the spectator that there is more to be felt and understood, is insistent, even transcendent. Similarly, O'Connor perceives "a strong vein of the metaphysical" in Guinness's performance as George Smiley; the "isolation" that the actor is said to project speaks to the sense in which Smiley's pain arises from a universal and irremediable existential fact (237). An early version of such a resonant impersonation is *Last Holiday*'s George Bird, an everyman in the sense that, in Ehrenberg's formula, he is beset by "all the tensions of the modern individual" (xxx). His Ealing performances withhold such resonance in the service of dramedies with no use for the hidden pain that Guinness as an actor could bring to a performance.

In *The Lavender Hill Mob*, the absence of depth in Holland is in fact "commanding," perhaps even foundational. Guinness suspends the inner truth of Holland's character. He makes him engagingly sympathetic, if thoroughly remote and in no way an indictment of the inevitable deprivation of ordinary men who find themselves at the bottom of the social order. Holland's unrealizable refusal to be ordinary (and in his own mind "nothing") speaks not to character in the deeper sense of that term, but rather to the darker side of the *mentalité* of the early 1950s, a time during which the wartime emphasis on working collectively for national well-being still wielded considerable authority. *The Lavender Hill Mob* deploys Guinness's ability to project dullness ironically, and this neuters its expressive power.

As *Last Holiday* opens, however, Bird is empty of, not filled with, intentions of self-fashioning; he is in fact sleepwalking through life, ordinary in the sense of being submerged in the spirit-deadening, if responsible, routines that everyday living demands we follow. Importantly, it is not the prospect of impending extinction that troubles him, but the bringing to the surface of his awareness that he is a failure. By the matter-of-factness with which he expresses this perception, Guinness makes it clear that Bird has always sensed this truth, which, once again, reflects Ehrenberg's understanding of the modern condition as demanding that individuals enlist themselves as agents of their own destinies. Even after more than a decade of adult life, he has not yet gotten "properly started" on the project of making something of himself, a thought that, instead of being self-deflating, inspires him to action. "Depression," in Ehrenberg's telling metaphor, "is the guardrail of the person with no road map" (233). But Bird quickly finds direction in the banality and spiritual vacuity of the doctor's recommendation that, with no future, he might as well enjoy himself in a seaside resort. He surrenders to good fortune (agreeing to the peddler's offer of an appropriate wardrobe) and takes useful advice (the housekeeper tells him to be "open" to connections with his fellow guests). Bird achieves a sense of self, and Guinness's subdued and restrained performance, ensures that this attainment of an engagement that confers a certain power over others remains sympathetic rather than seeming a Dale Carnegie power grab. He does not "win" friends or set out to "influence" people. Like the actor who embodies him, Guinness is by nature suited only to embody E. M. Forster's famous dictum, "Only connect."

Carpe diem

And yet most important is that wistful sadness at Bird's center, a quality palpable to the actor himself and often remarked upon by critics and biographers alike, as noted earlier. It is a quality of self perceptible in his best performances, while constituting a "commanding absence" in the others. *Last Holiday* achieves its emotional and spiritual power through an endorsement of life's goodness yet unavoidable sadness. Crowther captures the film's quality perfectly in judging that Guinness manages to convey of "serene despair," only rarely seen in screen performance (one thinks of James Dean and Marlon Brando). The pain that Guinness projects is poignant in the etymological sense, that is, "piercing." Bird obeys Horace's famous admonition: the day was always there to be "plucked." But the rest of that lyric line, usually not quoted, also seems to define his experience. Why should we attend to the day we now have? The answer is simple: *quam minimum credula postero* (because only a minimum of trust should be placed in what is to come [my translation]). As Bird discovers, we must act now when the day is "ripe," but there will be a time of "afterwards" (*postero*), even if we cannot trust to it more than necessary in order to go on. However shaky and uncertain, these grounds provide our only basis for action, and this is worthy of celebration, because life can be "good," even if brief and also an occasion for regret.

O'Connor suggests that it is as a "master of disguise" that Guinness best succeeded as an actor. There is abundant evidence in his screen and stage career to support that view. But then life is all about unrealized hopes, the failure of expectations, and a death that takes us unawares. These are the most important aspects of that ordinariness Guinness was so suited by nature, experience, and talent to portray. It was no accident that he was often selected for roles in which these duller, if always already transcendent, aspects of the human condition were the focus.

Works cited

Barr, Charles. *Ealing Studios*. Woodstock, NY: Overlook Press, 1977.

Ehrenberg, Alain. *The Weariness of the Self: Diagnosing the History of Depression in the Contemporary Age*. Montreal: McGill-Queen's University Press, 2010.

Harper, Sue, and Vincent Porter. *British Cinema of the 1950s: The Decline of Deference*. Oxford: Oxford University Press, 2003.

Klevan, Andrew. *Film Performance: From Achievement to Appreciation*. London: Wallflower, 2005.

O'Connor, Garry. *Alec Guinness: Master of Disguise*. London: Hodder and Stoughton, 1994.

Rawlings, Roger. *Ripping England! Postward British Satire from Ealing to the Goons*. Albany, NY: SUNY Press, 2017.

Richards, Jeffrey. *Films and British National Identity: From Dickens to Dad's Army*. Manchester: Manchester University Press, 1997.

Taylor, John Russell. *Alec Guinness: A Celebration*. London: Pavilion, 2000.

Chapter 8

Ingrid Bergman in *Stromboli*

Victoria Duckett

For an actress who won a remarkable three Academy Awards for acting (Best Actress for *Gaslight* (1944) and *Anastasia* (1956), and Best Supporting Actress for *Murder on the Orient Express* (1974)), there is surprisingly little written about Ingrid Bergman's acting. Perhaps her peripatetic career, her tumultuous personal life, and her capacity to defy what was expected of a female celebrity in the mid-twentieth century can explain this. Indeed, the fact that this Swedish actress—considered the "first lady" of the American screen in the mid-1940s (Breen, quoted in Doherty 288)—chose to partner with Italian neorealist director Roberto Rossellini means that it is often an interest in her biography that is brought to an analysis of their work together (Barbas 288–96; McLean; Thomson). This preoccupation is particularly true of their first collaboration, *Stromboli* (1950), pivotal as it was to the establishment of the Bergman/Rossellini coupling. As Elena Dagrada explains in her discussion of Bergman's role as a Lithuanian refugee in this film, "Karin's difference echoes that of Ingrid, venturing into a world she does not know to follow a man, pregnant like her at the end of the film and sure she wants to keep her baby" (Dagrada 27).

The "Ingrid Bergman: The Early Years" programme screened at Cinema Ritrovato in 2015 is important because it marks the centenary of Bergman's birth and gives us a fresh vision of Bergman's acting. Significantly, the programme highlights Bergman's pre-Hollywood skill in developing the role of "a woman with un-revealed secrets, finding herself in contexts and milieus where she feels out-of-place" (Wengström 252). If we consider *Stromboli* in the context of this programme, Bergman's performance confirms her capacity to explore alterity within the postwar context of European exile and modern marriage. We might consequently ask: how does Bergman's character negotiate the insecurity of an Italian internment camp and the social and geographic desolation that follows in her married life on Stromboli, a remote volcanic island? What costumes, props, and music are used to bring nuance and depth to her troubled character? How does Bergman use gesture and voice to express emotion? Finally, how does Renzo Rossellini's symphonic score work in relation to her acting? There is a strong case to be made, I believe, for the need to celebrate the skill that Bergman brought to her first collaboration with Roberto Rossellini. To turn a familiar argument on its head, I suggest that the maturity and integrity Bergman displayed in her personal life is mirrored in the professionalism and care she brought to her performance of Karin in *Stromboli*.

Introducing Ingrid Bergman

We are introduced to Bergman inside an Italian refugee camp for displaced people. As a title announces, it is spring, 1948. The opening shot of volcanic smoke is followed by an exterior night-time view of a tall wall bordered by a barbed wire fence. The camera fades into an interior shot of a woman regarding herself in a hand mirror. She combs her fair hair as she walks towards a group of seated companions discussing—in a telling mix of German, French, Spanish, and Italian[1]—the returned prisoners of war with whom they share the camp compound. A woman who is marked as a lesbian through her short boyish hair, her mannish dress, and the fact that she alone is smoking, turns to address someone offscreen. "Karin," she states when a male voice is heard singing in the distance and as the camera pans right, "That is your troubadour."

Isolated within a separate physical and psychological space, Bergman makes her first appearance. Introduced through a woman who is herself marginal in the refugee group, Bergman's Karin has her difference from the women reinforced. She is detached from their banter and stretched across a single bed, playing cards. Bergman pauses her solitary game, looks up, cocks her right eyebrow, gives an amused smile, nods, packs her cards away, and with a smooth sweep of her arm reaches up to grab a cardigan from the bedframe. She then stands. In these few succinct movements, we see that Bergman is calm and confident. She is not combing her hair nor borrowing clothes in anticipation of courtship; nor is she pacing outside, seeking her lover. Instead, with a quick glance in the direction of the group of women, she says a brief "See you" and saunters away.

Bergman remains a solitary figure throughout the film. Indeed, on Stromboli—an island on the margins of continental Europe and filmed in the temporal margins of the war's conclusion—Bergman is isolated. She is shut within her home, she lounges alone by the seaside, she is the only female who visits the fishermen at sea, and she ascends the arid volcano alone in the film's climactic finale. In this opening scene, however, she is located in a communal space. Moreover, Bergman's northern complexion does not mark her as "different" in the dorm. Nevertheless, Bergman emerges as a singular and powerful presence. When she moves outdoors, for example, the other women follow. The only person to address her while they exit the building together is her lesbian companion, who wishes her (in German) "good luck." With her cardigan now slung casually across her shoulders, Bergman briefly turns and says a quiet "I'll try." At this point, just as she expresses some uncertainty, Bergman makes a gesture towards her physical appearance. Unlike the other women who use a comb and mirror, Bergman distractedly smooths her hair off her face as she strides away.

In the next scene we see Bergman in a full-length shot for the first time. She is tall and walks confidently; she seems unaware that she is watched by scattered clusters of women sitting in doorways in the compound. Tellingly, she is the only woman pictured alone. Others walk or sit in groups; even the lesbian character joins a group of women. Bergman's isolation is reiterated in the following medium shot, where we see her walking beside a wall. Her calm inscrutability is now replaced by a shifting, restless gaze. She suddenly pauses, as though unsure of where to go. Her arms cradle her stomach and her left thumb and index finger are laced awkwardly into her cardigan. She turns her head right, left, and then right again, the suggestion of a frown creasing her brow. Slowly she continues to walk forward. Bergman looks around, using her considerable height to peer at the men on the other side of the barbed wire. We see her gaze left, pivot decisively away from the row of couples who are illuminated by the overhead lights, and stride urgently into the dark night. Through all of these minute actions, we can note that in transitioning to key events in the film, Bergman is cleverly acting and not just "walking through" the moments. To see her movements in detail is to see her agency and work, plainly, and also to see evidence of her meticulous thinking through how to walk, how to use the hands, how to turn the head, and so on.

It is relevant that at no point in this sequence of turns does Bergman call out or ask where her troubadour Antonio (Mario Vitale, in his first film appearance) might be. It is her roving gaze, the small turn of her head, the speed and confidence with which she walks, and the play of her hands on her cardigan slung across her shoulders that indicate how she is feeling. The soundtrack—a male voice singing a distant ballad, with no instrumental accompaniment—accentuates both the confidence and the hesitancy that Bergman is enacting. Indeed, the soft call of the diegetic song functions like a sonic lighthouse to Bergman's searching walk. She does not know where she is going yet she is nevertheless secure that she will indeed arrive. Renzo Rossellini's symphonic score, opening the film with such dramatic aplomb, is silenced during this opening sequence of shots. It resurfaces only at the point that Bergman understands where Antonio is: as soon as she turns and hurries towards him the score (now playful) recommences.

The light tone of the music in this scene emphasizes Bergman's newly relaxed attitude. Her left hand plays with her cardigan, her right arm swings loosely beside her as she saunters along. She stops when she reaches Antonio, rests her hand invitingly on the barbed wire, and lightly says, "Ciao." She playfully follows her greeting with a comment about the weather, shaking her head, saying, "Brrrrrr" and miming the physical experience of cold. We hear Rossellini's score mimic her actions with rapidly ascending and descending wind instruments, playfully "sounding" a winter's chill. The banter that ensues is interrupted only when Antonio asks if she will marry him. After expressing light-hearted incredulity, Bergman's voice softens and she asks, "What if you're making a mistake?" This quiet question, posed to a man exuding determined optimism, reveals the hesitant insecurity of Bergman's character. We knew—when she paused and looked around as she walked into the courtyard—that she was unsure of where to go. Now that she has found Antonio and he has offered her a way out of the camp, deeper and more profound uncertainties are expressed.

"I want to get out"

In the shots marking her arrival in Stromboli, Bergman's cultural and social difference is accentuated through her clothes. Her turtleneck top, long buttoned-up trench coat, seamed stockings, leather shoes, and tightly gripped handbag and purse stand in contrast to Antonio's lack of accessories, bare feet, open collar, and casually rolled up pants (with the "PW"—prisoner of war—stamp visible on them). The ragged crew of boys and young men that meet them on the shore and who carry their luggage attenuate Bergman's formality. It is only the town priest, wearing a clerical shirt, cassock, and biretta, whose clean, neat attire matches Bergman's own. However, like Antonio's aunt (the only other neatly dressed figure in these framing shots on the island), he is dressed in black. It is therefore not just Bergman's fair complexion and dismay at the barrenness of the island that differentiate her from the bustling group of locals around her, but her attire. Indeed, her light-colored trench coat, checked headscarf, and striped handbag indicate an urban cosmopolitanism out of place in the dirty streets of the local town. Her dress is stylish and fashionable; it represents a foreign origin and a bourgeois past, as well as her distance from the religion and traditions of this remote community.

Bergman's difference from the locals on Stromboli is further elaborated on her first morning in the town. Restless during the night, she awakens to argue with Antonio. For the first time, she elaborates her thoughts, telling him that she is his wife but that she is different and belongs to "another race"; that she is a civilized human being "used to other things." Soon after, Antonio angrily departs and she walks outside. This first scene of Bergman moving outdoors and alone into the compound of her adopted village is, in some ways, similar to the sequence of shots described above: she prepares to exit her home only when she hears a voice from outside (in this instance, a baby crying), and is unsure of where to go once she exits. She walks alone across a shared compound, feeling trapped and wanting to leave.

In this scene, however, Bergman is visibly distressed. Her playful uncertainty about marriage has been replaced by tearful despair. As she slowly exits her home she opens the lower section of her double-hung wooden door, then pauses outside, her head tilting downwards as her right hand sweeps up across her face to cover her forehead in a gesture of distress. Bergman develops this gesture, distractedly resting the palm of her hand across the left side of her brow, sliding her fingers down through the underside of her unkempt hair. As Bergman runs her hand through her hair she closes the open half-door behind her. Bergman's eyes are downcast, opening briefly to look rightward just as she reaches across her face. The contrasting directions of her eyes moving rightward as her hand moves leftward underscores the disequilibrium she is feeling. Bergman holds her eyes closed or downcast in the remainder of this shot. The shifting uncertainty of her gaze in the camp compound has been exchanged for symbolic blindness: this is a gaze that refuses to search or to see.

In these first moments outside her front door, Bergman exhales soft sobs. She takes heavy steps, literally swaying from foot to foot as she walks. She comes to a halt after a few paces. The non-diegetic score is somber; strings play a sad and solitary lament. Bergman then pulls herself upright and bends forward, her actions synchronous with the rise and fall of the score. In the final elaboration of this phrase, Bergman's head falls forward, following the collapsed contour of her upper body. Her head rests perpendicular to the ground. At this point, her face is obscured by the fall of her hair. In a few short steps, and even before she has walked down the stairs into the streets, Bergman has therefore moved from a woman gesturing and sobbing her distress in the doorway of her home to an immobilized silhouette of solitary despair.

The shot that follows is not just technically different—we move from a medium shot to a long shot that frames the village compound—it also shows Bergman as a trapped woman desperately trying to flee. Her statement about being civilized and from another race, noted above, is here ironically enacted. Indeed, while her uncombed hair, pants, and small buttoned top with a deep v-neck stand her apart from the traditional headscarves, black dress, and covered bodies of the island's female inhabitants, they also accentuate her alterity as she rushes around trying to get out. Sobbing "I want to get out" (tellingly, in English), Bergman scampers chaotically through the streets. She is lost, caged by walls, high stone fences, and a confused labyrinth of paths. She becomes an animal, disorientated in a new pen, bleating her distress as she tries desperately (but hopelessly) to flee. Again the musical score adds depth to Bergman's acting: loud and dramatic, it reinforces the tension and desperation she is feeling.

As Bergman hurries through the village, she repeats the sentence, "I want to get out," changing the intonation each time she utters it. On the first occasion, she speaks a hurried stream of words. She then sharpens the "t" in each word, so we hear "wan*t* to ge*t* ou*t*" as a staccato play on endings. In her third reiteration, Bergman emphasizes and slows down the word "out," so that it does not just conclude her cry but carries all of its meaning: "owwwt." In the final repetition, we hear Bergman sob as she speaks, her voice making the last "t" of the sentence close in an audible stutter.

In the following shot, Bergman comes to a standstill. Panting, her hand resting on a wall, she looks urgently ahead. We cannot see what she is looking at but it stops her in her tracks. Advancing slowly from behind the wall, she walks towards what we now see is a young boy sitting on dilapidated steps. Bergman carefully places her right hand on a step, swivels her body sideways to sit just beneath him, and softly asks if he is crying. Receiving no response, she again places her hand flat on the stair as she leans closer. She cups his face with her hands. Releasing him in order to trace her forefingers down her face, miming the fall of tears, she asks once more: "Are you crying?" This physical enactment of spoken meaning, this pantomime of what it means to cry, in a way repeats in close-up the "I want to get out" performance of her previous shot. In other words, Bergman performs simple, short sentences, as though hopeful that this doubling up of meaning will bring answers, resolution, and freedom.

Just as Bergman does not manage to get out of the compound, so too is she unable to locate the crying child who initially drew her outside or to elicit a response from the boy she has found. It is only when she walks dejectedly away and stops to rest her head on a wall that a hostile environment transforms itself—momentarily—into a sensual reverie. With prickly pear cacti dwarfing the background of the shot, Bergman plays with a sprig of rosemary she finds protruding between rocks. Renzo Rossellini's score, quietening here to soft strings and the single call of a calming flute, emphasizes the relaxed detachment of this moment.

Rossellini's calm melody accompanies Bergman's gestures throughout this scene. Plucking a twig of rosemary, Bergman spins it between her thumb and finger and gently raises it to her mouth. Lifting her head as though awakened by the touch and perfume of the plant, she plays her lips across it, softly biting some leaves and then playfully blowing them out.

Bergman traces the rosemary across her neck, chin, and jaw. She remains in this sensual reverie even as she stands and wanders along, dropping the rosemary only when she hears the hammering of workmen in the distance. Following this sound, we hear a mournful flute, its quietness reminding us that Bergman is returning home, having gone nowhere. Indeed, Bergman enters her house, her hand pushing open the bottom half of the double-hung door in a gesture that reverses the gesture of her earlier departure. In this re-entry we understand that Bergman's flight has led nowhere and might actually have alienated her further. Indeed, even the space of her home is now not her own: she enters to greet a group of unknown men working busily in her bedroom.

Eruptions and endings

In the final scene of *Stromboli*, Bergman's Karin has fallen pregnant to Antonio. Rather than celebrating her pregnancy, she solicits the advances of a man from the lighthouse (Mario Sponzo), who agrees to help her escape her claustrophobic confines. Organizing to meet him in Ginostra—a village that he tells her can be reached on foot and that has a port which promises passage out of Stromboli—Bergman departs from her house one final time. Unlike in the scenes above, she has planned her escape. Dressed in a matching skirt and short-sleeved shirt, she carries her suitcase and purse. As she sets out, she is a model of organization; even her hair has been brushed. If it were not for her furtive and hurried glances backwards or the ominous and suggestive music underscoring the tension of her flight, we might think Bergman was hurrying away on vacation. She turns to take a final look at the cluster of white houses that define the village. Raising her head she strides purposefully forward.

In the shots that follow, we see Bergman begin to climb the volcano. The terrain steepens, her shoulders drop, smoke begins to billow, and she pauses to drag a forearm across her nose, sucking her lips into her mouth in evident distaste at the fumes. Her figure becomes engulfed by smoke and we hear a series of short, dry hacks escalate into loud sobbing coughs. She emerges from the smoke, accidentally drops her suitcase as she clambers forward, and then stumbles on, pulling a scarf from her purse to cover her mouth. Losing her purse as she does this, she puts the cloth to her mouth. Later, this scarf will become the handkerchief that wipes her tears dry and the single object she clutches to her now-pregnant stomach. In a clever play with the symbolism of the white handkerchief of the melodramatic stage,[2] Bergman twists, clutches, and pulls at her dark piece of cloth, making it far more expressive than a utilitarian protection against acrid smoke.

When Bergman finally ascends the volcano, high enough now to be out of the smoke, she is a lone figure in an arid, primordial landscape. Against the backdrop of volcanic fumes, dark earth, and rocks, she appears a fragile presence. The music, strident and dramatic, reflects the battle she is now facing: her task is to continue even as she is pushed to her physical and existential limits. Overlaid with the gusting sound of wind, dramatic bursts of volcanic explosion, and Bergman's own sobs, pants, and cries as she collapses on the mountainside, the music expresses confusion and fear. This visceral response to the volcano is far removed from a communal prayer heard in an earlier scene, when the villagers calmly waited in boats as the volcano erupted. It is only when Bergman collapses and re-awakens to stare up at the night sky that the music softens and her cries become beseeching sobs to a possible God. "Give me, give me a little peace," she begs, sobbing, with her left hand covering her eyes as her head rolls gently from side to side. When Bergman awakens she is indeed peaceful, seeing the world anew in a whisper, after pulling herself to a seated position: "What mystery!" Glancing down at her pregnant stomach she rises calmly to her feet. In a matter-of-fact tone: "What beauty."

In the film's final shot, Bergman's demeanor changes. With her brows slightly puckered, she gazes down upon the village below. Slowly and clearly, in a tone of distaste, she states: "They're . . . terrible . . . It's all . . . horrible . . . They don't know what they're doing . . . but I am worse." This private reflection, shifting abruptly between who and what Bergman is addressing, serves as a meandering prelude to her final outburst. Wiping her tears, she shifts focus to her unborn child, running her left hand slowly and meaningfully across her stomach, her hand still clutching the dark scarf. In a softly determined voice she bows her head and vows: "I will save you, my child." Looking upwards, Bergman stridently demands: "God! My God! Help me! Give me the strength, the under-standing, the courage . . ." Closing her eyes and collapsing forward into her arms in sobs, Bergman makes it clear that her goal is no longer to reach a physical destination but to achieve self-determination.

The hesitant insecurity of her walk through the camp compound and the desperate circularity of her scamper through the village is finally replaced by this challenging climb and passage across the volcano, and this cry for agency. With no village priest to serve as intermediary to God, nor a husband to determine her place of worship, Bergman is finally free to take ownership of her future and her faith. "God, My God, Merciful God, God, My God!" she screams in this lonely place.

To argue that the range and depth of female performance was neutralized with the coming of sound film, or to suggest that "new, younger, more biddable starlets"[3] replaced the great divas of the early screen, is to ignore the power of this performance. If we join Cinema Ritrovato in looking again at Bergman as a mature and developed actress, she emerges as far more than a Hollywood scandale or a character in her husband's neorealist films. She is instead a woman who authors her actions. Narratively, symbolically, and literally Bergman confirms that an actress in the 1950s could indeed "get out."

Notes

1. Because the English version of the film was so heavily censored and changed, I am discussing the Italian version. In the English film, note that one woman speaks German, another a mix of Spanish and Italian, and another speaks dialect (Gelley 81).
2. The white handkerchief was a prop employed to great emotional effect by actresses on the late nineteenth-century melodramatic stage. Used in a variety of ways (for example, wrung between hands, used to wipe tears from eyes, and so on) it was integral to the expression of female psychological distress. This prop transitioned from the melodramatic stage to early film through the work of actresses such as Lilian Gish. In the kitchen scene in *Broken Blossoms* (1919), when Lucy (Gish) accidentally burns Battling Burrows (Donald Crisp), she makes her white cloth an active part of her choreography of dismay and fear (Duckett 45). In *Stromboli*, the innocent and pure white cloth of melodrama is now a dark piece of material expressively used by Bergman as she struggles, pregnant, to get away from her husband.
3. See Pamela Hutchinson's discussion of Louise Brooks in *Little White Lies*, online at pamhutch.wordpress.com/2016/11/14/louise-brooks-v-hollywood/ where she argues that "When female stars became too powerful, they were sidelined for new, younger, more biddable starlets—the type Brooks instinctively resisted becoming."

Works cited

Barbas, Samantha. *The First Lady of Hollywood: A Biography of Louella Parsons*. Berkeley: University of California Press, 2005.

Dagrada, Elena. "The Many Faces of Stromboli," included in *Three Films by Roberto Rossellini Starring Ingrid Bergman*, New York: Criterion Collection, 2013, 24–7.

Doherty, Thomas. *Hollywood's Censor: Joseph I. Breen and the Production Code Adminis-tration*. New York: Columbia University Press, 2007.

Duckett, Victoria. "The Silent Screen, 1895–1927," in Claudia Springer and Julie Levinson, eds., *Acting*, New Brunswick, NJ: Rutgers University Press, 2015, 25–48.

Gelley, Ora. *Stardom and the Aesthetics of Neorealism*. New York: Routledge, 2012.

McLean, Adrienne. L. "The Cinderella Princess and the Instrument of Evil: Surveying the Limits of Female Transgression in Two Postwar Hollywood Scandals," *Cinema Journal* 34: 3 (Spring 1995), 36–56.

Thomson, David. "The Art of Scandal," *The New Republic* 244: 18 (11 November 2003), 60–2.

Wengström, Jon. "Ingrid Bergman: The Early Years," in *Il Cinema Ritrovato XXIX edizione*, Cineteca di Bologna, 2015, 249–57.

Chapter 9

Toshirô Mifune in *Throne of Blood*

Douglas McFarland

In fashioning *The Tragedy of Macbeth*, Shakespeare took his plot from the sixteenth-century historian Raphael Holinshed, and added to it elements from demonologies, Roman tragedy, mystery plays (*The Harrowing of Hell*), and a variety of contemporary sources that included Michel de Montaigne, Samuel Daniel, William Camden, and others. Shakespeare's world was the theater, and his medium was, of course, language. His profound achievement, especially in the tragedies, was his ability through that medium to explore the depth of human subjectivity. What would it mean to erase that language and jettison the cultural materials from which he drew? In his film adaptation of *Macbeth*, this is precisely what Akira Kurosawa did. He replaced language and Western culture with cinematic images and the Japanese theatrical conventions of the Buddhist inspired medieval Noh drama. With respect to performance, this required a shift from a style of acting predicated, as Kurosawa himself put it, on "the psychology of men or circumstances" (Cardullo 65) to the highly stylized performance techniques of the Noh drama. To play the lead role Kurosawa chose Toshirô Mifune, an actor with whom he had worked in eight previous films. Mifune's performance, however, may or may not have resulted in what Kurosawa intended. In *Throne of Blood* (1957), two cultural performance styles exist in an uneasy dialectical relationship; one resting on the Western conception of the autonomous subject and the other on a depersonalized typological figure. Stephen Prince has argued that Kurosawa understood the problematic relationship between East and West in his filmmaking: "Kurosawa drew from . . . the western tradition where the autonomous individual is accorded a discrete place in the social arena, a positioning that is less problematic than in Japanese culture" (28–9). And Kurosawa himself put this in terms of the situation Japan found itself in after the War: "I felt that without the establishment of the self as a positive value there could be no freedom and no democracy" (146). Prince notes that this relationship between East and West yielded in Kurosawa's films "formal contradictions and dialectical tensions" (31). These "contradictions" and "tensions" are on full display in Mifune's performance, one in which his own status as an actor and film celebrity confront Kurosawa's insistence on traditional Japanese performance techniques. Moreover, in an almost uncanny way this relationship ultimately forms the basis for the tragic tale of Washizu, Mifune's Japanese Macbeth.

Noh theater

In preparation for filming *Throne of Blood*, Kurosawa informed the cast of his intention to set the play in the era of the civil wars in feudal Japan and to utilize the conventions of Noh drama, a genre of theatrical representation that includes song, poetry, elaborate costuming, a highly controlled and choreographed dance allowing little or no possibility for improvisation, and most importantly for Mifune's performance, the mask. Kurosawa recalls that, "I showed each of the players a photograph of the mask of the Noh which came closest to the respective role; I told him that the mask was his own part. To Toshirô Mifune, who played the part of Taketoki Washizu [Macbeth], I showed the mask named *Heida*. This was the mask of the warrior" (Cardullo 65). The *Heida* mask had thick eyebrows, slightly darkened skin to represent time spent in the sun, a large nose, and a gaping mouth with red lips and bared teeth. The principle actor or *shite* always wore a mask in Noh, and moved in a stylized dance that would at times demand quick, almost acrobatic, movements. The words that were ostensibly assigned to the main character could be taken up at various times by the chorus or, for that matter, by any of the other figures onstage. In other words, the *shite* was required to repress individual subjectivity and instead express one "all encompassing emotion that dominated the main character" (Dramatic Museum Realia 1). Actor and mask became unified. Moreover, the Noh stage was a minimalist, almost blank space reflecting the aesthetic of some *ukiyo-e* painting (floating-world pictures, such as by Hiroshige) in which individual figures appear as miniatures in an open and all encompassing landscape. Both Noh and *ukiyo-e* are informed by teachings of the Buddha, succinctly articulated by William Scott Wilson: "The Buddhist message was that life is unsatisfactory and that we suffer because of our ignorance, greed, and hate. His fundamental solution encompassed a radical rejection of attachment—from physical objects to notions of self" (Wilson 34). The task that Kurosawa set for Mifune was quite simply to abandon the discrete subjectivity of the Shakespearean tragic hero in favor of an acting style that minimized, to the point of elimination, the distinct personality not only of the character being played but of the actor himself, Washizu and Mifune together, including the actor's history of screen performances and his subtle under-standing of Westernized conventions of acting.

Mifune as Noh actor

In order to understand Mifune's performance as the *shite* in Kurosawa's Noh adaptation, one must first understand his history and identity as a screen actor. Mifune had served as a cameraman during World War II and intended to continue in that profession in the postwar years. In 1948, Toho Studios held open auditions in order to recruit new, young actors for their productions. Mifune was encouraged to enter one of these talent contests. An actor with whom Akira Kurosawa had worked earlier told him about Mifune and encouraged him to come to his tryout. Kurosawa describes what he observed on that day: "A young man was reeling around the room in a violent frenzy. It was as frightening as watching a wounded or trapped savage beast trying to break loose. I stood transfixed" (160). When Kurosawa was told that this young man had failed the audition, he went to the judges and convinced them otherwise. And indeed Mifune went on to make two films for Toho before Kurosawa, "deeply fascinated" by his performances, cast him to play a yakuza gangster in *Drunken Angel* (1948). That film opens with Mifune stumbling into a clinic in a slum district of Tokyo in order to have a bullet wound attended to. His hair is dark, thick, and slicked back at the sides in a Robert Mitchum or Marlon Brando style. He exudes a dark, dangerous, and compelling sexuality and generates an aura of existential fatalism. His presence tends to overshadow the other performers to the extent that Kurosawa felt caught in a dilemma. He was excited by "the wonderful qualities called Mifune" but was concerned that Mifune's "powerful and innate" screen presence might "warp the structure of the drama" (162). The key term here is "innate." Mifune's performance was not a form of Method acting, but rather a dynamic display of his own screen charisma, his own powerful presence onscreen.

When Kurosawa cast Mifune in the lead role in *Throne of Blood* seven films later, he was again forced to deal with Mifune's powerful charisma. In the meantime, Mifune had become an international star through his performances in *Rashomon* (1950) and *The Seven Samurai* (1954). But I want first to consider briefly the film they made immediately prior to the adaptation of *Macbeth*, *I Live in Fear: Record of a Living Being* (1955). Mifune plays an aging patriarch who has become excessively paranoid over the possibility of a nuclear war. Much to the astonishment of his children, he decides to sell the very successful family business and move them all to a farm in Brazil. The film charts his paranoid descent into madness and ends with a disturbing scene in the asylum to which his family has committed him. For his part, Mifune was required to wear heavy makeup in order to create the appearance of an old man, to the extent that he seems as if he were wearing a mask. Contributing to this effect is the essentially single expression that he wears throughout the film: his mouth is shaped in a diagonal slash across his face, his eyebrows are held in constant consternation, and his eyes are wide open conveying an intense ferocity to his paranoia. This expression persists until the end of the film when he has gone completely mad; his mouth is now horizontal, his lips open, his teeth bared, and his face frozen in terror. The audience senses Mifune drawing upon that earlier intense screen presence, first on display in *Drunken Angel*, as it simmers beneath the surface of the half-mask of an old man. There is a dynamic interplay between the mask and the actor beneath it.

In *Throne of Blood*, through the imposition of the Noh mask, Kurosawa takes Mifune one step further, almost as if there were a progressive elimination of the actor's own persona, of those "qualities called Mifune." There is a fascinating ongoing relationship between actor and director, both needing the other and both afraid of being controlled by the other. Years later they will have a serious and by all accounts bitter falling out (Galbraith, 523–4). And so it is not simply the subjectivity of the character Mifune is playing, but his own subjectivity as an actor that Kurosawa would suppress. What emerges is a performance that defies or at least compromises Kurosawa's conception of the film. Through the movements of his body, the gestures and physical responses to his environment, the tone of his voice, but most importantly the subtle shifts of his facial expressions, Mifune is able to provide an unconventional depth to his version of Macbeth, not the ritualized depth of the Noh character, but the psychological depth that Shakespeare had generated out of pure language. The physical aspects of performance open up a pathway to the interior. He turns, if you like, Shakespeare on his linguistic head. I want to go progressively through a series of scenes critical to understanding Mifune's performance and how he negotiates that space between his own identity as an actor and the figurative mask that Kurosawa has placed over his face.

Opening sequence

Throne of Blood begins with the aura of ritual. Instead of the eerie incantation of witches and a landscape imbued with blood that inform the first act of Shakespeare's play, Kurosawa opens his film with a fog that rolls across hilly undulations. The fog then lifts to reveal memorial markers, accompanied by the musical instruments typical of Noh (flute and drums) and the incantations of a choral chant. This place was once occupied by a great castle, feudal kings, and warriors. But all things pass; all things are consumed by time; all is vanity; ambition is inevitably frustrated by process. And then the fog lifts further. A figure races on horseback toward Spider's Web Castle where he delivers news to the King (Hiroshi Tachikawa) of the impending defeat of his army. A second, and a third, and then a fourth messenger bring increasingly good news. Under the leadership of Washizu (Mifune) and Miki (Akira Kubo) foreign and domestic enemies have been defeated. The exuberant king announces that the two warriors will be rewarded.

The film then cuts to the dramatic entrance of those warriors. They emerge on horseback out of the labyrinthine forest that serves as a protective barrier for the castle. They charge toward the camera but then abruptly halt in a clearing. Washizu and Miki seem disoriented and anxious, apparently unable to discover a way out of the confusing paths of the forest. In a medium close-up of Washizu, the audience sees the aggressive face of the warrior, very much in keeping with the Noh mask that Kurosawa had shown to Mifune. The aggressive expression of Mifune's mask-like face seems ready to forcibly clear a path through the forest. He then looks upward to the sky above the trees, stoically allowing the rain to pelt his face. He turns his head back to the horizontal plain and looks around him with a deliberativeness. The camera pulls back and the warriors return at full gallop back into the forest but then return to the location they had occupied earlier, frustrated with their inability to escape. Washizu's face conveys initial confusion (his mouth forms a perfect circle) but is followed by mixture of control and authority. He again surveys the horizontal plane of the forest and then bends his head upward to the tops of the trees. A fierce aggressiveness takes hold of his face, and he fires an arrow at the eerie voice that emanates from the canopy of the forest. Mifune fashions a human subject, not with words but with his eyes, his mouth, and his body. He is physically and psychologically in motion, darting from one expression to another. He is fierce, aggressive, anxious, deliberative, stoical, and analytical. The rapidity of these attributes as they come and go gives the impression that they are not discrete images of a mask but aspects of a human subject. Moreover, and subversively, we sense Mifune the actor struggling to come out from behind the mask that Kurosawa handed him on that first day of preparation. Multiple tensions have arisen between mythical ritual and naturalistic setting; between the impenetrable Noh mask and the subjective interiority of the modern screen actor; and between Kurosawa's explicit intentions and Mifune's own will. This dynamic, perhaps unperceived by either Kurosawa or Mifune, and yet felt by the audience, informs the thematic context of the scene. A warrior, fresh from his aggressive exertions on the battlefield, now must confront the perverse and otherworldly forces of the labyrinthine forest.

Season of the witch

The complexities in the relationship between actor and mask are reinforced in the ensuing encounter of Washizu and Miki with a supernatural prophetess (Chieko Naniwa). Led by Washizu, the two warriors suddenly turn their horses into a hollow where a ghost-like figure spins a wheel in an open hut-like enclosure. The camera faces Mifune on the level of his eyes and then moves in for a medium close-up. In his face are combined wonder, apprehension, and a fierce masculinity. His teeth are bared, his lips turned down at the corners, and his eyes opened wide. At this precise moment his face closely takes on the expression of the warrior mask. But that expression shifts and changes throughout the scene so that a greater sense of human agency is achieved. Washizu pulls out his bow and threatens a violent response to what seems to him the menacing supernatural figure who spins her wheel. But Miki holds him back, and they dismount. As he approaches the prophetess, Washizu wears a wary look. He stops short, with one extended leg conveying concurrently strength and trepidation. His forward movement is tentative, lest he be drawn into a supernatural trap. He stops and looks quickly back at Miki and then moves laterally as if, having reached some barrier, he can proceed no further. His eyes now are opened very wide, expressing fear and wonder and strength. He is like a fierce animal, aggressive and yet circumspect. And then he suddenly rushes forward, grabs at the gate of the enclosure, and jumps back, startled and confused. After the strange ghost-like spinner has told him his fate—that he will be promoted by the King for his success in the war—Washizu's face seems even more confused, his body drained of the fierce energy that has driven him. He looks over at Miki and then turns back to the prophetess to hear that he himself will became the next King, the lord of Spider's Web Castle. Suddenly he seems not simply weakened but impotent. He regroups, his body now rigid, his head moving up and down as if he were taking stock of the situation, with a fierce, aggressive expression on his face. The prophetess asks if he is "angered by this prophecy." Still upright and rigid, he points to the ground and says this space belongs not to him but to the King. "You are afraid of your desires," she replies, "you try to hide them." He thrusts his body forward with his battle face on, seemingly at war with the prophecy itself, at war with his own desire. Miki pulls him back and the prophetess vanishes upward into thin air. Unlike the case with Miki, whose expression remains essentially unchanged as if he were in fact wearing a mask, there is a range of Mifune's emotions and attitudes: aggression, anxiety, confusion, and most importantly dread over the exposure of the desires that lie hidden within him.

That night the two warriors are received by the King of Spider's Web Castle, who intends to reward them for their decisive victories against his enemies. These rewards fulfill the first part of the ghost's prophecy. The camera looks down on Washizu from the point of view of the King on a raised dais. Mifune's face is frozen in the expression of the Noh warrior, appropriate for this formal public ceremony. But when he hears the witch's prophecy fulfilled, Mifune's eyes momentarily twitch and then move laterally toward Miki. With this subtle and quickly terminated gesture, Mifune conveys Washizu's astonishment and furtiveness, and perhaps even the recollection that Miki has been promised greater things. Under the restraints imposed upon him by Kurosawa, with his marvelously expressive eyes, Mifune is able to negotiate that space between the restrictive Noh mask and his own expressive skills as an actor in order to create a multi-dimensional character.

In line with Shakespeare's Macbeth, Washizu murders the King so that he himself might rule, thereby insuring that the second prophecy is fulfilled. He brings the coffined body of the King to the castle where Miki awaits. Once again Mifune's face takes on the fierce and aggressive stare of the warrior mask as he approaches the castle with his entourage. But again he uses his eyes to express a hint of trepidation, moving them from side to side as if he were expecting some force poised to attack him. He arrives at the front gate and the doors swing slowly open to reveal Miki fronting his own troops. Miki stares at Washizu with one fixed expression, barely revealing his thoughts, a kind of opaque intent that Washizu must read. Miki, after all, is privy to the witch's prophecy and thus surely suspicious that Washizu is responsible for the murder of the King. But the effectiveness of the scene is conveyed not by Miki but by Washizu. Mifune uses his face in subtle ways to express a complex emotional and psychological response to Miki. He holds his face still and stares at his fellow warrior, mitigating his defensive aggressiveness with a slight uplifting of the eyebrows and relaxation of his mouth. In this moment time seems suspended as the two men share a memory to the exclusion of all others. Mifune conveys anticipation, an anxious fear of exposure and even guilt over the murder of the King. With a subtle gesture of eyes and face, he expresses the inner, nuanced, and subjective workings of his character.

In Shakespeare's *Macbeth*, the depth of human subjectivity is nowhere expressed more fully than in the "to-morrow and to-morrow" speech:

> To-morrow, and to-morrow, and to-morrow
> Creeps in this petty pace from day to day,
> To the last syllable of recorded time;
> And all our yesterdays have lighted fools
> The way to dusty death. Out, out, brief candle!
> Life's but a walking shadow, a poor player,

That struts and frets his hour upon the stage,
And then is heard no more. It is a tale
Told by an idiot, full of sound and fury,
Signifying nothing. (V.5.18–27)

Upon the death of Lady Macbeth, the King laments that our lives are nothing more than a "tale/Told by an idiot, full of sound and fury,/ Signifying nothing" (V.5.25–7). In Kurosawa's adaptation, these words, along with every other word, are lost, but the expression of the subjectivity of the character who utters them is not. Upon being informed that his wife has given birth to a stillborn child and that her own death might be imminent, Mifune the actor stares at his sword, the symbol of his political power, and the symbol of his masculine aggression, and cries out not with a speech in iambic pentameter, but with a single word: "Fool!" His face starts to dissolve as if the mask of the warrior were being pulled away. He begins to weep and then catches himself and turns from the political, moral, and psychological morass he has created and into which he is now entangled, to take up the sword and to replace the warrior's mask on his face.

Season of the witch II

Mifune brings his performance to a new level when Washizu returns to the forest to seek a second prophecy from the ghostlike figure that he and Miki had encountered at the beginning of the film. It is an episode ostensibly in keeping with Noh drama: a meeting between the natural and the supernatural, between the living and the dead. But Mifune takes things much further, pushing beyond the stylized ritual of the Noh, transforming the scene into a display of a deeply intense psychological collapse. Washizu falls into a Lear-like madness. He has discarded his helmet and exposed himself to the elements without his protective gear. He rushes toward the camera and in a medium close-up of his face we see that a manic terror has inscribed itself. But that aggressive expression of the warrior's mask is still present, so that madness and the aggression are melded together, the one feeding the other. Terror, aggressiveness, mania, paranoia, and the intensity of his need for stability, a need for reassurance all come to life in his face. Once again Mifune achieves this complex subjectivity by playing against the mask.

The alteration between fierce anger and terror had been established earlier in the banquet scene when the ghost of Miki appeared. Washizu oscillated between the two extremes, creating a second mask if you like, a mask of terror. He attacked the ghost with his sword but was then driven back into a corner, literally, his world becoming smaller and smaller, with him relying on violent aggression to break that enclosure open. The present scene in the forest pushes this further, adding a consuming mania almost as if Washizu/Mifune knew he had been and would continue to be the butt of some forces conspiring against him. But once reassured that he would not be beaten until the forest moved against him, he returns to his mask, to the fierce expression of the warrior, but now in an exaggerated version. Those wide, expressive eyes of Mifune convey madness, and in this case that madness is made palpable by his words: "I will kill them all." Of course, if he would do so, he would be surrounded by nothing other than mounds of skulls.

The final hunt

In the final set-piece of *Throne of Blood*, a version of the Noh mask asserts its final and absolute power over the face of Mifune, the actor. A one-dimensional mask of terror, of fear and trembling, usurps the depths of subjective expression. Washizu's face never changes in the concluding scenes of the film. Once he sees the forest literally moving against him, and perhaps recognizing that the arrows that come at him with rapidity and unrelenting repetition are made from the wood of that forest, the terror of not simply death but the knowledge that he is the butt of irony, that he is simply a player on this stage, that he has conspired with fate to bring about his own demise, spreads itself over his face and remains frozen there. With respect to performance, the subjectivity of the actor and the character he embodies is consumed by the mask. The Buddhist notion of self-erasure is used here in a harrowing way. That loss of self-identity, germane to the teaching of Buddha, is portrayed as something horribly violent. The loss of one's sense of self is after all a kind of death. Mifune's uncanny way of utilizing his own identity and skills as an actor, against and in conjunction with the Noh mask, signifies a great and unique performance, one that leaves the audience exhausted by what it has experienced.

Works cited

Baron, Cynthia and Sharon Marie Carnicke. *Reframing Screen Performance*. Ann Arbor: University of Michigan Press, 2008.

Buchanan, Judith. *Shakespeare on Film*. Boston: Pearson Longman, 2005.

Burnett, Mark Thornton. *Shakespeare and World Cinema*. New York: Cambridge University Press, 2013.

Cardullo, Bert Ed. *Akira Kurosawa Interviews*. Jackson, MI: University of Mississippi Press, 2008.

Dramatic Museum Realia. Columbia University Library, online at www.exhibitions.cul. columbia.edu.

Fujita, Minoru and Leonard Pronko. *Shakespeare East and West*. New York: Saint Martins Press, 1996.

Galbraith, Stuart. *The Emperor and the Wolf: The Lives and Films of Akira Kurosawa and Toshiro Mifune*. London: Faber and Faber, 2001.

Goodwin, James. *Perspectives on Akira Kurosawa*. New York: G. K. Hall, 1994.

Kurosawa, Akira. *Something Like an Autobiography*. Trans. Audie E. Bock. New York: Vintage, 1983.

McDonald, Keiko I. *Japanese Classical Theater in Films*. Teaneck, NJ: Fairleigh Dickinson University Press, 1994.

Ortolani, Benito and Samuel L. Leiter, eds. *Zeami and Nō Theatre in the World*. New York: Casta, 1998.

Prince, Stephen. *The Warrior's Camera*. Princeton, NJ: Princeton University Press, 1991.

Richie, Donald. *The Films of Akira Kurosawa*. Berkeley: University of California Press, 1965.

Wilson, William Scott. *The Flowering Spirit: Classic Teachings on the Art of Nō*. Tokyo: Kodansha International, 2006.

Chapter 10

Setsuko Hara in *Tokyo Story*

David Desser

She was called "the Greta Garbo of Japan." Where Garbo was thirty-six years old when she retired, the Japanese Garbo was forty-three. Neither woman ever married—rare in Japan. Garbo's famous line from *Grand Hotel* (1932), "I want to be alone," became something of Garbo's mantra and her lifestyle. And the same was no less true for Setsuko Hara. Best known for her work with beloved director Yasujiro Ozu, she retired the year Ozu died. Although there is no record of her saying, "I want to be alone," she went into a lengthy seclusion, rarely granting interviews or attending public events. She was ninety-five at the time of her death in 2015, by which time she had gone from movie superstar to mythical legend. Such was her fame and the link with Garbo that an obituary in the *Washington Post* noted, "Setsuko Hara, a Japanese actress who achieved international stardom and critical acclaim after World War II through her collaborations with directors such as Akira Kurosawa and Yasujiro Ozu, only to vanish, Garbo-like, from public life more than half a century ago, died Sept. 5 in Kanagawa Prefecture, Japan" (Adam Bernstein, "Setsuko

Hara, Japanese movie star of exquisite power, dies at 95," *Washington Post*, 25 November 2015, online at washingtonpost.com).

The beauty and even talent of many movie stars has much to do with what the French impressionist filmmakers of the 1920s called "photogénie" and which we in English call, a bit more prosaically, "the photogenic." For the impressionists, such as Jean Epstein, photogénie was the quality of the cinema itself that brought out the special characteristics of the object, whereas the photogenic is a quality inherent in the subject being photographed. Yet whatever term we wish to use, only a few movie stars have that ineffable essence that moves them from the realm of the popular to the realm of the transcendent. Garbo remains among the few in Western cinema and Hara perhaps the only Japanese star with that radiance that comes from within, a mysterious beauty that surpasses mere good looks. (Hara was hardly the most beautiful of Japanese actresses, even among her contemporaries.) Perhaps this inner spirit rendered her almost untouchable, one reason that among her many attributes was that:

> Ms. Hara was widely admired for her ability to convey the interior life of seemingly ordinary characters who exemplified archetypes of Japanese womanhood. Many of them struggled with tension between the desire for an independent life and traditional societal boundaries and family demands. She undertook so many demure or long-suffering roles that she was dubbed the "eternal virgin." (Bernstein)

Indeed, one of the many, and certainly the most handsomely produced, Japanese celebratory publications devoted to her career is titled *Eien no Madonna: Hara Setsuko no subete* (*The Eternal Virgin: All about Hara Setsuko*) (see Tadao).

Whether she was the eternal virgin or every man's ideal wife; whether she embodied the struggle between personal independence and restrictive tradition; whether her smile was "enigmatic" (Bernstein) or in keeping with Japanese ideals of emotional reticence, Setsuko Hara was both a Japanese superstar, voted the number one Japanese actress of the twentieth century in 2000 (Haukamp 4), and its first transnational star and still its most popular in the West. A number of her many films have become canonical. But is there something about Setsuko Hara in her role in Ozu's *Tokyo Story* (1953) that makes it No. 3 on *Sight and Sound*'s most recent poll of the fifty greatest movies of all time? Although its artwork is a bit unsatisfactory, the cover of the Criterion special edition two-disc set of the film features Hara. It is also significant that Hara is in the film for less than half of its 136-minute run-time, even disappearing for almost half an hour right in the middle of the movie. Yet, aside from the scenes with the old folks, Shukichi and Tomi, she is in every rich and significant emotional moment. If we take a look at her performance in the film perhaps we can discern something of what has made her the transcendent film star that she is.

The first time we see Hara, some thirteen minutes into the film, she gets both a star entrance—a bell rings, we hear her voice ("Gomen kudasai": excuse me), and her sister-in-law says, "That's Noriko"—and a modest one: she stands up in the frame in a long shot, her other sister-in-law in the frame, too. There's no close-up, only long shots as she briefly interacts with her brother-in-law in a shot taken from one end of a hallway. Can we say, as a matter of fact, that this is a star entrance given its actual treatment onscreen? For starters, Hara was undeniably a major star at this time. Her career began in the middle of the 1930s, the so-called "First Golden Age of Japanese Cinema," where she was highly billed in films by the likes of Tomu Uchida and Satsuo Yamamoto. Her star persona was sufficiently established as a traditional Japanese young woman that she could be cast in a Japanese-German co-production in 1937, *Atarashiki tsuchi* (*New Earth*) for Japanese release and *Die tochter des samurai* (*Daughter of the Samurai*) for German territories. The film was co-directed by Japan's leading filmmaker, Mansaku Itami, and by Germany's infamous Dr. Arnold Fanck, who helped Leni Riefenstahl's career. Important and prestigious films followed, such as an all-star production of Japan's most-filmed and performed tale, *Chushingura* (*The Loyal Forty-Seven Ronin*) in 1939 and *Ahen Senso* (*The Opium War*, 1943), one of the most interesting outright propaganda films of the war era. She also appeared alongside the later-to-be infamous Yoshiko Yamaguchi (aka Li Xianglan/Ri Ko-ran) in a film made in 1940 at the controversial studio Japan had set up in its puppet state in Manchuria, Manshu Eiga Kyokai (the Manchukuo Film Association, known as Man'ei).

Her appearance in propaganda films transferred easily into anti-war films and films about democracy in the postwar period. Unlike in Germany, film artists suffered little if at all for their pro-war movies and most indeed made the transition to postwar realities with ease. As for Hara, she appeared in Akira Kurosawa's angry condemnation of Japanese fascism, *Waga seishun ni kuinashi/No Regrets for our Youth* (1946) and *Anjô-ke no butôkai/The Ball at the Anjo House* (Kozaburo Yoshimura, 1947), a melancholy look at democratization and land reform in the immediate postwar era. She would work with Kurosawa again in his doomed adaptation of Dostoyevsky's *The Idiot*. Kurosawa desired a two-part release with a total run-time of over four hours, but the studio insisted on a release print with a run-time of 166 minutes, the only version available today.

By the time of *Tokyo Story*, Hara had become associated with Ozu, having starred in his most important postwar films. Both films had received the prestigious *Kinema Jumpo* Best One award and both featured Hara as a young woman named Noriko. *Banshun/Late Spring* (1949), *Bakushu/Early Summer* (1951), and *Tokyo Story* have since become known as the "Noriko Trilogy." Though they certainly did not refer to *Late Spring* and *Early Summer* in that way at the time, surely the Japanese audience, which had already made Ozu the most-awarded and among the most beloved of all Japanese filmmakers, would have been highly conscious of those films made previously in two-year increments.

Kindness

Shukichi and Tomi, long-married husband and wife, travel from faraway Onomichi by train to visit their married children Koichi and Shige, both of whom reside in Tokyo. When they arrive at Koichi's house, they are greeted by him, his wife Fumiko, and their daughter. Shortly thereafter Noriko arrives. Although Ozu does not make it explicit in Noriko's first scene that she is, in fact, the old folks' daughter-in-law, some clues are provided, such as Tomi saying that Noriko didn't have to come this evening whereas their actual children are there without question. More to the point, they know relatively little about her, asking if she works for the same company, for instance. And then, so important to identifying who she is relative to the family, but also, perhaps, the most devastating comment of all: "It must be hard to be on your own." This will be, along with Noriko's kindness to the old couple, the most significant leitmotif of her character. How Hara handles both of these qualities—kindness and sadness—makes this her most well-rounded character in Ozu's cinema, and her most tragic.

When Shige relates how, when she was a little girl, she was ashamed of her mother's size, we realize, obviously, that Noriko is not the couple's daughter and thus must be a daughter-in-law. In traditional Japanese society, the daughter-in-law becomes part of her husband's family in a way more profound and significant than in the US, for instance. Thus, despite her husband's death Noriko is strongly attached to his family. Darrell William Davis claims that with the husband's death/disappearance Noriko's kinship with the parents is suspended (82). But that is not actually true. Davis points out that, "Noriko *chooses* to play the role of dutiful daughter," but the fact is that such a role "is not one without significant precedent" (82; emphasis original). Yet, there is something to be said for Davis's point about the weakening of Noriko's kinship ties to the family, for as old Tomi notes, and as the film consistently demonstrates, "the world has changed." For Donald Richie, Ozu's primary theme in his postwar films was the dissolution of the family. Certainly, *Tokyo Story* is a great exemplar of this issue and while we see this dissolution clearly in the way in which the three older children—Koichi, Shige, and Keizo—treat their parents while also having their own lives to live, the moral and emotional focus of this concern rests on the slim shoulders of Setsuko Hara.

Tokyo Story is the story of the old couple, Tomi and Shukichi, perhaps a typical story of postwar Tokyo. To that end Ozu gives Noriko those moments in the film which attach to both the old Tokyo—the pre-war Tokyo of stable families, of marriage, of children, and of the passing seasons—and the new realities of the new world order. Thus the scene in which the old couple's children, Koichi and Shige, try to pawn them off on Noriko to take them on an outing. Despite having to ask for a day off from her boss, she smilingly agrees, making arrangements with Shige on the telephone from her office, the depth of her smile clear even as seen in a profile shot, since the smile moves from her mouth to her eyes, which seem to glow. Noriko agrees to take her parents-in-law on a tour, but in a typical Ozu ellipsis the next shot is of the tour bus, in medias res, with a guide who explains the city to the tourists on the bus, including Tomi, Shukichi, and Noriko. In some ways this seems a dispensable scene. It does not advance the story or lead to any revelations about character and relationships. Instead, this tour of the new Tokyo which celebrates the city's reconstruction since the war (unmentioned, but impossible not to realize) also implies the societal changes that Japan has undergone since the war, as well. The new city that literally rose out of the ashes brought with it unpredictable changes only now becoming clear (such as increasing internal migration to Tokyo and the hard work which led to the economic miracle that would slowly change traditional family relations). And here is Noriko, a Tokyoite—a working woman, an office lady in a transnational company—caught up in those selfsame changes but oddly being taught about them at the same time.

By any standards the next scene is certainly not dispensable. Following the tour Noriko takes Tomi and Shukichi to her apartment complex, a faceless, if rather weather-beaten structure. This sequence intends to show us both her sparse living conditions—she dwells in a one-room flat with tatami flooring and a kitchenette, lacking a bathroom—and her extraordinary kindness and solicitude toward them. She borrows snacks and sake from her next-door neighbor to give the old couple. They sit and talk pleasantly and sincerely to each other. But this scene is not merely intended to demonstrate the kindness of a former daughter-in-law who can probably ill afford the day off and the activities to which she has treated them. It also provides insight into Noriko herself. Here we see both her devotion to her former husband—his picture features prominently on her chest of drawers—but also her ambivalence about his memory. She recalls his fondness for drinking, just as Tomi notes of Shukichi, and how after a night of drinking he might bring home a group of his workmates for more drinking still. Yet she ruefully admits she misses that.

The performance in this scene is really rather extraordinary, but typically for Hara, very subtle. Watch how she responds to the discussion of her husband's likeness in that picture of him that she keeps. Her in-laws point to the tilt of his head to one side, noting that he always stood like that. At which point Hara casts her eyes downward, the smile drifting away as she tilts her head slightly downward. Then she puts down the bottle of sake, raises her head with that smile back on her face and rushes out the door. Perhaps we might think she is going to cry out of sight of her in-laws. Instead, she goes back to her neighbor to ask for a *tokkuri*, the little carafe in which sake is served, as well as *ochoko* (the tiny sake cups). Strange that she wouldn't have a complete set of her own or that she would have forgotten this when she borrowed the bottle of sake in the first place. How was she originally intending to serve the sake to them? And was the memory of her husband's drinking suddenly upon her as she remembered she needed a sake set?

As she warms up the sake and serves it with the snacks her neighbor also gave her (we are in the new Tokyo, where neighbors become like family and look out for each other) Ozu places her facing the camera with Shukichi and Tomi sitting opposite each other across the small table, Noriko centered between them, sitting at a ninety-degree angle. At the moment the question of drinking comes up, Ozu switches the camera and character placement by using a 360-degree cut, with Noriko's back now to the camera, and Tomi and Shukichi thus flipped horizontally in screen space. This shot is held in a fairly long take (twenty-one seconds). Noriko is still centered in the frame and thus the ensuing discussion of Shukichi's drinking focuses not on the couple but on Noriko, though now Hara is, so to speak, acting with her back and the tilt of her head. She doesn't simply turn her head to look at each of them. When Tomi mentions how much Shukichi used to drink and how she feared he'd become a drunkard (we will see later that he still has those tendencies) there is a small tilt to Hara's right and though we cannot see we know that she is laughing ever so slightly in sympathy with Tomi. And when Tomi continues in this vein, Hara nods her head to Tomi in that peculiar way Hara has of acknowledging the other person. But when Tomi asks Noriko if her husband liked to drink (Tomi has not quite come to terms with the disappearance of Shoji, whose body was never found), we get a full-on close-up of Hara's face as Noriko raises her head and eyebrows, and smiles as she says Shoji did. This is a brief shot of her, but with Tomi's follow-up question, we get two more close-ups of Noriko, interrupted by shots of her in-laws, and her face keeps the smile, but now it doesn't reach her eyes as closely, as deeply, as earlier. Even more extraordinary, however, is how she again acts with her back and neck when Ozu's camera returns to the long shot as Tomi mentions Shoji's absence. As Tomi speaks from Noriko's left, Hara moves her head slowly to her right so that now her head is straight, looking away slightly from Tomi (who holds onto a fading hope). We think she is beginning to look at Shukichi, who replies that surely Shoji must be dead, now eight years after the war's end. But Hara continues her head movement down to the right and past her father-in-law, eyes obviously downcast. Shukichi apologizes for his son's behavior, and a close-up finds Hara/Noriko lifting her head, gently insisting that he was never a problem. But now she cannot hide her sadness, eyes and head tilting down, as she moves her head slowly left to right, no longer smiling.

Ozu holds this shot for a brief moment longer, just enough to insist we acknowledge Noriko's look, when the doorbell rings interrupting the moment: her food delivery has arrived. Just when she ordered this (and how; she has no phone and this is long before the days of cellular service) we do not know, but three bowls of noodles have appeared, no payment necessary at that time. (It was common for small restaurants to deliver and for the proprietors to keep a tab and collect all at once at a later date.) First with her facing the camera and then with her back to it, Noriko serves her in-laws the food and her father-in-law more sake. This shot, with her back to the camera, lasts for twenty-three seconds, the longest take in this almost six-minute sequence, the average shot length of which is 7.9 seconds. Noriko picks up a paper fan and begins to fan them, her own food prominently left untouched on the tray in the right foreground of the frame. As she fans them left to right and back again, her head also moves, though more slowly as she companionably and with love comforts her in-laws. The length of the shot is important, here and elsewhere in this film and in Ozu. It gives the audience time to look at, to contemplate, and to feel for the younger woman, who is so kind to these people.

The layout and sparseness of Noriko's apartment as seen in this scene sets the stage for her next interaction with her in-laws. They have gone off to the Atami hot springs, but returning early the old folks are again dismissed by their busy children. Except this time, they have to separate, to spend the night in different quarters, Shukichi with an old pal from their hometown and Tomi with Noriko. Although the scenes with Shukichi and his old friend have an important thematic resonance, the scene between Noriko and Tomi is every bit as heartrending as Tomi's later death and its aftermath. We haven't seen Hara/Noriko for some twenty-seven minutes by this point in the film and when we do, the scene is in medias res, with both Noriko and Tomi in nighttime kimono, Noriko massaging the older woman's shoulders. This scene lasts for four and a half minutes, with an average shot length of 13.5 seconds, long for Ozu but as befits a scene of such nostalgia: happiness, as the old woman says, to sleep in her dead son's bed, but sadness, too, on the part of both women, the older one who feels sorry for Noriko and encourages her to remarry and Noriko, who knows she won't. Ozu's framing at the end of the scene is meant to recall the penultimate scene of Late Spring, where father and daughter go to sleep next to each other with close-ups of their faces as they lay awake on the tatami, each with their own thoughts until the famous cutaways to the vase (see Nornes for a full discussion of the possible meanings of the two shots of the vase as Noriko lies awake). Here there is no vase and only Noriko gets a close-up, in profile, as she lays awake in a near-agonizing fourteen-second shot which refuses to look away. Although later in the film, and then still later, she will cry, here she blinks back her tears. Yet there, just in the corner of her eye, a small tear appears.

Zurui

In the thirty-three minutes that comprise the film's ending section, from the time all of the children (except Keizo) and including Noriko sit as Tomi slowly passes away to the moment of Noriko's departure, it is only Noriko who shares intimate moments with many of the protagonists. When all of the children are there, Noriko stays out of the conversations, as does the youngest child, Kyoko. She is seen in the background of the predominant shot of the sequence where the children gather over Tomi's supine body as they await her death and after she has died. Other segments feature the other children speaking together, especially Koichi and Shige.

The film's oddest scene, at least on the surface, also involves Noriko along with Shukichi. In the previous scene Koichi has asked, "Where is father?" A direct cut reveals the answer. He is standing on a bluff above the bay, posed between two stone lanterns. Noriko rushes up to him in a long shot and then there is a cut to a closer two-shot as Noriko tells him that Keizo has just arrived. Shuchiki's response is just, "Is that right?" Noriko is watching him until he looks off and, with a bit more emotion, exclaims, "It was such a beautiful dawn." Noriko then gazes off to her left in the same direction, and then pivots so that her whole body is turned to face the bay to the west. Shukichi follows up with, "I'm afraid we'll have another hot day today." He then moves his body slightly, pivoting away from the direction of the water in order to walk back in the direction from which Noriko came. This two-shot lasts twenty seconds. But as Shukichi begins to walk toward the camera in the long shot, we notice that Noriko sees him leave but hesitates a brief second before walking back with him. The whole scene is merely three shots lasting a total of thirty-nine seconds. Of course this is the shortest scene in the film, but it inspired Hasumi Shigehiko to wax poetic about Shukichi's commenting upon the weather on this, the morning of his wife's funeral (see Hasumi 118–29). But it isn't the weather or Shukichi's comment that is most interesting; it is that Noriko is the one to whom Shukichi can express his deep sadness via his seemingly innocuous non sequiturs about the weather, Noriko, through Hara's subtle body movement, who reveals her deepest understanding of the old man's true meaning.

A quite long take (forty-eight seconds) from Ozu's characteristically low camera level provides us with the beginning of another of the film's most famous and touching scenes: Kyoko's lament about the insensitivity of her siblings. Noriko defends their actions, especially Shige's, with the idea that a woman of Shige's age has a life of her own, separate from her parents. Kyoko's youthful outrage is tempered by Noriko's worldly wisdom (although she is only a decade or so older than her sister-in-law; the actresses were eleven years apart in age). The only conclusion is that life is disappointing, but for Noriko in her experience, inevitably so. The scene lasts for three minutes and is capped by a twenty-seven-second take of a close-up of the two young women, with Noriko's face slightly toward the camera, so despite the balance of the frame we look at her. It seems that she continues to have that almost-smile that has characterized virtually all of her intense moments up until now.

What follows is an intimate scene between Shukichi and Noriko, one that in its quietude and emotional content recalls the famous climactic inn scene in *Late Spring,* bringing with it an almost erotic tension between the older man and the younger woman (an eroticism palpable when the pair play father and daughter in the earlier film and perhaps even clearer—because we allow it to be—here). It begins with Noriko's confession that she is *zurui,* translated as "selfish" in the subtitles but, as Davis notes, meaning something closer to duplicitous (82). One thing she confesses is that: "I'm not always thinking of your son, though you think I am." Clues have been left throughout the film that Noriko was not always joyfully happy in her (brief) marriage; but this is, in fact, the same thing we learned about Tomi and Shukichi. Ozu, who never married, always posits the ambivalence of marrying and marriage. (Setsuko Hara took this to heart; she, too, never married.) When Shukichi says, "I'll be happy if you forget him," we recall Tomi's comments that she, too, encourages Noriko to remarry. Noriko, of course, entertains no thoughts of staying with Shukichi to care for him: that will be Kyoko's position until she, too, will be encouraged to marry and will reluctantly agree at some later time in the Ozu universe. But there is something in both Chishu Ryu's and Setsuko Hara's being together, their companionable togetherness, that leads us to think, for just a second, this is what Noriko wants; her leaving has to do with her not wanting to leave him. Tomi's watch that Shukichi presents to Noriko is described by him as "old-fashioned." It is, therefore, more than a keepsake, but an acknowledgment that Noriko, in her piety towards him, is herself old-fashioned. More importantly, in Shukichi's transferring Tomi's watch to her, there is also a sense that he might wish Noriko to take the older woman's place, and that Noriko might want to do so. And this is why, in a rare (though not unprecedented) moment of overt emotionalizing, Hara/Noriko breaks out in sobs.

And then there is Noriko's final scene, the penultimate scene of the film, a brief sequence only about half a minute long. It begins with an exterior shot of a train hurtling past Onomichi—a shot recalling what we saw at the start in this film and thus bringing us full circle—then the interior of the train car, seeing Noriko in medium close-up. She takes out the watch that Shukichi gave her and for the next twenty-five seconds we see her looking up and into the distance. What is she thinking? Are we reminded, coming full circle ourselves, of Greta Garbo and of Rouben Mamoulian's famous suggestion that at the end of *Queen Christina* (1933) she should think about nothing and avoid blinking her eyes, so that her face could be a blank sheet of paper and every member of the audience could fill in the emotional undertones themselves? Or are Hara's widened eyes still filled with sadness and regret? And how appropriate is it that, in a film so concerned with train travel—the old folks' discussing their upcoming journey to Tokyo; the trip from Tokyo and the unexpected stop in Osaka when Tomi takes ill; Keizo's missed opportunity to take an earlier train to arrive before Tomi died—the only time we actually see someone on a train is with Noriko's departure. And do we fill in her expression of sadness and regret, for surely this is the last time she will see Tomi, who has died, and Shukichi, who is old and who will never return to Tokyo just as she will never return to Onomichi? Is she sad at her sense of being *zurui,* moving off into her own life, removed now from her in-laws, or is it something even deeper? It is virtually certain that Noriko will not remarry. There are many reasons to be certain of this, ranging from the image and status of widows in Japan, to her age, to the shortage of marriageable men due to the war, to the fact that one feels that despite her emotional outbreak, despite the fact that she doesn't think as often of her husband, she has no real desire to marry again. She knows the course her life will take. Will she be lonely when she is old, as Tomi predicted?

Ten years after the release of *Tokyo Story* Ozu would pass away and Hara would retire: never married, old, alone, but, should we assume, not lonely? Such is the quality of photogénie that Hara possesses that we think of all these things in the half-minute we see her near-expressionless face. Such is her star quality that the character of Noriko effortlessly slips back into the persona of Setsuko Hara, Japan's greatest screen star.

Works cited

Davis, Darrell William. "Ozu's Mother," in David Desser, ed., *Ozu's* Tokyo Story, Cambridge: Cambridge University Press, 1997, 76–100.

Hasumi, Shigehiko. "Sunny Skies," in David Desser, ed., *Ozu's* Tokyo Story, Cambridge: Cambridge University Press, 1997, 118–29.

Haukamp, Iris. "Fräulein Setsuko Hara: Constructing an International Film Star in Nationalist Contexts," *Journal of Japanese and Korean Cinema* 6: 1 (2014), 4–22.

Nornes, Abe Mark. "The Riddle of the Vase: Ozu Yasujiro's *Late Spring* (1949)', in Alastair Phillips and Julian Stringer, eds., *Japanese Cinema: Texts and Contexts*, New York: Routledge, 2007, 78–89.

Richie, Donald. *Ozu: His Life and Films*. Berkeley: University of California Press, 1977.

Sato Tadao, ed. *Eien no Madonna: Hara Setsuko no subete*. Tokyo: Kyodosha, 1986.

Chapter 11

Marcello Mastroianni in *8½*

Adrienne L. McLean

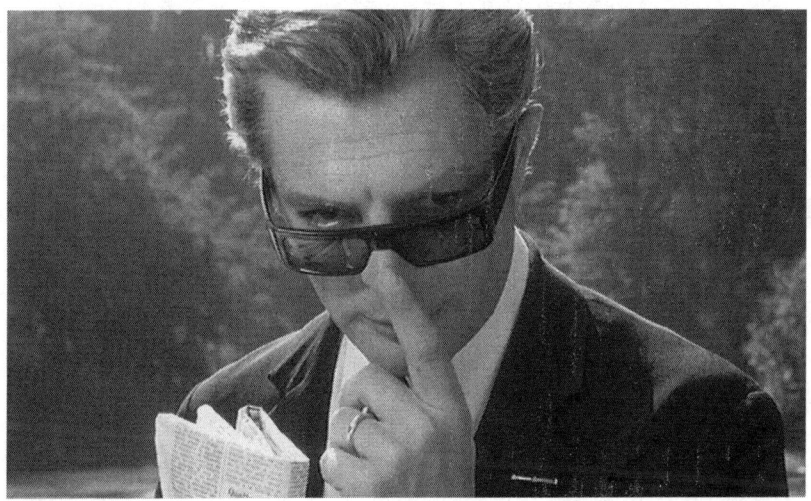

Peruse newspaper obituaries of Marcello Mastroianni and you will soon come across the anecdote that Federico Fellini hired him to play the jaded celebrity gossip journalist—also named Marcello—in *La Dolce Vita* (1960) because of Mastroianni's "terribly ordinary face." The critical and box-office success of *La Dolce Vita*, the first of their four director-star collaborations over the years, did give Mastroianni an international cachet he had not quite experienced before, but one can only imagine that Fellini's remark was made partly, if not wholly, in jest. Mastroianni's face was anything but ordinary; it had helped propel him to stardom in theater as well as the Italian film industry, where he had made some forty feature films already and become the most popular co-star of Sophia Loren (they partnered in twelve movies together from the 1950s through the 1970s). It is true that Mastroianni himself thought his countenance "likeable, pleasing" rather than handsome, claiming that his "upturned" nose disqualified him from the ranks of leading men like Alain Delon, Tyrone Power, or Vittorio

Gassman ("*they* were handsome" (Dewey 46)). But Mastroianni had also, quite convincingly, uttered the line "I am one of the most handsome men in Europe" in the 1958 film *Un ettaro di cielo* (*A Hectare of Sky*) (Hochkofler 15), and was not infrequently called the "Italian Cary Grant" to boot. It seems likely, in other words, that Fellini chose Mastroianni for *La Dolce Vita* precisely because of his beautiful—and already relatively famous—face; and the film's success made Fellini even happier to cast him again as director Guido Anselmi in *8½* (1963), Fellini's "ideal autobiography" (Hochkofler 53) and arguably most renowned work.

As is well known, the title of *8½* is just the first marker of the film's explicit self-reflexivity; it denotes its placement in Fellini's oeuvre to that point (he had directed six features and parts of two others). And as is also well known, *8½*—the story, which Fellini also wrote, of a blocked director confronting his inability to make decisions about his life, his relationships, or the film he is working on—is ironically itself assured and confident and was instantly recognized by critics and audiences as a masterpiece of postwar art cinema. To pay attention to Mastroianni's performance in *8½*, then, feels like a somewhat fraught undertaking. More than is usually the case with any art film, a mode which, in David Bordwell's words, "foregrounds the *author* as a structure in the film's system," here the star is playing the director who is "his" author as well; and while Bordwell writes that such films tend to "solicit confessional readings" that exceed the art film's characteristic interest in "authorial expressivity" (59–60), the confessions we seek are presumably not those of any actor but of the director himself (with few exceptions the postwar art film is a male preserve).

Fellini's own ways of working also complicate analysis of acting and performance generally in his films but certainly in *8½*, for example his preference for shooting scenes without scripts and dubbing in the dialogue later: "The actor plays better that way, not having to remember his [sic] lines" (Fellini 110). Thus, it isn't just that Mastroianni's lines are looped in postproduction to adjust for problems in recording sound on location—common with all films—but that he is often obviously speaking lines that are not those we hear, and the sometimes discomfiting lack of synchronization of lips and sounds, while the choice of the director, clearly can affect our evaluation of the actor's skills. And finally, we surely need to take account of what Fellini has written about Mastroianni, "a friend, a mate," who "helps" him "not just by being professionally good, but by abandoning himself confidently to me, which means that I can do risky things. This often happens quite naturally, without any of the sort of commitment that can be very chilling; I mean fanatical professional commitment" (Fellini 105). According to Fellini, "everything about" Mastroianni is "calm, malleable, relaxed and natural, so natural in fact that he sometimes dozes off during shooting, right in one of his own scenes, and even when he's being taken in close-up" (Hochkofler 11). This sort of characterization would suggest that, for 8½, Mastroianni was happy to have his chest hair removed, to lose weight, and to have gray streaks put in his hair and bags under his eyes so as to seem "older, less virile, and more fragile, as Fellini saw himself"; Fellini also had the actor "imitate his own behavior: his tics, facial expressions, and habits; he even had him raise his voice in order to resemble Fellini's higher pitch" (Reich 82).

But I invoke Fellini's remarks about how easy he found it to turn Mastroianni into his "screen alter ego" (Dewey, n.p.) in 8½ in order to dismiss them, at least for the purposes of this chapter. Here, I don't care whether Mastroianni physically resembles Fellini, other than to say that in several extreme close-ups the heavy makeup in the hair and around the eyes, meant to make the thirty-nine-year-old actor into the forty-three-year-old Guido (roughly Fellini's age at the time), perhaps intentionally but nevertheless distractingly ends up drawing attention to its own artificiality. Nor am I interested in how Mastroianni functions as a sign of Fellini's authorship or in how Guido Anselmi (who is also portrayed by a child actor) represents Fellini's own youthful dreams and disappointments, or that the weird science-fiction elements of Guido's incomplete project in 8½ refer to a "spaceship film" Fellini was to have made but never did following *La Dolce Vita* (Costello 82). Instead, I work to understand what Mastroianni does with his face and body formally in the contexts of the film's plentiful narrative ambiguities to make us care about Guido and his sometimes frankly despicable behavior—to worry about what is happening to him and what he is doing to himself and to others, to be upset when he appears to commit suicide, to feel some relief when he learns, if only in death, that "life is a celebration." Fellini by most accounts (other than his own) liked to play his actors against one another on the set of 8½, doing his best to seem "Federico the God" to his *bravo ragazzo* star while ridiculing and humiliating others (see the remarks made by Mastroianni's co-stars in Dewey 151–70). But in channeling himself through a star who he believed possessed a face with "no personality" (Dewey 17), Fellini instead, and not wholly unexpectedly in the case of

Mastroianni, has with the passage of time ended up being substantially overshadowed by the star himself.

That said, Mastroianni did state publicly that his roles in *La Dolce Vita* and particularly *8½* were "part of [his] development as a man, as a human being" (Dewey 82). Indeed, doing the part of Guido was

> like looking into a mirror, observing, getting to know oneself. It was like a psychoanalysis session, or rather a form of self-psychoanalysis, because Guido was a man of my own generation, a sensitive, intelligent man, a very particular kind of anti-hero. He was the prototype of that generation which is now entering its forties, with all their fragility and confusion; the kind of man who is useless now. Today they need men who are much more sure of themselves. It was an effective X-ray. (Hochkofler 71)

And it is true that Mastroianni also helped promulgate the notion of an essential malleability and amiability in the hands of his directors—that film acting was a "pleasure," a "fantastic game," and as such not to be taken very seriously: "Assume that you have some basic training, that your diction is intelligible, that you can walk across a room and not fall over your feet, that you're not up there to make a personal spectacle of yourself and that you're dedicated to doing your part, not some clown show for your friends. From that point on, all an actor really has to do is to develop his intelligence, to cultivate it as he needs for his work" (Dewey 80). Famously contemptuous of Method acting—which he called "nonsense"—Mastroianni claimed,

> I'm content to be myself on the screen—the myself who can get into the feelings and emotions of a given character but who remains Marcello Mastroianni. If a director doesn't want that, he doesn't hire me for the part. If he does hire me, he knows that he will not get an impersonator, a mimic. It is the actor *acting* as a character that makes for what some people call art in this business, not the actor *becoming* a character, which probably means that he belongs in a loony bin. (Dewey 83)

Taken together, these remarks suggest that we might still best approach Mastroianni's performance as Guido through the lens of ambiguity—not, or not primarily, the ambiguity that arises from the interaction of realism and authorial expressivity and that marks all art cinema, as Bordwell claims. But rather the ambiguity that is produced by considering an actor who felt he was being "himself" rather than an "impersonator," who felt that his part was like "looking into a mirror," and yet who believed, according to Sandra Milo (Carla), that "Federico was god, the gospel" (Dewey 151) and who did allow himself to be somewhat passively shaved, dyed, shaped, and otherwise molded physically to be a stand-in for, an avatar of, Fellini. Through Mastroianni, the director could represent— in more prepossessing form—*his* corporeal features, tics, gestures, and even voice in addition to his own obsessions and "expressive" ideas and concerns. Though hardly a revolutionary claim—it is probably true of most director-actor collaborations in art cinema—my conclusion is that *8½ should* be less interesting as a Mastroianni vehicle than a Fellini film, but that without Mastroianni's beauty, skill, and personality it would not be the masterpiece it has generally, since its release, been taken to be (with naysayers who did reject it doing so on the basis, in one reviewer's words, of the film's "complete surrender to narcissism" (Dewey 151)). The passage of time has been arguably less kind to Fellini than to Mastroianni, in other words, whose "luscious ease, vitality, and naturalness" on the screen (Kaufman 64) enable him, along with the audience, to transcend, or at least to ignore, *8½*'s outmoded sexual politics—women as lovely young goddesses, erotic grotesques, demanding shrews, or gentle but devouring old mothers; gay men as effete and decadent phonies; women of color or the working class as earthy or superficially "authentic." And, of course, the bad voice dubbing, from which admittedly Mastroianni is spared the worst, whether because his lines were later made part of the script or because he was performing dialogue Fellini had already written.

The opening of *8½*, which has no credits other than the title card announcing the producer and the film as "by Federico Fellini," is justly famous: almost silent, the sound—dark drums, or perhaps a heartbeat— sneaking into the image of a traffic jam in a tunnel. We know the character whom we see only from behind is important because of the point-of-view cutting, as though he is looking and being looked back at (with repeated brief freeze-frames in the POV shots drawing attention to the film as a film). Whoever this is, soon, in a brief montage, he responds with terror to smoke filling his car, beating and clawing at the windows before magically exiting and floating away out of the tunnel over the stalled traffic, arms outstretched and black coat streaming behind him, fedora on his head. He flies through clouds to the noise of wind, arriving at a beach with a guy on a horse, a priest who reads from some documents, and another guy who tugs at a rope attached to the airborne character's ankle and that he struggles unsuccessfully to untie. The few lines of dialogue from the men on the beach end with "Down, definitively"—the Italian can also be translated as "permanently"—from the priest, and in an extreme bird's-eye shot we watch the character fall into the sea.

By this point, we're clearly watching a dream sequence, a conclusion cemented by the moaning gasps that bridge the cut to a shot of a clutching arm reaching up from a bed. The dialogue of the doctors and nurse who then enter the room, speaking to the man in formal rather than familiar Italian, suggest that whoever this is is a film director— "What are you preparing for us now, another film without hope?" one doctor quips—and the point is underscored by the glossy head shots of beautiful women ("Nice merchandise," the same man says appreciatively) littering the bed. (Later, Guido will somersault slowly over the photographs on the bed and fall asleep to dream again before being awakened by a phone call about a crisis with Carla, the mistress he both depends upon for escape from his troubles and of whom he is tired.)

But while we have heard Mastroianni's voice in the frenzied breathing of the opening, the gasps as he wakes, and his response to questions and orders from the doctors and the nurse, still we have not seen his face nor heard his name. Now we again see him from the back, his head turning this way and that after he erupts from his nightmare and is bombarded with questions and comments from his visitors—they are joined by a dour man (Jean Rougeul) in pyjamas and robe who enters and sits against the wall in a chair; he is soon to be identified as a movie critic and writer of a sort (and is particularly cursed, here as in all his scenes, in the bad dubbing department). When we finally see our man from the front, his head is hidden under a white and then a dark cloth (this seems to be a continuity error) for a physical examination ("Breathe deeply," "Cough"). Finally, as the exam ends and the critic suggests meeting later instead, Mastroianni lumbers out of bed in long shot, shakes the hand of one of the doctors, and shuffles slowly toward the bathroom putting on his robe while the other doctor dictates his prescription to the typing nurse. Only in the bathroom, as he flicks on the hard but dim overhead light—hard overhead lighting marks many tight shots in later scenes, too—do we see Mastroianni's haggard face clearly, in the mirror, as Wagner's "Ride of the Valkyries" begins on the soundtrack. He shuffles away from the mirror as what seem to be vastly brighter studio set lights loudly buzz on above him, the floor littered with newspaper and torn photos, as the phone rings and his posture sinks comically lower and lower with every ring.

With a straight cut we move outdoors to the spa grounds and characteristic Fellini slow pans along with deep-focus and often expressionist compositions in depth—actors suddenly appearing between the camera and what had seemed to be the focus of the shot, or the camera swooping down from on high to land in close proximity to a face or body—in a rhythmically edited montage of a variety of people and faces of all classes, ages, genders, and occupations. Some gesture at the camera or blow it kisses, others ignore it; a few wave the glasses of mineral water the spa proffers and that have been prescribed for Mastroianni's character. Wagner still dominates the soundtrack, the music's status as apparently non-diegetic undercut only slightly by the revelation through panning of a conductor waving his hands in time to the music. Because so many of the faces we see look directly into the camera, clearly we "are" still the man we've been observing so far; but not until the music crashes to an end, replaced by an excerpt from the overture to Rossini's *The Barber of Seville*, do we see Mastroianni's face again.

No longer haggard, now he's slickly coiffed and handsomely dressed in a dark suit and tie, eyes hidden by the sunglasses he will don regularly in other scenes. He's in a line of people moving slowly forward to the stone counter where they will be handed glasses of water by uniformed young women working the taps. He scans the crowd, smoking the end of, and extinguishing, a cigarette. He starts suddenly and pulls the glasses down his nose to uncover his eyes, gazing just to the side of the camera, swiveling his jaw slightly from side to side, and the music stops. We cut to barefoot Claudia Cardinale posing head down in the trees, then back to Mastroianni tapping his nose as he gazes at the silent apparition who then glides toward us on tiptoe, her beautiful smiling face intercut in tight close-up, to offer up to Mastroianni his glass of restorative water. "Grazie," he slowly and beatifically says, and as he does so the world snaps back into a reality we only now are certain we had departed, Cardinale replaced by one of the harried servers who tells him to take his glass. He shoves his sunglasses back up his nose, grabs his water, and we cut to an extreme long shot as he walks slowly across the stone platform and down the steps to meet the gaunt critic he has asked to read, and possibly collaborate on, the screenplay of the film he is trying to make but can't seem to finish. (It will be quite some time before we learn who Cardinale's character is—Claudia, a possibly real, possibly imaginary, muse.)

In the hilarious scene that follows, the critic obligingly proffers the opinions—all negative—that the director has asked him for. He waves his notes like a limp flag in front of the barely attentive and lounging Mastroianni as he pontificates about the utter worthlessness of films that lack a philosophical premise, that are nothing but a series of completely gratuitous episodes, that have all of the limitations of the avant-garde but none of its strengths, and many other such comments that could easily pass as the clichéd criticisms of all art cinema generally. After declaring that the script has made him absolutely certain that cinema is fifty years behind the other arts and that he can't imagine why the director would have thought of him as a collaborator on a project that he obviously doesn't see as being anything other than a disaster, he drops down beside Mastroianni and hands him the notes. Mastroianni is still slouched, eyes obviously roving behind his sunglasses, against the curved back of a moderne white bench—jacket open, legs crossed and foot jiggling, glass of water in hand, and a folded newspaper under his arm—and he makes a comical moue as he reads; and when the critic at last stops speaking, Mastroianni looks up with a start, plants his feet on the ground, and tries tentatively to explain what this film means to him, rubbing his mouth and moving his head from side to side as he makes a few halting remarks. But we don't find out much—Mastroianni looks past the writer, calls out a name, and excuses himself to run excitedly toward an old man, Mezzabotta (Mario Pisu), he has seen in the woods. Another apparition, we wonder? No, it seems to be an old friend. And at last we learn that Mastroianni's name is Guido, and we see him smile.

I describe this scene in such detail because it contains many of the expressions, gestures, and movements that Mastroianni makes in the rest of the film, and because it gives us a characteristic chance to examine him closely while learning very little about "what's happening" in narrative terms. The withheld access to Mastroianni's face and eyes, especially, during some five minutes in which we watch or listen to him in action, creates a suspense that appears to lead nowhere but to the unexpectedly haggard countenance we see in the bathroom mirror. The overhead and low-key lighting in that shot both hoods his eyes and draws attention to the applied wrinkles and bags under them, a scheme reproduced in many other scenes as well, for example when he impulsively telephones his wife, Luisa (Anouk Aimée), and invites her to visit him on location even as he consorts with the mistress he has ensconced nearby in a cheap railroad hotel; or when he's driving (escaping) with his muse Claudia, as well as their subsequent conversation in which her answer to all of his complaints about the indeterminate motivations of the main character in his film is, "Because he doesn't know how to love." In daylight scenes, the lighting is no less hard, which allows even the smallest movements to register with the force they do here and for Mastroianni to make full use of his mobile face and eyes. In the noisy and chaotic scene where he is pulled this way and that by film personnel and opportunistic hangers-on, all asking him questions he doesn't want to—or can't—answer, he finally agrees to see three actors who might play the (really "his") father; and there's a nice play of emotions across his lopsidedly and tentatively smiling face, his eyes darting from one to another, the smile becoming tighter with a quick anger and head shake as he tersely rejects them all as "not old enough."

Mastroianni himself thought of his eyes as "his main physical asset" (Dewey 47), and the covering or framing of Guido's eyes in *8½*—through not only sunglasses but inconsistently donned glasses (they sometimes look like bifocals) with thick black frames whose purpose is never explained (does he need them, and if so, to do what, and why wouldn't he wear them for the same activities all the time?)—is balanced by lengthy close-ups that allow us to examine the specific contours of his symmetrical but slightly top-heavy face and head: the abundant hair (though again usually swiped with thick gray dye) and widow's peak, the single vertical crease between his large dark eyes, the curving horizontal furrows of his forehead and his well-shaped eyebrows, the slightly curly mouth marked by the prominent tubercle of his upper lip and tiny dimples in the corners, the mole on his right cheek, the cleft in his chin. He looks like a dazzling matinee idol in some shots, inordinately silly in others where he wears the thick glasses, a Pinocchio nose mask, the fedora, and sometimes a scarf that looks like an old man's shawl—occasionally all at once. Whether the forelock-tugging, nose-tapping, face-rubbing, and hangnail-biting are his tics or Fellini's (Mastroianni has a huge repertoire of gestures in other films), they help make Guido seem not only uncertain but boy-like, an important component of a character whose childhood is shown to have been the source of so many of his actions and reactions in the present as well as of the imagery and events that he is putting—or trying to put— into his film.

The editing of *8½* adds to this feeling, not only through dreams and flashbacks to Guido's boyhood but in abrupt juxtapositions that emphasize his inconsistency and flightiness, all mechanisms he seems to adopt as ways to distract himself from the project and the people who are complicating his life. In the scene with the three old men, Mastroianni suddenly turns with a small double-take (one of many; the actor is a master of them) and starts loudly keening some vaguely "Arab" noises, his arms raised like a supplicant, before dropping to his knees and bowing before the corpulent man in a Fellini-like cape whom we know to be Guido's increasingly irritated producer. And of course in the famous "harem fantasy" in which all of the women in Guido's life, past and present, torment him about his attitudes towards them, Mastroianni at one point is dressed in nothing but a towel that hangs down his front like a bib, a sheet round his waist, and his fedora (the brim curled up so that it resembles a small cowboy hat), his skinny arms and hairless chest undercutting the masculine authority of the whip he cracks to keep the unruly women in line.

Although Fellini reportedly had the phrase "Remember, it's a comedy" taped to his camera during shooting (Reich 78), and one might—albeit uneasily—laugh at the absurdity of the harem scene as well as at the grotesques or poseurs that surround Guido, it is only Mastroianni who comports himself physically in a way we might find conventionally amusing. Like Cary Grant, Mastroianni looks tall on the screen (he was reportedly a little under six feet), has a somewhat sunken chest, and is a bit pigeon-toed. But Mastroianni's joints are much looser, his ankles and feet floppier (Guido fidgets constantly). Although he is obviously in control of his body, the looseness—most visible in long shots, or when he melts against the wall and sits, legs akimbo, in discouragement or despair—also, along with the fidgeting, makes him seem callow and uncertain rather than authoritative. Immediately after a psychologically complex dream sequence with his dead parents on what might be a ruined exterior film set, Guido comes walking down the hall of his hotel to the elevator vaguely "da da da da da"-ing the Rossini overture we've already heard, slapping out Keaton-like steps in his fedora to which he supplies his own mickey-mousing in the form of sharp whistles. And of course near the end of the film, as the now-dead Guido apologizes to and frolics with all of his loved ones and colleagues, past and present, on the beach, his movements become even looser, but now they are joyous.

At the conclusion of 8½, as the circus on the beach comes to an end and the little crew of musicians diminishes to one small boy that we assume is the child Guido, Mastroianni has disappeared once more; he is absent from the final shots, completely now, rather than with the tease of the back of his head and body as in the opening scenes. In a sense, Fellini started his project by making us want to know who that man was, and while the ambiguities of the film's construction and its interweaving of past and present, reality and fantasy, never allow us to understand all of his problems or motivations, Mastroianni serves his director well. Guido becomes, and remains, fascinating, and it is hard to imagine that this will ever change, especially as the number of people who care whether the character acts like or resembles Fellini himself becomes smaller and smaller. Through Guido's dialogue, Fellini makes the statement, "I'm putting all kinds of things in this film." Although *8½* is rich and complicated, by far the most significant "thing" in it is Marcello Mastroianni.

Works cited

Bordwell, David. "The Art Cinema as a Mode of Film Practice," *Film Criticism* 4 (Fall 1979), 56–64.

Costello, Donald P. *Fellini's Road*. Notre Dame, IN: University of Notre Dame Press, 1983.

Dewey, Donald. *Marcello Mastroianni: His Life and Art*. New York: Birch Lane Press, 1993.

Fellini, Federico. *Fellini on Fellini*. Trans. Isabel Quigley. New York: Delacorte Press, 1976.

Hochkofler, Matilde. *Marcello Mastroianni: The Fun of Cinema*. Trans. Jocelyn Earle. Rome: Gremese International, 2002.

Kaufman, Sarah L. *The Art of Grace: On Moving Well Through Life*. New York: Norton, 2015.

Reich, Jacqueline. *Beyond the Latin Lover: Marcello Mastroianni, Masculinity, and Italian Cinema*. Bloomington: Indiana University Press, 2004.

Chapter 12

Jeanne Moreau in *The Bride Wore Black*

Adrian Danks

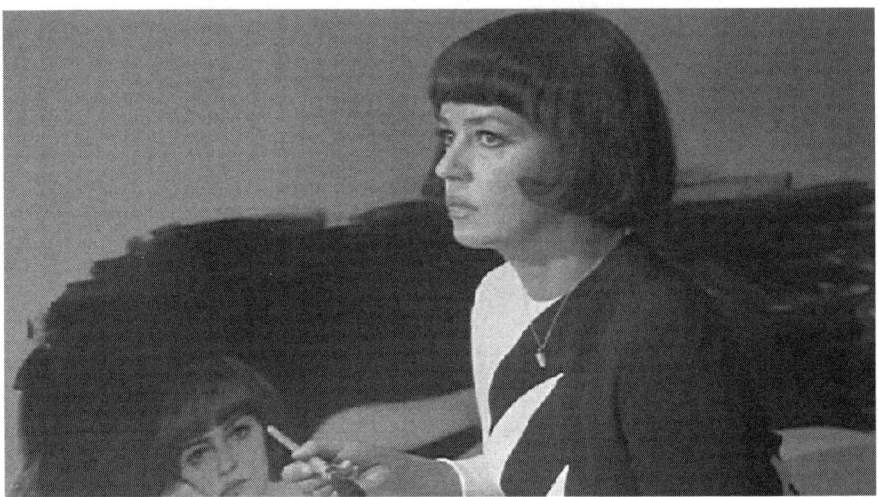

La mariée était en noir (*The Bride Wore Black*, 1968) opens with the sound of a photographic printer producing image after image of a nude painting of Jeanne Moreau's titular character, Julie Kohler. This curiously blank and evidential black-and-white reproduction points towards the theme of relentless repetition that drives François Truffaut's adaptation of Cornell Woolrich's 1940 crime novel. This credit sequence also emphasizes notions of the copy, variation, and serialization and their significance to the processes of adaptation, the "pulp" form of the crime fiction source material, and the endless play of similarity and difference that typifies the performances of any true star, particularly one of Moreau's magnitude. But this staccato stream of photographs also suggests the animated materiality of the film itself and its preoccupation with the star "identity" of Moreau. It is almost as if the film is willingly animating her fantastical and largely immaterial character into being while trying to contemplate, pin down, and even caricature the essence of the French actress's cinematic form.

Julie looks out from the image towards both the artist and the audience, while her undecided expression sits somewhere between a characteristically indeterminate Moreau frown or smile. The mask-like quality of her expression, painted from memory (as viewers learn) after she leaves the artist's studio, as well as the overall design of the composition, place her character somewhere between the modern and the archaic, between a cosmopolitan, highly professional, and contemporary, woman and a timeless avenging goddess.

This gambit also points back to Moreau's defining role as Catherine in Truffaut's *Jules et Jim* (1962), undoubtedly one of the key works of the *nouvelle vague* and European art cinema more generally. The photographic moment here is particularly reminiscent of a scene where Catherine attempts to distract *and* attract the attention of Jules and Jim by affecting a series of quizzical poses that are then frozen as the film's forward momentum is briefly arrested. Both of these moments reinforce Molly Haskell's view that Moreau's piercing gaze and domineering countenance define her star persona. Her work is not marked by the occasional striking close-up, *à la* Garbo, but defined by an all-encompassing proximity: "Moreau's face is at the center, the lyrical driving force, of . . . almost every movie she made" (Haskell 20). As Ginette Vincendeau also claims, "Moreau's face connotes interiority and soulfulness" ("Indiscreet Charm" 34). But her mercurial expressions and quizzical facial gestures do not generally promote singular interpretation.

But the difference between these two sets of arrested images of Moreau, appearing across the space of six significant years in her truly international career, speaks volumes about the self-conscious relationship between these two Truffaut films as well as their core variations in tone, style, performance, and sensibility. The steely gaze and clear, almost monomaniacal motivation of the painted Moreau sits in contrast to the flighty, mercurial, and patently unreadable Catherine. The disarming simplicity of this reproduced image matches the relentless symmetry of the film's narrative. As the various pieces of the puzzle are put together we come to realize that Truffaut's film is a relatively streamlined revenge narrative that follows the murderous actions of Julie as she systematically executes the five deeply chauvinistic men responsible for the unintentional death of her husband on their wedding day. The fascination of the narrative is dependent not on the suspense of whether she will be able to fulfill her task but on how, when, and where her retribution will take place. Woolrich's novel concludes with the thudding irony that Julie killed the wrong men, and more readily draws upon such noir tropes as the femme fatale and the relentless hand of fate, but Moreau's imperious character and performance are much too driven, pure, and "modern" to countenance such radical uncertainty. The film concludes with the successful completion of her momentous task and her complete departure from the scene.

When planning *The Bride Wore Black*, both Truffaut and Moreau were very conscious that they were creating a character who sat in contrast to the domineering and sexually experienced Catherine, as well as the litany of similarly worldly, highly sexualized, and sometimes ethereal characters embodied by Moreau in such films as Louis Malle's *Les amants* (1958), Michelangelo Antonioni's *La notte* (1961), Joseph Losey's *Eva* (1962), and Jacques Demy's *La baie des anges* (1963). As Vincendeau argues, Moreau emerged as one of the key international stars of the late 1950s and early 1960s and

> came to embody the ideal New Wave woman in her combination of the sensual and the cerebral. She offered an image of Parisian sophistication and amorous passion, performed with great charisma in a naturalistic style. She also displayed commitment to the new auteur cinema. ("Paradox" 378)

In many respects, *The Bride Wore Black* is a very conscious attempt to question and probe this dominant and restricting star image while still working within an identifiably "auteur cinema." As Truffaut stated, "We were trying to find a new subject for Jeanne Moreau that would have nothing in common with *Jules et Jim*. No laughing or smiling; this time I asked her for an absolutely neutral face, that of a professional absorbed in her work" (Jacob 165). Although I can see how the character they shaped together sits in contrast to the shifting fathomless depths of Catherine, as well as other Moreau creations, Julie also reinforces many of the same ideas about the performative nature of femininity, the reflective relationship between men and women, and the tantalizing ungrasp-ability of Moreau's onscreen persona. The film offers a more grounded, relentless, and meticulous representation of its central female character, and Moreau's performance is remarkably attentive to behavioral detail, but I'm not sure that Julie is any less a fantasy than Moreau's mercurial Catherine. The difference may well boil down to the purpose, origin, and orientation of this fantasy.

As I will go on to argue, Julie is constructed very consciously as an "artifact" *of* the cinema. Although the credit sequence featuring the swiftly multiplying image of her provides a particularly strong instance, there are many other aspects of the film that reinforce the totally constructed and even desiccated nature of her character and how it appears *on* film. For example, the film's first major section features Moreau dressed seductively but incongruously in a gossamer-like white evening dress. She often startles the other characters by seemingly appearing out of nowhere, and her physical actions (such as the moment where she pushes her prey from an apartment balcony or unconvincingly, even unhurriedly, runs from the scene of the crime) are never quite grounded in a commonsensical understanding of physical or even intellectual reality. Throughout, Julie also changes her appearance to suit her surroundings. We even see her preparing herself for the next role she is to play, for example, how she familiarizes herself with a particular Vivaldi recording before luring a subsequent victim to a concert of the same piece (a tiny Truffauldian homage to Hitchcock). She also brings this recording with her to score the murder of her victim, bringing the film closer to the stylized mechanics of one of its key offspring, Quentin Tarantino's *Kill Bill: Vol. 1* (2003; which similarly shares a preoccupation with feet).

As Penelope Houston claims, "Moreau doesn't come on to a set: she materialises, suddenly there, with her Bette Davis basilisk stare" (188). In attaining this magical, almost transcendent feeling for space and time, Truffaut was plainly after a very particular dreamlike affect: "*The Bride* can seem simplistic and mechanical to whoever refuses to admit that an adult film can begin with 'Once upon a time . . .'" (quoted in Baby 26). This fairytale-like sensibility is reinforced by the singularity of Moreau's actions and motivations, as well as by the insularity of the film's mise-en-scène. In the opening sequence we quickly witness Julie economically packing her exclusively black-and-white designer wardrobe (the framing of objects, hands, and gestures at this point is consciously from *Marnie* (1964)). She also divides up her savings into five bundles, carefully divvying up the financial cost of each act of revenge. Although the pursuit of the five "killers" will take some time, it is as if she is just packing an overnight bag with the essentials she needs for her ruthless task and nothing more. The economy and purity of Julie's actions, and Moreau's very limited range and precise performance of her character, seem to infect the broader world of the film. The blue pattern of the wallpaper in Julie's room miraculously reappears on the curtains in the first victim's apartment as well as in the discarded bra of his fiancée. Despite the fact that Julie seems to take time traversing the country in seeking out her victims—one of whom admits that the only connection between the group is their shared interest in "women and hunting"—the police inspector who haphazardly pursues her just happens to be an acquaintance of two of them.

The Bride Wore Black was made after the peak of Moreau's stardom and in the wake of the commercial failure of Truffaut's *Le peau deuce* (1964) and his similarly oneiric *Fahrenheit 451* (1966). Although the film was a relative commercial success in France, and was made by Truffaut as a "tribute" to his close friend Moreau, its critical reputation has always suffered in comparison with the earlier *Jules et Jim*. Many of the initial reviews of *The Bride Wore Black* also remind readers that Truffaut had only just published his interview book with Hitchcock in English. This provides an opportunity for critics to compare the two filmmakers, mostly to the detriment of Truffaut, and provide a compendium of elements that betray the influence of the "master's" work. For example, Andrew Sarris, discussing the pathological and solipsistic sexual fantasies shared by Truffaut and Hitchcock's male characters, highlights the "fact that Miss Moreau, like Miss Novak [in *Vertigo*], is too substantial for the ethereal spirit of the illusion," heightening "the resemblance" between the directors' work (162). While Sarris equally argues for the shared humanism between Truffaut and Jean Renoir, other critics such as Peter von Bagh and Tim Hunter position *The Bride Wore Black* as an explicit piece of Hitchcock criticism ("*The Bride Wore Black* at the Charles," *Harvard Crimson*, 30 July 1968, online at thecrimson.com/article/1968/7/30/the-bride-wore-black-pthe-influence/). Although there are significant points of correspondence between the two directors, particularly relating to the way that Truffaut frames specific objects, the use of Bernard Herrmann's familiar-sounding score (repeating some motifs from *Marnie*), the revelation of key plot information midway through the narrative, and the characterization of Moreau's Julie, *The Bride Wore Black* is generally unconcerned with notions of guilt, suspense, or even psychology and is more mannered in its visual style (and often, too, with a more free-floating camera than is characteristic of Hitchcock).

Although I don't think that such comparisons can get you very far in appreciating the particular qualities of Moreau's performance or Truffaut's film—which is itself a work of multiple competing authors— the director himself later soured in his view of his achievements:

> The only film that I regret having made is *The Bride Wore Black*. I wanted to offer Jeanne Moreau something that didn't resemble

any of her other films, but it was badly thought out. Here was a film where the color was an enormous mistake. The theme lacks interest. An apology for idealistic vengeance shocks me in reality ... One doesn't have the right to take vengeance. It is not noble" ("Interview" 124)

Truffaut also later claimed that Moreau was "badly miscast" (Ingram and Duncan 47), a curious admission considering that the whole film is built around her screen persona. Although it would have been interesting to see the results of casting a cooler, more reserved actor in the role of Julie—say Catherine Deneuve, who did feature in Truffaut's subsequent Woolrich adaptation, *La sirène du Mississippi* (*Mississippi Mermaid*, 1969)—it is almost impossible to contemplate this film without Moreau. She is the vortex, black hole, or blinding star around which everything else orbits and ultimately depletes. Even the idea that using color was a mistake seems bizarre in light of the key contrast the film draws between the monochrome costumes and even mise-en-scène of Moreau's Julie and much of the rest of the film. In contrast to Deneuve, Moreau still manages to bring a core physicality to the film that helps ground this often immaterial character and her actions. Her "domestic" earthiness is a defining feature of Moreau's screen persona. For example, Marguerite Duras claimed that she wanted Moreau to star in her 1972 film *Nathalie Granger* "because she knows how to clear a table" (Vincendeau, "Indiscreet Charm" 34). Although Moreau's Julie is characterized by an uncanny ability to move through space and truly command her environment, she is also marked by a meticulous adeptness to carry out tasks, perform domestic chores, take on roles, calculate what is required, and systematically and unfussily commit multiple murders. These qualities are why Moreau can be convincing as such varied characters as the maid in Luis Buñuel's *Le journal d'une femme de chambre* (*Diary of a Chambermaid*, 1964), the bourgeois wife in *Les amants*, the earthy, even bawdy Doll Tearsheet in Orson Welles's *Chimes at Midnight* (1965), the weary, aging and TB-infected prostitute in *Monte Walsh* (1970), and the more mercurial Catherine in *Jules et Jim*. Her performances often move beyond "acting" and are grounded in the quotidian immediacy of the present moment. The determined Julie is torn between the memory of her romantic past and the material necessities of her dogged place in the here and now.

Although Moreau came to prominence as the very modern star of Malle's *Ascenseur pour l'échafaud* (*Elevator to the Scaffold*, 1957) and *Les amants*, she had already had a significant if somewhat underwhelming film career over the previous nine years. She was also a substantial figure on the Parisian stage. By the time *The Bride Wore Black* started filming in mid-May 1967, Moreau was already thirty-nine years old. A key preoccupation of some of the initial responses to the film was how old and "haggard" she looks in the movie, and the problems this induces considering the film's overriding premise and its reliance on the sexual allure of her character. An extreme version of this troubling "critique" is offered by Vernon Young: "But Jeanne Moreau is really quite confoundedly ugly; she looks as if she'd been saved from drowning but not quickly enough to erase the expression of horror stamped on her features" (338). Although Young's misogynistic account of Moreau's performance and her broader star image is plainly beyond the pale, it does link up with a more common attempt to pinpoint the shifting appearances and allure of the actress's onscreen image. As David Thomson more acceptably claims,

> Moreau is one of the most challenging of screen actresses. Far from beautiful, she sometimes seems plain-faced, dumpy, and sullen. But when her personality is engaged, we have the feeling of an intelligent, intuitive woman wanting to commit herself to the inner rhythms of the movie. (612)

Although Thomson is ultimately critical of *The Bride Wore Black*, her performance certainly taps into the "inner rhythms of the movie."

Nevertheless, I would also argue that Moreau's performance in *The Bride Wore Black* transcends or defines the character she is asked to play. The figure of Julie in Woolrich's novel is plainly younger than Moreau and capable of more significantly transforming her appearance to suit the sexual predilections of her five victims. All of the five incarnations of Julie constructed for Truffaut's movie are variations on Moreau's star persona and can never truly move beyond the corporeality of the actress. They are all plainly Moreau. Although she does wear a series of different wigs, varies her makeup, and modulates her facial expressions beyond the "neutrality" claimed by Truffaut, the differences in her physical appearance and even manner are minimal from section to section of the film.

In many respects, *The Bride Wore Black* can be seen as a marker of the resilience of Moreau's indelible stardom and her embrace of the processes of aging (for a fuller discussion of Moreau and aging, see Kaplan). The male victims in this film are seduced by the generally vaporous figures Moreau incarnates, but also by the residual power and allure of her designer-clad stardom. It is as if they are watching a carefully staged movie. Several of these characters act as if they are literally starstruck when first eyeing Moreau's Julie. But I don't want to suggest that Moreau's performance is one-dimensional or lacking in any further depth or complexity—even if it is pointedly monomaniacal in some respects. Although Julie is a particularly driven and emotionally resolved figure, she does display moments of kindness and true humanity. As Graham Petrie argues, "Jeanne Moreau with her haggard beauty, her cold detachment, the glimpses she gives of warmth and tenderness beneath the self-imposed *façade*, is a most magnificent presence" (151). For example, the post-credit sequence begins startlingly with a shot of Julie posed against a garish backdrop of flowery blue-and-white wallpaper before she dashes to throw herself from the window in a self-conscious demonstration of her abject despair at her husband's recent death. Thwarted, the following moments show that she does have a degree of care and kindness for both her mother and niece, but that these won't halt her singular pursuit of revenge. While Moreau is able to convincingly convey these snatched moments of emotion and despair—she also cries when revealing her motivation to the victim she suffocates by entombing him under his staircase—the character of Julie mainly draws upon the implacable demeanor familiar from Moreau's most famous roles. These opening moments also highlight the importance to the film of setting and objects and the ways in which they are responded to and manipulated by Julie's character. These range from the modern, alienating apartment blocks of Cannes and a comfortable artist's studio to the grim, dirty minimalism of the final prison setting. Each of these environments feels both organic and staged, a vehicle for Julie's organizing will and for the messiness of life.

It is intriguing to note that *The Bride Wore Black* was released in France a month or so before the first television screening of Orson Welles's short feature *Histoire immortelle* (*The Immortal Story*), also starring Moreau as a character a little too old for the role she is asked to play. In both films Moreau's character is motivated by revenge and is seemingly spent once she has carried out her task. But the most fascinating correlation between the two films is the way in which they both explore the nature of role-playing and stardom. Each self-consciously draws on the mercurial qualities of Moreau's onscreen persona and noticeably aging star image and body as well as her ability to channel and question male desire. Nevertheless, there are very few moments in *The Bride Wore Black* where Julie falters or steps outside of the largely fetishized series of roles she carefully and studiously plays. Like Virginie in Welles's film, she is a kind of actress tailoring her performance for the gaze and pathetic desire of men. This is reinforced by those moments in *The Bride Wore Black* that isolate aspects of Moreau's body or appearance, and that are designed to appeal to the taste of her character's various victims. But these moments also point to the distinctiveness of Moreau's star image and the particularity of her face and diminutive body, full but often-down-turned mouth, voice, and walk. Buñuel once claimed that what drew him to cast Moreau in *Diary of a Chambermaid* was the way that she walked with a slightly crooked or unstable gait (241), and many of her most famous films feature her striding, running, or ambulating through a mostly urban environment. Movement is central. It is revealing that the police detective in *The Bride Wore Black* first starts to realize Julie is the same woman he saw in the first victim's apartment when he sees her walking away from the fourth victim's studio. His first instinct is to chauvinistically comment to the painter Fergus (Charles Denner) on the quality of her legs, but it is obvious that this vision has triggered another more unsettling memory.

The penultimate section of Truffaut's film, featuring Julie's pursuit and eventual killing of Fergus, is the one that most directly addresses and stages the questions and issues noted above. In this long section of the film Julie is asked by Fergus to pose for a painting of the virginal Diana the Huntress. She becomes quickly aware that to continue to attract Fergus she must retain her role as a model and not respond to his requests to extend their relationship beyond the studio. It is in this section that the film also comes closest to some of the thematic preoccupations of Hitchcock's work, in relation to the obsession of this male artist and his wish to transform, capture, and mold Julie's appearance. But what seems to momentarily and uncharacteristically disturb Julie is her partial loss of control in shaping her own image as well as her "shocking" identification with the figure of Diana. She is also somewhat thrown by the genuinely surprising and out-of-character dedication and emotional commitment Fergus pledges towards her.

Moreau's performance in *The Bride Wore Black* draws upon a number of her previous roles, including those in films like *Eva* and *Elevator to the Scaffold* that emphasize her duplicity, sexual allure, and destructiveness. The steely blankness of much of Moreau's performance also self-consciously holds back the excess of emotion and quixotic feeling that characterize her more unstable roles in films like *Jules et Jim* and *Eva*. But Julie is equally a schizophrenic concoction who is both highly sexualized and virginal, a femme fatale and a righteous avenging angel. The strength of Moreau's performance is contained in this will to block out emotion and the more expressive dimensions of her performance. There is some variation as she attunes her appearance, expressive range, and physical capabilities to suit the immediate desires and environs of her various victims—the cosmopolitan apartment, the family home, the tawdry bachelor's bed-sitter, etc.—but she is always defiantly the same character and actor.

The final section of the film provides a neat and provocative correlative to the opening credit sequence. In a significant departure from Woolrich's novel, Julie manufactures her own arrest at Fergus's funeral so that she will be taken to prison to mete out her final revenge on the last killer of her husband, now incarcerated. In the novel, we are often taken outside of Julie's perspective and experience to follow the ongoing and painstaking police investigation of these outwardly random and unconnected homicides. Truffaut's film is much more preoccupied with the purity of Julie's actions and Moreau's meticulous preparations, while also making some attempt to reveal the bumbling if chauvinistic humanity of several of her victims. It also has a greater sense of compassion and materiality than Woolrich's nightmarish and pitiless book. But this final sequence is also remarkable for its pared-down simplicity. Much of the rest of the film has contrasted the black or white outfits carefully worn by Moreau with the warmer and more varied color palettes of the male milieu. As it reaches its conclusion, the overall color of the film moves closer to the monochrome range favored by Julie. As in the opening shots of the photographic printer, the film "becomes" Moreau in these final moments. In this methodical exchange of shots, we follow Julie as she painstakingly positions herself to be able to exact and complete her revenge. The final moment when this occurs is registered by a medium long shot of a prison corridor, the movement of Julie offscreen, and the inevitable scream of her victim as she stabs him with some purloined cutlery. Where can the film go from here?

Julie has been created from the stuff of cinema. Her only motivation is to carry out this revenge. As she herself claims at one point, she is already dead and animated only by the will to carry out these acts of retribution. She is a cipher for the self-fulfilling nature of narrative itself. It is in this regard that the film becomes a true homage to and vehicle for Moreau, a confirmation and pointed depletion of her established screen image. There is a kind of purity to its system of representation: a key characteristic of Moreau's persona is its messy embrace of life and liveliness, even if there is often also a strong, even umbilical tie to death, but Moreau's

Julie is a much more commanding, limited, and centripetal force than is common in the actress's work. Her role in Truffaut's film is both a palimpsest of her screen image and a distillation and negation of several of its most distinctive features. Once her goals have been reached, and Moreau has left the frame, all that is left is the dank mise-en-scène of the prison corridor and the void of a completed narrative. Her final victim artfully killed and his name crossed out of her little black book, there is nothing left for her to prepare or see. While *The Bride Wore Black* is rarely singled out as one of Truffaut or Moreau's best films, it is a confirmation of Moreau's stardom and a dramatization of how that stardom is willed into being. Pure, unadulterated Moreau.

Works cited

Baby, Yvonne. "*The Bride Wore Black* is a Film of Pure Sentiment," in Ronald Bergan, ed., *François Truffaut: Interviews*, Jackson: University Press of Mississippi, 2008, 24–7.

Buñuel, Luis. *My Last Breath*. Trans. Abigail Israel. London: Fontana, 1985.

"François T: Interview with *L'Express*," in Ronald Bergan, ed., *François Truffaut: Interviews*, Jackson: University Press of Mississippi, 2008, 114–27.

Haskell, Molly. "La Lumière." *Film Comment*, 26: 2 (March–April 1990), 20–6.

Houston, Penelope. "Hitchcockery," *Sight and Sound*, 37: 4 (August 1968), 188–9.

Ingram, Robert and Paul Duncan, eds. *François Truffaut: The Complete Films*. Köln: Taschen, 2008.

Jacob, Gilles. "Hollywood sur Seine," *Sight and Sound*, 36: 4 (Autumn 1967), 162–6.

Kaplan, E. Ann. "Wicked Old Ladies from Europe: Jeanne Moreau and Marlene Dietrich on the Screen and Live," in Murray Pomerance, ed., *BAD: Infamy, Darkness, Evil, and Slime on Screen*, Albany: SUNY Press, 2004, 239–53.

Petrie, Graham. *The Cinema of François Truffaut*. New York: A. S. Barnes, 1970.

Sarris, Andrew. "Violent Genres: *The Bride Wore Black*," in Hollis Alpert and Andrew Sarris, eds., *Film 68/69*, New York: Simon and Schuster, 1969, 162–4.

Thomson, David. *The New Biographical Dictionary of Film*. 4th edn. London: Little, Brown, 2002.

Vincendeau, Ginette. "The Indiscreet Charm of Jeanne Moreau," *Sight and Sound*, 8: 12 (December 1998), 32–5.

Vincendeau, Ginette. "Between Renoir and Hitchcock: The Paradox of Truffaut's Women," in Dudley Andrew and Anne Gillain, eds., *A Companion to François Truffaut*, Malden, MA: Wiley-Blackwell, 2013, 375–87.

Von Bagh, Peter. "The Bride Wore Black," *Movie* 16 (Winter 1968–9), 34–6.

Woolrich, Cornell. *Four Thrillers by Cornell Woolrich: The Bride Wore Black, Phantom Lady, Rear Window, Waltz into Darkness*. London: Zomba Books, 1983.

Young, Vernon. *On Film: Unpopular Essays on a Popular Art*. Chicago: Quadrangle Books, 1972.

Chapter 13

Michel Serrault in *La cage aux folles*

Kyle Stevens

"J'ai cassé le biscotte!"/"I broke the toast!," exclaims Albin (Michel Serrault) during a decisive scene in Édouard Molinaro's famous French farce *La cage aux folles* (1978). This is no mere confession of gastronomic slaughter. Albin confesses it, whispers it with the intensity and inflection one might expect from a person who has accidentally murdered a lover. Serrault's delivery may make us laugh, but how are we to understand his ostentatious style? Is it the kind of "excessive" behavior that requires no explanation because it relies on the offensive conception that detectably homosexual males are theatrical, easily distressed, lily-livered nellies? And, in turn, does *La cage* belong in a long line of films that merit inclusion in a history of queer visibility in mass culture, but which, since it deploys stark stereotypes, has little to recommend itself to presumably sophisticated audiences today? In this chapter, I will argue that when we attend closely to Serrault's performance, Albin emerges as far more than cliché, and, in fact, that it is Serrault who merits credit for the film's progressive sexual politics. Moreover, Serrault's work provides an important case study for thinking not just about performance within farces, but also about performances that are farcical. In order to do this, I will return to the significance of what it means for Serrault's Albin to care so much for a piece of toast.

Relatively speaking, the filmic farce has had difficulty finding a devoted audience. It leans further toward "theatricality" than cinephiles have traditionally favored, and this sensibility bleeds into evaluations of performances and performance styles. Part of the problem is the ambiguity of the word "theatricality" in this context. Invoking this ancient art should not be pejorative, yet it usually refers to a metonymic chain that leads to the presumption that some expressions, or, more accurately, some ways of expressing, are ostentatious, excessive, or broad (according to a tacit and highly personal standard that goes unarticulated). In opposition to this, performances deemed successful, which are usually dramatic, are typically judged on the perceived convincingness or sincerity of the expressive actions that comprise them—a function of what particular audiences find familiar or plausible.[1] This binary leaves no space for thinking about styles that rely on intentionally unconvincing expressions, and so, implicitly damns the style of performed actions common to farce. But the size or scale of an expressive action need not render the expressed inauthentic or untrue. When watching Serrault's performance, as with many valuable comic ones, we need not decide on a single direction to explore; we can go broad *and* deep. His expressions are sometimes small and precise, but they are often grand and expansive, too, and this is not to suggest that Serrault switches styles. Expressions can be big and true, unconvincing and accurate within the same acting style. Realism and naturalism (or minimalism) are not coextensive.

It is especially crucial not to confuse grandness and inauthenticity in *La cage*, lest we misapprehend Serrault's work as predictable, clichéd, and, worse, potentially harmful for reinforcing behaviors judged negatively at the time and used as evidence by social conservatives (such as the stiff character played in the film by Michel Galabru) for the oppression of homosexuals. In fact, in terms of visibility, Serrault's is arguably the most decisive gay characterization in Western film history. Given this weight, understanding the effect of Serrault's choices matters. In part it matters because *La cage* was a *hit*. French cinema historian Rémi Fournier Lanzoni writes that *La cage* is "one of the most celebrated successes of French comedy" (296). Serrault in fact won the César Award for Best Actor in

1979. Moreover, the film fared just as well in the US (which allows me to feel comfortable viewing it through an American lens). Albin was, for the majority of American viewers, the first onscreen "sissy" character who was also sympathetic—though his sissiness is, as in previous examples, also offered up as object of laughter, a point to which I shall return. *La cage* was, as Benshoff and Griffin point out, "the most successful foreign film release in American history (to that point in time)" (184), and it remains in the top ten box-office successes by a foreign film in US history. *La cage* won the Golden Globe for Best Foreign Film, and it broke through the Motion Picture Academy of Arts and Sciences' historical ghettoization of the "foreign film" category to be nominated for three Oscars: Best Director, Best Adapted Screenplay, and Best Costume Design. More important than money and awards, though, Benshoff and Griffin attribute to *La cage*'s popularity the move away from tortured, murderous, or murdered gays to a kinder, gentler depiction of homosexuals. Still, they note that queer audiences at the time—who saw the film as something like the *Amos 'n' Andy* of gay culture—were largely offended by its use of stereotypes, and that "the film does invite straight audiences to laugh at the swishy antics of effeminate gay men and drag queens, and both central gay roles are played by heterosexual actors" (184).

To be fair to these objections, there is, after all, no anti-gay epithet that one could throw at Albin that would not stick: flaming, screaming, fairy, etc. Such terms of offense rely on laughing at effeminacy, and are, especially in the logic of the times, at base anti-woman (and here just at the time that second-wave feminists were fighting hard, and ultimately failing, to pass the Equal Rights Amendment in the US). This retroactive status puts a great deal of pressure on the ethics of the characters' representation. Lives were (and remain) at stake when so few individuals were out that mass culture's few queer film characters shaped the public's definition of the homosexual. I should also point out that the provocative fact of homosexual content was rendered "safe" both by its *Frenchness* (French films had been identified and even marketed as sexually progressive since the 1960s in the US) and by the way the characters' age was presented as an erotic obstacle. Albin worries that Renato (Ugo Tognazzi) no longer finds him attractive, assuring the audience that the couple are not sexually active. This also makes Albin and Renato comprehensible to moviegoers steeped in the heterosexual imaginary whereby aging couples struggle to sustain sexual aspects of their lives, and aligns Albin with the female role in the marriage (since twentieth-century fiction and consumer culture maintained that it was women's task to stay attractive for their husbands—to "keep a man," as the saying went). To put it another way, the two men are not coded sexually passive and active; they are coded woman and man. While this projection of gendered behavior onto sexual difference is disagreeable, it also exposes that woman and man can *be* coded, and are not essential features of persons.

It is in such ways that *La cage* encourages audiences to be aware of its depiction of gender and sexuality, but I want to consider Serrault's Albin not just according to a politics of representative inclusion—that is, how *La cage* encouraged audiences to conceptualize real-life homosexual men (as though we could construe a one-to-one ratio between fictional and real persons or that we should police the past according to today's virtue of inclusiveness and attention to bodies). I want to examine how, when given a controversial character, a performer might successfully negotiate stereotypy.

The joy of hostility

The film takes its title from its primary diegetic setting, Albin and Renato's home and place of business, a renowned queer-oriented cabaret club in which Albin performs nightly in drag as the queen Zaza. Renato is the club's manager and director. He has also raised a son, Laurent (Rémi Laurent) (the byproduct of his one experiment with heterosexuality). On the evening of the story's beginning, we meet Renato and Albin having what appears to be a nightly ritual: Renato pleads with Albin to perform while Albin, in full diva mode, bemoans his age, weight, and looks. This night is different, though. After Albin takes the stage, Laurent appears. For a time, because we do not yet know who Laurent is, the intimate dialogue between father and son suggests the kind of romance of which Albin suspects Renato. This scene is, in fact, the film's only sexually suggestive one, indicating its skittishness toward Renato and Albin's sexual natures, but, beyond that, it reveals how rarely men, fathers, are pictured being intimate with their adult sons. Laurent next informs his *papa* that he wants to wed and that his fiancée's parents—Simon (Galabru) and Andréa Charrier (Luisa Maneri)—are leading-light political conservatives, experts on the "defense of morals." Laurent requests that Renato secret Albin away. Albin's presence would reveal the truth. The threat to moral order is not homosexuality but the appearance of homosexuality.

Since the narrative hinges upon Albin's flamboyance, one might assume that Serrault has the choice part, the flashy part. However, playing this stereotypical role is tricky if one does not want to insult the homosexual and drag queen communities (which is a large presumption, given that in the 1970s there was no widely felt ethical obligation not to do so). But there is a greater difficulty to playing Albin. Unlike the heterosexual characters and Renato, who are given objectives in each scene (usually to get rid of Albin), Albin wants very little. He simply wants to *be*, which was in itself a radical socio-political polemic but is a serious actorly challenge. At the same time, the film positions Albin as reacting to the others' desires, aligning him with the stereotypical notion that effeminate (homosexual) men are passive, and that the passive are de facto powerless.

Serrault, however, surmounts this reductive narrative situation in multiple ways. Perhaps most obviously, and most broadly, he performs in a farcical mode. This may at first go unnoticed, as it functions so organically close to the diva/drag queen mode. The presence of a drag queen onscreen was, at the time, a sufficient condition for titillating humor, and Albin's style of drag (and he is often presenting *as though* in drag even when not costumed as Zaza) performs womanliness and femininity in such an exaggerated fashion that it combats the very conventionality of gendered actions. Because of this extravagance, we might consider Serrault's performance, his outwomaning of womanliness, itself farcical. Eric Bentley, building on the theories of Vsevolod Meyerhold, states unequivocally: "Farce is acted ... Melodrama belongs to the words and to the spectacle; the actor must be able to speak and make a handsome or monstrous part of the tableau. Farce concentrates itself in the actor's body, and dialogue in farce is, so to speak, the activity of the vocal chords and cerebral cortex" (208). Bentley's point is that farce is character-centered, and audiences follow along the quixotic movements of characters' minds. This is why successful farcical performances usually take on a *feeling* of being improvised, unlike the case in other genres, where characters' deeds (especially their utterances) can feel preordained.

The ultimate purpose of farce, according to Bentley, is aggression: "If in melodrama fear enjoys itself, in farce hostility enjoys itself" (210). Farce is about the style of violence taken toward its subject. It is a perceptual aspect of the fiction, as we take pleasure in the mockery undertaken by the text's exaggerations, ironies, paradoxes, and so forth. Farce thus serves subversive, countercultural stories well. It combats authority and convention (and the authority of convention), and, what is more, requires its audience to be intellectually engaged in order to get the humor.

But if farce is intrinsically hostile, and traditional masculinity is defined in part as an attachment to aggression, is farce necessarily masculine? And hence indicted within the terms of *La cage*? This possibility presents Serrault with a dilemma, and in order to see how he tempers his character without undermining the farcical mode, I want to return to the example of him knifing the toast. This moment follows the revelation from Renato and Laurent that they wish to banish Albin from the premises. Renato takes Albin to a nearby café to collect himself. Serrault plays the moment as humiliated, then depressed, then indignant, and, finally, resolved to prove to the Charrier family, to Renato, and to himself, that he can perform heterosexuality as well as anyone can (signaling again, before Judith Butler, that both gender and sexual identity are culturally and historically specific). As in all good realist performances, there is a logic to his emotional progression, and one that refers to plausible sequences in which emotions occur and shade into each other—in this there is realism, not in spite of but because of the grand scale of the performance.

Taking sympathy on Albin (and slowly acquiring the ability to properly acknowledge their couplehood), Renato decides to direct him in how to act like a man. This set-up allows the two performers to improvise and react to one another "in the moment," as Renato gives Albin a series of seemingly simple tasks.[2] One is the task of spreading jam on toast, which goes horribly wrong when Albin's anxiety about completing the task butchly causes him to smear, and then snap the toast. As scripted, the line "I broke the toast" could have been delivered in a number of ways: to demonstrate Albin's disappointment in himself for failing to be butch or to please Renato, or to express irritation at his failures. Serrault, though, paints Albin's distress at having injured the innocent bread. That is, his energy is not directed toward himself at all. Serrault creates an Albin who is so loving, so nurturing, that he becomes distraught at this slight loss. These sorts of moments, sprinkled throughout the film, are absolutely essential to understanding Serrault's accomplishment, for within the terms of the story—not to mention society at the time—nurture is defined as a feminine quality. That is, Serrault does not just perform effeminate gestures but effeminate *choices* to make these gestures. To put it a different way, his actions are not just adjectivally effeminate; they are *formally* effeminate because they are the product of "feminine" motivations.

We are now in a position to see that Serrault creates a dynamic tension between the formally gendered values of the masculinity of the farcical mode and the femininity of care. (In addition, this propensity to protect stands in tension with the vanity of Albin's diva side, deepening our impression of his psychological depth.) Through Albin, Serrault is hostile to gender norms, and revels in that hostility, while, and at the same time, offering up the supposedly feminine quality of care— even for a pet piece of toast—to balance the hostility. In doing so, he depicts a pleasing symmetry, and in modernist fashion makes form echo content—not in the mere reflexivity of performing a character that performs but in crafting an androgynous character that is also *androgynous in form*.

Controlling the rhythm

At a more detailed level, the most trenchant way that Serrault overcomes Albin's lack of agency in the narrative (until the climactic dinner scene where he decides to impersonate Laurent's mother) is that he controls the rhythm of scenes. Serrault often indulges Albin with lengthy silences, like musical rests. Other characters must wait and attend to his dramatic pauses while he ensures that they have registered the new way that they have cut him to the quick (however true or intentional the offense), while at other moments, as in the hissy fit Zaza throws during rehearsal, Serrault charges through the scene at breakneck pace, barely allowing others to wedge in counterarguments. He who controls the rhythm controls a lot (even if we extend the dominant/submissive metaphor to its sexual conclusion), and, in this way, Albin's performance of submissiveness becomes paradoxically dominant. Serrault's pauses are also crucial to our sense that Albin is thinking, measuring even his tantrums. Without them, Albin might appear merely foolish, ridiculous. Instead, Serrault contrasts him with the Charriers, who are ridiculous because we believe that although they are capable of a knowledge better than their homophobia and hypocrisy they act as though they are not (and in general we laugh at those deluded about their own wisdom). Albin, though, could not know better, because what could be better in this context? Better than him being himself?

There is another way that Serrault helps Albin escape his narrative subjugation. Besides pauses, Serrault's most consistent performative addition is a repetitive yelp—sometimes little, sometimes big—that Albin gives as an expository reaction to practically anything. The yelp is not exactly effeminate, though it is farther from the realm of the "masculine" than from the "feminine." It evades the binary. What is more, it is *funny*. Like a pun, the yelp reveals language's fragility. It points to the limits of language, simultaneously being uttered and outside of speech, outside the grammar of the sensible. One might be tempted to claim that through these yelps Serrault plays Albin as constantly surprised, but it is more accurate to say Albin is constantly startled. A surprise occurs when a person has a belief, probably about how the world will be, and then experiences the world not conforming to that belief. Albin's reactions, though, appear less conscious than this. His yelps are bestial, and, indeed, those around him treat him like an animal. Laurent and Renato want to kennel him for the weekend when guests who are allergic visit.

The question thus emerges—with a yelp!—whether Albin is a man or a beast. This is the question at the heart of all stereotypy, and one that takes on particular force with publicly self-identifying homosexuals, those who lay claim not just to minority identities but to identities claimants know will introduce animus into their lives. In the café scene, when Albin takes a sip of tea, Renato chastises him for raising his pinky along with the cup to his lips. Albin's response is simply: "It does that by itself." That Albin observes his body moving seemingly on its own is a curious figuration of embodiment. The raised pinky takes on the status of instinct, or reflex. There is no intimation that Albin's body learned the behavior through habit, like choreography. Moreover, this behavior is confirmed as innately homosexual when Renato unconsciously raises his pinky when lifting his own drink moments later.

Unlike Renato, who is surprised at his own pinky when Albin points it out, Albin seems to comprehend that his body simply does such things. In this moment, like the yelps (and to a lesser degree the pauses), Serrault situates Albin as living in the present, which marks him as different than other characters. Renato expects certain things to occur or not occur; he is forward-looking. The Charrier clan, worried about the patriarch's career prospects, the family legacy, and their potential grandchildren, are also concerned with the future. The narrative thus situates Albin—who, remember, desires nothing *further*—as radically queer in the sense that Lee Edelman imagines in his book *No Future*, which stations queerness opposite dominant culture's concentration on procreation and future-thinking directives. It is Serrault's genius to replicate this logic at the formal level.

Within the terms of this narrative, being entirely present is essential to successful performance, too, and performance is essential to survival (for all of the main characters). This is the main evidence that the film, and not just Serrault, is on Albin's side. The climax of the narrative comes as the characters assemble for dinner (this is farce, remember), each intent upon improvising. Here is a method of performance that requires players to remain firmly situated in the present, reacting moment by moment to co-players. Renato and Laurent stammer and pause, hem and haw. Andréa and Simon drone on and falter. The day is saved by Albin, who charges ahead with their collective deceit, advancing it by his ability to be solely *present*, to relate to others as the millisecond dictates. This is not only a sign of his intelligence and wit—valuable commodities in a comedy—but of his bravery and self-assurance. He never doubts his own abilities. It is revealed in contrast that Laurent, Renato, and the Charriers are the ones that need rehearsal.

The happiness of each member of the ensemble ultimately depends on his or her ability to perform well, and the task will fall to Albin to teach them how to do so (in drag, no less) in order to avoid further harm. Key to the satisfaction of this culmination is the greatness of the irony on which it depends: the bulk of the movie has been a plot to keep Albin away, yet he is the best performer there. And of course he is: Albin knows how he appears to the world, because the world forces him to know. Renato does not. Renato does not *feel* the implications of the fact that his pinky pops out. Albin knows precisely the importance of both belonging and standing out, of blending in and impressing. We feel not only that the past few days, but Albin's whole life, have led to this culminating dramatic event. As Robert Dawidoff writes of queers living in an antagonistic culture, the homosexual stands outside of the language and gestures dominant culture might perceive as "natural": "One had to rely on interpretation and tone . . . The translation of the felt language of love and custom was something homosexuals understood by doing without. This creates an almost instant doubleness in one's awareness" (86).

Entailed in this awareness is a sense of place and moment, Albin seeming to know at the dinner party that conservatives like the Charriers need and depend on him for existence. At least, that might be one explanation for the bravery in his penchant for performance. He knows exactly what others think of him and what his world will afford. In a way that is deeply sad, but also funny, he expects no particular consequences from his actions, because he doesn't expect them to make claims on others in the normal way. He doesn't expect others to see his actions as having been done by a person, as worth anyone's caring to respond to. *La cage* thus portrays a world that diminishes the weight of intention, which is to say, a world of levity, where one may act mistakenly and things may still turn out all right. Farcical performances need this light atmosphere, and Serrault creates it; and in doing so he moderates the inherent vanity or meretriciousness in Albin's diva-ness. The emotions that are at the surface for Albin make his shallowness a paradox. He lives life not just *as* surface, as one might assume of a drag queen who specializes in appearances, but *at* the surface—and his interior life is no less real for this, nor is our sympathy for him less deep. Seemingly every expression lies in wait. His mind is at the tip of his body. His emotions are not buried within, needing to be pumped up like oil by the extreme pressure of circumstances; they are right there at the ready. Rare is the man, in life but especially onscreen, who can call forth emotional intensities so readily. One must be in touch with one's self, *know* who one is.

At a more abstract level, Albin's knowledge that to continually reinvent the self is to acknowledge life-in-death allows for his generosity with others, which is central to the beauty of Serrault's performance. Prior to the toast scene, when Laurent and Renato kick him out, Albin is genuinely devastated, only half kidding that he might kill himself. Serrault chooses to play Albin in this moment as humiliated and pathetic, yes, but with resolve, too, preparing us for Albin's later refusal to modify his effeminate behavior, when he doubles down on it to masquerade (to everyone else's surprise) as Laurent's mother. I mention this as a potent example of Albin's experience. We see at different points in the story Albin's lover, his maid and friend, his child, his law enforcement, his co-workers, his patrons, and his enemies all laugh at him, degrade him.

Humiliation

In a homophobic world, straights like to see gay suffering, and audiences of *La cage* could laugh and see suffering, suffering precisely for the kind of self-knowledge that gays usually have: a power over the social mores under which straights continue to labor. And it *is* funny to see a person who has so conquered arguably the most entrenched social institution of all in Western society in the 1970s—gendered behavior—yet who struggles nightly to go onstage, to accept middle age, or to spread jam on toast. Serrault grounds Albin's personality in this reality, not just "humanizing" him by demanding audiences find it within their hearts to love even a stereotypical being, but by playing Albin as one who *embraces* humiliation. Albin always subsists and never holds a grudge (not for more than a second anyway). There is a painful and real history to this inurement. Albin feels unentitled to claim the respect of others. Serrault could have played the moment of exile as a tantrum, a breakdown, a defensive lashing out. That would have made perfect sense: Albin's way of life, his identity not just as half of a pair but as a radical member of society with the wherewithal to *lead* his life, is at stake. Instead, by announcing Albin's tenacity, Serrault uses the occasion of humiliation to reveal the character's nobility, perhaps reminding us that humiliation can be a virtue, as it was within Kant's moral system, where it takes on the vital role of constraining and "undermin[ing] all other vehement states based on self-love, pride, self-affirmation, or any merely personal search for happiness" (Fisher 238).

In closing, I want to take a moment to consider the politics of Serrault's casting. Arguing whether those with particular sexual self-identities may rightly play a character with a designated sexual identity different than their own gets us nowhere and denies the very nature of acting, fiction, and talent. However, given that the film was made at a time when a major "out" homosexual actor did not exist in the public sphere, it is worth appreciating that whoever and however Albin was played, the experience would be that of a straight actor's interpretation. And anyway, Serrault was famously heterosexual. One wonders amidst Albin's sensitivity and generosity: where is the anger? Should not there be anger when asked to leave one's home? At being denied by lover and son? I am tempted to see in this absence a pernicious fantasy that minorities freely accept their subjugation. After the ravages of AIDS, the reporting of hate crimes like Matthew Shepherd's murder, and the 2016 Orlando massacre, a performance this sweet may never again be seen as anything but wanting.

Notes

1. For more on the logic, and the history of critical thought about the logic, that subtends these criteria, see Pomerance 42.
2. For more on the importance of teaching scenarios in the history of improvisational performance, see Stevens, 75–8. I discuss this with regard to Mike Nichols's 1996 remake of *La cage: The Birdcage*.

Works cited

Benshoff, Harry, and Sean Griffin. *Queer Images: A History of Gay and Lesbian Film in America*. New York: Rowman & Littlefield, 2006.

Bentley, Eric. "On Farce," in Robert Corrigan, ed., *Comedy: Meaning and Form*, New York: Harper and Row, 1981, 193–211.

Edelman, Lee. *No Future: Queer Theory and the Death Drive*. Durham, NC: Duke University Press, 2004.

Fisher, Phillip. *The Vehement Passions*. Princeton: Princeton University Press, 2003.

Pomerance, Murray. *Moment of Action: Riddles of Cinematic Performance*. New Brunswick, NJ: Rutgers University Press, 2016.

Stevens, Kyle. *Mike Nichols: Sex, Language, and the Reinvention of Psychological Realism*. New York: Oxford University Press, 2015.

Chapter 14

Madhubala in *Mughal-e-Azam*

Corey K. Creekmur

The Hindi film star Madhubala's role as the servant girl (*kaneez*) Anarkali in K. Asif's *Mughal-e-Azam* ("The Great Mughal," 1960), one of the most celebrated and popular films in Indian cinema history, is undoubtedly her most famous performance. A massive hit following a difficult production extending over nine years, the film remained India's box-office champion for a decade after its release. Given the film's sheer visual spectacle, including two elaborate color sequences (the original black and white movie was unfortunately colorized for a 2004 revival), it might be easy to overlook the performances it contains, which risk being overshadowed by the ostentatious display of crowds, costumes, and décor, culminating in an ornate *sheesh mahal* ("palace of mirrors") featured in the color sequences. But the film's epic grandeur is consistently grounded by its powerful performances, especially those of its romantic leads Dilip Kumar, as the historical figure Prince Salim (later Emperor Jahangir), and Madhubala. (Rumors and gossip about the offscreen romance of the onscreen couple circulate to this day.) The equally legendary stage and film star Prithviraj

Kapoor, in a part justifying bombastic theatrics, embodies the film's other major role, the "great Mughal" Emperor Akbar.

The film's plot, based on slim historical evidence, pits Kapoor's powerful father against Kumar's headstrong son over the latter's forbidden love for the strikingly beautiful but lowly young woman who threatens to distract him from his noble duties or to become his Queen. Eventually, affairs of state collide with affairs of the heart, requiring a series of painful decisions and noble sacrifices by the lovers and within the royal family. (History confirms that Salim indeed led a rebellion against his father, whom he eventually succeeded in 1605.) At first glance, Madhubala's distinctive success in her role stems from her ability to carefully balance her character's erotic allure with her dignified assumption of her tragic fate, the latter mythologized in Indian popular mythology as a vivid demonstration of the power of "eternal love" even though it is thwarted in this world by the apparent impossibility of reconciling political strategy and personal desire. In a film that dramatizes the clash of the stubborn, immobile wills of two powerful male leaders, eventually on the battlefield as well as in the Mughal court, Madhubala's humble servant girl functions as the most (literally) moving, humanly approachable, and memorable performance in this Indian cinematic monument.

As a major star of the era now celebrated as Hindi cinema's post-Independence "Golden Age," Madhubala remains famous in South Asia for her beauty, in effect preserved by her untimely death at the age of thirty-six. As an iconic figure, she has been persistently celebrated for her sensuality, charm, and charisma, but not necessarily for her skills as an actor, despite a career that included a remarkable range of roles that began when she was a child and eventually encompassed contemporary, historical, comic, and tragic roles. Although she made a few films following *Mughal-e-Azam*, her performance in it is widely acknowledged to be her career highlight, and images of Madhubala that continue to circulate in South Asian popular culture typically derive from it. Like many other female stars, Madhubala's exceptionally glamorous image has ensured her lasting fame but has also unfortunately deflected appreciation of her remarkable skills as an actor, an oversight this chapter hopes to help correct.

However, before attending directly to Madhubala's performance in *Mughal-e-Azam*, it's worth emphasizing that "good" or appropriate acting in popular Indian cinema is not generally expected to be subtle or restrained. Unlike the aesthetic norms for India's art (or "parallel," or "third") cinemas, best known internationally through the realist films of the Bengali master

Satyajit Ray, the performance codes for popular Hindi cinema (at least until recently) might be described in Western terms as melodramatic or emphatic rather than nuanced or subtle. In Indian popular cinema, and perhaps especially in genres like (what in India is called) the historical, acting styles veer towards the stentorian or declamatory, with dialogue delivered emphatically, as if in a rousing public speech or, more often, to resemble a dramatic recitation of poetry (or *mushaira*). *Mughal-e-Azam* is highly celebrated for its elevated, evocative Urdu dialogue, some of which remains elusive for modern Hindi speakers, and the male stars of the film often deliver their lines as if they expect listeners to pause to admire their powerful eloquence before they continue. If women are somewhat more restrained when speaking in Hindi historical films, this is largely because they are expected to be so offscreen as well, although the female performers in *Mughal-e-Azam* are also often required to deliver impressive gems of Urdu wisdom. Moreover, since the conventions of Indian popular cinema demand a more presentational than representational style, a self-aware exhibitionism or openly acknowledged display—rather than the complicit, disavowed voyeurism characteristic of Hollywood cinema—defines their performances as well. In this film, like most of her others, Madhubala is overtly a glamorized "object to be looked at," a status enhanced by the ways in which she is carefully adorned, posed, framed, and lit to signify levels of exceptional beauty lifted beyond her "natural" attractiveness. However, and most significantly, as a Hindi film star she is also a subject who often looks back, and who performs with the full knowledge that she and her character are being gazed upon by characters onscreen and spectators in the cinema. This self-awareness is obviously most evident in scenes in which she is performing within the narrative for an onscreen audience, and of course for us as well, her (visually) acknowledged albeit offscreen audience. In this regard, Madhubala often takes advantage of the tendency of popular Indian cinema to allow its actors to directly meet the gaze of the camera, a practice scholars have linked to the Hindu (but also secularized) practice of "taking" or "giving" *darshan* (literally "looking"), which describes a direct visual interaction between a devotee and a god or goddess in the form of an embodied object or image (*murti*), but which can also summarize interaction between two human beings, perhaps of unequal social rank: Indian fans seek to take *darshan* of popular movie stars. In short, performance as such in popular Indian cinema is frequently self-aware and explicitly acknowledged, rather than driven by the realist goal of a performer's full immersion into a role and narrative that typically earns the praise of Western filmgoers when evaluating actors. Although it is not a self-reflexive film per se (of the sort where actors play actors), in *Mughal-e-Azam* Madhubala's performance nevertheless develops as a performance about performance or, more broadly, about the roles demanded and enacted by her character's difficult negotiation of the competing poles of emotion and obligation.

Mughal-e-Azam begins audaciously with the nation (*Hindustan*) itself literally rising to speak to the audience in order to introduce its epic tale, grounded in history but fashionably tailored by romance. Following a fairly lengthy exposition that establishes its prideful male characters, the film's female star's entrance is delayed and (like the prologue featuring an inanimate object coming to life) highly unconventional: it also might not promise the great performance by its female star which is eventually delivered. The character played by Madhubala, whose actual name is Nadira, is first briefly heard (in reel three) but remains unseen until (in reel four) she appears as a stark white statue, dramatically unveiled in the Emperor's courtyard by an arrow fired by the Prince, that releases the pearl-bead curtain surrounding it. Salim has already peeked at the statue, which held him in rapt fascination, though we were not allowed to see the image that transfixes him. Although the "angelic" statue soon startles the court by beginning to move and speak, our desire to see the character and star remains frustrated, as Madhubala remains caked in white plaster and thus emphatically inexpressive. Like Pygmalion's statue, however, she assumes human form, and insists upon her humble status.

Madhubala's first onscreen line of dialogue, contradicting a pronouncement of the Emperor himself, is now famous: "*Kaneez farishta nahin, insaan*" ("This servant girl is not an angel, but a human being"). Akbar, still impressed by the young woman and her surprising entrance, names her Anarkali, or "pomegranate blossom." (Whether such a historical figure actually existed remains debated). His smitten son, Prince Salim, smiles slightly at the young woman's gentle boldness before the Emperor declares that Anarkali will dance at the next day's festivities, a ceremony to honor Lord Krishna and thereby the Emperor's wife and Queen, Jodha Bhai (Durga Khote), a devout Hindu in this otherwise Muslim court. Despite her assuming human form, our next glimpse of Madhubala remains somewhat obscured: at the start of the film's first major song sequence (one of the defining conventions of popular Indian cinema), the camera tilts down to reveal her seated on the ornate floor in an elaborate costume, with her face covered by a sheer veil. After a series of three shots of her appreciative audience—father, mother, and son, but occupying their august roles of Emperor, Queen, and Prince—a now-famous close-up depicts Madhubala slowly raising her veil and glancing to her side with a slight, crooked smile that by then was the most celebrated, oft-noted characteristic of the star's famous face. (In this moment, the audience also hears the voice of the legendary playback singer Lata Mangeshkar, whose importance for the impact of this role and film cannot be underestimated: however, as this sound cannot be attributed to the performer Madhubala, employing a conventional separation of sound and image fully known to Indian audiences, I will set this significant component of the film aside.) This close-up certainly functions as a "star entrance," but the unveiling of a woman also functions as a powerful narrative trope in Indian cinema, especially within the once-popular genre termed the "Muslim social" (the latter term designating a contemporary rather than historical setting). But even outside of its specific cultural milieu the moment evokes the theatrical punctuation of a curtain raising, marking a narrative transition from one realm to another.

From this point forward, Anarkali, embodied by Madhubala, will remain largely revealed to us, although performative strategies will allow her to "re-veil" or mask herself in plain sight when necessary before a literal, rhyming re-veiling near the end of the film. Now that the curtain has risen on her face, the narrative and film that perversely withheld her arrival will largely revolve around her.

This sequence is the first of twelve song and dance sequences (or what in Indian cinema is called a "picturization") that punctuate the film. Unlike many Hindi films, which shift between male and female musical performances or include romantic duets by couples, *Mughal-e-Azam* is dominated by the female voice and body: eight of the dozen songs feature Lata Mangeshkar and Madhubala. In this first number, "Mohe Panghat Pe" ("Krishna teased me at the bank of the river"), Madhubala is required to be simultaneously reverent (she is singing a religious song in honor of a Hindu god, although one about being teased by him) and alluring (she is winning a Prince's love). Luxuriously dressed and filmed, she appears to be a very confident and skilled performer, well aware of her impact upon her rapt audience. However, the following scene quickly reveals how much her stage persona constituted a performance, for the sexy courtesan is shown to be a soft-spoken, demure young woman, now in marked contrast to her more confident and impudent sister Surayya. When Surayya presents Anarkali with a love letter from the Prince (written with a white-feather pen) Madhubala finally allows her character's deeper emotions to surface, after the character has shorn the successive layers of plaster, veil, and choreographed theatricality through which the film has heretofore contained her.

Yet, despite our new, greater access to her, she reads the letter behind closed doors, and—in a remarkable sequence for the presentation of a movie star—with her back turned to the camera, permitting only a brief glimpse of her face in profile that reveals she is nearly overwhelmed, emitting an audible sigh and permitting a slight shudder of her body to break into her measured reading of Salim's exquisite poetry. Presented within an ornate work of art (the highly stylized film itself) and as an artwork herself, this is the first scene in the film to depict Anarkali as a conflicted and emotional human being, at last demonstrating the status she declared for herself when mistaken for a beautiful if cold piece of marble. From this point forward, Madhubala's performance consistently renders Anarkali, introduced as a beautiful artwork and then as a skilled artist, as an accessible, sympathetic, and vulnerable woman, a crucial shift for a character whose initial distance from a common audience might otherwise seem unbridgeable.

The sequences following this key scene emphasize that Anarkali's overriding fear of the social transgression her love for the Prince represents freezes rather than frees her: only the subsequent musical performance, in this case a friendly *qawali* competition commanded by her jealous rival Bahaar, will snap her out of her apprehension and self-marginalization, and as in the previous song sequence Madhubala's exuberance while singing now underscores her timidity when her character is not performing. The moment and space of performance allow her to assume a status that cannot be sustained in privacy, where her distance from the Prince is bluntly reasserted. For instance, when Salim dares to suggest that she could become Queen of India, she replies *"Paaon ki khaak ko sar ka taaj na banaaiye"* ("Do not make a crown out of the dust that lies beneath your feet"). Throughout the film's first third, Madhubala consistently reinforces Anarkali's humility by lowering her head and eyes and quieting her voice, signs of discretion again enhanced by the much bolder demeanor of the film's other female characters. Musical performance, in contrast, requires but also emboldens her to make the eye contact that she avoids "offstage," when her social status fully defines her. Similarly, her lowered voice in private is inappropriate for the public activity of singing, and so Indian cinema's most famous female voice emerges from her image onscreen.

Following these contrasts in Anarkali's characterization, the film as a whole decisively pivots on Madhubala's facial expressions in a love scene that has become famous for its restrained yet palpable eroticism. Overcoming repressive decorum and risking scandal, Anarkali meets Salim in the palace conservatory while the legendary historical figure Tansen (voiced by classical singer Bade Ghulam Ali Khan) sings "Prem Jogan," a classical song identifying Anarkali as a "devotee of love," while the Prince gently brushes her face with the white feather he used earlier to pen his love poem to her. The scene, reminiscent of silent cinema's reliance on the affective power of the actor's face, is built around five extreme close-ups of Madhubala registering ecstasy, intercut with Dilip Kumar's more static, slightly smiling face. After initial reluctance, signaled by turning her face away from him, the first tight close-up shows Madhubala with her eyes closed and mouth slightly open as the feather crosses her face, functioning like an old-fashioned wipe. However, the next close-up is startling: now meeting Salim's gaze directly, Madhubala smiles her crooked smile with an expression that seems suddenly knowing and mature before she returns, under another swipe of the feather, to a downward gaze. The next close-up is similar to our previous view of her until it ends with her almost nibbling at the feather as it makes another pass. Another brief close-up precedes the final one, now without the feather, which in effect renders the moment post-coital, even wistful of something now past. No longer smiling, Madhubala's half-open mouth and eyes suggest that this brief moment has been concluded even though it is the film's first scene establishing a physical relationship between Anarkali and Salim. The short but powerful sequence concludes with the camera moving back in order to view the couple, with Salim leaning in to kiss her, an action obscured by the feather and a cutaway to the jealous Bahaar witnessing the forbidden scene from a distance: the full sequence ends, it seems, a short while later (despite the continuous song) when the couple wakes together, now covered in fallen flower petals, and sense that they have been spied upon.

It's tempting to claim that much of the plot of the film is condensed in the minute changes traversed over these intimate close-ups: Anarkali's shy reluctance based upon respect for Salim's standing gives way to romantic and even erotic abandon, concluding with a hint of melancholy if not anticipatory dread. Even if this summary of the film's narrative arc seems fancifully encapsulated by this brief scene, its catalogue of facial expressions confirms that Madhubala's performance thereafter will not be one-note, even if her character, like most in popular Hindi cinema, embodies a familiar type.

Whereas the first third of *Mughal-e-Azam* seemed to require two markedly different performance styles to distinguish Anarkali's restrained private self from her more expressive public one, after her daring expression of passion in private it's appropriate that the next song sequence, of her singing "Mohabbat Ki Jhooti Kahani Pe Roye" ("I cry over this false story of love"), is *not* another public performance but takes place alone in her cell, where she has been tossed in chains after the Emperor discovers his son's transgressive romance. Singing through tears, eyes half-closed, Madhubala lurches clumsily from grabbing massive chains to falling against rough walls, in troubling contrast to her gracefully choreographed movements in the previous two numbers. Brought back to court in chains, the ethereal beauty is now disheveled, sweaty, and dirty as she wobbles, barely able to stand or walk, again undermining the "angelic" image and skill to which the film introduced us.

Despite her abjection, however, the once self-effacing Anarkali now faces the Emperor defiantly, her gaze at him just a few inches away from directly piercing the camera and audience, too. Freed on the condition that she deny her own heart and serve the Emperor by deceptively convincing Salim that her love was untrue, Madhubala returns to her demure self-presentation, once again shyly avoiding direct looks at the Prince. Crucially, what we took to be genuine expressions of Anarkali's humility in earlier scenes are now visible to us as a ruse, a performance enacted in private by a character we earlier saw explicitly only taking on roles in public. As in any film which positions us to witness actors acting, this fundamental shift renders much of the rest of Madhubala's performance in the film double-edged: we are now attuned to view Madhubala act as Anarkali acting.

Her next song in the film, "Humain Kash Tumse Mohabbat Na Hoti" ("If only I had never loved you"), facilitates this sharpened focus. Following the Emperor's command that she tell his son she never loved him and was only seeking social advancement, "Humen Kaash Tum Se Muhabbat Na Hoti" ("If only I had never loved you") is performed for Salim only. Madhubala's body is now largely static (slowly walking and kneeling are her only actions) and her expressions are introspective, with her eyes no longer staring down but gazing blankly into space rather than at her lover. While this is ostensibly a love song (but with elusive lyrics), Madhubala appears continually distracted as she sings it, and seems to forget that she has an addressee in Salim, who has to gently touch her in order to regain her attention. When the song ends, she turns her passive face away from his, leaving him devastated: she is no longer the singer who solicited him and won his heart. Unlike the Prince, we now understand even this apparently intimate act to have been a powerful performance, calculated for results rather than simply the expression of emotion.

At Bahaar's devious suggestion, following Akbar's plan, Salim soon comes to believe he has indeed been deceived by Anarkali's performance and so, given the increasingly multi-layered scenes in which acting by characters within the narrative is made visible, we find ourselves glimpsing the truth behind the performance which was staged to *appear* to reveal the truth: we view Anarkali denying her love for Salim out of her love for him, while he can only see one level deep, leading him to cruelly curse rather than appreciate her self-sacrificing deception. Again, we are located in a privileged position that allows us to see Madhubala performing Anarkali performing, a somewhat dizzying perspective appropriate for a film leading us to a hall of mirrors.

The film's first color sequence continues this pattern of requiring us to negotiate simultaneous, multiple meanings. Serving as both a command and farewell performance by Anarkali in Akbar's court, it echoes the film's first song sequence while also being designed to showcase the film's lavish, Islamicate sets and décor even more boldly. In the *sheesh mahal*, which will eventually fragment her wildly dancing body into dozens of replicas, Madhubala performs what became a signature song, "Pyar Kiya To Darna Kya" ("If one has loved, what is there to fear?"). This performance is again targeted at its internal audience (especially Akbar and Salim, whose momentary reconciliation the song will break apart), but is also often aimed at us, as the filmmakers persistently have Madhubala look directly into the camera. Her renewed defiance, emphasized in her bold, direct address, lands her once more in chains and an underground cell. By this point, the once shy, self-effacing slave girl has fully taken control of the film's love story, even if she cannot be allowed to also seize control of the historical, political narrative with which it tragically intertwines.

Again, Madhubala's unusual task is also now to continually establish meaning on two levels, ostensibly affirming the duty in which she has been commanded while continuing to express her true feelings, with only the film audience allowed to easily view her slippage between them. (Salim, on the other hand, cannot negotiate his role as effectively as Anarkali: his adherence to his emotions requires him to reject his father and his duty.)

While the male protagonists fight their battles over her, their positions remain firm, a narrative element reinforced by the consistent performance styles of the male actors, who are not asked to demonstrate much range. Madhubala's Anarkali, however, has become a much more mutable, multi-layered character as the film unfolds. It's not just that the central conflicts of the film—love versus duty, the personal versus the political, or family versus nation—revolve around Anarkali, but that she embodies a complexly mobile center, signaled by the only performance that shifts notably across the film. Once more, the narrative's Father and Son, both burdened with pride as well as obligation, are stubbornly stable, despite their moments of conflicted regret. Madhubala's Anarkali isn't simply a fought-over prize for the winning male, but a condensation of the film's thematic tensions and a warning of the impossibility of the narrative finding a fully acceptable resolution to them. (The film in fact ends quite unsatisfactorily, caught in a desperate desire to mask its contradictions: apparently sticking to his promise to let his son live if Anarkali misleads Salim by participating in a sham wedding and then sacrificing her own life by being buried alive, at the last minute Akbar shows a traumatized Anarkali and her mother a secret passage leading away from his kingdom, where they will be allowed to live in anonymity. Everyone lives, but love loses.)

In a sense, and despite the unsatisfying ending that rescues Anarkali and Salim but requires their separation, *Mughal-e-Azam* brings Madhubala full circle, from imitating a statue to our final vision of her as a traumatized, zombie-like figure whose bestowed identity has been stripped away from her. But her dramatic transformation between these poles is surely the beating heart of this legendary love story. While the film's presentation of family tensions that threaten to destroy an empire seems designed to remind us that even ancient emperors, princes, and queens faced human problems "just like us," their historical and social distance from virtually all audiences for the film remains difficult to bridge. It's Madhubala's character and performance that offer an available route into the film's agonies and ecstasies, allowing a mass audience to project their own less celebrated experiences of love and loss into a film that in its historical splendor is designed to remain at some remove from contemporary and everyday experience. While her movie-star glamour certainly remains one of the principal visual attractions within one of India's most resplendent spectacles, Madhubala's complex performance is absolutely vital to securing the film's ongoing status as one of popular Indian cinema's emotional touchstones.

Chapter 15

Michael Caine in *Alfie*

Jason Jacobs

According to one of his books, Michael Caine's first challenge was getting his character's direct address to the audience, for which Lewis Gilbert's *Alfie* (1965) is famous, tonally correct. The film starts with Caine, as Alfie Elkins, after extracting himself from his car where he has been lovemaking with a married woman, adjusting his trousers, noticing "us" across the barrier of the screen, and then talking directly at us as if fully aware that he's a character in a movie. "I suppose you think you're gonna see the bleedin' titles now? Well you're not, so you can all relax," he says in a broad and upbeat southeast London accent. It's as if he is in charge of the content of the movie as it is projected to us: how much does he know about what is to come? We feel safe in his "hands," and that is partly to do with the assumed intimacy he strikes with us from the beginning. Here is Caine's account of the process:

> When you flesh out a character to make him real, your tools are aspects of yourself that apply, and your role models. People always think the character Alfie was close to my own personality, but while I understood Alfie, I wasn't like him. I based him on a guy named Jim Slater, my best friend when I was young. I could never get any girls, and Jim got them all. He would have been perfect in the part,

except that he was always too tired ... I also used Jim as the person to whom I was talking when I had to speak directly to the camera. Normally when you look directly into the lens, the effect will be very phoney because the filmmaker is breaking the illusion of eavesdropping on reality. But in *Alfie*, my character spoke to the audience through the camera, a bit like the technique of "asides" in the theatre when a character detaches itself from the action and addresses the audience directly. In fact, when I first spoke directly to the camera, I treated it like a large audience. The director, Gilbert Lewis [sic], said, "Cut! Come close to the camera. Do it as if you were talking to just one person, so that every member of the audience feels as if you're singling him out personally." Then I played the moment as though I was talking to Jim. We liked each other, and Jim was really interested in what I had to say. He would have especially appreciated remarks like, "She's in beautiful condition," when Alfie was running his hands over a woman's bum, because Jim used to say things like that. That confidence in Jim's appreciation is what won me the collusion of the cinema audience, even when they didn't really approve of Alfie's goings-on. (Caine, *Acting* 96, 98)

This was Caine's technique in order to achieve a level of intimacy with his audience in an ongoing one-to-one relationship, while the rest of the diegetic world continued around them, without being theatrical or mannered. He literally treated the camera as a friend, which is pretty much the general advice Caine gives to budding actors earlier in the same book:

If your concentration is total and your performance is truthful, you can lean back and the camera will catch you every time; it will never let you fall. It's watching you. It's your friend. Remember, it loves you. It listens to and records everything you do, no matter how minutely you do it. If theatre action is operation with a scalpel, movie acting is an operation with a laser. (9)

But many new to the practice and study of film or television neglect to remember that moving pictures have an ear as well as an eye: the sound, modulation, and amplitude of Caine's voice is extraordinary in this film and throughout much of his career. Somehow his voice provides emotional weight that other aspects of his body and movement seem to lack or avoid. This is something Caine acknowledges in a 1998 interview, when responding to a question about why many impersonators enjoy "doing" him:

It's a compliment to be sent up so much. I must have some kind of personality, otherwise people wouldn't recognize it. You can't impersonate a lot of stars because their voices are straight. Mine is different. It's my fortune really, although I've done accents all over the place. (Duncan 15)

What is in and behind that voice is a disarming undercurrent of wanting to teach and to help the listener: to instruct them on what David Thomson, describing Caine's books and videos on acting, calls the "clever, if rather obvious" aspects of human life learned through his experiences (144). In print and in character, often Caine's voice seems in possession of information that is at once a product of observation or experience anyone could have and also authoritatively sincere, blessed with just-discovered information that—one does not wish to point out to the excited messenger—everyone already knew anyway. Despite the banal or offensive content it is called upon to deliver, Caine's voice has a peculiar confidence and charm, and this is fully exercised in *Alfie*. The voice can be loud or quiet but it never wavers from testing and checking the world against the experiences its holder has had. Married women for example, need a laugh but, "Of course it don't work with a single bird—it starts you off on the wrong foot. You get one of them laughing you won't get nothing else. [We see Siddie (Millicent Martin), the married woman, happy and laughing] See? Just listen to it. It was dead glum when I met it tonight. I listened to all its problems then I got it laughing . . . It'll go home happy."

So, Alfie is confident we will not have to sit through the "bleedin' titles" and the first half of the film has him tell us about, and let us watch, his various systems, theories, and approaches to bedding women married and single. Caine uses his personal address to us to carve out, and to color with his view, the public and private spaces in which he uses it. *Alfie* the film uses its mise-en-scène to attempt to distance or comment on what might well be our hesitations in endorsing this unremorseful, destructive, and misogynistic—as well as lively and hedonistic—litany of sexual pursuits and conquests. Women are treated explicitly as objects in a world of other objects—"it," "it," and "it"—a transactional world where ideally everyone has a bit of fun and no one gets hurt. But all the while the film's distance is crudely established, Caine's voice, its content however offensive, never pushes us away, never alienates itself, however "loudly" it gets.[1] For example, his long-term single-woman relationship with Gilda (Julia Foster) is conducted mostly in her small flat. As Alfie sits on her bed and complains about the hot water bottle in it, we see a large porcelain doll on her side of the bed, above the lower half of a painting of two dogs. The juxtaposition of these objects in this context is clear: Gilda is a kind of object, and for Alfie the world is, too, just like the doll, one that needs to be "fiddled" or controlled, like a dog. Soon he checks her menstruation status by consulting his little red book (which he carries everywhere, presumably a diary for this purpose): "Shouldn't our little friend have arrived on the nineteenth?" Her period didn't arrive on time, though. Human beings are not mere passive objects that survive by instinct or nature, nor do they run solely by calendar or clockwork, as Alfie's notebook implies. Caine's voice is recruited here to use its strongest attribute, which is not so much charm as instruction itself, its capacity to tell one what one needs to, but may not, know, even elliptically. A common catchphrase adopted by impersonators of Caine was, "Not a lotta people know that," and the pedagogical tone of the sharing of the discoveries of experience is common throughout the actor's written work on acting and cinema.

He goes on to instruct Gilda on "fiddling" (that is, stealing from) the cash register (the "till") at work: "Nobody helps you in this life. You've gotta help yourself. Everybody should take an interest in their work." These are hardly the sort of maxims that would bolster the Kantian categorical imperative, but it is clear that Alfie has developed a series of systems or ways of living that take advantage of the emergence and prominence of transactional services tuned to individual self-presentation during the 1960s. As Christopher Bray puts it in his excellent biography of Caine, Alfie as depicted in the original version (first a radio, then a stage play) is a "satisfied consumer fetishist," and Caine plays this up by wearing a gorgeous selection of suits, jackets, and accessories that directly work against the usual hostility to "stuff" expressed in the British kitchen sink genre (Bray 81).

Indeed the attention to fine clothing is woven into an early medley of sequences that shows Alfie's "system" of transactional rewards (otherwise known as sex for services, or prostitution; or capitalism) in action. We begin with a shot of the exterior of a dry cleaners shop (again, in typically British-cinema fashion the mise-en-scène *underlines* the latent sexual point by having a sign prominent in the window that says, "Prompt Service Within"), followed by a witty moment as the camera pans along a rack of cellophane-wrapped clothes as Alfie canoodles with the shop assistant behind. We hear him declare in voiceover, ". . . And I was getting a suit cleaned in the bargain," as he emerges (and the pan completes its motion) on the other side of the rack in a gorgeous navy blue terylene and mohair jacket. Time and transaction are compressed, and what emerges looks great: it is capitalism at work, with human beings wrapped in the "shiny packaging" so berated by Richard Hoggart in his attack on the Americanization of culture in *The Uses of Literacy*. But with the Technicolor printing we can almost feel how good that jacket feels.[2]

Next we see Caine in scarlet (again: no subtle gestures!) wearing a dressing gown as he has his feet seen to by a female chiropodist who "cut me corns handsome." Another exchange, but this time Caine deploys one of his finest physical assets as he delivers the lines to camera: his heavy eyelids, which help provide an air of calculated menace.[3] As he grins like an imp, he notes that despite the fact she is not perfect he is "prepared to overlook the odd blemish as long as they have something to make up for it. Well, that's what we're all here for innit?—to help one another out in this life." In the space of minutes, Alfie has gone from his advice to Gilda (nobody helps you in this life) to a new sense of what "help" really is about: the weighing of exchange value. Here Caine looks at us under those eyelids with the calculating certainty of an economist, Adam Smith or David Ricardo, perhaps. Value always and exclusively exists for Alfie in relation to a commodity. Any associated sentiment, emotion, or feeling is weighted and weighed in tune with one's convenience and pleasure in enjoying said commodity and ensuring that the time invested is rewarded with pleasure or services provided. Alfie just makes clear, with Caine's voice of experience, what human relationships are really like. And it is here that Cavell's astonishingly accurate point about leading men hits home hardest:

> We no longer take it for granted, that a man who expresses no feeling has fires banked within him; or, if we do grant him depth, we are likely not to endow him with a commitment to his own originality, but to suppose him banking destructive feeling. (67)[4]

Where is the destructive feeling in Caine's Alfie, a man who by my own back-of-the-envelope calculations was "having it off" with at least one different woman a day (and "on top of them was the odd bird that came my way by chance") during the time we observe him? Is it the annihilation of self in partnership (even if that means only crude coupling), that Matthew Arnold observes in his poem "Dover Beach"—

> And here we are as on a darkling plain
> Swept with confused alarms of struggle and flight,
> Where ignorant armies clash by night.

—or something far more unsettling even than that? For Alfie's sexual rapaciousness and consumer appetites are ultimately cashed out, not so very many decades later, in fictional figures such as Patrick Bateman in Bret Easton Ellis's *American Psycho* (1991; on film in 2000), as if the containment of masculinity in contemporary culture cannot function without monstrous distortion.

Part of the answer to this paradox—in so far as there is one—lies in the way Caine's voice is able to maintain its privacy with us even in very public spaces or, worse, in those intimate private spaces where public conversation—with, say, a film audience—should be well out of bounds. His voice commodifies human privacy, and makes that commodification attractive. We have necessarily different registers of locution in public and private; Caine's Alfie erases those, which may well be why the film appealed internationally, and especially in the US, in the way that it did. His address to us contradicted, but also re-domesticated. It embodies that essential characteristic of English life that George Orwell described as "the *privateness* ... All the culture that is most truly native centres round things which even when they are communal are not official—the pub, the football match, the back garden, the fireside and the 'nice cup of tea'" (15). Alfie "commercial-izes" that native privacy and does so in a film that should by rights belong to a distinctively English genre—the kitchen sink melodrama, part of the British New Wave—but really has its heart and soul elsewhere. *Alfie,* then, is a kitchen sink drama, a naturalistic depiction of working-class life that is also transitional, in that the sexually explicit aspects of the genre are amplified and other elements (the struggles of work, money, marriage, family, and faith) are played down in relation to that. *Alfie* strongly individualizes what, up to now, had been situations whereby the leading (mostly male) characters carried the burden of representation (*Saturday Night and Sunday Morning* (1960), *A Taste of Honey* (1961), *The Loneliness of the Long Distance Runner* (1962), *Room at the Top* (1959)). Funded by Paramount, *Alfie* marked a real shift for that kind of British film, following *Tom Jones* (1963) in courting an international export market that universalized what were distinctively provincial or national narratives. It even internalizes its own interna-tional target audience in the character of the loud, sexually rapacious businesswoman Ruby (Shelley Winters). Most "kitchen sink" efforts after *Alfie* avoided London as a setting, and tried regional locations: Ken Loach's *Kes* (1967), for example, or Peter Hammond's *Spring and Port Wine* (1970).

Nevertheless, *Alfie* keeps one foot firmly in the British kitchen sink genre as well as confirming Deborah Thomas's argument that the melodramatic element or lining of any genre tends to be expressed through the resistance to containment or domestication that the male characters are depicted experiencing. Arthur Seaton (Albert Finney) in *Saturday Night and Sunday Morning* is played as a hell raiser, but his confrontation is with the pressures of work *and* home to contain him within a conformist culture that is hostile to individual expression, inimical to fighting back. As the character says (also in voiceover: as in *Alfie*, what these men are "banking" is directly communicated to us), "I'm me and nobody else. Whatever people say I am that's what I'm not. Because they don't know a bloody thing about me." For Seaton and other male figures in this genre, it is domestication, the femininity of modernity and consumer culture that is as much a downfall for the individual as the more legible aggressors of authority figures at work, or the police or military. For Alfie, what is to be avoided is the control of women—*at all*, quite apart from their evocation of consumer culture (in which he is a full and willing participant) or other kinds of social and political control. But what that means, by the end—when he is free of women—is that he is in fact far more confined, trapped, in a world devoid of meaning apart from his own sense of observation and the systems he has created around that. Caine presents us with a figure who is outwardly confident but fragile, and, unlike Seaton, physically cowardly: consumer culture has not quite made him effeminate, but it has made him oddly, narcissistically effete.

Since in these fictional settings "expression" means sexual freedom, a key complication was pregnancy, since contraception and abortion were not, until the late 1960s, freely or legally available in Britain. This is where *Alfie* cashes out its distance from Alfie; it is also the point where Caine himself met a challenge to his acting. As he put it:

> Things were moving along easily, too easily in fact, until I was at a stage where I was trailing through the scenes with all the confidence of a Spencer Tracy, when in came an actor called Denholm Elliott as the abortionist, who started to act me off the screen. Socks were pulled up and shoulders put to the wheel to combat this extremely charming new menace, but to no avail. I never managed to top him, only just managed to hold my own, in fact. (Caine, *What's* 218)

There is an apt correspondence between the performative challenge, for Caine, of Elliott's upstaging and Alfie's own confrontation with the consequences of his promiscuity. Since pregnancy was a complication plausibly arising from sexual adventure, and abortion illegal in the UK until the late 1960s, kitchen sink genre plots would often recruit the moral and legal forces ranged against sexual expression as part of their narratives. But *Alfie* does this particularly strongly, since the rest of the contextual stuff (work, family, tradition) has literally dropped away in its fiction even if we see and hear aspects of it residually (most famously the pub brawl sequence, which arrives as if from another film altogether). Alfie is just a young man in London who has sex with many women, some of them married. The abortion scene stands as the payoff, when the moral position of the film, rather than that of the character, is asserted.

Alfie is a womanizer (the most polite way to put it)[5] who is briefly "contained" after being diagnosed with an unspecified lung problem which requires him to spend time in a convalescent home. Health problems aside, he continues sexual adventures with the nursing staff, but also meets Harry Clamacraft (Alfie Bass), a very domesticated man suffering from a lung complaint. Married with children, Harry is dedicated to his wife Lily (Vivien Merchant) and, as Alfie points out to us, literally distracted by his own nervousness as he awaits her visit. After Alfie gets out of the institution, he visits Harry, whose "condition" (never specified) keeps him there. Lily is visiting, too, as the dutiful wife. Alfie kindly offers her a ride home, which becomes a kind of adventure. He takes her on a very romantic boat ride down the river, where we see her watch the sunshine peek through the leaves as she relaxes in the punt. It is clear that Harry has never so much as considered something like this for Lily. She and Alfie have tea and then sex (as Alfie says to us directly after they hug, "It'll round off the tea nicely"), and the issue is confined to one more notch on Alfie's bedpost.

Much later on, however, and out of the blue, the film shows us Lily coming to Alfie's dingy little flat. There they await the arrival of Denholm Elliott's backstreet abortionist. Elliott is a mirror to Alfie: he gives Alfie's menace, seediness, and hypocrisy a concrete, maliciously self-righteous form. The scene is unusual in that Caine has no moments where Alfie breaks the fourth wall to talk to us directly but we *do* hear him talk to us in the more conventional manner of a voiceover (the film is quite inventive in mixing the two kinds of address). He says of the event—looking back across three months—"That was something I thought I got for nothing but it don't never work out that way does it?" Again, a vague "law" of transactional equilibrium is evoked.

When Elliott arrived on set as the abortionist he effectively did to Caine what Caine's character had been doing to other men. The part of the abortionist requires a peculiar mixture of sleaze and priestly self-righteousness. Coming toward the end of the film the sequence is intended to teach us and the character a moral lesson in the consequences of having a "bit of fun": these are pain—especially physical pain (vividly expressed by Vivien Merchant as the contractions of the induced labor begin)—and moral disorientation. It is the latter quality that Caine's performance brings to the genre, in such a way that it transforms the genre's combative fists-up, chin-down stance into something far darker, if superficially more playful. In Alfie's moral disorientation we can grasp that the entire film is framed as a false equilibrium based around allegory: it begins with two copulating dogs, the bitch being enticed away by a charming third, leaving one behind alone. This is what Alfie does to married men, except that they are so involved in the routines of their domesticated lives (e.g. gardening catalogues, the routines and security of house and home) that they do not notice. According to Walter Benjamin:

> Any person, any object, any relationship can mean absolutely anything else. With this possibility a destructive, but just verdict is passed on the profane world: it is characterized as a world in which the detail is of no great importance. But it will be unmistakably apparent, especially to anyone who is familiar with allegorical textual exegesis, that all of the things that are used to signify derive, from the very fact of their pointing to something else, a power which makes them appear no longer commensurable with profane things, which raises them onto a higher plane, and which can, indeed, sanctify them. Considered in allegorical terms, then, the profane world is both elevated and devalued. (175)

Or, in a slightly different translation:

> Every person, every object, every relationship can stand for something else. This transferability constitutes a devastating, though just, judgment on the profane world—which is thereby branded as a world where such things are of small importance. (Lukács 42)

As Lily goes through with the induced labor, Alfie goes for a walk; here improbably he witnesses the baptism of the second child born to Gilda, and sees his son, Malcolm, who has been adopted by Gilda's husband, the ever devoted and domesticated bus conductor, Humphrey. We see Alfie hear Malcolm refer to Humphrey as "Daddy." Caine watches the group leave the church: he is wearing his navy mohair jacket, his smart watch, his pinky ring. The handsome profile is still and unreactive, except for a small movement of his thumb on his chin. Yes, this movement tells us, thought continues. But it is withheld from us.

Only on his return to his flat, and his sighting of the dead fetus in his bedroom, is this brilliant performance unfolded for us emotionally. The scene is touching because Caine's accumulation of restrained performance gestures are cashed out here, loading Alfie's tearful, distraught, and overt reaction at the moment of his breakdown in the context of loss of *two* children. We have seen Alfie at his happiest when he is also at his most silent toward us: when he played with the young Malcolm, slow-motion action and black-and-white still shots provided a sense of enraptured fatherhood, one based on Alfie's strong sense of Malcolm's similarity in nature and mood to himself. Now, even that kind of growth—or outgrowth—is lost forever. He has lost a future where values could be passed on to real people, not the fake imaginary friend he appears to be talking to throughout the movie. That is why he does not talk to us at this point: he has nothing to teach us, nothing to pass on; and we, imaginary listeners, have become hollow to him and irrelevant. The transferability of things is given a dead halt with a dead life: stopped in mid-growth, murdered, and paid for by money borrowed from Alfie's friend Nat (Murray Melvin).

After he sees the fetus, but before Lily leaves, Alfie goes downstairs to visit Nat and it is to him, rather than us, that he tells about his distress caused by the abortion. Nat's flat is neat, and has a small balcony where we see him watering an impressive display of potted plants as Alfie talks. This is one man who can grow things, enjoy himself (it is Nat who recruits Alfie as a tourist photographer), and remain loyal—he lends Alfie the twenty-five quid he needs in order to pay Lily back for the abortion. In true kitchen sink style, they go for a walk along a canal, in one of the most touching scenes in the movie. The abortion and his responsibility for it mean that Alfie is confronted with a question about which there can be only a moral response. "It could never have had any life in it . . . I mean, not a proper life of its own," he says aloud. And then he steps forward into close-up and contradicts that: "Still, it must have had some life, of course."

Alfie has learned to have a private conversation with a friend about what has moved him most deeply. At the conclusion of the sequence, he stares beyond the right side of the screen, but we do not hear what he may be thinking; Caine leaves us to believe he is thinking, but this time, it is for him only. He no longer has the confidence, arrogance, and certainty to share with anyone but himself.

After the abortion scene, Alfie experiences one further rejection. His "servicing" of the older American businesswoman Ruby is brought to an abrupt end when he discovers her with another man. He has gone to the trouble of buying her flowers—not a good sign for someone who, as we know, is as rapaciously promiscuous as Alfie himself and has a similar "doggy" sense of the dangers of commitment—when he discovers another man in Ruby's bed (an electric guitar nearby indicates he may be a band member). He asks her, "What's he got that I haven't?" "He's younger," she replies. And so at last he has lost everything: in Malcolm, the mirror of himself and his playfulness; because of the abortion, the pleasure of sex; the sense of a system of transferability and equilibrium where "everyone helps one another," everything balances, without anyone being hurt.

Like Caine, Alfie is someone who seems compelled to pass on the lessons of his hard work and experience to anyone who will listen, however obvious or banal the content. Caine tells the story about Denholm Elliott coming on set as a part of his telling what he learned during his career. One of Caine's strengths as an actor is his capacity to embody a person who has at some point in the unseen past learned a lesson from events we may never know or hear about. He often needs to "do" very little in order to convey this, as in *Gambit* (1966) and *The Italian Job* (1969) and *Sleuth* (1972), where his characters are those of a clever, dashing crook who, on the brink of being outwitted, learns quickly and makes good, or nearly good. The lesson is that hard work and the drive to achieve can get one far even without the inherited advantages of others.

But *Alfie* ends with a genuinely unsettling delivery to us, this time with Caine alone (a young couple canoodling nearby providing some glimpse of an alternative to what we hear), once again next to the Thames after he's tossed into it the flowers he bought for Ruby. He addresses us for the last time, this time expressing the modernist confusion that he has been banking up, where everything is a question: "I ain't got my piece of mind. What's it all about? Know what I mean?" He meets the same dog we saw at the beginning, and the allegory collapses on itself.

But not for Caine: *Alfie* made him an international film star in a way the kitchen sink dramas did not for Alan Bates or Albert Finney (but in the way the part of James Bond did for Caine's close friend Sean Connery). Caine's performance internationalized a provincial narrative by adding the standing modernist puzzle of ultimate meaning to a tale of consumption and hedonistic pleasure that was equally garnished with sentiment. When Caine says to the dog, "Come on, boy," and the dog follows, we see that animal's loyalty without judgment. Caine has been taken by his biographers and others as the epitome (allegory) of the British working-class loyalty without judgment: seduced by the hedonistic pleasures and consumer sparkle of US culture and British Thatcherism, he abandoned the good municipal commitment to nation and culture. Christopher Bray has described Caine as "perhaps the sixties'" most crucial fore-runner of the Thatcher era" (75n). As Caine told that pillar of British culture at the time, the BBC's *Radio Times*:

> You get an especially bad press in England if you're successful in America. They like an actor to be old, broke, humble, decrepit and to have had his day. Well, it isn't like that for me … I didn't expect to get this far, so I was never jealous of anyone who went farther. I'm jealous of me really. How the hell did he do it? I'd like to be able to bottle it and sell it. I learnt how to do something and I've done it to the best of my ability for the longest amount of time. That's all. I have no regrets. You know what happens if you look back? You trip up. Keep going forward and you'll see where the stumbling blocks are. (Duncan 18)

One thing is another: this could be Alfie Elkins telling us about his great acting career. Thus, at the end of *Alfie*, the man we see walking off into the distance over the river is Caine, confident, heading toward a mixed commercial and critical career but one that rarely took a breath over the next fifty years.

Notes

1. In their competitive attempts to depict Caine's voice in *The Trip* (BBC, 2010) Steve Coogan tells Rob Brydon that when "it gets loudly it gets very loudly indeed."
2. The review of *Alfie* in the British *Monthly Film Bulletin* berated the way the film betrayed its genre through "impressive" production values: "one is left to wonder," it concludes, "whether a good, unpretentious little black-and-white film may not have been smothered under those very values" (1 January 1966, 70).
3. In his second autobiography Caine tells us that Robert Mitchum asked him to present his Lifetime Achievement Award at the Golden Globes: "'Did you pick me because I had heavy eyelids like you?' I asked him. And he said, 'Yes. You're the only one you know. People were always talking about my eyelids and then I saw you in *Alfie* and I thought to myself: this guy's got heavy eyelids, too. They're not as heavy as mine, of course, but they're quite heavy. It's all to do with the eyelids'" (*Elephant* 3).
4. Cavell mentions Sean Connery and Caine as examples of the "distance we have come, along the line of silent strength" from male hero types like Gary Cooper, Henry Fonda, James Stewart, and Humphrey Bogart.
5. A more vernacular set of words at the time would have included "cocksman," and "pussyhound."

Works cited

Benjamin, Walter. *The Origin of German Tragic Drama*. London: Verso, 1998.

Bray, Christopher. *1965 The Year Modern Britain Was Born*. London: Simon and Shuster, 2014.

Bray, Christopher. *Michael Caine: A Class Act*. London: Faber and Faber, 2006.

Caine, Michael. *Acting in Film: An Actor's Take on Movie Making*. Rev. and expanded edn. New York: Applause, 1997.

Caine, Michael. *What's It All About?* London: Arrow Books, 2010.

Caine, Michael. *The Elephant to Hollywood*. New York: St. Martin's Press, 2010.

Cavell, Stanley. *The World Viewed*. Enlarged edn. Cambridge, MA: Harvard University Press, 1979.

Duncan, Andrew. "Interview with Michael Caine," *Radio Times* (7–13 March 1998), 15, 18.

Hoggart, Richard. *The Uses of Literacy*. Harmondsworth: Penguin, 1960.

Lukács, Georg. *The Meaning of Contemporary Realism*. Monmouth: Merlin Press, 2006.

Orwell, George. "The Lion and the Unicorn," in *Why I Write*, London: Penguin, 2004 © 1940, 11–94.

Thomas, Deborah. *Beyond Genre*. Moffat: Cameron & Hollis, 2000.

Thomson, David. "Michael Caine," in *The New Biographical Dictionary of Film*, New York: Knopf, 2010, 143–4.

Chapter 16

Amitabh Bachchan in *Deewaar*

Ulka Anjaria

Possibly his most famous role, Amitabh Bachchan's performance in Yash Chopra's *Deewaar* (1975) is certainly one of his best, in part for how it reinterprets the "angry young man" from the earlier film, *Zanjeer* (1973), in which Bachchan made his name as Hindi cinema's top superstar. The angry young man is a figure largely credited to the writing team of Salim Khan and Javed Akhtar, known as Salim-Javed, who are seen to have given expression to the voice of subaltern discontent in a 1970s India increasingly disillusioned by the failure of the state to follow through on the promises made at independence. Many have praised Bachchan's performances in these films, but little attention has been given to the role of his performances—in *Deewaar* in particular—in modulating the affect of anger and thus shaping the angry young man as more than merely "angry." *Deewaar* is a particularly good example of how restraint and dispassion are even more central to imagining subaltern discontent than actual rage, an interpretation which allows for a broader understanding of the affective aspect of vigilantism and enables a recognition of the continuity between 1970s Bollywood films and today's "middle-class" cinema. Bachchan's ability to move between these different affective registers is central to how he builds this version of the character Vijay and the angry young man more generally above and beyond *Deewaar's* brilliant script and direction.

The antinomies of performance

Bachchan's great performance in *Deewaar* can be considered in relation to the various other performances that exist in the film. Performance is built into the text from the very first scene of the extended flashback that constitutes the entirety of the film, when we see Anand (Satyendra Kapoor), who will turn out to be Vijay (Bachchan) and Ravi's (Shashi Kapoor) father, making a rousing speech to a crowd of workers who are shouting, "Anand babu, zindabad [Long live Mr. Anand]!" Anand is an organizer of a union of coal miners striking for better pay and access to good schools and hospitals. He gives a convincing performance, encouraging the workers to continue with their strike, offering rousing but stock promises like, "A new morning . . . will come when workers will receive their rights and a fitting reward for their hard work!" Large crowds gather at his speech and his performance is so successful that news of it spreads beyond the workers: his sons come home from school reporting that their teacher was praising their father's "true principles." But very soon into the film, Anand's performance collapses. His performative persona dissolves once he enters the mine owner's lair, where he becomes weak and sniveling and helplessly sells out the union to save the lives of his wife and sons. The problem is not the nature of Anand's performance per se—it made him a local hero—but the fact that his agitating was *mere* performance, thus inherently weak and unable to withstand the pressure of the mine owners' corrupt machinations. Unable to face his humiliation, he abandons his family, criss-crossing India for the next few decades on the trains that become his new home (Joshi 12). Ravi and his mother feel the loss of Anand, but it is on Vijay that his abandonment makes the biggest imprint. Not only does Vijay have to become the man of the house (11), he is forcibly branded with his father's shame in a tattoo that he lives with for the rest of his life, which reads: "Mera baap chor hai [My father is a thief]."

The fact that Anand is played by Satyendra Kapoor highlights the perennial minorness of his character in relation to Bachchan's star persona. Kapoor played hundreds of small character roles in Hindi cinema throughout the 1970s and 1980s, perhaps most famously the loyal servant Ramlal in *Sholay* (1975), the mega-hit released the same year as *Deewaar* and in which Bachchan starred as well. In *Zanjeer* (1973), the first "angry young man" film, in which Bachchan made his name, Kapoor had played the policeman who finds the recently orphaned Vijay (here, too, Bachchan plays a Vijay, in a not uncommon repetition that suggests a metafictional gesture in the various films) as a child and kindly takes him into his home. But Kapoor in *Zanjeer*, sanctioned in his generosity by the state, is but a weak substitute for Vijay's real father, who had been killed by a corrupt gang leader; thus it is outside the law where the loss of the original father must be avenged. In this scenario, there is little room for Kapoor's good-hearted policeman. In *Deewaar* as well, Kapoor's quick fall from union leader to the victim of workers' violence suggests a chiastic relationship with Bachchan that unfolds both in the story and in the parallel text: Vijay gains his rebelliousness from his father's failure, and Bachchan's stardom requires the minor status of a range of lesser artistes. Whereas in *Deewaar* Kapoor plays Anand as a man of many words and little charisma, Bachchan's Vijay is the opposite, and it is that affective laconicism—seen through contrast against Kapoor's work—that sets the groundwork for Bachchan's success in this film.

Bachchan's performance can also be seen in relation to that of Shashi Kapoor, a well-loved actor at the time, known for his off-beat films and classic good looks. Kapoor plays Vijay's brother Ravi as charming and likeable but completely lacking in anger or rebelliousness. At times, he seems ineffectual and almost pathetic, recalling his father's failure. At other times, he provides much-needed relief from Bachchan's brooding Vijay. He is the only one who gets a fulfilled romance, a middle-class job, and a song-and-dance sequence to which every Bollywood hero is entitled—but that is here denied to Bachchan's Vijay. This despite the fact that Ravi's life, like Vijay's, is marked by the loss of his father and by a social context in which there are very few opportunities for educated men and women that do not involve special favors or corrupt connections. But Ravi reacts to these obstacles with a light-hearted affability that contrasts with Vijay's aloof bitterness. After graduation, the series of missed chances to find work make Ravi neither angry nor frustrated but bemusedly resigned, so that when one interviewer tells him not to feel bad about not getting a job he has just given to someone else Ravi responds, "No sir, how can I feel bad? It's my fault. My file contains degrees and certificates, but no letters of recommendation. Thank you sir." His affect here is so lacking in anger that in the very next scene, he moves believably into a love song, with Kapoor shifting seamlessly between the sense of injustice and that of romance. Ravi thus seems to embody the "affable young man" that Satish Poduval opposes to the angry young man in the 1970s popular cinematic imaginary: "a distinctly ordinary 'hero': clumsy but well-meaning, self-absorbed but likeable, vulnerable but determined, bungling but triumphant" (43). For the affable young man, frustration is channeled into light comedy, and patience is "deemed more acceptable than . . . disruptive public activism" (44). Indeed, the fact that Ravi does end up finding a job, as a police officer no less, suggests that affability can be put to the service of the nation. This is not an option available to Vijay. For Poduval, affability represents a "counterpoint" to the angry young man's anger; but here, *both* anger and affability are contained within the same text, and Bachchan is able to channel the competing energies of both his father and his brother into his own contrapuntal characterization of Vijay.

While it is sometimes assumed that Bachchan's stardom is founded in an epic "antiheroism" (Mishra 128), a foundation of numerous films, that represents the rebelliousness of the Mahabharata's Karna rather than the more typical heroism of his brother Arjuna, we can see how heroic counterpoints are also constructed within individual texts. For Bachchan in particular, the creation of the kind of brooding persona that had never been seen to this extent in Hindi film requires counterpoints within various films and even various scenes in *Deewaar*. Even in *Anand* (1971), before the "angry young man" persona had been created, we can see, underlying Bachchan's performance, "the same anger, the same unease with the definition of the heroic role" (133) that appears in the later films. In that film, too, Bachchan works to harness and redistribute the charismatic energy of Rajesh Khanna, at that time a much bigger star than he, and in doing so transforms his minor position in the film into a much more significant one. In *Deewaar*, the close-knit nuclear family with its allegorical resonances (Joshi 11) and the deeply relational structure that binds this unit inextricably to each another, even when perhaps it is not in their interest, only heightens this antinomical structure of characterization to suggest a potentially asphyxiating national unit.

Turning away

The first time we see Bachchan's Vijay he has his back turned away from the temple his mother and brother are visiting, and consequently away from the camera. There are numerous scenes throughout the film where Vijay's back forms a communicative boundary between himself and others in the scene or the audience. Thus we have a spatial representation of Vijay's sense of alienation from his family, from civil society, from god and religion, and even from the cinematic spectator, giving his star's body a certain materiality that refuses immediate interpretation. But at the same time, Bachchan allows us to access the affective stance of his character even in his turned back. In the temple scene, the zoom compels us to follow Ravi's gaze down the temple steps where Vijay sits at the bottom, his face turned mostly away. His unsmiling countenance and his hunched posture suggest defiance and refusal, even though we cannot fully see his face. Later, at home, he is sleeping facing the camera, but his face is shrouded in darkness; his back is turned away from the rest of the room, where Ravi stays up late to write a few more applications in his seemingly endless search for employment. This posture, turned away from Ravi, suggests a refusal of the bourgeois citizenship in which the latter's job search implies inclusion. In another scene, this time in the gangster Dawar's apartment, Vijay's back is turned away from both Dawar and the camera as he faces Bombay's iconic Marine Drive to ponder his turn to criminality. In all these scenes, Bachchan's back functions as a sort of *deewaar* (wall/boundary) that suggests that the character's emotional state might not be immediately accessible. The fact that it is Amitabh Bachchan's back suggests that the oversignified, recognizable body of the star might itself be at odds with the full interpretation of the character. Bachchan's own well-known brooding, inaccessible nature thus becomes an obstacle to Vijay. Alienation seems to be the dominant trope here. We see this also in refracted images, such as when Vijay finishes his first assignment for Dawar and sees the money he is owed laid out on a glass table; the camera shows Vijay's face from the bottom up, *through* the glass table scattered with wads of cash. Vijay cannot believe that all this money is his, but the face we see mediated through the glass table is one of sadness rather than joy. The table here becomes another *deewaar* that suggests layers of psychic angst that lie between the character and his performance.

The famous bridge scene where the brothers part ways for the last time is an interesting exception and marks a shift in the filmic economy of turning away. It begins with Ravi at the center of the frame, lighting a cigarette as he waits for Vijay to arrive. But his centrality is quickly displaced as Vijay's car pulls up. As the brothers occupy the same frame but bring to it opposing interests, their bodies are positioned in opposite directions. But uncharacteristically, it is Vijay who is turned towards the camera and Ravi who is facing away. This suggests that the chronotope of the bridge, a dark space outside of civil society, and also of course the site of their shared past (they had slept under the bridge with their mother when they first moved to the city), allows for a temporary reversal of the alienation trope, with Ravi being ill fit in the space and Vijay marked by his comfort in it. This chiastic arrangement characterizes the dialogue as well, as the two negotiate their relations to one another in spatial as well as social terms ("Who is it listening to me now? A brother or a police officer?" Vijay asks. "As long as a brother is speaking, a brother is listening. When a criminal will speak, a police officer will listen," is Ravi's pointed reply.) Vijay's new stylish appearance, his relaxed pose with his hands in his blazer pocket, and his relative position vis-à-vis the camera which exaggerates what is already a significant height difference between the two actors suggest to a first-time viewer that this might be the incipient moment of Vijay's moral victory. But in fact, this scene is precisely where this gestural economy reverses itself, signaling exactly the opposite: the beginning of Vijay's decline. As he is increasingly caught off-guard by Ravi's calm demeanor, he steps closer to the camera and further from Ravi. As Ravi rotates his body in small degrees towards him and the camera, the film suggests for the first time that the increased availability of Vijay's body marks not a resolution of his alienation but its perpetuation.

How angry is the angry young man?

In his chapter, "How Angry Is the Angry Young Man?" in *The Secret Politics of Our Desires*, Fareeduddin Kazmi debunks the idea of Hindi cinema's angry young man as representing subaltern protest, arguing that he is instead a much more conformist figure. Here, I am more literally interested in the question of how Bachchan plays Vijay as a particular kind of angry young man, encompassing a range of emotions of which anger is not always the most important one.

Most critics take the angry young man's anger for granted, assuming, as does Sudhanva Deshpande, that the 1970s Hindi cinema hero exhibited "a poor man's anger towards an unequal and exploitative society" (187). This generalized formulation deserves complication, however, as the various characters termed "angry young men" are not always poor and, as we will see, not always angry. In *Zanjeer*, in which Bachchan also plays a character named Vijay, it is the psychic trauma of having been orphaned by Teja, an underworld don, that gives him his explosive anger and leads him to enact justice outside the law. Bachchan plays this first Vijay as plagued by an anger that erupts sporadically, often in response to instances of injustice; but there are only momentary expressions of social awareness, and the anger is largely portrayed as irrational. Otherwise, *Zanjeer*'s Vijay has a calm demeanor which, as his wife Mala points out, rarely breaks into a smile, and thus the anger signals a deeper depression or malaise. Fittingly, then, it is assuaged neither by enacting social justice nor even by the vigilante killing of Teja but through the action of throwing away the white horse bracelet (the eponymous *zanjeer*) that Teja wears, and that haunted Vijay in his nightmares. The healing here is as much psychic as it is political.

But in *Deewaar*, Bachchan's sense of loss is simmering throughout and exhibits itself in an affect of aloofness and "cool" that only occasionally turns to anger, and that, too, only in moments of weakness. Bachchan's common pose of keeping his back to the camera is a gesture of alienation and distance more than irrational rage. His shoulders and his head are always still, even when his face is unreadable. As a dock worker, he is largely indifferent to what he sees around him. Only when he sees a new worker killed as a result of refusing to give the local gangster a portion of his paycheck does Vijay decide that something needs to be done. But again, his determination to get rid of the gangsters once and for all is born not of anger but of something more like true grit. When Rahim Chacha warns him to flee because the thugs are after him, Bachchan's Vijay calmly walks away, leading the audience to believe that he has heeded Rahim's warning. But in fact, he goes straight to the warehouse where the thugs are gathered, so that although they are looking for him, it appears as if he is the one lying in wait for them. This reversal of the typical gang/individual power structure is captured in what has become *Deewaar*'s iconic image, of Bachchan sitting with his back leaning against the warehouse wall, his dock worker's rope coiled up around his shoulders, smoking a cigarette with his feet up—a pose of supreme self-possession which sets the stage for the calm affective register that defines his character for most of the rest of the film.

The fight scene that ensues, which might be seen as Vijay's initiation into manhood—the moment when he has the chance to redeem his father's life but chooses to go in another direction instead—is also performed with a surprising coolness. Even in the most extreme moment of the fight, when Vijay's own rope is tightened around his neck as he tries to stave off at least half a dozen men, Bachchan performs Vijay not as angry or trapped like a caged beast, which is how the gangsters want to make him feel, but as someone who is desperate to summon the mental and physical energy to throw off his attackers. The affect is one of strain rather than rage. Once he wins the fight there is a scene that mirrors the strike scene early in the film, where as Vijay unlocks the door of the warehouse and walks out towards the water tap, he is greeted by a gathering of fellow workers cheering, "Vijay zindabad!" in a replay of the earlier refrain, "Anand Babu zindabad!" But rather than stepping into a potential role as a leader, Vijay quickly walks through the crowd and away from the chanting, collapsing under the tap and reconfirming his ethos as one of apartness rather than solidarity.

Even when, due to his success in the fight, he is invited into Dawar's living room and offered a job, he remains heavy-lidded and morose, remembering what his family suffered, and resigned to transforming that sense of injustice into a life of syndicate criminality. When he hears his brother got the police job, we see another example of Bachchan's acted impassivity; even though the focus of the scene is Ravi, excited to have finally landed a job after years of patient affability, we cannot turn away from Bachchan, who plays the turbulence of emotions that lie under the surface just as perfectly as he plays impassivity on his face.

Real anger erupts for the first time only when Ravi, now a policeman, has discovered that Vijay is part of the smugglers' syndicate and asks him to sign a confession and name his associates, a conversation in which Ravi names the eponymous *deewaar* for the first time as the "wall between us." It is in this scene that Vijay erupts with an articulation of his sense of injustice, that before had lain under the surface of his demeanor, appearing only in the hieroglyph of his shameful tattoo: "Mera baap chor hai." Now, however, he reveals his belief that his own criminality is inextricable from the myriad wrongs that his family has borne:

> I will sign this, but I won't do it alone. I won't be the first to sign it. First go get the signature of the man [the mine owner] who took my father's sign [selling out the union]. Go get the signature of the man who insulted my mother and fired her from her job. Go get the signature of the man who wrote this on my arm. After that—after that—I will sign whatever you want me to.

The speech crescendos until Bachchan is almost shouting. This seems like the moment when the angry young man first becomes the angry young man, but ironically this has the effect of *weakening* Vijay's character rather than motivating it: this eruption of anger—when Vijay loses his cool—is actually the moment when he starts losing his moral authority as a repository for alienation and simmering discontent. It is the moment when he reveals his own somewhat utilitarian morality, when he expressly justifies his own criminal activity, and, of course, when he loses his mother, who chooses to leave his house in protest at his actions. His anger thus precipitates his gradual decline. When his mother turns her back on him at the end of this scene, he resorts to begging and childlike desperation: "Ma, you can't leave me! I know you love a lot and you can't leave me! . . . No, Ma, you can't go! . . . Ma, I did this all for you! This house, this car, this money, it's all for you. And you're leaving me?" These desperate words suggest a muddying of moral authority that anticipates Vijay's untimely end.

Bachchan thus interprets anger as an emotion associated with weakness rather than strength. Vijay's rage next erupts when Jaichand, a fellow gangster, suggests assassinating Ravi as a way to stop the police's effective stranglehold on their smuggling operation, an idea which Vijay immediately dismisses as impractical and dangerous. But Jaichand, who knows that Ravi is Vijay's brother, eggs him on: "Is that the only reason you don't want Ravi to be killed? Isn't there another reason?" At first, Vijay remains characteristically impassive but is finally goaded to exploding, "Yes, because he's my brother! And if you say anything else about him, I'll kill you!" before storming out of the room. Here, as Sumita Chakravarty writes of Bachchan more generally, it is Bachchan's eyes in particular, seen here in a characteristic close-up, that register the transformation "from a 'normal' state to one of rage and vengefulness" (229).

The rage Vijay exhibits opens up a new emotional register, a tragic weakness born out of his ties with, maybe even his *love* for, his family, despite his permanent alienation from them. This is the "impossible" quality of the gangster film that Warshow aptly identifies (quoted in Banerjea 170), which here signifies at the level of performance as well. Bachchan might have insistently turned away from them/us but he cannot remain that way for too long without losing his sense of self. The anger brings together both diegetic levels to mark an ironic recognition of this dilemma. The explosion of anger is a break in Vijay's character as well as in Bachchan's performance, following which we have the film's climax: Vijay seeks out his brother to warn him about the threat to his life; when his mother gets sick he uncharacteristically visits the temple to pray for her; he agrees to marry Anita; and finally he meets his mother in the temple to die there, in a self-defeating return "home." This might also offer another explanation of the changed positions vis-à-vis the camera in the bridge scene, with Vijay facing the camera as part of a new version of himself that at some level seeks engagement rather than disaffection, and that the moment at which he names the *deewaar* reflects a subconscious desire to see it broken down, even though it is by then too late.

It is this *new* Vijay who is the angry Vijay, the one who loses his cool and his self-control, and slowly spirals into the inevitability of his own demise. Under the bridge he tells Ravi that for all his moral posturing, Ravi has nothing to show for himself except his worthless principles:

> Ugh—your principles and your ideals! Of what use are your principles? All your principles can't feed you for one day! These ideals for which you are willing to give up your life, what have they done for you? . . . Look at me. This is me and this is you. We grew up on this same footpath, but look where I have come, and look at you. Today I have buildings, properties, bank balances, houses, cars, what do you have?

This listing of his material possessions feels very different from the Vijay who looked out of the window in Dawar's apartment and saw his own penniless and helpless childhood, and who agreed, with tears in his eyes, to accept Dawar's offer to join the ranks of the underworld. It is not surprising, then, that, with a rare upper hand against his more charismatic brother, Ravi rightly identifies this listing of possessions as an indication of Vijay's moral decline, and responds with the cutting—and justifiably famous—line, "Mere paas Ma hai [I have Mother]." The rise of anger represents the loss of everything, most importantly the maternal tie.

Vijay's final explosion of anger takes place at the temple, where he makes an exception to his hatred of religion and goes to pray for his mother's health, in a desperate bid to reclaim the loss of her. Here his anger is evident right when he enters the sanctum and begins yelling at the Shiva statue. His anger is mixed in with a deep sense of failure, as he sarcastically shouts at the image of the god, "You must be so happy today, since today I have lost . . . What is [my mother's] crime? What sin has she committed? Is it that she is my mother? Is her crime that she gave birth to me? Is her crime that I love her? What crime is she being punished for?" The camera's abrupt movements in this scene, the low lighting, and the shifting angles underscore the connection between anger and Vijay's decline. He shifts almost manically between anger and contrition: "Give me my mother back!" and in this case, at least briefly, it works. His mother does not die, but he does, and the vengeful god suggests that he must give up his own life to save his mother's. But it also marks a limit to anger as a human emotion. Far from giving him power, it tires him out existentially. When he finally returns to the temple to reunite with his mother and simultaneously to die, having been fatally shot by his brother a few minutes before, he is no longer angry but exhausted: "I have arrived, Ma. I am very tired, Ma."

Bachchan's Vijay in *Deewaar* suggests that the "angry young man" formulation deserves additional nuance. While these films are said to represent subaltern discontent, Bachchan plays Vijay not as an uncontained vigilante or vengeful figure but by crafting a new aesthetic of aloofness and distance that marks the rebel as more inaccessible than hotheaded. This foreshadows the direction the vigilante takes following the 1970s, and the path of Bachchan's own trajectory. From the cool unreadability that he perfects in *Deewaar* and *Sholay* (1975) to his middle-aged rebelliousness in *Main Azaad Hoon* (1989) all the way to his grandfatherly vigilantism in *Viruddh* (2005), we see how central Bachchan has been not only to developing the affective masculinity of Hindi cinema but to defining an affective ethos for the political actor in India outside the bounds of the law.

Works cited

Banerjea, Koushik. "'Fight Club': Aesthetics, Hybridisation and the Construction of Rogue Masculinities in *Sholay* and *Deewaar*," in Raminder Kaur and Ajay J. Sinha, eds., *Bollyworld: Popular Indian Cinema Through a Transnational Lens*, New Delhi: Sage, 2005, 163–85.

Chakravarty, Sumita S. *National Identity in Indian Popular Cinema: 1947–1987*. Austin: University of Texas Press, 1993.

Deshpande, Sudhanva. "The Consumable Hero of Globalised India," in Raminder Kaur and Ajay J. Sinha, eds., *Bollyworld: Popular Indian Cinema Through a Transnational Lens*, New Delhi: Sage, 2005, 186–203.

Joshi, Priya. "Cinema as Family Romance," *South Asian Popular Culture* 10: 1 (2012), 7–21.

Kazmi, Fareeduddin. "How Angry is the Angry Young Man?: 'Rebellion' in Conventional Hindi Films," in Ashis Nandy, ed., *The Secret Politics of Our Desires: Innocence, Culpability and Indian Popular Cinema*, New Delhi: Oxford University Press, 1998, 137–60.

Mishra, Vijay. *Bollywood Cinema: Temples of Desire*. New York: Routledge, 2002.

Poduval, Satish. "The Affable Young Man: Civility, Desire and the Making of a Middle-Class Cinema in the 1970s," *South Asian Popular Culture* 10: 1 (2012), 37–50.

Chapter 17

Catherine Deneuve in *The Umbrellas of Cherbourg*

Alexia Kannas

Absence is a funny thing

Geneviève (Catherine Deneuve) exhales; in one fluid movement she wets her bottom lip with her tongue and lets her teeth pull at it gently while she coifs her hair and sits at the table. She looks up at Guy (Nino Castelnuovo) and smiles. As they plant soft kisses on one another's hands, the band begins to play a mambo and they get up again to dance. Geneviève bends gently to adjust her heel and sings that she should have changed her shoes, while a barely perceptible but playful frown colors her face. Deneuve's gestures in this moment exceed the innocence that has characterized Geneviève so far, but embody the charged mood of early love with delicious accuracy.

Her roles in Roman Polanski's *Repulsion* (1965) and Luis Buñuel's *Belle de jour* (1967) may have cemented the icy eroticism of Deneuve's star image, but it was this performance as teenager Geneviève Emery in

Jacques Demy's incandescently melancholy musical film, *The Umbrellas of Cherbourg* (*Les parapluies de Cherbourg*, 1964), that catapulted the then nineteen-year-old actress onto the international stage and mobilized her exquisite beauty as an icon of unattainable refinement. Demy's homage to the classical Hollywood musical celebrates the "bright new mood" of MGM's postwar output—films like *An American in Paris* (1951) and *Singin' in the Rain* (1952)—through the dazzling color of its hyper-stylized mise-en-scène, the unforgettable themes of composer Michel Legrand's jazz-inflected score, and, most distinctively, the fact that every line of dialogue is sung. But the film's glittering aesthetic and Deneuve's restrained elegance are famously contrasted with a story and characters who could not be more ordinary. Geneviève is a shop girl who works with her mother (Anne Vernon) selling umbrellas in the rainy French coastal town of Cherbourg. She has fallen in love with a mechanic named Guy, who works at the local garage. The two plan to marry, but Guy is called up for military service and must leave Cherbourg to spend the next two years in Algeria. On the eve of his departure, the young couple spend a single night together and Geneviève falls pregnant. As the months pass, his absence begins to take its toll, and the growing distance between them—which she swore she would not permit herself to feel—leads her to accept a marriage proposal from Roland Cassard (Marc Michel), a soft-spoken Parisian jeweler. In the film's final act, Geneviève and Guy meet a number of years later, but the once star-crossed lovers have little to say to one another.

If this extraordinary film set the course for Deneuve's illustrious career, it also marked the development of a rift between her covetable elegance and what Ginette Vincendeau calls her "naturalistically 'innocent' performance style" (202). This is a tension hinted at in Germaine Greer's characterization of her as "impassive" and foregrounded in the writing of critics like Manny Farber, who once described her performance in *Belle de jour* as the "mechanical-doll act" of a "porcelain dummy" (Germaine Greer, "Siren Song," *The Guardian*, 31 December 2006; Farber 274). But in *The Umbrellas of Cherbourg*, a film that pivots on a refusal of catharsis, Deneuve's understated performance style is—perhaps ironically, but not accidentally—instrumental to the film's affective poignancy. As the emotional register shifts from the honeyed love-forever delirium towards the anti-climactic acceptance of love's fading away, Deneuve's restrained performativity helps to induce a destabilizing effect, pushing us out of the film's story and pulling us further into its emotional landscape, all at once.

Sites of contradiction

Despite the humdrum circumstances of the film's characters, Demy's dedication to reproducing the spectacle and quality associated with the classical Hollywood musical meant that the film's production was an extremely challenging project for the young actress. The musical is conventionally defined by the way it oscillates between the contradictory modes of realism (the narrative) and fantasy (the musical numbers), but to Demy this classical form felt disruptive; in a 1972 interview he described *The Umbrellas of Cherbourg* as the fulfillment of his "dream . . . for a seamless work." So, as with the production of the great musicals of Minnelli, Demy's actors memorized the film's pre-recorded score with the aim of achieving perfect synchronicity between sound and image during shooting, but, unlike most classical Hollywood musicals, *The Umbrellas of Cherbourg* is performed entirely in recitative—that is, every word of dialogue is sung. Nobody "breaks into song" in Demy's film: they are always already singing. The film's sung dialogue pushes back against our expectation to hear its characters speak, defusing the contradiction we expect to encounter in the conventional musical's switch between spoken and sung dialogue. Richard Dyer points out that films which eliminate this sense of contradiction and collapse the conventional musical's dual modes indicate that "the world of the narrative is . . . (already) utopian"; instead of retreating into spectacle to escape the everyday, such films suggest that their story plays out entirely in the realm of fantasy (28).

But if Demy's blending of ordinariness and dazzling artifice suggests a utopian playground for the petite bourgeoisie, Amy Herzog reminds us that "the overwhelming thrust of the film . . . is not an ironic gloss on cinematic conventions" (120). Despite the fact that, in one sequence, Guy and Geneviève are so swept up in their romance that they literally float down a cobbled side street, in *The Umbrellas of Cherbourg* the contradiction is located elsewhere. Amidst the chromatic wallpaper, the matching suits, and the multi-colored umbrellas, there is the smooth, white face of Deneuve. She looks up into the camera: golden spun hair pulled back off the face with a colored bow, arched brows that frame the shiny pools of her eyes and the mouth that doesn't smile and doesn't frown. In the la la land of young love, Deneuve's face becomes a locus of ambiguity—the figure on which thwarted futures will eventually unravel and turn cold.

When Deneuve first arrived to begin work on the film, Demy had quietly expressed his distaste for the way the actress was wearing her hair: the bulk had been teased up into a fashionable beehive and a tapered fringe, which brushed her eyelashes, concealed her forehead. Deneuve sat in the courtyard of Demy's house that afternoon while Agnès Varda took a stiff brush and dismantled the bouffant, combing the fringe back off the face to reveal in full the actress's porcelain complexion and to draw further attention to her distinctive bone structure. Deneuve likened this treatment to being undressed: "a fringe is a kind of protection," she complained. "Having one's face suddenly stripped bare is difficult when you're being looked at" (1983 interview at National Film Theatre, London). But if the actress had felt exposed, her performance transformed this sensitivity into matchless manifestations of Geneviève's devotion and then, the waning of her desire.

In the scene with which we began, Geneviève and Guy are out on the town one night visiting a club after taking in a performance of *Carmen* at the theatre. As they dance, the camera waltzes around them. Holding Guy close, she expresses concern that her mother knows about their relationship. As they turn on the dance floor, their faces appear and disappear behind one another's heads and those of the other couples flitting past. As with the other actors, Deneuve's face never conveys the effort of producing the melodic dialogue, but that face, especially in the film's first act, also rarely acknowledges the position of the camera.

When we first meet Geneviève, she is looking out of the window of her mother's shop, waiting for her sweetheart. Her lemon yellow cardigan enters the playful window display of red, blue, and white umbrellas. As she spots Guy pulling up on his bicycle she smiles and gives a discreet, excited wave, before darting across the street and colliding with him in a gleeful embrace. From this moment, Deneuve expresses Geneviève's besotted state by withholding her gaze from us and directing it instead towards Guy. With her arms around his neck she looks up into his eyes and sings that she loves him, while Demy's Ophülsian long take winds us around the young lovers. Nothing can come between them: as they turn a corner, Geneviève turns away from us and leans into Guy's shoulder to inhale the smell of gasoline that perfumes his clothes. Instead of feeling their intimacy through its register on her face, we watch from outside the whirlwind of their romance and receive affective direction from the score.

When Guy receives his draft notice and tells Geneviève he must leave, Deneuve's performance turns even further inwards. In the tender close-up at the café where we first encounter the dramatic strings of Legrand's theme "I Will Wait for You," Castelnuovo expresses Guy's distress by alternating between holding his face close to Deneuve's and looking out into the uncertain future that now lies ahead of them. But Geneviève, who must remain in Cherbourg, cannot accept their impending separation. Collapsed into his chest, she sings with eyes closed that she cannot live without him; as she grasps at his collar her eyes search his shoulders as she implores him not to go. Only at the mention of the two years they will spend apart does Deneuve reveal her tear-stained face, which, now staring blankly into the abyss, reflects the suspension of desire she is about to endure. In breaking the established rhythm of her downcast gaze and averted glances, Deneuve's blank expression takes on a revelatory quality. Geneviève's eyes soon close once more as Guy wipes away her tears, but the impassive gaze haunts this moment like a prophetic ghost.

Lawrence Shaffer has suggested that although the face in cinema is "more epistemologically valuable than the other surfaces on the screen," it "remains an impenetrable surface" despite its potential to express (4). If Deneuve's restrained performativity confronts us with this impenetrability, the effect is amplified by Demy's near-overwhelming mise-en-scène, in which every surface competes for our attention. As Madame Emery sails through the back room of the shop, her lipstick red suit buzzes against the hallucinogenic red and purple floral wallpaper; later, Madeleine waits for Guy in a café, camouflaged by the perfect match between her orange dress and the café's bright orange wall. And while Geneviève contemplates the diamond ring she has received from Roland, her blue shift dress festooned with magenta flowers harmonizes with its look-alike wallpaper in the bedroom. As Herzog writes, "The surfaces multiply, overwhelm, and dwarf the actors, whose own costuming is often hyperstylized and utterly divorced from the reality of middle-class existence in Cherbourg" (130). As much as this aesthetic evokes the "charmed space" of the traditional musical, the juxtaposition of its blatant falsity and the unfolding story's dark themes undermines the expectation of utopian harmony that we inherit from the musical genre (Grant 2).

Deneuve's performance foregrounds this unsettling falsification most explicitly when her figure is staged to replicate the life-sized articulated commercial dolls we know as mannequins. As Guy's absence begins to wear on her, she increasingly inhabits the space of the shop window—principally in her mother's umbrella store, but also at the dressmaker's where she has a new dress fitted to accommodate her growing belly. In this shot, she models the dress for her mother on a raised platform in the shop window beside a dressmaker's mannequin, as the seamstress pins the hem. Later, Demy's camera follows Madame Emery as she inspects a group of mannequins assembled in a bridal store, before finding Geneviève standing amongst them in her bridal veil. As the score builds to a gentle crescendo, the camera moves in to frame Deneuve in close-up. In response, she looks up and gazes directly into the camera, through the gossamer veil that amplifies both her serene beauty and the inscrutability of her expression.

Making the strange familiar

Such self-consciousness is not the "conservative reflexivity" of the classical Hollywood musical, which Jane Feuer has suggested helps to achieve a sense of generic continuity through its citation and celebration of other musicals (102–4). While *The Umbrellas of Cherbourg* is clearly colored by its affection for *Singin' in the Rain,* the spirit of its cerebral intertextuality would seem to resonate more with the films of *Cahiers du cinéma* directors like François Truffaut and Jean-Luc Godard, who were Demy's contemporaries. Accordingly, Rodney Hill has attributed the film's moments of direct address to its "quasi-Brechtian program" that, he explains, encourages us to recognize the film's artifice, intermittently pushing us out of our engagement with its story and alienating us from that which should feel familiar. But gazing into Deneuve's eyes I feel my own begin to swell with tears; instead of the strangeness of her looking at me, I feel a surge of affinity swirling between us. Demy's self-consciousness does not produce the effect of distance, but, as Herzog explains, works "to destabilize the viewer's relation to the film through emotional resonance" (116).

We can observe this profound effect in the scene where Geneviève and Madame Emery have Roland Cassard at their home for dinner. It is the evening of Geneviève discovering she is pregnant, as well as the celebration of Epiphany. Madame Emery serves "Galette du roi," traditionally eaten at this time of year. Seated at the table, Roland looks at Geneviève; Madame Emery looks at Roland; Roland looks at Madame Emery; and Geneviève stares at her plate. With bowed head and lowered eyes she chews politely, but Deneuve's pinned back shoulders give Geneviève an air of cool indifference. When she leaves the table, Roland will ask Madame Emery for Geneviève's hand and, without realizing, force her to choose between the idealized romance of her relationship with Guy and the comfortable future he hopes to provide.

But if we must root for the triumph of romantic love, we must do so without guidance from Deneuve, whose performance does not allow an easy assessment of the characters or their situation. When her mother declares she hasn't found the *'fève,'* the treat that comes hidden in the cake, Geneviève—with a sudden smile—counters that it is in her portion. Deneuve's cool restraint focuses into an expression of delight as she sets the tiny plastic figure down on the plate. As her gaze lingers on the tiny "bean," Geneviève privately recognizes her joy in carrying Guy's child (a "little bean"). Although this discreet cue from the actress suggests the resilience of romantic love, when her mother insists she choose a King, Geneviève intones that she has "no choice" before looking up at Roland, whose point of view we have assumed. As Madame Emery places a gold foil crown on Geneviève's head, Roland's melodic motif gives way to a wistful reprise of the theme that heralds "I Will Wait for You," conflating Guy's absence with Roland's desire. Deneuve lifts her head once more. She looks directly at Marc Michel's Roland—at us—again, and her eyes shine while the corners of her mouth curl gently upward. It lasts only a moment, but her smile betrays an ambivalence that feels devastatingly true: we don't doubt her love for Guy, but neither can we pin Roland as a one-dimensional agent of her unhappiness. Geneviève neither condones nor exhibits any aversion to Roland's efforts to court her and Deneuve's restraint intensifies the emotional complexity of her predicament through its refusal to express certainty.

Although the quadrilateral staging is ostensibly dictated by the table at which the characters are seated, the 180-degree cuts to Deneuve's face feel particularly unfamiliar after the ceaseless movement that has otherwise characterized the behavior of Demy's camera. With the gold crown on her slightly bowed head and her downcast gaze restored, Deneuve's smile falls away. Even Roland seems to sense the incongruity of this moment: fixated—as we are—on Geneviève, he sings that she reminds him of a painting he saw in Antwerp depicting the Virgin with Child. At once, her restraint and solemn serenity take on the celestial quality of the painted holy figure. But while this intertextual reference functions as a moment of self-consciousness, it also brings us face-to-face with Geneviève's internal struggle in its simultaneous allusion to the unborn child she carries. This moment of emotional intensity works not in spite of Deneuve's restraint but because of it; it is so palpable that Madame Emery must emit a high-pitched cry and quickly tell us she has had too much to drink, to puncture its expanding force.

"A finite forever"

In her 1965 review of the film on its theatrical release, Elisabeth Sussex observes that *The Umbrellas of Cherbourg* contains "none of the exuberance characteristic of the best American musicals; unlike them," she writes, "Demy's film never, so to speak, explodes" (21). In this sense, Deneuve's performance manifests the rhythm of the film's narrative, which, as Herzog points out, "though chronological, is marked less by action and progression than by loss, decay, and the failure to overcome difficulties" (126). Both the inter-titles that tell us the month and year of sequences and the shots of Cherbourg amidst the changing seasons mark the passing of time, however they also underscore the duration of suspension that the characters endure.

As Geneviève and Guy's dream to be married and have a family moves further from sight, their desire, which had driven the film's action, begins to wane. As the months roll by and Geneviève receives little word from Guy, she feels the intensity of their romance begin to fade. By March, her reserved disposition has taken on an air of indifference as she wanders around the shop, with her growing belly always one step ahead. When her mother asks if she's still waiting for Guy, she can only dip her head in a half-nod of helpless resignation. Deneuve shifts the register of Geneviève's forlorn countenance by holding her head slightly higher now: with her face bared her gaze tends to linger, reflecting on the sense of loss which now permeates the film. As time passes, this loss relates less to Geneviève missing Guy and more to the lack of certainty in their union. "Absence is a funny thing," Geneviève sings to her mother, "I look at this photograph and I forget what he really looks like."

As the intensity of her desire is displaced, time begins to take on the swirling, repetitive tendencies of Legrand's score. Beneath the matching wallpapers and costumes, we begin to notice repetition and coincidence in the story's patterns of action. When Geneviève, now heavily pregnant, strolls with Roland along the wharf, she traces the same path she had walked with Guy the night they went dancing. But where she had skipped and twirled along the beams of a railway track, she now treads cautiously, weighing up her new suitor's offer. Because his character hails from Demy's directorial debut *Lola* (1961), Roland's presence superimposes an additional cyclical temporality over this moment, articulated through the repetition of his musical theme from the earlier film. But Geneviève doesn't know this. These cycles of remembering are our cross to bear—not the characters'—and in our drive to resolve the disorder of their world we are confronted with the film's ultimate contradiction: that the "forever" of Geneviève and Guy's love is finite.[1]

Demy knows that, as Feuer writes, "the classical musical ends at that moment of perfect equilibrium when the couple is frozen into the eternal embrace, the show frozen into a perpetually triumphant curtain call" (87). This is why it is snowing when, in *The Umbrellas of Cherbourg*'s final scene, Guy and Geneviève meet again. Several years have passed when her car pulls up at the little Cherbourg gas station that Guy owns with his wife, Madeleine. A moment earlier Madeleine had finished decorating the Christmas tree, when Guy had come up behind her and wrapped his arms around her waist. Expressing Madeleine's infinite joy, Ellen Farner smiled the kind of smile that Deneuve cannot: huge and true, all teeth and gums. This is an imperfect equilibrium.

As Guy comes over to attend to Geneviève's car, she coifs her glamorous updo in the rear-vision mirror, while their daughter Françoise beeps the horn. Guy walks around the car to meet her at the window and as his shadow suspends the illumination of her face, her cold distraction freezes into an expression of restrained recognition. They don't talk about what happened. Instead, anger, regret, shame, and the pain of their separation play out in the reticence of their performance. Deneuve clutches at the collar of her fur coat as they head into the office, wiping snowflakes from her face instead of tears. Geneviève finds herself standing in a shop window once more, unable to transcend this mode of cold display. In their brief exchange, her eyes search Guy's face and his shoulders, but there is no urgency in her gaze now. He asks her to leave and she walks back to her car as the score revisits the melancholy refrain of "I Will Wait for You." Deneuve bites her bottom lip as she puts the car into gear and drives away, just as Guy's wife arrives home with their son, François.

In her refusal to perform Geneviève's emotional turmoil as an explosion of heightened drama, Deneuve presents a kind of paradox: in order to work, this existential exploration of the waning of desire requires that we project our own emotional experience onto the film. In this exchange, we are not alienated from the narrative but, as Herzog argues, "implicated in the journey that [Demy] constructs" (118). One afternoon, while Guy is in Algeria, we confront with Geneviève the unanswerable question: "I would have died for him," she sings. "Why am I not dead?" If the bitter note of the film's aftertaste lingers longer than the sweet, it is because there has been no catharsis. And, after this emotional investment, we must confront the fact that, despite the film's glorious artifice, this lack of resolution feels unwaveringly true. Sometimes, love doesn't last.

Note

1. Jim Ridley describes this contradiction at greater length in his review "*The Umbrellas of Cherbourg*: A Finite Forever" on the Criterion website, at www.criterion.com/current/posts/3235-the-umbrellas-of-cherbourg-a-finite-forever.

Works cited

Farber, Manny. *Negative Space: Manny Farber on the Movies*. New York: Da Capo Press, 1988.
Feuer, Jane. *The Classical Hollywood Musical*. Bloomington: Indiana University Press, 1993.
Grant, Barry Keith. *The Hollywood Film Musical*. New York: Wiley-Blackwell, 2012.
Herzog, Amy. *Dreams of Difference, Songs of the Same: The Musical Moment in Film*. Minneapolis: University of Minnesota Press, 2010.
Hill, Rodney. "The New Wave Meets the Tradition of Quality: Jacques Demy's 'The Umbrellas of Cherbourg,'" *Cinema Journal* 48: 1 (2008), 27–50.
Shaffer, Lawrence. "Reflections on the Face in Film," *Film Quarterly*, 31: 2 (1978), 2–8.
Vincendeau, Ginette. *Stars and Stardom in French Cinema*. London & New York: Continuum, 2000.

Chapter 18

Jean-Pierre Léaud in *Stolen Kisses*

Aaron Taylor

What opportunities are afforded to a poor schmuck who nevertheless wants to be taken seriously as a lover? For those wishing to look beyond the idealized manifestations of romance "successfully" achieved, where might we find a seriocomic representation of clumsy male amorousness instead—one that acknowledges the quotidian difficulties of learning how to love? The achievement of Jean-Pierre Léaud as a star of the French New Wave is to articulate this very possibility, particularly within his collaborations with François Truffaut in the Antoine Doinel series. Over the course of five films—*The 400 Blows* (*Les Quatre cent coups*, 1959), *Antoine and Colette* (*Antoine et Colette*, 1962), *Stolen Kisses* (*Baisers volés*, 1968), *Bed and Board* (*Domicile conjugale*, 1970), and *Love on the Run* (*L'Amour en fuite*, 1979)—we bear witness to Antoine's evolving sentimental education (from the age of fourteen to thirty-four), but also to Léaud's developing talents at dramatizing inexpert romantic maturation. In particular, his work in *Stolen Kisses* (our first introduction to Antoine's "grownup" incarnation) is invaluable for its layered exhibition of budding adult love. In this film, Léaud offers a remarkable characterization of a romantic soul on the cusp of maturation, and in so doing provides an indelible portrait of a nebbish stricken with a laboriously theatrical love—a role model, as it were, for wallflowers everywhere, aching to bloom. These dimensions—awkwardness, work, performativity—will be considered as instrumental components of Léaud's third outing here, as Antoine.

Awkwardness

We cannot fully appreciate Léaud's accomplishments in *Stolen Kisses* without first briefly acknowledging the rare appeal of his performance: that it stands as an episode within a broader, serialized project dedicated to observing the maturation of a single character (and performer) from boyhood to adulthood. Beginning with *Antoine and Colette,* the series is principally focused on Antoine's amorous endeavors and romantic mis-adventures. *Stolen Kisses* is a more expansively comic study of Antoine at twenty-three, in which "Léaud does age as Antoine Doinel, but the child of *The 400 Blows* is still alive in his older . . . face" (Dalle Vacche 413). Here, his longings for love are finally rewarded—by the student violinist Christine Darbon (Claude Jade), and by the older wife of a humorless salesman, Fabienne Tabard (Delphine Seyrig). However, while Antoine is possessed of a florid imagination—aggrandizing both his yearnings and their objects—this shiftless young man is no Casanova. The film follows him through two interrelated endeavors: to find gainful employment (after being ejected from the army, he tries his hand at being a hotel night clerk, a private detective (who poses as a shoe-store stock boy), and a television repairman), and to choose between two equally enticing romantic partners.

By the film's end, it is evident that he is not altogether successful in either of these enterprises, nor, perhaps, will he ever be. On the one hand, he does come to terms with his anxious feelings for Christine and proposes marriage. He also acquits himself of his obsession with Fabienne via the generosity of her own proposal: a liberating, one-off affair. On the other hand, Antoine emerges as a petulant and feckless lover. Although the film treats his diffidence affectionately, we also apprehend Antoine as being eternally out of place, always on the move. Indeed, in *Bed and Board,* he strays from Christine soon after she gives birth to their son, and by *Love on the Run,* the couple have amicably divorced. Antoine receives many lessons in love, but he remains, as in his youth, a perpetually bad pupil. As Bart Testa asserts, "Whereas Antoine grows up to be slight, nervous, and awkward, the young Antoine is sturdy, self-contained, and deliberate. Antoine/Léaud is a 'little man' who grew up into an adult little boy" (100).

Generically speaking, Léaud is a boy among men. The history of the romance genre is largely a parade of heartthrobs: a veritable pageant of virility, exoticism, ruggedness, charm, resplendence. We might conjure such exemplary visions as Rudolph Valentino, Clark Gable, Cary Grant, Rock Hudson, Sidney Poitier, Amitabh Bachchan, Denzel Washington, Brad Pitt, Leung Chiu-wai, or Ryan Gosling. Edgar Morin writes, "The great lovers rule the screen, focusing love's magic upon themselves, investing their interpreters with divinizing virtues . . . The star is above all an actress or an actor who becomes the subject of the myth of love, to the point of instigating a venerable cult" (40). If the movies are a forum for the cultivation and perpetuation of the romantic imagination, the afore-mentioned romantic leading men serve as some of their more fantastical ambassadors.

But while "Hollywood film . . . can be seen as an institution that aids in the formation of . . . a *habitus* by modelling appropriate courtship behavior," what kinds of roles exist for the maladroit, the uncouth, the embarrassed and embarrassing, the timid, the unlovable (Wexman 5)? That is, the tendency in writings about romantic representations in the cinema, and the performers that embody images of adoring or adored men, is to treat upon their most ideal exemplars. Those for whom love is a struggle—Harold Lloyd, Charlie Chaplin, Eddie Bracken, Jack Lemmon, Jerry Lewis, Woody Allen, Dudley Moore, Adam Sandler, Seth Rogen, or Michael Cera—are typically addressed as clown figures within the hybridized genre of the romantic comedy. While love's foibles can certainly be a laughing matter, these frequent casualties of romance are typically relegated to more explicitly comic terrain instead of being regarded as idealized or mythic figures. Contrarily the romantic leading man personifies the venerated object. His acts of ritualized courtship, ambitions for coupling, or efforts at achieving the requisite sensitivity have a degree of solemnity and affect that are almost always denied the lovelorn clown.

At first glance, Antoine might seem a counterintuitive nominee to proffer as a template-setting paradigm for "serious" depictions of non-idealized romantic figures. After all, *Stolen Kisses* is widely noted for its comic dimensions, and certainly the film can be characterized by its liveliness, frothiness, and knockabout pratfalls. Yet its viewers should not willfully forget the agony of Antoine's loveless childhood in *The 400 Blows*, nor overlook the gravity of *Stolen Kisses*'s romantic intentions, despite its frequent frivolities. *Kisses* is exemplary for its iconic role as precursor to the seriously lighthearted or lightheartedly serious contemporary romance film (or, "dramedy" if you like). Léaud's influential work here as a struggling romantic anticipates such twenty-first-century iterations of this type as Jay Baruchel, Zach Braff, Xavier Dolan, Donald Glover, Jesse Eisenberg, Neil Patrick Harris, Tobey Maguire, Dev Patel, Daniel Radcliffe, and Jason Schwartzman.

Léaud's portrait of the twenty-three-year-old Antoine is indelible in its iconic emblematizing of ungainliness. To be awkward is to exist in a state of gracelessness. You are at home neither in your body nor in your environment. You find yourself unable to orient your physical being towards the world adequately and, ontologically, your sense of self is untethered from a stabilizing milieu; you are, as they say, out of place. Awkwardness manifests itself in numerous ways. On film, we observe it as malfunctioning physical coordination, the breakdown of judgment and timing, propulsive energy without direction, flinching contractions inward away from convivial connections, nervous fidgeting as the traitorous body refuses to adjust to its external conditions, or the jagged repudiation of relaxation. Moreover, the discomfited individual instills discomfiture in others. To observe another's inept gaucheries is to risk infection, a consequent collapsing of always-already precarious self-confidence. Defensive responses can be cruel (laughter, sadism) or compassionate (pity, nurturing), near-instinctive urges to re-place the displaced other or to mitigate the circumstances that cannot accommodate the other's aberrant corporeality and comportment. Léaud's floundering Antoine is an invaluable admittance that, for many, love can and does afford awkwardness. The emotion does not inherently instill confidence in those who experience it, or, should we say, are afflicted by it.

One of Léaud's most defining characteristics, then, is his elegant inelegance—the near-balletic fluidity underlying Antoine's rigidity. As an actor, he nearly always seems ill at ease, "like a startled being caught in the haunted house and never able to find the exit" (Thomson 605). He seems constitutionally averse to relaxation—a condition often deemed by acting coaches to be essential to an actor's concentration, pliability, receptivity, and conveyance of authority (Barr 35; Caine 53–5; Haase 9–17). Stasis for Léaud is an utterly alien condition. He is nearly always in motion:

bobbing, weaving, twirling, fiddling, his fingers raking through ever-flopping hair. His gestures sometime occur in spastic bursts, like wayward toddlers escaping from the confines of a play circle. Some of his directors have spoken of their struggles to contain his paroxysmal propulsion, of "how difficult it is to frame the actor, who has the tendency to veer to the edge of the frame or to wander beyond the blocked boundaries of a set-up" (Darke 39). Manny Farber offers the most exhaustive description of Léaud's awkwardness as,

> a passionate decision that peaks his frenzied exasperation, physical compulsiveness. His taunted, berserk, exhausted moods [impart] … the sense that everything around them is insipid, banal, and what they need, crave, is a release to some glamorous scene. With Léaud, the release never comes; he's a sort of Lilliputian given a streak of go-go energy, trying to keep from sinking in the middle-class sloth, a near paranoid who's dead if he ever sinks down. (228)

A remarkable example occurs in *Stolen Kisses* just after the opening scenes. Immediately following his discharge from the army, Antoine follows his former comrades' advice and literally sprints to a brothel. Anxious for another kind of discharge altogether he jabs a fistful of francs at the madam, rat-a-tats his fingers over his watch, yanks at his tie, grabs his change, thrusts back a tip, and lurches up the stairs behind the sex worker. On his way up, unable to contain his excitement, his hands flutter up and down in the air and behind her back—as if urging the girl up more quickly, undressing, and fondling her at the same time. Antoine desires everything all at once, wishes for every pleasurable moment to occur impossibly at the same time. His impatience for a deliverance unto "some glamorous scene" is thwarted by the "insipid, banal" squalor of the hotel, and the economic limitations of his exchange with the girl. Bursting with an idiot passion, he lurches from a jaunty whistle to a ravishing, thrusting kiss—its inept intimacy rebuffed by his unwilling partner. Looking for love in all the wrong places, clearly, but Antoine never was a quick study: sulking out of the room, he almost instantly turns heel and follows a second girl up the stairs to her room. On their way back up, Antoine looks her up and down, up and down, up and down—his appraisal becoming boyishly compulsive in its mechanic repetition.

This early scene primes us for the graceful gracelessness of Antoine's flirtatious tea with his adored Fabienne. He is in the employ of her husband, Georges (Michael Lonsdale), in two senses—one real (as the private detective he has hired) and one fictive (as a stock boy who actually spies on George's employees). Left alone with the radiant Fabienne, the subterfuge and subservience has Antoine on edge. He stirs, and stirs, and stirs his cup of coffee, sipping at it absentmindedly from his spoon, darting furtive looks at her as she puts on a record. When she asks if he likes music, he distractedly replies, "Yes, sir,"—ever the dutiful pupil but momentarily forgetting that this "he" is, in fact, a she. The faux pas is enough to cause him to violently spill the hated cup, and propel himself from the room (urged by sympathetically horrified non-diegetic music) and down the stairs—hair flopping, fingers raking. Happily, Antoine is eventually redeemed by both Fabienne and Christine, as these extraordinary women acquiesce and adjust to his awkwardness. Fabienne proposes one afternoon of mutual carnal delight, even while Antoine yanks the covers up to his nose and peeks out at her goggle-eyed. For her part Christine eventually accepts his tenderly silly marriage proposal: a bottle opener slipped over her finger in lieu of a ring.

His convulsive action, propulsive fervor, and automatous replications are signs of Léaud's meaningful awkwardness. His gift is to show, painfully, drolly, how love's fervor can make boys out of men. Or prevent males from ever showing themselves not to be boys. And while the temptation is to regard him as yet another romantic clown, unlucky in love, his work in *Stolen Kisses* primes us to acknowledge clowns as plausible lovers, however gawky. He clears a path, then, for many equally immature and amateur infatuates to come. For while it is the gentleman who fancies, it is the lad who adores. Antoine's boyish affection spills out everywhere and in all directions. Thus, this directionless naïf perhaps makes for a lousy lover, and noncommittal fiancé. Leave it to the romantic leading alpha male to be ardor's master. In the wake of Léaud, many can only ever remain recalcitrant students.

Work

Stolen Kisses is just as concerned with Antoine's efforts to find gainful employment as with his efforts to find love. Rather, Antoine learns how grownups love by simultaneously learning how grownups work. Just as romance does not come naturally to him, neither does professionalization, and he labors—largely in vain—at both enterprises. As above, Léaud's accomplishment lies in denaturalizing labor—making work look like work, so to speak: effortful, studied, and technical. In so doing, his performance helps expose the illusionistic and tacitly ideological connotations of classical cinema's representation of skilled work as naturally attainable and morally bracing.

We are accustomed to actors sliding into the roles of professionalized characters plausibly and smoothly. In many films, we are presented with the professional business of a character skilled in some craft or trade, and it is the actor's responsibility to depict working habits in a manner that appears automatic rather than practiced. Recall John Wayne on horseback, Steve McQueen behind the wheel, or Sylvester Stallone in the ring. In many such cases, the ease with which an actor displays professional talents is a byproduct of offscreen interests and activities. But the plausible representation of a working professional is also contingent upon a "natural fit" between an actor's physiognomy and our stereotypical preconceptions of what a member of a certain profession is supposed to look like. Thus, "looking the part" also means eschewing awkwardness—appearing to know your craft: how to handle the reins, make a hairpin turn, deliver an uppercut. The professionalized body appears acclimatized to its tasks, engaging gracefully with every affordance the work environment provides. Exertion—the crude admittance of toil or pain—is minimized, or at least kept in check by an intense (and intensely watchable) concentration. In cases where we are privy to extensive training regimes, or periods of tutelage, the undisciplined and inexperienced body is brought to heel and attains maturity. As these actors portray the transition from amateur to pro, their mastery appears inspiring because their singular focus dispels the specter of failure that haunts every undertaking. Work's drudgery is elided by montage. Lo and behold: it looks easy.

Of course, professionalized characters have the benefit of singlemindedness. But contrarily, as we have already noted, Antoine rattles about from one job to another in *Stolen Kisses*. Because we are accustomed to seeing actors portray characters at work in but one job, this film's depiction of Antoine's sequential and multiple failed careers is strikingly unusual for its time. Thus, we are prompted to note how Léaud lays bare the physical drudgery, mental burden, and onerous demands of professionalization. Many viewers relate to Antoine's lack of careerism and flightiness, and critics frequently remark upon his ordinary shiftlessness. "For all his charm he is a mediocrity," writes Don Allen, "inspiring in an audience not the wish to emulate him but a recognition of the ordinary man's limitations" (51). Even Truffaut expressed some ambivalence toward his co-creation: "I felt that the cycle as a whole was not successful in making him evolve . . . I never wanted to give him ambition, for example. I wonder if he's not too frozen in the end, like a cartoon character" ("Closing").

Little wonder that some, like Pauline Kael, find Antoine a disappointment; we are accustomed to success stories in film (Kael 175–81). By contrast, *Stolen Kisses* is a story of failure—or, more charitably, irresolution. In dramatizing Antoine's lack of resolve, Léaud shows us that many are ill-suited for the careers upon which they embark, and that practice does not always make perfect. Sometimes our bodies betray us. Try as we may, we never acquire the precision, finesse, dexterity, and coordination required in complex, technical trades. Antoine only ever plays at working; he is even hired to pilot toy boats in *Bed and Board*. Like a little boy at a costume trunk, *Stolen Kisses* shows him to be repeatedly ill-suited: to a soldier's uniform, to a private detective's cover garb, to a TV repairman's coveralls.

While we may find Antoine's antics at playing dress-up to be charming, his superiors rarely find his boyishness adorable. Earlier, upon dishonorably discharging him from the army, Chief Warrant Officer Picard (François Darbon) sardonically berates him for his abysmal service record and ridiculous motivation for enlisting (he had hoped to impress a girl). As Picard cites each instance that Antoine went AWOL, our naughty little soldier casts his eyes downward even as he visibly fights a compulsion to grin. Told he will neither be fit for civil service nor work with a "respectable company," Antoine mock-frowns (*Oh, well*), rolls his eyes and prods his tongue into his cheek (*Whoopee-doo*), indulges himself a grin (*Je m'en fou*), and drops his eyes again (*Sorry, sir, I couldn't help myself*). Léaud's delightful performance choices in these reaction shots both essay Antoine's playful spirit and telegraph a late 1960s blasé attitude towards establishment work.

Léaud's inspired ineptitude is also showcased in a scene in which Georges pretends to hire him as a stock boy for the rather posh shoe store. Lined up alongside four other contenders for the position, Antoine and his "rivals" are instructed to wrap equally sized white shoeboxes in tissue paper. The camera laterally tracks across their busy hands—Antoine's clumsy crinkling offset from his competitors' purposeful pleats—and tracks back across their intent faces, observing that Antoine's brows are almost as furrowed as his tissue paper. Georges observes the wretched package and declares it "fine." Antoine cannot stop himself from lifting his chin and grinning proudly, and Truffaut punctuates the moment with a brief freeze frame—a grace note accentuating Léaud's inspired comic touch. In addition to serving as a parody of nepotistic hiring practices, this misplaced pride is characteristic of Léaud's boyish gift for being simultaneously endearing and infuriating.

Antoine is equally useless as a night watchman at a hotel, but it is as a would-be private detective that his incompetency is at its most pronounced. While Antoine is chronically ineffectual, he nevertheless is often entranced by the prospect of a job well done. Léaud essays Antoine's gormless zeal during a sequence in which the fledgling gumshoe tries to surreptitiously tail a woman along a street. His director provides a skillful context for Léaud's comedy, as "Truffaut's long takes and depth-of-field composition . . . allow the viewer to place Antoine in a rich diegesis while Antoine himself acts as if he were the absolute centre of his world" (Testa 98). Dollying along in front of Antoine, the wide framing betrays his every effort at sneakiness: a wide open, unbusy street in broad daylight does not afford a private dick many opportunities for covert action. Antoine's movie-mad imagination propels him to imitate his noir-ish idols, but Léaud shows us that overheated fantasy is rarely conducive to the genuine goal orientation a job demands. He uselessly covers his face with a newspaper, zigzags across the boulevard, needlessly bolts toward an open door then jogs out again, slips behind trees, pretends to read, and darts for cover behind a police signal post. This last hiding place proves ironic; his freaked-out quarry alerts a cop, and they see no intrepid investigator, but only a persistent pervert. In turn, Antoine does the only thing he does well: he flees.

Performativity

Léaud's "uncanny ability to make a mechanical physicality appear full of grace and fluidity" reveals itself most visibly in his depictions of the awkwardness of love, and the laborious mechanics of professional work (Graham). These talents are also employed in his depiction of Antoine's penchant for self-dramatization. To that end, Léaud's work in *Stolen Kisses* is invaluable for its cogent illustration of the demonstrative tendencies of the love-struck—their predilection for treating themselves and others as actors in films of their own making. In this concluding section, then, let us suggest a further connection between Léaud's inspired depiction of artlessness in both love and work: its relation to performativity in cinema.

Performativity here simply refers to an actor's basic essential task of creating and enacting a fictive identity. From here, we can recall the familiar mandate of classical, illusionist drama, which is to minimize the ontological gap between the identity of actor and character (so that the actor appears to "be" the character), and to obscure evident signs of the actor's work (the technical craft the actor employs to instantiate a character). By contrast, other traditions (e.g., modernist and melodramatic) are said to foreground the distinction between player and possible person, and direct viewers' attention to an actor's purposeful effort. Léaud's skills as a performer are amenable, then, to directors interested in the exposition of performativity, as his turns for Olivier Assayas, Jean-Luc Godard, and Jacques Rivette demonstrate. Indeed, Léaud is frequently described as an emblem of the New Wave's reflexive inclinations (Darke 36; Hawker; Neupert 161). His propulsive instincts "represented cinema itself to Truffaut, and [he] was in that respect the perfect cinematic figure" (Pomerance 233). In *Stolen Kisses*, then, Léaud allows us to apprehend Antoine both as a histrionic personality and, more broadly, as a type of lover who stages his romantic affairs.

Rhys Graham describes Léaud's work as "performed performance": "a verbally and physically precise sense of movement and interaction." Such precision is evident in "gestures and movements [that] are excessively self-aware in postures of cool and defiance," but actually "betray the emotions and vulnerability beneath" Antoine's fluidly mechanized activity (n.p.). Unlike the spiky didacticism of his work for Godard, Léaud's recurring collaborations with Truffaut have less polemical motivations. Rather, his performativity in *Stolen Kisses* is in the service of Truffaut's preference for love (and cinema) over politics. Consequently, Léaud shows how romance can inculcate performativity in some jejune lovers. For Antoine, to be besotted is to try a turn as a romantic lead, whether one has the skill or not. The results are, unsurprisingly, awkward and labored—two of the very qualities conducive to a performance that exposes the creation and enactment of an identity.

Testa aptly describes the "charming awkwardness" of Antoine's physicality as "essentially a theatricalization of himself" (96). As Antoine tries out various professional roles, and oscillates between various women, Léaud's very deliberate and mannered performance choices are embodied metaphors for the character's own self-dramatization. Antoine views love as a pretext for role construction within his own private film, and his self-dramatizing inclinations are most evident in his hyperbolic descriptions of Fabienne. Delivering a field report over the phone, he describes her "luminous skin *lit up from within*," with accompanying declamatory gestures that would do any melodramatist proud. Contrarily, Christine proves resistant to his aggressive aggrandisements, rebuffing his guided-missile kisses and mocking his habit of writing her nineteen letters per week. Antoine mostly responds to this with apoplectic sulks. At the film's end, however, an abashed and newly-engaged Antoine recognizes the obsessive declamations of another weirdo, a man in a trenchcoat (Serge Rousseau) who has been stalking Christine, for what they are: the all-too-familiar performative utterances of an infatuate, an actor in love with the idea of being in love instead of living the part.

While it may have been enough to essay a portrait of the *artiste* as a young man, Léaud takes things a step further. He occasionally lays bare his own construction of Antoine as a role. Two scenes feature a pyjama-clad Antoine engaged in repetitious speech while preparing his toilet—exactly the sort of thing an actor might do when learning his lines. In the first, he is simply practicing his English whilst shaving. In the second, though, he gazes intently into the mirror, one hand raised in a gentle crescent, repeating "Fabienne Tabard" at varying speeds, volumes, and intensities. Occasionally, he drops his eyes, curls his fingers into a revolving fist and impels the mantra forward. He shifts to "Christine Darbon," and repeats the ritual, sometimes pointing a finger, sometimes cupping the air, sometimes pumping the fist—the circumvolving of the hand conducting the passion of his declamations. At times, his eyes are both frightened and frightening, those of a man horror-struck by his own self-possession. As he takes up his own name, the repetition builds to a fever pitch: the voice quavers then crescendos maniacally, the cords stand out in his neck, the pumping hand forces out continued reprises of "Antoine Doinel" until the name degenerates into meaningless syllables. The accumulated effect is of a man falling under the spell of his own cultivated performance. Shuddering slightly, he abruptly rubs his face, splashes water on it. The spell is broken.

As Léaud works to become Doinel, a bounded sense of where one begins and the other ends dissolves. At times, Léaud's gestures "have a strange life of their own, a characteristic pace and rhythm: sometimes a somnambulistic quality, sometimes incorporated into a frantic routine," and he gives the sense that "a character is speaking words that were not his, but that he has in a way made his [own], has absorbed, processed and projected them back out again" (Hawker). This is, of course, what an actor is, at heart, required to do. Thus, Léaud occasionally reveals just how mindless, repetitious, laborious, and sometimes mania-inducing "creating a role" can be. To be sure, acting is entrancing for those who uphold its magical dissolution of one self into an other. But acting, like love, can also be self-entrancing, and the process can be awkward, laborious and, in the end, delirious. If Jean-Pierre Léaud draws us in through his work in *Stolen Kisses*, he does so by offering a romance that spares us none of love's discomfiture, its struggles, or its madness.

Works cited

Allen, Don. *Finally Truffaut*. Rev. edn. London: Secker & Warburg, 1985.

Barr, Tony. *Acting for the Camera*. Rev. edn. New York: Harper, 1997.

Caine, Michael. *Acting in Film*. Rev. edn. New York: Applause Theatre Book Publishers, 1997.

Dalle Vacche, Angela. "Directing Children: The Double Meaning of Consciousness," in Dudley Andrew and Anne Gillain, eds., *A Companion to François Truffaut*, Malden, MA: Wiley Blackwell, 2013, 403–19.

Darke, Chris. "Jean-Pierre Léaud: Lord of the Left Bank," *Sight & Sound* 16: 10 (2006), 36–9.

Farber, Manny. "New York Film Festival – 1967," in *Negative Space*. Expanded edn. New York: Da Capo Press, 1998, 225–30.

Graham, Rhys. "Because of Tenderness: Thoughts on the Performance of Jean-Pierre Léaud," *Senses of Cinema* 8 (18 July 2000), online at sensesofcinema.com/2000/jean-pierre leaud/tenderness.

Haase, Cathy. *Acting for Film*. New York: Allworth Press, 2003.

Hawker, Philippa. "Jean-Pierre Léaud: Unbearable Lightness," *Senses of Cinema* 8 (18 July 2000), online at sensesofcinema.com/2000/jean-pierre-leaud/lightness.

Kael, Pauline. "Three," in *Reeling*, New York: Marion Boyars, 1976, 175–81.

Morin, Edgar. *The Stars*. Trans. Richard Howard. New York: Grove, 1960.

Neupert, Richard. *A History of the French New Wave*. Madison: University of Wisconsin Press, 2002.

Pomerance, Murray. "Antoine Doinel, Antoine Doinel, Antoine Doinel," in Claire Perkins and Constantine Verevis, eds., *Film Trilogies*, London: Palgrave Macmillan, 2012, 226–42.

Testa, Bart. "Un Certain Regard: Characterization in the First Years of the French New Wave," in Carole Zucker, ed., *Making Visible the Invisible*, Metuchen, NJ: Scarecrow Press, 1990, 92–142.

Thomson, David. *The New Biographical Dictionary of Film*. 6th edn. New York: Alfred A. Knopf, 2014.

Truffaut, François. "Interview: Closing the Doinel Cycle," *Cinéscope*, 1980.

Wexman, Virginia Wright. *Creating the Couple*. Princeton: Princeton University Press, 1993.

Chapter 19

Isabelle Huppert in *The Piano Teacher*

Alison Taylor

> This face is never made up; even when it's made up, it's not made up, so that it can work out from inside, so that something can "work its way out" from inside, so that a personality other than that of the actress can be worked out, can be worked out by itself, as if of its own accord. (Jelinek 23)

In her essay, "The Defenseless Face," Elfriede Jelinek describes Isabelle Huppert's style of performance as a splinter in the skin: something that is evacuated and externalized as by a process of friction, working its way out. Huppert's skill is not to portray a character so much as it is to disguise such a process of incarnation as unconscious and obligatory. Astutely observed by Jelinek, Huppert's capacity to bring interiority outward—often barely moving a muscle—is what makes her performance in Michael Haneke's *The Piano Teacher* (2001) one of the most iconic of her career.

Adapted from Jelinek's novel *Der Klavierspielerin*, *The Piano Teacher* is the first of Haneke and Huppert's collaborations—she subsequently appeared in *Time of the Wolf* (2003), *Amour* (2012), and *Happy End* (2017)—and of these the role that best showcases her talent for realizing characters poised between stony aloofness and bare expressivity. Huppert plays Erika Kohut, a conflicted soul both sexually repressed and desiring, her competing impulses revealed in the fraught public and private identities that she embodies. To her colleagues at the illustrious and sterile Vienna conservatory, she is talented and serious, pursuing perfection with a requisite coldness. In secret, however, Erika seeks out confrontation with, if not gratification from, baser pleasures; sniffing used tissues in sex shop viewing booths; self-mutilating her genitals in the bathroom; or stalking the drive-in to snatch a glimpse of teenage coitus. Huppert's is a performance built on contradictions, the origins of which are never fully explained in the film's plot. Erika seems to occupy a precarious identity between child and adult, prudish spinster and melodramatic heroine. Her only truly private moments must be stolen by lying to the oppressive, overbearing mother with whom she shares an apartment. Any equilibrium we might assume Erika has cultivated over years of dysfunction is unsettled with the arrival of Walter Klemmer (Benoît Magimel), a handsome and talented young student who pursues her romantically, piquing both her interest and her self-preserving disdain.

To appreciate Huppert's performance in *The Piano Teacher* is to attend to the precision with which she balances extreme control with controlled extremity, never quite relinquishing herself entirely. At times, Huppert's Erika is stiff and guarded, holding her head aloft as though in spite of her slight stature she might look down upon others. Alternately, she displays a pained vulnerability, doe-eyed and girlish, transforming her appearance to look younger than her years. Characteristic of Huppert, Erika's eyes bespeak a soul that is ruthlessly intelligent and hardened by experience at one moment, and innocently childlike at the next. One gets the sense that inside, however, is a tensely knotted psyche; like scar tissue that has formed over years, the spirit beneath yearns to stretch and split but is condemned always to retract to its habitual, burdensome, familiar condition. Her moods are equally variable; moments of harshness with students are often tempered with just enough warmth to stop them from being simply bitter reprisals, just as the brief glimpses of acquiescence quickly retreat back into her carefully crafted self-composure.

Acknowledging Huppert's capacity for both cold impassivity and impulsive flashes of emotion risks underestimating her talents. These are not merely two alternating registers, rather Huppert manages to retain a complexity, since not once is she wholly one or the other. In part, we can attribute this distinction to the nuances of both Huppert's performance and Haneke's rendering of it. Haneke's restrained camera affords us access to Huppert's sheer responsiveness. For Haneke's part, there is no stylistic intrusion or rescue; static shots of Huppert dominate the film, giving the performer nowhere to hide. Lingering takes reveal the slightest of movements like a study of micro-gestures. While the subtle twitch of an eye or tensing of a cheek muscle communicates a wealth of feeling, it is remarkable that Huppert's sensitivity is just as perceptible in the instances when her back is turned. The quietest of adjustments that would go unnoticed if not for the camera's fixed attention are paradoxically amplified, Huppert's presence remaining fierce regardless of her position within the frame. Even with several scenes played against piano pieces from some of the greatest classical composers, the music feels like something that must be lived up to rather than imbuing a performance with unearned gravitas. In the hands of a lesser actress, the film would surely fail, Erika's transgressions ringing absurd or unduly comical were they not handled so deftly. Huppert's gift is to rise to the challenge of being held under such sustained scrutiny.

We glimpse the competing impulses in Erika's character early, on the evening of her first meeting Walter. After hearing her play at his aunt and uncle's charity recital, Walter is immediately infatuated and eager to praise her talents. In response, Erika publicly humiliates him, curtly dismissing his compliments as "unfashionable enthusiasm" and his attempts at jest as immature and precocious. Moments later, however, we see a shift in her persona. With her students having drifted off into other conversations, and her watchful mother preoccupied, Erika is afforded a private moment with Walter, which she urgently seizes. Ignoring Walter's feeble attempt at casual conversation, she stares up at him intensely and abruptly changes the subject: "Have you read Adorno on Schumann's Fantasia in C Major? He talks of his twilight." Noting that this piece was composed in a state of lucidity before the artist succumbed to madness, she offers: "It's being aware of what it means to lose oneself before being completely abandoned." Walter responds with quiet reverence: "I'd say you are a good teacher. You talk about things as if they were yours. It's rare." Erika shrugs off his compliment, stating that Schubert and Schumann are merely her favorite composers, then in an uncomfortable moment of revelation self-consciously mentions her father's own madness and death in an asylum, a disclosure the veracity of which is later undermined.

Here we might see Erika's already shrewd awareness of what a romance with Walter could mean. Perhaps she assumes it is simply her lot to be spurned and abandoned should she open herself to a world that has already dealt her half measures (the talented pianist who does not perform professionally but teaches; the desiring woman whose emotional reserves are consumed entirely by her mother). Or perhaps beyond this, she realizes that half measures are all that should be available to one who cannot bear to make herself vulnerable to a world that has more to offer. And so, Erika's interactions with Walter reveal her contradictory impulses, her desire to be swayed by the young man's attentions offset by an understanding that this would likely result in suffering as per the conventions of tragic romance. Huppert's inflection makes transparent Erika's own performance of the alluring but unknowable heroine, as though she is trying on a mask while simultaneously deploring its failure. If Huppert's performance as Erika is built on opposing tensions, in this instance we see them manifest as those unreachable aspects of herself that she is desperate to conceal, at odds with the desire to bear all: to truly lose oneself (if only to be aware of what truly losing oneself means). We are left with the resultant impression that neither impulse can be fully satisfied; Erika courts melodramatic archetypes but lacks the capacity to comfortably inhabit them.

While Erika's narrative trajectory aligns with her reference to Adorno on Robert Schumann, we might consider Huppert's performance in relation to Adorno on Arnold Schoenberg, for both critiques operate around the problem "of mastering the contradiction between essence and appearance" (Adorno 153). Adorno describes Schoenberg's ability to reveal an inner coherence via musical structures that initially sound disjointed: a process by which "the inward dimension moves outward" (153). Indeed, Huppert's mastery of the contradictions within Erika is evident in the nuances of discomfort, as latent desire surfaces against Erika's will. While in her early conversation with Walter Erika toys with disclosure, albeit contrived, for much of the remaining film she is at pains to conceal her interiority, performing a blankness that is increasingly undermined by the obstinacy of her body.

Seeing Erika affectively moved against her will becomes a crucial motif in the film. Huppert manages to exude inner tension with such precision that it seems involuntary—a process perhaps best revealed during the scene of Walter's audition to be accepted as one of Erika's students. Along with nine or so colleagues, Erika awaits Walter's performance. Haneke's framing in this scene signals that there are multiple performances being observed: Walter's onstage, heard rather than seen; Erika's in the audience, as she endeavors to conceal her fascination both from Walter and from her colleagues; and of course Huppert's under the relentless gaze of the camera. The commencement of his playing triggers the scene's three central shots—all static long takes. With each, the camera is figured at the same angle, but has moved closer to its subject: not Walter, but Erika as she observes from across the room. The first is a wide shot: Erika looks away from Walter, listening to the young man's impressive rendition of Rachmaninoff with calculated disinterest. Then something in her shifts and she allows herself to watch him, adjusting her posture slightly. The next shot takes us ahead in time—Walter has shifted to the more delicate meditation of a Schubert Andantino. It is clear that he has her attention now, but that her responsiveness is in spite of herself. Erika's neck is held stretched out and upward, and while her focus is on Walter she would still rather look from the corner of her eyes than turn her head to a more natural position. Her strain to preserve a rigid posture is palpable, but over this shot and the next, we glimpse tiny traces of her composure begin to slip. The intricacies of Huppert's expression here are remarkable. In a seemingly absentminded gesture, her eyes drift toward the ceiling, her tongue wetting her lips before her thoughts return, a transition registered by a self-conscious swallow. She gives the air of one who knows she is being scrutinized but is unwilling to let her emotions be read. Yet, in the slight purse of her lips, and the uncertainty of what to do with her restless hands, the discreet agitations of her body betray her.

Walter's audition marks one of several instances in which the competing tensions within Erika are worked out physically, her private self made public as if of its own accord. The effort to conceal her interest in Walter, not least from Walter himself, is evident in the small shifts in Erika's body which play out like a battle between the cognitive and the corporeal. Observing Walter comfort a nervous female student before a rehearsal, however, proves too much for Erika, moving her beyond discomfort to a spontaneous act of cruelty. As Walter helps Anna prepare at the piano, Erika holds the pair captive in her unblinking gaze. With the slightest of modulations, Huppert conveys Erika's deep suffering: tears well in her eyes; her eyelids quiver and twitch; her brow furrows. Such delicate adjustments would not be perceptible to Walter across the room, but in close-up they are imposing. We feel the pressure mounting until something inside her spills over, and, just before a tear can shed, in another kind of involuntary movement, she all at once whips herself round and exits the auditorium. The compulsion to take action animates her gait as she hurriedly skips down the stairs to the cloakroom. Here she pauses at its entrance for a moment. Inhaling deeply, an inner angst percolates before her body grows impatient. She scratches one hand with the other, absentmindedly, conveying a body determined to do *something*. But this something is an idea not yet fully formed.

Over the next few minutes, in an almost silent long take, we witness a transformative moment in which Erika's thought becomes action. Huppert exploits the full space of the frame, her restless body pacing and pausing as though private ideas are being shaped, measured, and discarded. The body's disarray is all the more tangible set against the rigid stillness of the empty concrete room, every step echoing, every fidget audible. It's a bravura bit of performance, particularly remarkable in that a good portion of it is played with Huppert's back to the camera. If we have already marvelled at the sensitivity of her facial expressions, in this moment we are given to appreciate just how much her body conveys when the face is unavailable. As she comes to sit on a bench in the foreground, facing a sea of student coats, her gestures appear impulsive and unaffected: Huppert wipes her nose, agitatedly rubs at her earlobe, inhales sharply, and arcs her shoulders. As though she is uncomfortable in her own skin, every stir signals a mind unsettled by competing notions until one notion is finally made manifest and suddenly she is in motion again. Having spied an empty glass, she delicately wraps it in a stray scarf, crushing it under heel to deposit the shards into Anna's coat pocket. Be it because of jealousy at Anna as the recipient of Walter's attention, jealousy at the girl's musical talent, recognition of Anna as her likeness (with a similar affinity for Schubert and a similarly domineering mother), or some combination of these, Erika's response in this moment is to disfigure her student. Having set this plan in motion, Erika's face is stony in resolve, but then as she turns to leave the room the restlessness of the body returns: a slight shake of the arms, an instinctive stroke of the collar bone, and after adjusting her sleeves a girlish swing of the hips in achievement as she exits.

Such gestures demonstrate Huppert's mastery, intuitively recruiting the vocabulary of the agitated body and preoccupied mind: the latter's tension necessarily expelled through the former. Through the subtlety of her movements, Huppert trains us to attend to the minutiae of expression and their revelatory potential. So sensitized are we to nuance in Huppert's performance that when Erika's body does best her, the result is jarring for lack of restraint. In one instance, during a piano lesson she berates Walter for not attending to the subtleties of Schubert's score, especially his indications of volume: "You gladly ignore the dynamics . . . Schubert's dynamics range from scream to whisper, not loud to soft." Walter, who by this point is in love with Erika, or at least believes he is, is wounded by the admonition, the very sting of her words registering on his face. By contrast, Erika's face fights to maintain composure as her body threatens to erupt in an involuntary coughing fit. As though in retaliation against herself, she projects her struggle in a renewed wave of acerbity, the pace and tone of her words hastening and sharpening, her attack on Walter becoming personal: "Schubert was quite ugly, did you know? With your looks nothing can ever hurt you." When Walter interrupts her tirade, confessing that he cannot bear to look at her directly lest he be driven to kiss her neck, Erika is no longer able to suppress her wayward body; retreating to the corner of the room, she is gripped by a wave of coughing so violent that her body doubles over, clutching the arms of a chair to steady herself.

This coughing fit moves her figuratively and literally; it signals an inability to express herself verbally—words catch in the throat—but it also moves her across the room away from Walter and toward her satchel, from which she pulls an envelope: a letter in which she can express her desires in writing. Interpreting this as a romantic offering, Walter attempts to embrace her but Erika struggles away and begins coughing again. Here, Huppert's performance erupts, her body beside itself for an instant, before Erika regains command. Indeed, by the film's end we will have seen all manner of involuntary ruptures of her body: from uncontrollable coughing to compulsive urination and unexpected vomiting. For all her attempts to contain her interiority through the forceful repression of mobility, the violent discharges threaten to turn her self inside out.

In Huppert's hands, even these severe expulsions resist becoming simply a grotesque catalogue of a character's eccentricities. Instead, these agitations are in themselves instructive. That Erika should point out Walter's failure to recognize musical dynamics as more than just a matter of volume, instead vesting them with human qualities, tells us of her deep affinity for the nuances of expression even as she is at pains to express herself. "You cough because you're uptight," Walter asserts, and while this statement is not untrue it is yet another failure to understand depth. For Erika, hearing music is of a different register to being moved by it, just as being seduced is of a different register to being loved. To the untrained ear or eye, however, hearing and being moved, being seduced and being loved may carry the same signifiers. Walter's confinement to superficiality—his confidence, charm, and effortless talent—is crucially at odds with Erika's better judgment and will to self-preservation. There is a desire in Erika to be swayed by Walter's romance, but there is a competing impulse to resist being swayed too easily. Huppert's capacity for expressive nuance deepens our understanding of Erika's contrary desires.

Erika's letter, it turns out, is not the romantic proclamation that Walter had hoped for, but it is a detailed list of instructions for him to follow. He is to bind, gag, and beat her to fulfil her sadomasochistic fantasies. In a harrowing scene, she insists he read the letter and we watch her wait as he voices her transgressive requests aloud with a mixture of bewilderment and contempt: "Next, take off the blindfold, please, and sit down on my face and punch me in the stomach to force me to thrust my tongue in your behind . . . Ask me why I don't cry out to mother or why I don't fight back. Above all, say things like that, so that I realize just how powerless I am." Again, the emphasis is laid on Huppert's responsivity, with the stillness of Haneke's frames in sync with her own attempts to maintain composure. In one revealing moment, a close-up from Walter's perspective has Huppert look directly down the lens. It is another instance of Erika's performative blankness, but Huppert's features betray a vulnerability that was not evident during Walter's audition earlier, where we witnessed the rigid posture of a stern headmistress straining to contain her feelings. Now Huppert sits upright, like an obedient schoolgirl, her wide-eyed expression open and alert, her forehead muscles held taught, suspending the eyebrows in anticipation.

Erika has shown her hand. These are the conditions under which she will agree to be loved by Walter. Walter, in turn, finds her active desire an affront. She is no naïve and skittish prize to be conquered but someone whose carnal desire eclipses his own. He spurns her in disgust, an event that forms the catalyst for two mirroring scenes of metaperformance with tragic consequences. In the first, Erika undertakes a desperate project to win back his affections, attempting to embody the role Walter desires of her: the swooning romantic heroine to his chivalrous champion in the tradition of courtly love. Her eyes tinged with a desperation on the precipice of madness, she finds him at an ice rink after hockey practice, declares her love, and begs forgiveness. Huppert's features are paradoxically pulled in opposing directions, somehow tense and fallen at the same time, as though desperate longing and pained resignation were competing for authority. To prove her devotion, she quite literally throws herself at him, kissing him wildly in a clumsy display of unbridled passion. As Walter returns her embrace, kissing her neck, Erika's mouth falls ajar awkwardly, her heavy breathing descending into animal whimpering. Just as it appears Walter might believe this unconvincing apparition of the devoted and passive heroine he longs for, a feverish attempt at fellatio— Walter pushing himself atop Erika, who lays prone—causes her to gag and vomit unexpectedly and Walter attacks with a renewed wave of verbal cruelty.

This scene is echoed the following night, when Walter, with Erika's fantasies playing on his mind and driving him to desperation, attempts to embody the role she has crafted for him: the cruel dominant to her obliging submissive. Bursting into her apartment, he recounts lines from her letter as though rehearsing a script, before beating and raping her. It is here that we see Erika's performative blankness peak. In every other instance, her attempts to conceal interiority manifest as a gradual push from within, that reveals her discomfort and desire in barely perceptible shifts. Here however, we see a reversal of sorts. As Walter forces himself on top of her, Huppert's physical presence gradually diminishes as her emotions retreat back into hiding—her quivering lip stills, the protruding veins in her neck recede, the hand unnaturally curled like a dead spider on her chest falls to her side. If only for this moment Erika goes limp, as though the connection between mind and body has been severed. Walter heaves above her, periodically pausing in futile attempts to revive her responsivity.

For all of her contradicting impulses to reveal and conceal herself, to permit and resist being moved by a desire that is unworthy of her, Erika's reluctant attempt at openness is monstrously distorted. Walter has again misunderstood the dynamics of her direction, failing to recognize that there is a vast chasm between the consensual submission to a lover's dominance and being the unwilling subject of a brutal assault. It is of course, a deeply unsettling scene, not least because we have been made so sensitive to the capacity for Erika's inmost self to be worked out through Huppert's expressive fluctuations. In the preceding one and three-quarter hours, Huppert has delivered a master class in expressive range. To suddenly find ourselves searching these vacant eyes and this immobile face, unearthing absolutely nothing, is harrowing by contrast.

From this quietest moment of Huppert's performance comes its most thunderous. With the film drawing to a close, the climactic concert her students have been training for is about to begin. Erika's mother has already gone into the hall accompanied by Mrs. Schober and her daughter Anna—the girl Erika has surreptitiously injured with the broken glass and is now replacing in the performance. There's a flurry of movement, voices and footsteps echo in the grand foyer as the last of the audience members hurry to deposit their coats. Expertly choreographed, this sequence unfolds not unlike a dance, the expansive space serving as the setting for its players to move towards and away from each other before the surge of noise and activity will eventually recede into a private setting for Erika's final gesture.

Erika's wide eyes desperately search for Walter's arrival. One eye hardly conceals a bruise delivered the night before, the other is framed by an eyebrow held arched in defiance of the symmetry of her face. There's a suddenness to her movements now. While her eyes retain the intense stare and her neck is still held taught, she is just as liable to pivot suddenly so as to not neglect the other side of a room too grand to possibly take in at once. Curiously, where it was the muscles of her porcelain face that betrayed her interiority earlier in the film, they now seem fixed; all of Huppert's expressiveness emanates from the eyes. Her face anxiously teeters forward and back in close-up as she adjusts her stance to better glimpse the door. And then spying Walter's aunt enter, she begins a steady pace across the room. Aunt and uncle hurriedly deliver polite well wishes as they rush up the stairs. Walter, accompanied by a young lady we haven't seen before, passes Erika without stopping, expressing his eagerness to hear her play and regarding her with his familiar cocky smile as though the previous night's brutality had never happened. Clutching her purse Erika turns away from us, her gaze following Walter up the stairs as he hurries to his seat.

A cut takes us to a close-up of Erika, alone now in the foyer. The pained micro-movements of her facial muscles return. Her brows furrow slightly, tears well in her eyes, her tightly pressed lips amount to quiet devastation. We trace the mute anguish upon her features as the bustle of hurried footsteps and trailing conversations subsides to silence. Without averting her gaze she opens her purse, feeling for the knife inside, and in a fluid motion, drives it firmly into her shoulder. Simultaneously her formerly composed features distort into a monstrous grimace, the upper lip pulled upward bearing her top teeth, the lower pulling her mouth ajar. The eyes crumple into a pained squint, and with a momentary halt in her breathing, the face flushes with blood.

It is an astounding moment for its sheer contrast in emotional expressivity. Compared to the level of restraint she has exercised thus far, here Huppert's face scrunches like paper in an extravagant display of anguish. Driving the blade into her shoulder and removing it just as quickly, Erika affects a histrionic gesture of defiance, a performative affront to the world, significantly witnessed by no one but us. That Erika should stab her shoulder in an empty foyer only moments ago bustling with people, points to the failure of this gesture and its impact upon the world. This deliberately private performance has all the makings of a liberating act—the spurned melodramatic heroine's final paroxysm, channelling a lifetime of misery into a cumulative and irreversible self-obliterating statement. And yet it falls short, for even now Erika does not have the capability to surrender herself completely. Huppert gives the impression this gesture is rehearsed: a feeble and self-conscious imitation of torment, a failed attempt to be aware, as Erika enunciated early in the film, "of what it means to lose oneself before being completely abandoned."

The wound is not serious; this is not the passionate surrender of Emma Bovary, but an abrupt and fleeting tear in the fabric of Erika's day. Placing the blade back inside her purse, her blank expression returned, Erika turns to assure the act hasn't been witnessed, and self-consciously covers the bloodstain forming on her blouse with a hand. A cut takes us outside to gaze upon the foyer's vestibule. Erika briskly exits, walking out of view. The doors remain but our protagonist is gone. Erika, Huppert's splinter, has been worked out.

Works cited

Adorno, Theodor. *Aesthetic Theory*. Trans. Robert Hullot-Kentor. London: Continuum, 2002.

Jelinek, Elfriede. "The Defenseless Face," in Elfriede Jelinek and Serge Toubiana, *Isabelle Huppert: Woman of Many Faces*, trans. Simon Jones and Steven Lindberg, New York: Harry N. Abrams, 2005, 21–8.

Chapter 20

Emma Thompson in *The Remains of the Day*

Timotheus Vermeulen

In this short chapter, I look at the performances of Emma Thompson as Miss Kenton in James Ivory's 2003 film *The Remains of the Day*. I use the plural "performances" here as opposed to the singular "performance" to address Thompson's acting achievements, because in Ivory's film, in fidelity to the Kashuo Ishiguro novel from which it was adapted, there appears in many a sense to be more than one Miss Kenton. Of course, most performances aspire to be more than a type; indeed, there are plenty of performances that are complex and layered and ambiguous, in which with their bodies actors portray conflicting states of mind, playing out whims and musings, dreams and demons. But in the case of Thompson's portrayal of Miss Kenton, multiplicity is inscribed in the narrative, if you will. For one, *The Remains of the Day* shifts, often imperceptibly, between various experiential registers: that of Miss Kenton herself, through the letters she is heard narrating; that of the film's protagonist, Mr. Stevens (Anthony Hopkins), whose memories we see; and a third—extradiegetic, omniscient—point of view. To further the sense of heterogeneity, the film also visits Miss Kenton at different stages in her life, covering a period of over twenty years. What this means is that there might well be four or five or eight or ten Misses Kenton: the Miss Kenton who reads out the letters today, as it were, musing backward in time; the one she talks about in those letters, a maturing, emancipated woman; the one Mr. Stevens appears to remember; a Miss Kenton at a job interview in the late 1930s; one running the country house (in which we continue to see her) a few years on; the grandmother in 1958, and so on. To study—and do justice to—Thompson's performance therefore, I wouldn't think it feasible to concentrate on one performative moment in isolation. What should be scrutinized, rather, so as to appreciate the performance fully, are the relationships of some moments to other moments, some contexts to other contexts. What I look at here, in moderation, is the interaction between a few of these moments, trying to tease out some of their respective nuances.

Three faces of Emma

As I was researching the scholarly literature in preparation for this chapter, I was somewhat surprised by how little critical attention Thompson's performance of Miss Kenton has thus far received (or indeed, it must be said, the film itself, especially if you compare it to the extensive and prolonged discussion the novel seems to have provoked). Many popular reviews seem to overlook the actress's achievements, too, focusing on the skills of her male counterpart instead. The reason that this took me slightly by surprise is that Thompson spends nearly as much time onscreen as Hopkins. It could be argued that it is the male point of view that dominates much of the narrative—though certainly not, as is the case in the novel, all of it. In any case, by most accounts. *The Remains of the Day* tells the story of Mr. Stevens, a devoted butler, who abandons his private dreams—above all his romantic feelings for the housekeeper, Miss Kenton—so as to fulfill those of his employer, Lord Darlington (James Fox), only to realize that it was all for nought. In this personification, this incarnation, of an age of hierarchy and Empire, Stevens literally isn't able to embrace, to open up his body to, to stretch his limbs around, the collapse of all distinctions—class, generation, morality (Lord Darlington sympathizes with Nazism)—at the onset of modernity. This is the case even, or especially if, his mind has already understood modernity's implications, so that we find him stiffening his muscles, as it were, as his bones crumble, imposing a rigid order on a busy house that no longer follows his rules. Eventually he stays behind weak and, in many a sense, alone.

The film follows in the novel's footsteps in portraying its characters through multiple points of view and at various stages of their lives. It navigates these different spatio-temporal registers differently, however. In the novel everything is resounded through Mr. Stevens's voice, like a faint echo, or rather still, a late-arriving message in one of those "telephone" games where people keep altering the message as they hear it. The letters by Miss Kenton, for instance, appear in the novel only insofar as they are read by Mr. Stevens. In the film, however, it is far less obvious who is speaking at some moments, whose gaze we are following, in whose story we share. Though it might be a remark in a letter by Stevens, or a fleeting glance, that introduces a scene, there isn't nearly enough use of point of view or voiceover or mise-en-scène to suggest all of the ensuing images are shared by him, nor does the content necessarily and always seem his to share. Indeed, the film's opening statement simultaneously appears to see with Stevens's eyes—remembering Miss Kenton walk the halls—and speak with Miss Kenton's voice—reminiscing about the household. That is to say: the film uses POV both more democratically and more diffusely than the novel, shifting, or rather still, sliding, almost imperceptibly from one character's position to the gaze of another. I would suggest, in this respect, that the many Miss Kentons in play are not separate: they overlap, slip in and out of each other, very like the bodies, the correspondences of hair and skin and muscle, to be seen in a Francis Bacon portrait, or indeed, like Nunnally Johnson's three faces of Eve.

It is telling that Thompson's first go at Miss Kenton is bodiless, that is, literally without body, a floating voiceover unaccompanied by images of the person in question, that draws out the contours of a character without detailing them, without coloring them in, without ossifying them—just, indeed, as Bacon often paints what Gilles Deleuze calls the "ring" behind and around his subjects: an oval, evenly colored space that at once delimits these subjects' movements and enables them (it is from this "patch" that they are scratched out, as if it were); or, to make the metaphor musical (acoustic rather than optical, finally), a staff yet to be notated with pitches up and down the lines and in between. To my admittedly foreign ears, Miss Kenton's voice here, reading out a letter she has written to Mr. Stevens, is a measured but unpracticed voice, trained classically but straining slightly into dialect, suggesting the speaker is someone who once moved in certain circles but now moves in others. Similarly, Thompson intones with a timbre that alternates between formal (a reading voice), professionally glossing over the words, and more affective, one that offers occasional changes of pitch and tempo to imply an intensity and depth of emotions. "Dear Mr. Stevens" is gradually exchanged for "Oh, Mr. Stevens" and "our Mr. Stevens," and a casual reading of a newspaper story about the history of Lord Darlington and his residence turns into a series of elongated vowels, disbelieving sighs and even scuffs, finally leading to the admission it made Miss Kenton's "blood boil." Indeed, if the voice suggests a subtly torn personality with respect to social mores and emotional restraint, the words themselves imply a tension between a professional self and someone longing for, or in any case short-circuiting into, intimacy.

My point in explicating, indeed emphasizing, that Miss Kenton is introduced through sound and not image, through her words and not her looks, is above all that this creates a pulsating resonance, that is to say, a sense of a person, a corporeality, the space of a body and not the physical appearance of the body, itself; in other words, she inhabits a kind of acoustical sphere, yet to be sounded, yet to be punctured and punctuated with her humanity, a staff still to be annotated, nor with one melody exclusively, but with the possibility of any melody at all. The film suggests that it's these punctuations, these annotations, that will make up the body, perhaps less as a figuration than as a melody. Miss Kenton's body isn't a given. What the film does is to instruct the audience, literally and metaphorically, to listen to her before it sees, to listen to her movements, her expressions, and her indicative gestures, before forming an image. Indeed, intended or not, one of the film's most powerful effects is to portray Miss Kenton from the beginning as a woman who is more than an object to be looked at for Mr. Stevens, or to be overcome.

Thompson plays within and towards these contours, this oval, on and around the musical staff I am hypothesizing, as the film proceeds, here centering on social uptightness, there using another brush to foreground intimacy; sometimes she feels blue, at other instances she rejoices in higher notes. In most cases, Thompson presents a singularly nuanced picture, mixing the sonic "palette," thickening and complicating the melody. There are a few scenes, however, where she makes a clear mark, where one color or indeed one pitch dominates all others. Towards the end of the film, Miss Kenton meets with Mr. Stevens in a dreary tearoom several years after having left her job as a housekeeper at Darlington's. Her accent has unmistakably slackened—the clipped perfectionism is no longer a requirement—so as to suggest a loosening of the class relations that defined her former life, a loosening of the stiffness and rigidity by which Mr. Stevens, by contrast, still abides, or rather, one might say, by which he is tightly bound. It is not only her voice that denotes relaxation. Her whole appearance bespeaks a liberation of the class signs it communicated in Darlington Hall: her hair is coiffed back, fixed with hairspray; she wears large, shiny earrings and a broad, even somewhat gaudy, necklace; her lips are painted red as are her nails; and she smokes. Most noticeable, however, is Thompson's use of her body, especially in relation to the man seated opposite her. She seems at ease now, portends to be at ease, her posture at rest (that is, not on show), her movements assured, smooth, as she subtly leans in from her chair, head nodding sympathetically—all too sympathetically at times, too emphatically sympathetic—gazing straight into her companion's eyes, warmly, understandingly, but also daringly, gazing this way to demonstrate that she can, her arms open, her elbows on the table, at once leisurely and demonstratively, in defiance of etiquette, as she holds her cigarette nonchalantly, fingers fiddling absentmindedly yet assertively, pointedly, indeed occasionally pointing towards her companion to stress an argument. Thompson's performance here reminds me in some sense of a teenager pretending to be a grownup: she overemphasizes her familiarity and comfort with the rules of (lower) middle-class life, whilst expressly dispensing with the signs of the rigid class system, its cutting distinctions between working class and upper class, that lie far behind her. The audience, Mr. Stevens, sits straight and mostly still in his chair. Tellingly, his elbows do not seek support on the table. The few moments he does move, to look around or away or to order tea or ask for the bill, he doesn't so much turn as he jolts, jerks, like a Claymation character in a stop-motion film. He appears to be both anxious and appalled by the surroundings, too much a servant to dare take his part in this tearoom yet also too much a "gentleman," as he once referred to himself, to deem it worthy to participate at all. Unlike Miss Kenton, for whom this is obviously a private meeting, Stevens also cannot distinguish private life from professional life, retaining his professional restraint throughout. Miss Kenton's forehead wrinkles whereas his remains even, at all times. Her eyes are steady upon his, empathetically so, while he shifts his gaze distractedly from left to right, keeping his emotions at bay. She grimaces when she worries and smiles when she is pleased. But Mr. Stevens's expression rarely changes from its cool placidity.

Another extreme is introduced ten minutes into the film. As Mr. Stevens, in one of his letters, calls to mind the first time he met Miss

Kenton, the camera turns its gaze to their job interview. Fading from an extreme long shot of Darlington Hall, it briefly depicts Thompson's face in close-up (so that the house and her face overlap) before gradually zooming out to a medium close-up of her sitting in Mr. Stevens's office. If the fade is interesting, so is the close-up zooming out, suggesting that she occupies the house but doesn't own it, and making manifest that she is in someone else's office, still wearing her hat and coat, like a guest, framed in on all sides by furniture, appliances, and decorations which are not hers. If Thompson's movements at the end of the film are frictionless and fluid, seeming to flow naturally from the character's thoughts and feelings, here they are straight and stiff. Her arms press narrowly against her sides, her hands are clasped tightly in her lap, her head nods curtly, her eyes gaze downwards, toward her feet, as though, it seems, she is afraid to come across as too assertive. She clenches her jaw as her mouth trembles. I do not mean to suggest that Miss Kenton is insecure here. She is nervous, but she doesn't at any moment lack confidence. My point is that, in line with the editing and the mise-en-scène, Thompson portrays a person who is looking to restrain herself, seeks to accommodate her body, her being, to her surroundings. And that this accommodation takes some effort. She uses her arms as a straitjacket; her mouth trembles, twitches, not because she is afraid of him, but because of herself she is forcing her lips to stay shut. Indeed, when Mr. Stevens tells her that there are no "gentleman callers" allowed, Kenton nods her head vigorously in agreement, almost as a release, closing her eyes to suggest commiseration, whilst turning the corners of her mouth in disapproval. Who could even think of having a gentleman caller in such a house! When he shares his frustration about, and disdain for, housekeepers looking for romance, she even interrupts—a recurrent trope—to verbally offer support. After all, a "house is in sixes and sevens once the staff start marrying each other." In interrupting Stevens, however, Miss Kenton makes manifest that if she may be dependent upon his approval for the job, nevertheless she otherwise isn't reliant on his validation, nor should he feel reason for a moment to believe that she feels she is. Indeed, it is at this moment that, briefly, she does stare him in the eyes, only to look away once she's had her say. When I say that through her voice Thompson sketches out the contours that circumscribe her physical performance like a Bacon painting, I mean that, without losing sense of her character's corporeality she allows for, is able to accommodate, these opposed bodies of hers, obedient and self-assertive, receptive and contributory: these dissonances.

I would very much be inclined to suggest that if it could be argued that the voiceover demarcates the range of Miss Kenton's character, or, in more discipline specific terms (narrative terms), of her development, across points of view and through time, her two bodies stand—and stand firmly—at that development's end and beginning, like bookends, keeping her other bodies upright, balancing their weight by pushing them inwards, into one another. Thompson's other performances in *The Remains of the Day* are negotiations, compromises between the manner in which the actress uses her eyes, mouth, jaw, arms, and hands in the film's closing minutes and her gestures and gesticulations in that early scene in Mr. Stevens's office. This is not simply to say that if she stares Stevens in the eyes by the end of the movie whilst she doesn't dare to look in his direction in that early scene their interactions in between are characterized by a gradual increase in eye contact, although this is certainly the case, something which is, *pace* Griselda Pollock, a valuable achievement in itself. Rather, Thompson uses different strategies so as to suggest a loosening of her restraints. An exchange between Miss Kenton and Mr. Stevens in his office, about fifteen minutes in, is a case in point.

This exchange differs from the one a few minutes previous in many respects. For instance, Miss Kenton knocks on Mr. Stevens's door, but now doesn't wait for his reply before entering. She also places a vase with flowers on his mantelpiece without asking. The film makes manifest, it would seem, that she no longer is, or in any case no longer feels, like his guest, like a stranger. Indeed, it seems the scene's narrative rationale is to directly present Miss Kenton's struggle to loosen up, as well as Mr. Stevens's battle to prevent it. For it is with her sense of familiarity that Mr. Stevens takes issue, reacting in surprise to her presence and responding dispassionately to her efforts to spruce up the place, before going on to berate her for using the Christian name in talking to an elderly employee, in fact his father. Thompson and Hopkins are both particularly impressive in performing this stand-off. The latter, just to say a few words about his performance, expresses his reticence by keeping his distance, both verbally and physically. Verbally: he speaks, if not in tongue then at least in a language so formal and abstract that it sounds as if drawn from another time, as if written by an nineteenth-century philosopher, emphasizing and repeating terms like "one" and "such." "One such as yourself," for example, or "someone such as my father." Explicitly spelled out is the extent to which the syntax is in the subjunctive, distanced even grammatically. Hopkins's pronunciation is deliberate, precise, and prolonged, like that of an Oxford don. The physical performance extends and expands this sense. Tellingly, the first thing Hopkins does is to take a seat behind his desk. What is most noticeable about his use of his body here is the manner in which he moves his hands. Seated in his chair, cigar in one hand, glass of Scotch in the other, the only attribute absent being a scholarly robe, he at once underscores and overwrites—indeed, overplays his hand—by rolling out his wrist, not so much unfolding as uncurling, gently opening his palms to dispense his wisdom, as if he explaining an intricate treaty eloquently to a naïve student.

Thompson's performance in reaction here is, I think, exceptional for many reasons, but the one aspect I'd like to single out is the way in which she uses her body to enact in quick succession, and in subtle, that is, natural, transition, a varied range of emotional states. In chronological order: confusion, discomfort, displeasure, annoyance, anger, and outrage. As Mr. Stevens fires off his opening salvo, telling Miss Kenton off for calling his father by his first name, Thompson momentarily wrinkles her forehead while lowering her eyebrows, her face struggling to find a form, and looks down in confusion, not so much to her feet as to invisible depth, where there is presumably to be caught an answer somewhere deep, deep below. Then, seconds later, she rolls her eyes to the side and presses her lips stiffly together, pushing down her cheeks whilst pulling up her chin, her whole expression tightening contortedly so as to suggest the dawning of disbelief, discomfort, and finally displeasure. Indeed, as she informs Mr. Stevens that she doesn't "quite get it," that *she* is the "housekeeper, and your father is the *under*butler"—that in "other houses I was accustomed to address the *under*servants by their Christian names"—her voice gradually transforms from hesitation, as she interrupts her "I don't quite . . . understand" with a pause and an "uhm," to annoyance, stressing the "I" in "*I* am the housekeeper," tightening her jaw so that the words come through her teeth, whilst at the same time cocking forward her head and opening her chest, releasing her hands clasped in front of her to sway tensely along the sides of her body. When Mr. Stevens continues his assault on Miss Kenton by suggesting that if she "would stop and think for a moment, you would realize that [*sic*] how inappropriate it is for one such as yourself to address as William someone such as my father," Miss Kenton's expression transforms from annoyance to anger. Thompson's performance of emotional distress is measured less by grand gestures than by short, staccato movements: the eyes blink rather more often; the eyebrows are repeatedly raised, in quick succession, each time pulling up the upper part of the cheeks and wrinkling the forehead; the mouth jerks left and right, and with it the lower cheeks and chin, since the teeth remain gritted and the jaw stays clenched. In a sense Thompson's whole head jerks along, straining her neck, almost pulling muscles and glands through the skin. It is this tension, this conflict between movement and stillness, stiffness, or restraint that signifies Kenton's anger, or that in any case signifies the form her anger can publicly take. For certainly, if Murray Pomerance is right in pointing out that gestures may well be taken as indexes of characters' interior states, they are also indices of their bodies' external relations, of the skin's contact with the outside world phenomenological, physical, and social. In the Dutch language there is the expression "uit je vel springen," which translates roughly as "to jump from your skin." We use it to describe a situation where someone is either so angry or so afraid that they could literally rattle their muscles and bones loose from their skin, like a cartoon character. As I was watching Thompson's performance here, I was reminded of this expression: it is as if all her muscles, as if her entire bodily apparatus wants to jump from a skin that doesn't bulge, that cannot, not here at least, not in this office, at this moment in time.

There is much more to be said about Thompson's performance in this film, some of which I would like to think I might have said had in more space; and plenty of which, I realize, I would have undoubtedly overlooked even had I all thinkable space and time on my hands, but which hopefully will be said by others elsewhere. At any rate, the above reading of Thompson's performance in four single scenes can't do justice to her achievements in the film as a whole. What I haven't discussed here, for instance, are two separate scenes in which she is not berated by Mr. Stevens, but instead tells him off; nor have I managed to look at a splendid scene in which she breaks down in front of him; nor indeed, those scenes in which Miss Kenton interacts with persons other than Mr. Stevens. I am certain that readings of each of these moments would raise new questions with respect to the particularities of Thompson's performance, or even open up discussions about more general issues around the nature of acting. What I hope to have achieved here, is to think through, or help the reader think through, or inspire the reader to think at all about, the manner in which Thompson performs a character across points of view and temporalities, that is to say, a character that is never the same, is always already someone else, without that character herself, of course, necessarily realizing as much. I have found that Thompson accomplishes this sense of multiplicity not simply by changing tack, by using one tic here and there another, but rather by playing out tensions on and around a spectrum which is itself less a character outline than an emotional sketch, a tonality, if you will, or, indeed, that oval that Bacon frequents. What makes Emma Thompson's performance of Miss Kenton so spectacular, in my view, is not her ability to portray a character who has emotions but rather her talent to use her emotions to portray a character, here defined as a series of interlinked, overlapping bodies in very human form.

Works cited

Deleuze, Gilles. *Francis Bacon: The Logic of Sensation*. London: Continuum, 2003.

Pollock, Griselda. *Vision and Difference: Femininity, Feminism and the Histories of Art*. London: Routledge, 1988.

Pomerance, Murray. *Moment of Action: Riddles of Cinematic Performance*. New Brunswick, NJ: Rutgers University Press, 2016.

Chapter 21

Tilda Swinton in *I Am Love*

Murray Pomerance

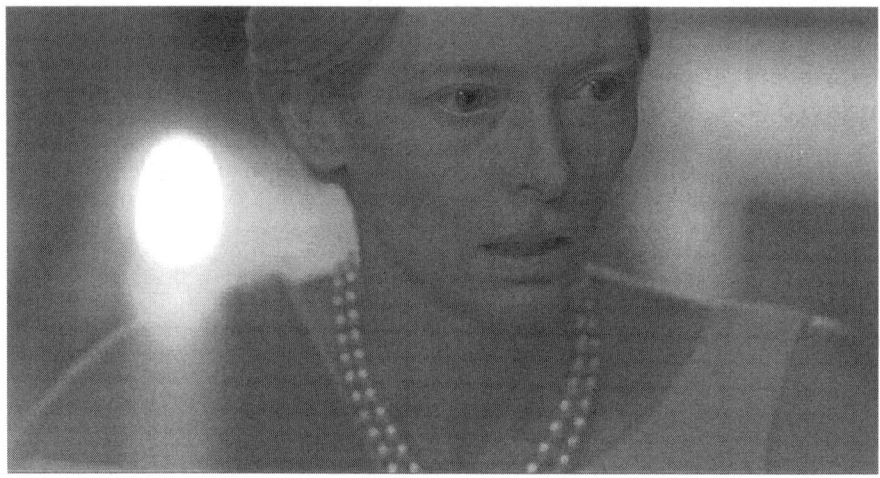

There is a great deal of brilliant, uncompromising work one must lay aside to appreciate the turnings and surprises of Tilda Swinton's performance in Luca Guadagnino's *I Am Love* (Io Sono l'Amore, 2009): her gender-bending, eye-opening eponymous work in *Orlando* (1992), her Lady Ottoline Morrell in *Wittgenstein* (1993), her guru-retreatist Sal in *The Beach* (2000), her depressive maternal Margaret in *The Deep End* (2001), her comfortingly maternal Audrey in *Thumbsucker* (2005), her chilled and chilling White Witch in *The Chronicles of Narnia* (2005), the scathingly bitchy lawyer Karen in *Michael Clayton* (2007), her loyal but vitiated vampire in *Only Lovers Left Alive* (2014), among considerably more stunning performances. All to be laid aside. All to be turned away from.

I Am Love is a difficult film, in that it is necessary to attend closely to what is shown, and the way it is shown, to make sense of its mystery and feel completion with its stunning resolution. There is a kind of doubling, or metamorphosis. The larva becomes the butterfly. Norman O. Brown:

"Every sentence is bilingual, or allegorical: saying one thing and meaning another . . . Every sentence a translation" (9). Two in twinning, two in the prelude and fugue. Two acts, two palettes.

A study in blue, white, and gray

We fall upon the Recchi estate in Milano, after a snowfall and by gliding through the city—its long, empty vias—to the haunting strains of John Adams's "The Chairman Dances: Foxtrot for Orchestra" from *Nixon in China*. A huge, brutalist, yet utterly majestic house set behind dense evergreens—these latter tall, dark, thick with snow—blocks of cement perched upon one another and graced with fittings of polished mahogany softly lit. (The Villa Necchi Campiglio, regarded astutely by Swinton, who co-produced the film, as "part palace, part museum, part prison" on the DVD commentary). The evergreens heavy with snow, the long boulevards heavy with snow, the sky white with the promise of snow. Inside, helping the maids fold laundry, nothing, it seems, of the aristocrat who is the matron of this palace, Emma Recchi is safe, poised, warm (Swinton, ironically, comes from Britain's aristocracy). Companionable, direct, with an athletic build, she seems handy and alert; indeed in a recurring performative gesture, Swinton keeps Emma's eyes open and hungry; and she displays, above all else, a peaceable softness without ever turning sweet. Swinton performs Emma largely without makeup, relaxing into this not-quite-known woman who is relaxing into what is for her, perhaps, a not-quite-known wifely role. She sees to the small, domestic things. Encourages the children.

Tancredi, her husband (Pippo Delbono), runs the textile business his father built, and brings the family its notable fortune. Edoardo, the oldest son (Flavio Parenti), a Donatello in Armani, is bringing his fiancée to dinner, here, now, tonight, and the grandparents are coming: guests of honor, because the old man is having a birthday. It's one of those distinctively composed, sedate parties, everyone smiling, all the pleasantries respectfully whispered, the tranquil waters. The old man (Gabriele Ferzetti) grinning silently on his throne, Serenity in bronze. He may well have studied his Pascal: "Nearly all the ills of life spring from this simple source, that we are unable to sit for long in a quiet room."

The celebratory laughter is a little forced, actually. The bustling servants damp with anxiety: aristocratic life. Emma seated next to her father-in-law, her vivid crimson dress well cut but unornamented. Smiling graciously, saying nothing audible. Edo's girl Eva (Diane Fleri) is—forgive her!—an Ugolini, not, perhaps, quite the right kind of family although they're cute enough together (especially at a brief moment much later, on a stairwell, alone, in fancy clothing, when they grab at each other below the waist), but Eva does behave respectfully to the old man, she's definitely good-looking, clean, polite, properly subservient. Tancredi, motionless at the far end of the table, is a mute pasha: tall, somewhat fleshy, one suspects not a great thinker: no Moravia. The youngest child, Elisabetta (Alba Rohrwacher), has artistic talent. Every year she gifts Nono a framed drawing (he plans to open a gallery and make people pay to see them) but this year something new, something daring: she has branched into photography. "Very nice," with a tepid half-smile, but then a rich giggle as he warns, "You still owe me a drawing!" Hollow laughter all around, except that the loyal Emma, seeing the girl blush with mortification at this familial brutality, announces that it's beautiful. The old man has risen with his glass. Time to retire, pass on the textile company to . . . Tancredi and . . . Edoardo, because "It takes two men to do the job I did!" A very chummy Mussolini, in his palace. The court assembled all around. Emma the sparkling ruby in the crown, hesitant, observant, perfect in every respect, although it is manifest that she is not feeling joy.

She is young by comparison with her husband, fresh as wildflowers in springtime yet somehow, in this domain, carefully arranged, placed in a crystal vase through which she is fully visible, yet also, in ways not to be speculated upon, warped by the faceting. Emma has the great household of Recchi entirely upon her elegant shoulders. From her minimal movements, her graceful silences, her retreating to the top of the stairs, her non-stop observation—not to miss a flicker of life—we can deduce: responsible, careful, practical, practical, careful, responsible. And responsible. And practical. To whom, finally, will she owe this duteous responsibility? And in what venue will her practicality show itself most gloriously, if at all?

A nighttime visitor. Edo's new friend Antonio (Edoardo Gabbriellini), to whom he just lost a sporting competition, has baked him a cake. A prodigy of cuisine, this one, a connoisseur of fruit. Introduction to the mother, hello, nice to meet you, but swiftly as a sylph she retires upstairs, the muscular Swinton thighs producing invisible thrust as the poised Swinton torso maintains its form. What is it about the way Swinton ascends here—from above, we watch—that conveys in the tiniest gestural nuance her sudden, overwhelming sensation of this stranger: that in her mind his ripe young face has been imprinted? Antonio leaves as Emma reaches her sanctum, as downstairs the generations intermix in this grandiose, this much-polished, this socially elevated house. Emma is at a height, the top of Milan society. Antonio has come from the streets. Here is George Orwell writing in the *Tribune* (3 January 1947) of a shipboard memory then almost twenty-five years old, that involved a quartermaster, whose job was to take the wheel:

> I came up from lunch early. The deck was empty except for the fair-haired quartermaster, who was scurrying like a rat along the side of the deck-houses, with something partially concealed between his monstrous hands. I had just time to see what it was before he shot past me and vanished into a doorway. It was a pie dish containing a half-eaten baked custard pudding . . .
>
> It took me some time to see the incident in all its bearings: but do I seem to exaggerate when I say that this sudden revelation of the gap between function and reward—the revelation that a highly-skilled craftsman, who might literally hold all our lives in his hands, was glad to steal scraps of food from our table—taught me more than I could have learned from half a dozen Socialist pamphlets? (404–5)

As to Tancredi, he is proud and pleased to have as wife so charming, so svelte, so modest, so accomplished, and so tactfully helpful a woman—a woman his judgmental parents have accepted and seem to love, a nourishing mother to his duteous children, a completely loyal partner for his life.

What is it about Swinton's graceful stance and sculptured face in the Recchi mansion that conveys, repletely and unmistakably, the depths of sadness in her soul? Is it that for all its stateliness and form, for all its composure, her body is only her body, glowing but limited; while all around her this palace seems to stretch endlessly into the space of its modern times?

Study in springtime green

But after some months, the old man is dead. Captivated by the talented and unpredictable Antonio, Emma has found herself panicky to be with him and taste his concoctions, has confided him the story of her life. She lived in Russia. She had no name: people called her "Kitesh." Tancredi arrived on a business tour, met her father, an appraiser of art.

He brought her back to Italy. She is Tancredi's *objet d'art*, then, has long been. Antonio is a vigorous and passionate one—he has a young man's desire, neither callow nor mature. In lovemaking, he is predictably inexhaustible; they tear at one another in his little hut near San Remo, with the springtime hills and glades all around. She must pay a ransom for his sunshine, however, the recipe for that soup she makes, Edo's favorite food. She details the making of *ugha,* which involves a distinctly clear broth and numerous kinds of freshly caught river fish. Here is the intimate architecture of a monumental triangle: mother, lover, son.

Easy enough—because of Guadagnino's structuring but also because Swinton gives no hint that any other dynamic might be moving her—to believe that it is Antonio's youthfulness to which Emma has succumbed; that he substitutes for the enchanting but forbidden son; that she is something of a cougar in training, exercising her talents and drives by playing out love with this innocent artist. She lets him cut her hair. She makes excuses so that she can travel to him in San Remo.

Elisabetta makes a confession: she is in love with another woman. Emma naturally becomes her confidante, a mother's duty. And not to tell papa. Not to tell Edoardo. They wouldn't understand!

With her mother-in-law Rori (Marisa Berenson) and Eva, Emma lunches at Antonio's father's restaurant, where Antonio prepares a seductive meal. *Gamberoni*, pink as sunset! Important to note and consider that in all of what I have described, even—perhaps especially—in Emma's lovemaking with Antonio, Swinton works without enunciation, without gesturing placements or expressive ornamentations, without ever permitting Emma to behave in such a way as to make a show of herself. If there is anything at all that will identify Emma in her colossal modesty—as seems—that might afford her some real background and allow our empathy, it can be only the situation in which she finds herself, only the vast array of geographic, characterological, and social details orbiting her consciousness, because Emma's strategy in life is to permit situations to impose themselves upon her. She is one of David Riesman's other-directed folk:

> The other-directed person must be able to receive signals from far and near; the sources are many, the changes rapid. What can be internalized, then, is not a code of behavior but the elaborate equipment needed *to attend* to such messages and occasionally to participate in their circulation. As against shame and guilt controls, though of course these survive, one prime psychological level of the other-directed person is a diffuse anxiety. The control equipment, instead of being like a gyroscope, is like a radar. (41–2)

In Milan Emma is the mistress in the Recchi household, she is "Mrs. Recchi," she is what Tancredi needs and expects her to be, and what her children need and expect, too. With Antonio she is his "girl."

If she has her own hungers and passions, still she has not learned to openly desire.

Pure cinematic acting

Guadagnino's design for the cataclysmic ending of *I Am Love* involves Swinton in a chain of events, at each link of which she performs what can only be called "pure cinematic acting." In coining this phrase I mean to point explicitly: not to one particular, isolated idea or intent on Swinton's part, but to ideation in a number of different modes, in all of which her performative effect is distinctly heightened because she makes herself subservient to the camera and the techniques that flow from camera use. This film produces Swinton as much as she produces this film. I think of Pirandello, of course; that she serves what he calls "the machine" so faithfully that Emma's sense of reality and being come to be defined according to the "desire" or "need" of the project. This passivity, as we may estimate it, is crucial to what will be revealed at the film's end, when, as it were, the "curtain goes up."

Soup

Tancredi is giving a gala dinner, to celebrate his sale of the company to an international conglomerate headed by Shai Kubelkian (Waris Aluhwalia). Emma has asked Antonio to handle the food. She either does not know, or by the time of taking her seat has forgotten, that he intends to serve nothing other than the *ugha*, needless to say in a special version only he could create, one that will astound the diners at the same time as giving unmistakable sign of his authorship (and culminating pleasure to his friend Edo). Emma's traditional version was golden and clear, yet very simple, rustic. Antonio's broth is clear as diamonds, with various exquisitely shaved pieces of fish and punctuating vegetables arranged in its depths, this whole concoction radiant in the candlelight like an elaborate edible crown. The soup is delivered to the guests one by one, and the last to receive it is morose Edo, disarmed by his father's insistence on selling, regretting Kubelkian's presence in his house, and feeling cut off from meaningful action. This young man has his eye on tradition, after all. He looks to the worker with concern, as in a feudal relation, and thinks of himself as carrying on his grandfather's ownership habits, this noblesse oblige notwithstanding a provocation from his younger brother Gianluca (Mattia Zaccaro) that the grandfather was as unconcerned with his workers as any factory owner would be, was indeed something of a secret tyrant. Edo, at any rate, had only valorous intent, but this intent has been stolen, the ground upon which he builds his moral edifice has been trespassed upon.

He flashes in shock when he sees the soup. Antonio; Antonio's place in the hills; the ring of hair, his mother's hair, he found there! Rather than delighting in his favorite dish he has read its character *as sign*. How *could* Antonio know about *this soup?* Seeing him withdraw, Emma opens her eyes wide and stares down. We look at her face looking down. We look at the *ugha*, its makeup, its colors, its creative uniqueness, its undeniable signature. She gasps when the puzzle comes whole. Edo has already backed away and strides manfully out of the room, hissing sarcastically at Emma as he passes, *and in Russian*, "Spaciba, mamma" ("Thank you, mother!"). She gets up to follow as Tancredi makes a smarmy remark about this perfect display of the Russian character.

But Emma and that soup: Swinton's performance of the sudden realization—that Edo must know she has been making love to his friend (and been unfaithful to his father)—is accomplished in two shots, laid upon one another like two hands clapping. First Emma noticing Edo and pulling back in fear, her mouth agape. Then we have the soup Emma is looking at, its character spelling out the situation. Her face becomes the register of reaction, the embodiment of knowledge. Swinton is able to use only the slightest modulation of mouth and eyes, since the magnification of the moment is produced by the close-up lens, first on her face, then on the *ugha*. One might see her work here as "acting *with* lens," rather than acting for the lens. This is the minimalism of an actor's "action" before the camera, of which many have written, yet it goes to a special depth because the party ceremonial and her relation with Edo are constraints. Her seeing is everything. The bowl of *ugha* is Swinton's scene partner.

Pool

Edo has gone outside the glassed front doors, to a cement bench. We see Emma still inside, searching for him, partially ascending the stairway then coming back down and gazing into the twilight. She emerges, beckoning (still in Russian); sits by his side. He is caustic in reproach: she is no more faithful than the rest of them. As he stands she tries to grab at him and he falls into the pool, striking his head on the concrete edge. She freezes.

Here, a matter of posture in a wide shot showing only part of her body and Edo floating face-down, in the dim light. Through her complete inability to take action, indeed even to cry out, we see the magnitude of the revolution of consciousness that has beset her with terrible swiftness—the secret love made open and undeniable; the cherished child fleeing from her and rejecting her; his beautiful body floating in the pool, as though dead.

At the hospital the family members sit in silence. A surgeon delivers the fatal announcement. There is no reaction—a scathingly authentic moment for Swinton's Emma, whose world has been utterly destroyed. For Emma, not only is there nothing to express, *there . . . is . . . nothing.*

Then she is embracing Elisabetta. What is remarkable here is the telltale desperation in that embrace, the muscularity, shown from behind Betta and in a close shot to emphasize Emma's hands. The grip is fierce. Only a gripping hand to convey female bonding in a tumultuous male world. Emma clasps more than the young girl's physical form; she draws to herself all the energy that innocent youth might offer, all of the variform possibility implicit in breaking away from convention. Betta was also Edo's confidante, and so Emma, in clutching at her, tries through the age-old magic of the flesh to bring the dead boy back into the world of the living. The hands, the fingers, the sinews, the bloodlessness, now that hope is gone.

Sleep

Emma takes herself to Edo's bedroom and curls up on his bed, perhaps to dream . . . She is clutching his stuffed dog, she has looked at his framed photographs, everything perfunctory. Curled there, she is lost, and curled in Emma's body Swinton, too, is lost. Performance is abrogated. A hand covering the face. That same clutching hand, covering the unsigning face. What a courageous, wholesome, true thing to do, only to lie upon the bed, to make no gesture, to be subject only to gravity.

Funeral

Outside the chapel, the family gather in the sunshine around Tancredi. Everything is as it would be for them now, as it has always been, can only be, given the prevailing disbelief. Except one thing. On the steps of the chapel, still in shadow, is Emma. Standing, moving a little, turning, turning, then turning back, but not emerging. No thread binds her to these people now. Something has changed in the center of Emma's earth. She runs off.

Cupola

Tancredi finds her in a Russian Orthodox church, a great hexagonal vacant echoing space, under a massive cupola painted royal blue with a million stars. She has dropped her shoes and waits in a ray of sunlight. He approaches. She is wet from rain, soaked through. He places his jacket over her shoulders protectively, gazes at her in anguish and what he would surely call beneficence. But now something happens to trigger the event that could only have been waiting in preparation, not unlike Antonio's majestic food preparations set out on the kitchen table. Something magical and horrifying. There is a flutter. Emma looks up.

A pigeon has been trapped in the cupola.

She faces Tancredi. "Io amo Antonio."

His voice becomes a blade. "You do not exist." He steps toward her. She flinches in reflex, from the slap she expects upon her cheek. (It is as though Swinton knows what it is to be slapped, shocking as the thought may be for her legion fans who dote on her dignity.) But Tancredi merely reaches out to take his jacket back. He walks away.

That pigeon. It is the clear and unadorned symbol, the objective correlative perhaps, of her condition. Trapped in this Russian crystal. So trapped that for ages even the thought of escaping was beyond the pale, but now it is trying to get out. Emma must be receiving this impression, wholly and deeply. Betta has found her own way out. Emma knows she is flapping like the bird, however. Her position in the Recchi family, her being nothing but a souvenir from a business trip, is now brought sharply to consciousness in all its stagnant filth. In Russia she was content, but Tancredi took her away. She learned Italian (all through the film, we can have noticed how her conversation, while competent, is a little lacking). She bore him three children, and took up the position as mistress of his august household, while in fact being completely unprepared for the status, unaccustomed to incalculable wealth, nervous in the regal presence of his mother and father. All of the poise we have been seeing, the grace, the warmth, the comfort—a show! Regardless of the fact that her husband could claim to love her; regardless of the fact that Rori could deign to accept her; regardless of her loyal and adoring children, especially the glorious Edo; still, on foreign soil, away from the soil of her homeland, as it were (and the soil around Antonio's place in San Remo must remind her of home), she is alone, trapped, cut off from her deepest root in reality. All of this is in that pigeon.

And what is marvelously cinematic about the acting here, what is not only pertinent to cinema but built out of cinema, is Swinton's conscience that she will be edited, that editing will build the moment. There are two gestures that must be made to occur, one before the other; one immediately following from the other; and the editor will cause that sequencing to happen. She need but provide unequivocal clarity in each of two shots. She must look up. She must confess to her husband. In the first moment she need not, nor should she, signal the approach of the second. And in the confession, she need not, nor should she, reflect back on the truth of the first, the bird. The moments should be isolated, encapsulated. There will be continuity (time will pass, life will continue), but cinema itself (the editing) will provide it.

Home

Now she is seen approaching the Recchi home, from a camera position near the sitting room where we can spy all of the members of the family seated in grief near the windows. She runs in, still sopping wet, dashes upstairs, races with the help of her maid Ida (her real, but entirely unacknowledged, friend) to pack, Ida (Maria Paiato) anticipating Emma's every move. When she walks out we are left with a medium close shot of Ida sobbing. Swinton knows that she need not confide emotion in this poignant farewell, because Paiato will convey emotion reflexively. This is acting by reverse shot. Stand pat, let your scene partner create the character you are.

Downstairs near the door a bravura finale. The shots cut through the family, from face to face, close shots, then back to Emma in long shot as she stands so far away, in the atrium, gazing. Gazing without recognition, gazing without a past. Pompous Tancredi, his lips turned down in distaste. Haughty Rori, superior, staring at the perfect justification for her own self-anointment. Betta welling with tears at the loss of her chief ally but certain that she can go out into the world as the person she wants to be. Gianluca sullen, uncomprehending, too young to understand complexity. And Eva, from the wrong kind of family, revealing to them all that she is pregnant and thus imprisoned herself now, in this great bourgeois fortress. But catching her breath, Emma knows the change has come upon her, here, now. There is nothing for her in this house anymore. Swinton makes no expression, not even a widening of the all-seeing eyes.

Someone in the drawing room calls out her name, but it is no longer her name.

Guadagnino cuts back to the atrium as the music culminates with a trumpet blare, and we see the open door, the airy world outside. Emma has gone.

Swinton's acting in this scene is thunderous and powerful, working with the ineluctable crescendo of the music to mount in intensity and desire. Yet the actress has understood, has given herself to, a cinematic construction. She will be seen standing and watching. Her face will appear to react against the various expressions on the family faces. But she will not be there at all. The marvel is that in the film's final shot, we can believe we see her walk through that door to freedom, but we do not. She is already gone, gone before we permitted. And then it can become shockingly apparent what we have been seeing through the entire film:

That Swinton's Emma has never for a moment been at home here.

That she has been modeling as Tancredi's wife, Rori's daughter-in-law.

That the environment, for all its perfection of design, is her bleak cell.

That her etiquette came from the heart, but covered for her fear.

All of her being in this place has been Emma's performance, and Swinton has been secretly performing this performance that is fully evident only when Swinton is onscreen no more. Knowing in advance that only in the finale would it all become clear, all of her presence with the Recchis, she knew that the apotheosis of the act would be to vanish. When Emma finally comes alive, comes into her own, it is only as a ghost.

Works cited

Brown, Norman O. *Apocalypse and/or Metamorphosis*. Berkeley: University of California Press, 1991.

Orwell, George. "Extracts from 'As I Please,' 66: The Gap between Function and Reward on a Luxury Liner; Persecution of Writers in USSR," in *Seeing Things As They Are: Selected Journalism and Other Writings*, sel. Peter Davison, London: Harvill Secker, 2014, 404–7.

Pirandello, Luigi. *Shoot!* Trans. C. K. Scott Moncrieff. Chicago: University of Chicago Press, 2005.

Riesman, David, Nathan Glazer, and Reuel Denney. *The Lonely Crowd: A Study of the Changing American Character*. New Haven: Yale University Press, 1950.

Chapter 22

Denis Lavant in *Holy Motors*

Nick Davis

Leos Carax's surrealist mosaic *Holy Motors* (2012) is nothing if not a "glorious, go-for-broke actor's showcase" for Denis Lavant (Justin Chang and Peter Debruge, "Perf Turf Not Always an Even Playing Field," *Daily Variety* 312: 32 (2012), 11). Adopting a dozen personas across different sequences, from laconic banker to knife-wielding gangster to subterranean troll, Lavant seizes center stage for nearly the entire runtime, excluding the preamble and finale. The main link among otherwise unrelated, generically disparate vignettes, Lavant's theatrical skill manifests not just in the vocal, gestural, and cosmetic leaps he takes with each new character but in the camera's recording of his painstaking preparations for each shapeshifting feat.

In any other movie, watching Lavant study scripts, run lines, remove dentures, peel off prosthetic noses, and affix fake scars and fingernails might have a demystifying effect—spoiling a magician's act by exposing all the mechanics. The enigmas of *Holy Motors*, however, prove more intractable than most, encasing Lavant's exploits and backstage rituals within a mise-en-abyme of open questions. Who is Lavant playing? Writers typically refer to his character as "Monsieur Oscar," the name most frequently ascribed to him by his associates, but even this moniker may be a pseudonym, as well as a flagrant pun on awards-caliber performance. Who, furthermore, schedules Oscar's appointments around Paris, each entailing a radical makeover? What purpose could it serve, and what income could it possibly provide, for him to wander from arrondissement to arrondissement, perpetrating acts of imposture and tomfoolery before clambering back into his limousine? By the internal (il)logic of *Holy Motors* and in the eyes of the film's awed but confounded audience, Lavant's virtuosity constitutes an entertaining end in itself. The misalignment, though, between what we see and what we know—our copious, close-up access to Lavant's thespian exertions versus our unalleviated bewilderment at Carax's larger scheme—fosters an imbalance in most analyses of the film. Critics posit various through-lines and theoretical contexts to make Carax's experiments more legible, a goal that fixes the director, not his star, as the riddle to be cracked. Even articles that promote *acting* or *performance* as keywords for decoding *Holy Motors* frequently short-shrift Lavant's specific contributions, adulating him as a brilliant executor of Carax's cryptic designs but not quite a co-creator.[1]

This chapter consequently aims to recuperate aspects of Lavant's performance that remain unsung despite the many hosannas it attracted, including his first nomination for the César, France's version of the Academy Award. I argue first that Lavant, tempering his signature athleticism with persistent notes of exhaustion, fashions *Holy Motors* into a playful yet melancholy elegy for his own career as well as Carax's—thereby certifying his physical body *and* his body of work as crucial frames of reference in evaluating *Holy Motors*. Next, without begrudging all the well-deserved acclaim for Lavant's astounding versatility, I spotlight some quieter shifts and pregnant ambiguities within each characterization. I thus expand the scope of Lavant's achievement beyond his animation of such massively divergent personas. Finally, to the extent that these subtler strata in Lavant's performance suggest something like an "inner life" for Oscar, I contend that seemingly old-fashioned values like *interiority* remain pertinent to the flagrantly post-human, post-millennial *Holy Motors*, even amidst its shattering of selfhood paradigms and its vehement embrace of surfaces over depths.

Who is he/who was he/when he was/who he was/ back then?

Holy Motors is scarcely conceivable without an actor who is equal parts stuntman and sphinx, tender but insolent, fearless exhibitionist and fathomless withholder, plausible as both the father of a teenaged misfit and the husband of a chimpanzee. Bulldoggish, press-shy, an early pupil of mimes and circus performers, a steadfast accomplice to outré auteurs, Lavant would fit this bill to a tee even without the further credential of having headlined most of Carax's other films. He and he alone, then, can fulfill every high-wire task the movie devises for its star while helping to frame the project as Carax's skeptical prognosis on his own career and his medium—surveying cinema's incipient decrepitude but also its untapped promise, figured through the body of his perennial alter ego.

When a performer becomes emblematic of a director's repertoire, though, the perceived inevitability of his or her casting can pull focus from finer-grained particulars of their work, or displace attention away from the actor entirely. *Holy Motors* exacerbates this tendency by cuing viewers to read Lavant's protagonist as a surrogate for the filmmaker. For one thing, "Oscar" and "Alex," the names most often attributed to Lavant's various guises, are a joint anagram for "Leos Carax." For another, the opening scenes suggest a porous boundary between these men, with the director appearing as himself, seeming to dream Oscar up while sleepwalking around a seaside suite and stumbling into a secret cinema hidden inside the hotel walls. Lavant arrives into the film three shots later, exiting a strange domicile with porthole-shaped windows and other nautical motifs, similar to that which hosted Carax's meta-cinematic hallucinations.

Rather than passively inhabit symbolic frameworks that the prologue erects around him, though, offering his body as a stand-in for Carax's or a metonym for all cinema, Lavant's hunched shoulder, tight carriage, and noticeable limp in his first scene bespeak a specific corporeality: not a blank slate awaiting an imminent decathlon of performative trials but a site of already-accumulated stresses. These hints of fatigue contrast pointedly with the smile on Oscar's face, the green oasis of bourgeois comforts surrounding him, and the stream of numeric, faux-corporate abstractions that pour from his mouth during his first phone call: "187 per cent, I think, at 5009 . . ." Like Robert Pattinson's much younger but similarly limo-bound financier in David Cronenberg's *Cosmopolis* (2012), unveiled at the same Cannes Film Festival as *Holy Motors*, Monsieur Oscar has somehow incurred a physical toll from the dubious "labors" of gliding around town, managing other people's wealth. This curious paradox, unvoiced by the script, arises purely from Lavant's choice of mien. Before we can unpack its implications, Oscar's awkward embodiment invites additional readings. Once initiated to the character's peculiar itineraries, we wonder if his stiff waddle at the outset was an aggregated consequence of days', weeks', even years' worth of strenuous play-acting. In a film that moves strictly if elliptically forward, Oscar's comportment suggests an inheritance of unseen pasts that cannot be dispelled overnight.

Just as likely, viewers may respond to Lavant not "in" character but as himself, like the nude subjects of Étienne-Jules Marey's proto-cinematic life studies, which pop up occasionally in the montage of *Holy Motors*. If we assume that Oscar's white hair and hypertonic gait are "really" Lavant's, we may gasp at how he has aged—this actor who works frequently but mostly off the mainstream radar, and whose fitful notoriety over three decades has hinged on calisthenic displays. For Carax, he spat fire and galloped across the Pont Neuf in *The Lovers on the Bridge* (*Les amants du Pont Neuf*, 1991); he stormed around the Japanese capital in *Tokyo!* (2008) as an evil imp named Merde, a character he briefly reprises in *Holy Motors*; and, most iconically, undertook a sprinting, exuberant dance in an uncut dolly shot down the streets of Paris in *Mauvais sang* (1986), scored to David Bowie's "Modern Love." Now the same man looks slightly cramped just walking to his car. For Harmony Korine, Lavant played a Charlie Chaplin impersonator in *Mister Lonely* (2007), a reverberant association insofar as you can almost see a subdued version of the Little Tramp in Monsieur Oscar's penguin-like shuffle down his driveway. Many viewers will know Lavant best as the disgraced Legionnaire in Claire Denis's *Beau travail* (1999), which notoriously ends on Lavant's three-minute, schizophrenic breakdance inside a doorless disco, a scene that recent film scholars have canonized as a modern classic. Elena del Río, among Lavant's most influential champions, grants his wild gambol in *Beau travail* a philosophical weight that transcends its text, insofar as it "demonstrates the immanence, rather than the opposition, of movement and rest, speed and slowness" (164).

Ghosted by past performances and by their continued uptakes in theory and culture, Lavant's stilted entrance into *Holy Motors* simultaneously invokes and deflates his reputation for physical extravagance. His evident depletion, whether faked or not, even carries a feminizing connotation in a medium where male stars' illusion of hardiness is regularly maintained well into their dotage, while women either fail to get parts or are forced to play mawkish scenes of rueful self-scrutiny, despairing before mirrors or at old photos of themselves (though this pattern is less stark in French cinema than in many others). This gendered element adds further ironies to the spectacle of Oscar being driven like Miss Daisy by a spry older woman, and to his first costumed appointment playing a wizened crone who shills for coins beside the Seine.

Any perception of Oscar's or of Lavant's nascent infirmity may seem misplaced once we arrive at the second "appointment," where he dons a sensor-covered bodysuit for his gig as a motion-capture actor. The character negotiates an ambitious schedule of martial arts, cardio exercises, and contortionist choreographies that unseen animators will repurpose into videogame set-pieces; in the process, he revives the supple, somersaulting Denis Lavant his audience knows so well. That said, Lavant complicates the dichotomy between his successive portraits of decline and agility. The crone may radiate weariness, yet Lavant plays up Oscar's energy in assembling that character, for instance by yanking his comb through her knotted wig in strong, forceful strokes. Even her broken-backed posture, tilting dangerously forward on her cane, legs splayed widely and her toes pointed inward, requires a deceptive amount of yogic stamina to maintain. Conversely, despite approaching the motion-capture facility with a new spring in his step, Lavant noticeably slows his pace after Oscar climbs all the stairs to the specific booth where unseen motion-capture technicians will record his performance. Well before his ill-fated treadmill exercise, which ends with Oscar tumbling off the machine (an especially pointed failure, in light of his immortal sprint through *Mauvais sang*), Lavant's heavy breathing and some wobbled landings already suggest the character's fatigue, notwithstanding that balletic prowess he exhibits in the same shots. Lavant, fifty years old when filming *Holy Motors*, can still roll and flip like someone three decades younger, but his character will pay for these strenuous exertions tomorrow.

Holy Motors places Lavant's most athletically daunting routines early in the film, to include the sclerotic shuffling of Merde, the red-headed troll, through sewers and cemeteries, and also Alex's rumbustious entr'acte through an empty cathedral, during which Lavant plays his accordion with blaring, bicep-flexing, pirouetting gusto. Because the film's second hour favors quieter scenes, as well as some blunt dialogues about Oscar's mounting ennui and possible retirement, the movie might have implied a broad arc from verve into lassitude. Lavant instead insists upon recurrent, unpredictable oscillations between these poles, suggesting in myriad ways and at unexpected moments that Monsieur Oscar is dwindling but always capable of mighty rebounds. The running, head-first leap Lavant takes into his limousine after his soulful, sung-through interlude with his ex-lover Jean (Kylie Minogue) offers another example of the actor boosting his energy just when the film seems designed to suppress it, or vice versa.

This dialectic of waxing and waning in Lavant's performance echoes what most critics took to be *Holy Motors*'s position on cinema itself, rendered here as a much-eulogized medium that nevertheless yields two hours' worth of startling new potentials. The same swings govern Carax's bipolar self-portrait, brimming with auto-allusions. He casts his career in retrospective terms, shutting off all the lights for a surreal, valedictory epilogue where driverless cars gently talk each other to sleep, but simultaneously summoning "the pent-up energy of a first film" (Lim 41) and including, for the first time in any of his five features, "jokes, humour, burlesque, as if [he] were getting younger, like a comic going back to childhood" (Père 43). The crucial point is that Lavant's citations, extensions, and refutations of his own youthful glories are not subordinate to Carax's project but equally fundamental to the movie. As Jean sings her doleful ballad, asking "Who are we/who were we/when we were/who we were/back then . . . ," Oscar trails slowly behind her, as if inhibited by the paralyzing force of built-up regrets. However, he also impulsively punts a dusty mannequin's head like a soccer ball across a gutted department store—the kind of spontaneous eruption on which Lavant's fame has thrived. While *Holy Motors* musically challenges Oscar to measure his present against his past, and against futures he once imagined, Lavant continues elaborating a performance that synthesizes his livewire legacy, his inevitable humbling by time, and the alluring if optimistic notion that his motors are still warming up.

Surface, nuance, and the fantasy of internal life

Stealthy intimations of vigor within exhausted scenes and of exhaustion within vigorous ones are just two of the ways in which Lavant textures his performance, elevating it from the chain of grandiloquent tricks it might otherwise have comprised and making his close-ups as memorable as his back flips and nosedives. Carax encourages our wonderment at Lavant's metamorphoses, cutting abruptly from the actor in one guise to a shot of him looking drastically otherwise, and dwelling at length on his regimens of makeup, costume, and rehearsal. Playing each interlude of "getting into character" with a focused stare and methodical hand—instead of rushing through these protocols or seeming bored by them—Lavant further whets our appetite for each *coup de théâtre*, as did journalistic preoccupations with the actor's acrobatic training. Lavant, though, a longtime stage veteran with affinities for Shakespeare and Chekhov, has voiced desires to explore characters beyond his trademark gallery of oddballs. About his quieter part in Merzak Allouache's *Tamanrasset* (2009), for example, he enthused, "What I really enjoyed is that it was a more 'normal' role given to me, less extreme than the one I had in Leos Carax, Claire Denis, or Harmony Korine's films . . . [an] occasion for me to have the experience of a film dealing with a more conventional day-to-day" (Louise Catier, "Mister Lonely: Interview with Actor Denis Lavant," *FranceInLondon.com*, 19 March 2008, online at franceinlondon.com/en-Article-292-Mister-Lonely-Interview-with-actor-Denis-Lavant-Culture—film-cinema.html). *Holy Motors*, albeit the furthest thing from a "conventional day-to-day" occasion, nonetheless accommodates Lavant's underreported knack for behavioral nuance.

Even the episode where Alex becomes the flame-haired ogre Merde, the most patently "extreme" of Oscar's errands, showcases Lavant's ability to limn his biggest, crudest portrayals with meaningful gradations, treating them as occasions for acting, not as jokes. (When Oscar opens the case that houses Merde's latex mask, he pauses solemnly before removing it.) Reprised with some adjustments from Lavant and Carax's segment of *Tokyo!*, Merde's habit is to spring out of manhole covers in major urban areas, tear through each city in the spirit of that *Godzilla* theme which sonically accompanies all his appearances, terrorize passersby, munch on flowers and paper money whenever he discovers them (and, in one case, on two fingers of a dumbfounded observer), and emit shrill wails and glottal consonants that defy comprehension. *Holy Motors* captures not just the shock value but the taxing physicality inherent in this routine, as Lavant freezes every tendon in his legs, angles his knees and toes outward, and stomps on his heels throughout long tracking shots, similar to those Carax uses elsewhere to document Lavant's nimbler runs and ninja flips. While in character as Merde, Oscar conducts an assault on a film crew among the tombs of Père Lachaise and subsequently kidnaps the supermodel Kay M. (Eva Mendes) with all the vocal clamor and violent, arthritic movement that are Merde's hallmarks.

Despite his implacable anarchism, however, Merde is not a flat creation. Having brought Kay M. into his sepulcher, this singular being reveals an appetite for mimesis, crossing his legs as hers are crossed in a farcical but poignant pretense at shared glamour. After provisionally styling himself in Kay's image, Merde sets out to change hers, reassembling her satin gown into a burqa and deploying his talons as erstwhile scissors. What stands out is this beast's newfound fluency of gesture once confronted with beauty, draping Kay's fabric and adjusting its folds with unexpected precision and grace. Just as, having applied Merde's palsied claws in the limo, Oscar ably manipulates his chopsticks to consume a pre-performance bento box, Merde finds that his creatureliness need not obstruct his aspirations to elegance, however deplorably pursued. Anatomy is not destiny, in a film that valorizes the transformative potential in all bodies and art forms. Just as saliently, Merde's evident species difference from Oscar's other roles does not render him a breed apart. Having introduced Merde's strangulated idiolect of high-pitched howls in *Tokyo!*, Lavant revives it in *Holy Motors* not just for Merde but for the motion-capture actor's rendition of alien orgasm and for the dying gasps of Alex and Théo, the identical-twin gangsters, one of whom expires on the same warehouse floor. Lavant may assay a huge range of characters but defies any notion that they have nothing in common. His acting choices insist on the intersections between superficially dissimilar subjects, between sex and death, and between the human and its others.

Like the segue from the female pauper to the videogame performer, Oscar's consecutive appointments as a sewer-dweller and a suburban dad heighten our focus on Lavant's staggering elasticity. The astounding differences between these two characterizations should not, however, distract us from some subtle but resonant continuities between them. For instance, the emotional violence that gradually suffuses the vignette of Oscar and his "daughter" Angèle differs from Merde's physical assaults on Kay M. and others in the previous segment, yet the thread of aggression toward women links them, in more ways than might be obvious. As Angèle takes a seat in her "father"'s Peugeot, he strokes the introverted girl's hair and cups her cheek before inquiring about her evening. The pivot of the scene is a cell phone call that unwittingly exposes Angèle's recap of the party as a lie. At that moment, Oscar lunges for a cigarette with obvious agitation. The darkening mood and even the threat of cruelty from "Angèle's father" arise in part from his sudden switch in smoking comportment. Having previously let cigarettes dangle rakishly from his mouth while he drove, this character now pulls his whole, open palm to his lips for each drag, exactly as Lavant did in his immediately preceding turn as the monstrously volatile Merde. After a few sharp rebukes, asking Angèle how she could be such a "*conne*" (translated as "moron" for American prints, but closer to "bitch" in French) as to spend a whole party hiding in the toilet, Lavant sidesteps the expected, even clichéd tantrum by reverting to an even tone for the rest of the scene, but if anything, his ensuing castigations cut Angèle even more to the quick.

Curiously, once their long drive has commenced, this man never looks at his daughter, with either adoration or ire, even when he demands that she look at him. He delivers all his dialogue with the same straight-ahead, faraway stare that in other scenes connotes a trancelike introspection. Thus, even his sharpest words to Angèle—"Your punishment is to be you, to have to live with yourself"—double as a possible self-censure. If so, Lavant's character might be voicing a broad, existential self-loathing, consonant with Oscar's subsequent confessions of growing tired of his vocation and even of himself. Alternatively, we could project a nastier psychology onto Angèle's father, who admits his jealousy of his teenaged daughter's suitors, and who pulls her body toward him at one point along the drive, even while avoiding eye contact. Is "being himself" a punishment for this man, too? Could such a condemnation be linked to Angèle's anxiety around boys at parties, or to her defensive reflex in the face of her father's low-voiced, wet-eyed anger, crossing her arms over her chest as if to deflect unwanted contact?

Every aesthetic and structural premise of *Holy Motors*, its incessant underscoring of pyrrhic identities, and every contemporary missive about cinema's senescence and postmodernist flatness would seem to weigh against the minutely interpretive, psychopathologizing route I have just laid into this troubling tableau—Lavant's last performance before the jazz-punk entr'acte, itself a spume of improvised energies and nonsensical rallying cries ("3! 12! Shit! Go!") that spoofs any quest for underlying truth. It seems as silly to ask what or whom Lavant is "really" playing as to ask what *Holy Motors* "means." I acknowledge the folly of these questions while noting, too, how diligently the film spurs its viewers to pose them, not least through its mirage of privileged access to the "real" performer embarking upon all these contrivances. By cutting to Oscar (or is it Lavant?) as he gears up for new antics or pauses after finished ones, the film resuscitates that seductive figment of an underlying self that it constantly pillories. This is true even as Lavant induces enough inconsistencies in the "backstage" Oscar—who sometimes limps and sometimes does not, sometimes moves smoothly around the limo cabin and sometimes looks cramped, sometimes fumbles with the overhead light switch and sometimes flips it with practiced ease—that we know "he," too, is multiple and fabricated. Even so, the fact that an enclosed vehicle is where an actual Oscar is serially posited, if only to be undermined, reproduces the classic opposition of external façade/internal reality that structures old fantasies of authentic personality, latent textual meaning, and of privacy as a threshold of revelation.

Lavant's pugnaciously inscrutable face, taciturn manner, and emphatic embodiedness have aligned him, from the standpoint of screen performance, with a common twenty-first-century privileging of surface, ineffable sensation, and unknowability over stable narratives, psychic recesses, or exhumable truths. In analyzing *Beau travail*, however, Rob White highlights a contradiction whereby "the undemonstrative surface all the more powerfully suggests depth or psychic substance" (136). White thus seeks, in part through Lavant, a cinematic aesthetics that is neither a "conventional humanist" (136) project nor utterly inhuman in its formal or affective impenetrability. As a movie, *Holy Motors* makes some feints in the direction of psychological realism, a close cousin to what White calls "conventional humanism," before inevitably retreating from it. For example, the long deathbed scene Oscar plays as "Monsieur Vogan," whispering to a much younger niece about fateful bequests, cribs most of its dialogue from Isabel Archer and Ralph Touchett's final conversation in *The Portrait of a Lady*. Even as the templates of *Holy Motors* require that Oscar awake after "Vogan" dies and the niece reveal herself as the same kind of itinerant pretender that Oscar is, an extended homage to Henry James is hardly the behavior of a movie that regards "fully formed, psychological characters" as nothing more than "the sorry theatrical and novelistic legacy that cinema has had to fight for well over a decade now" (Martin 19). Granted, Vogan moves more slowly and acquires deeper wrinkles with every shot, and Lavant makes him sound sicklier with each line. The character withers before our eyes, arguably taking an entire formation of realist aesthetics with him. *Holy Motors* offers a dignified sendoff to this ambassador from a different artistic age, then proceeds in its penultimate sequence to cast humans as nothing more than marginally better-dressed apes and, after that, to cede its last words to some chatty, acerbic machines.

Lavant, though, even more than this movie, refuses to jettison the fantasy of interiority. In a film that favors serialism over logic or causation, his physical and verbal inflections suggest that old saw of narrative-realist acting, the subliminal character arc. Even in interstitial scenes, as Monsieur Oscar looks out the window of his moving limousine, Lavant's eyes dart around, roving and refocusing, implying a pensive headspace even if *Holy Motors* declines to access it. We cannot know whether Lavant has complicated or corroborated Carax's vision by insinuating, within the radically posthuman world of this film, that some vestige of internal life and coherent character progression survives. The text stymies such an inquiry. The actor seldom gives interviews. And on the few occasions when the director speaks about *Holy Motors*, he favors runic aphorisms. What Carax once disclosed, though, about his fascination with the limousine, which is "at the same time erotic and morbid, totally made to be seen and at the same time opaque, so you can't see what's in it" (Père 42), applies equally to his star. Lavant embodies the governing tension in *Holy Motors* between brazen spectacle and indecipherable signification. He also fosters some paradoxes of his own, cruising the middle lanes between eternal youth and creeping age, between drastic transformations and incremental shifts, between a steadily dehumanized universe and one where personality, however adumbrated or incoherent, can still be glimpsed—darkly, as through a tinted window.

Note

1. For instance, Saige Walton's superb essay on *Holy Motors* as an exemplar of twenty-first-century baroque privileges *embodiment* and *performance* at the outset, only to stress the "kinetic activity of the [viewer's] eye" (250) over Lavant's exertions. Later allusions to "metamorphoses of Oscar's body" serve mostly as metaphors for the film's generic shifts, and her invocations of "the body" as a crucial analytic quickly distinguish themselves from "the figure of the human body" (255–6).

Works cited

Andrew, Dudley. *What Cinema Is!: Bazin's* Quest *and Its Charge*. Chichester: Wiley-Blackwell, 2010.

Del Río, Elena. *Deleuze and the Cinemas of Performance: Powers of Affection*. Edinburgh: Edinburgh University Press, 2008.

Denby, David. *Do the Movies Have a Future?* New York: Simon and Schuster, 2012.

Hoberman, J. *Film after Film: or, What Became of 21st-Century Cinema?* London: Verso, 2012.

Lim, Dennis. *"Holy Motors," Cinema Scope* 51 (2012), 40–1.

Martin, Adrian. "Where Do Cinematic Ideas Come From?" *Journal of Screenwriting* 5: 1 (2014), 9–26.

Père, Olivier. "Anything but Cinephilia," *Cinema Scope* 52 (2012), 40–6.

Rosenbaum, Jonathan. *Goodbye Cinema, Hello Cinephilia: Film Culture in Transition.* Chicago: University of Chicago Press, 2010.

Shaviro, Steven. *Post-Cinematic Affect.* Winchester: Zero Books, 2010.

Walton, Saige. "The Beauty of the Act: Figuring Film and the Delirious Baroque in *Holy Motors*," *NECSUS: European Journal of Media Studies* 3: 1 (Spring 2014), 245–65.

White, Rob. "Forms of Beauty: Moving Beyond Desire in Bersani/Dutoit and *Beau travail*," *Journal of European Studies* 34: 1–2 (June 2004), 128–42.

Chapter 23

Choi Min-sik in *Oldboy*

Hye Seung Chung and David Scott Diffrient

I was Oh Dae-su when we were making the film. (Choi Min-sik)

The above statement, spoken by a charismatic Korean screen icon discussing his critically lauded, award-winning performance as the emotionally and physically tortured protagonist Oh Dae-su in director Park Chan-wook's *Oldboy* (2003), echoes a sentiment that has been put forth by other celluloid celebrities for decades; namely, that an actor can sometimes *become* his or her character when immersed in a particular role. Indeed, during a 1962 interview in which she discussed her process as an actor, legendary Hollywood diva Joan Crawford stated, "Once in a role, I eliminated myself completely. I became the character I played . . . I was the role and it was my life, for twenty-four hours a day" (190–1). Similarly, Jet Li, star of numerous Chinese martial arts films, claims that he "became the character" when playing the folk hero Wong Fei-hung in *Once Upon a Time in China* (1991) and two of its sequels (Yu 79). Choi Min-sik's comment is nothing new, merely an iterative account of how the dividing line between "actor" and "character" dissolves once the former begins to mentally inhabit the world of the latter. And yet, Choi's remark is noteworthy, for it encourages audiences to reconsider the themes of *Oldboy* in light of extratextual details that emerge during the actor's interview, which reveals that he "went to the extreme" during the film's production and frequently "thought of things not in the script."

Moreover, the power dynamic between Choi's character, Oh Dae-su, and his antagonist, Lee Woo-jin (Yoo Ji-tae), can be said to allegorically reflect the traditionally asymmetrical relationship between actor and director. This dynamic is on view during the two characters' final encounter, which shows the protagonist becoming deferential and dog-like at the feet of his "master," a former classmate, after a soul-shattering secret is divulged. If, on set and throughout the production of a motion picture, an actor is typically asked or expected to do the bidding of his or her director, then the ostensibly preposterous story that *Oldboy* tells is symptomatically grounded in the actual experiences of creative personnel who exert power through and against other members of a film crew. As such, beneath *Oldboy*'s admittedly beguiling surface is still *another* narrative: an equally profound and reflexive account of the ways in which actors and directors often engage in agonistic struggles during the making of a film.

In a public lecture on screen acting co-hosted by the Korean Academy of Film Arts in Seoul (August 28, 2013), Choi Min-sik referred to movie actors as "subcontractors" who play a subordinate role vis-à-vis directors, whose intentions are often singled out as the most dominant component of the filmmaking process (Yoon Hye-ji, "Authenticity Is Valuable, Treasure Yourself [*Jinjja neun gwihada, na reul gwihagaehara*]," *Cine21*, 12 September 2013, online at www.cine21. com/news/view/?mag_id=74351).

As for the creative freedom of actors in shaping or defining a character, the veteran actor elaborated by saying that "if a director demands an 'A' for a character, you could suggest an 'A+' or an 'A-' as an actor. If your suggestion is accepted, great. But if the director says no, that's it. You need to observe the boundaries of the [director's and actor's] roles" (Yoon). As we hope to show, though, Choi Min-sik's participation in the making of *Oldboy*, while characterized by a level of physical and mental exertion (and perhaps even exploitation) that exceeds most actors' assignments, enabled him to challenge and partially upturn the traditional hierarchy of on-set labor relations that posits onscreen performers as mere "pawns" or "puppets" of their directors.

Freedom and imprisonment in *Oldboy*

As an example of what some critics and fans refer to as "Extreme Cinema" (a branding to which the UK distributor contributed by way of its "Asia Extreme" line of DVD and Blu-Ray releases), Park's *Oldboy* revolves around a hyper-violent vengeance plot in which bloodshed and tears are conspicuous elements. A businessman named Oh Dae-su, is kidnapped and imprisoned for fifteen years, for no apparent reason, then freed by his unseen captor, a wealthy puppet-master named Lee Woo-jin whose motives are gradually revealed over the course of the narrative. Flashbacks fill in missing details about the two men's shared history—their experiences as students at the same high school, where Dae-su had spied on an incestuous incident between Woo-jin and his sister. Because Dae-su told their fellow classmates about it, Woo-jin's sister—believing that she was pregnant—took her own life out of embarrassment and guilt. Harboring resentment in the years since her death, Woo-jin plots to put Dae-su in a situation as compromising and painful as his own, first by locking him away in a personal prison and then by hiring a female hypnotist to guide the hero's actions following his release. Not long after gaining his "freedom," Dae-su finds himself trapped in a cat-and-mouse game in which he has five days to discover his captor's motives. If he succeeds, Woo-jin (who communicates incognito to Dae-su through a cell phone), will commit suicide. If he fails, Woo-jin will kill Mi-do, a young chef at a sushi restaurant with whom Dae-su has fallen in love. In fact, the attraction between the older man and younger woman was engineered from the start by Woo-jin's hypnotist, who guided the protagonist to the sushi restaurant. The narrative's most shocking revelation, reserved for its penultimate scene, is that in truth Mi-do is Dae-su's missing daughter, his own "flesh and blood" kin, for whom he had been searching prior to learning that she was adopted by a Swedish couple (misinformation designed to steer him away from the truth).

Hypnotism, it turns out, is an important if largely overlooked aspect of this film's incest plot, for it eventually functions as a way for Dae-su to wipe the traumatizing carnal knowledge from his mind. Although the film's concluding close-up of Dae-su's grimacing face (as he embraces his lover/daughter in a snowy forest) suggests otherwise, the hypnotist's final act—wiping away all traces of the incestuous act from Dae-su's mind—brings an ironic sense of completion to this open-ended story, sealing his fate and giving him (temporary) relief from the suffering that will likely return in the months and years to come. Warning Dae-su that her procedure could "go wrong and distort [his] memories," the female hypnotist proceeds to direct his attention to a nearby tree, which (in his mind) becomes a stone pillar. She rings a bell, saying the sound signals that he has "split into two people": one, a man who doesn't know the horrible secret; the other, a monster who does. "When I ring the bell again," she whispers, "the monster will turn around and start walking. With each step he will age by one year. When he reaches seventy, the monster will die." These words are delivered over an image of Dae-su's darkened reflection in a window looking out over the city from inside Woo-jin's penthouse. This shadowy figure, who represents the innocent man rather than the grinning monster (that is, the version of Dae-su that is shown walking away from the camera, each of his first few steps coinciding with a light being turned off inside the apartment), visually contrasts with, yet thematically complements, the shot of Dae-su that immediately follows, taken from a great distance, a bird's-eye view showing his small black figure spread out on the snowy white ground, meager and isolated. Having been reduced to a shell of his former self, the man is alone save for his daughter, who joins him in this final scene but remains oblivious of his painful past.

In a 2007 interview with the Korean film magazine *Cine21*, Choi confided his agony in searching for the right expression for Dae-su's final close-up as he hears his daughter's declaration of carnal love. Perhaps the hypnotist's trick finally did not work. We see Dae-su's smile dissolving in pain. Ultimately, he found inspiration in another big-screen performance: that of Mexican-born American actor Anthony Quinn, whose face, similarly framed in close-up, registers ambivalence—neither happiness nor sadness but something in between—in the final scene of the 1967 war drama *The 25th Hour* (Moon Seok and Kim Min-gyeong, "*Oldboy's* Man and Woman [*Oldeu boi eui nam gwa nyeo*]," *Cine21*, online at www. cine21.com/news/view/?mag_id=46023). This little-known Henry Verneuil film concerns a man's involuntary separation from his family during World War II, beginning with Nazi Germany's incursion into his home country, Romania, in 1940. Quinn's brick-maker, Johann Moritz, is forcibly imprisoned in a Jewish labor camp despite being Christian, and spends the rest of the narrative shuttling from one European locale to another, all the while searching for his wife Suzanna and their two children. When they are finally reunited at the end of *The 25th Hour*, a decade of living apart from one another has done irreparable harm to their marriage and to Johann's relationship with his children. Suzanna now has a third child, a blonde toddler whose father is Russian. As the members of the reunited family gather together next to the tracks at a train station, a US photojournalist spots them and asks to take their picture, forcing husband and wife to stand next to one another and inviting Johann to put his arm around Suzanna. The obnoxious American edges closer with his camera, clicking one photo after another of the visibly uncomfortable family. At this point, close-up shots of Anthony Quinn's face show a flustered look that is barely masked by his plastered smile. Clearly wounded but also happy to be standing next to his wife once more, the protagonist is similar to Dae-su insofar as the two actors' ambivalent expressions—snagged between pleasure and pain—reflect in microcosm the two men's liminal position throughout their respective narratives.

Performing pathos and pain

The two previously mentioned moments of separation in the final minutes of *Oldboy*—the hypnotic split between "man" and "monster"; the divergence of memory and experience on the part of father and daughter (who nevertheless hug each other at the end)—attain allegorical significance as metatextual nods to an audience that goes into this film-viewing experience with foreknowledge of Choi Min-sik's prior work as an actor who sometimes struggles to separate himself from his roles. Indeed, a similar "hypnosis" would be required to wipe away many Korean spectators' memories of his earlier films and performances, which, like shadows, haunt *Oldboy* much as Dae-su's own memories threaten to figuratively imprison him after he has gained his "freedom." Before starring in Park's film, the talented actor had appeared in *No. 3* (1997), *The Quiet Family* (1998), *Happy End* (1999), *Shiri* (1999), *Failan* (2001), *Chi-hwa-seon* (2002), and other motion pictures that showcased his knack for playing tragic, misunderstood, and/or hapless men who sometimes descend into violence and antisocial behavior. Indeed, the actor summed up his screen persona in one word: "pathos," a sentiment that links such disparate roles as the humiliated stay-at-home-husband/father who ends up murdering his unfaithful wife in *Happy End* and the good-for-nothing thug in *Failan*, a man who belatedly realizes that he missed out on his one chance at happiness with his Chinese paper-marriage wife after her premature death (Yoon).

This pathos-filled persona that Choi Min-sik has perfected over the course of his career is on view in *Oldboy*'s second scene, a flashback to the moments immediately preceding Dae-su's mysterious imprisonment at the hands of Woo-jin. We are inside a Seoul police station, where he awaits processing after a night of drunken revelry. Dressed in the attire of a businessman, but unkempt in a way that anticipates the physical transformation he will undergo once his fifteen years of solitary confinement are under way, Dae-su is belligerent toward the officers and attempts to urinate in the corner of the station. He curses loudly and throws a few sloppy, drunken punches at the men before ripping off his white dress shirt in a stupor. By the time he is shown wallowing in his own misery on the filthy floor, audiences will have witnessed the actor run the gamut of emotions, from paternal pride (that of a father showing a photo of his four-year-old daughter to the police staff) to childlike goofiness (as he goofily flaps some angel wings purchased as a gift for his daughter) to silent frustration (at not being able to leave this place). Such performative intemperance, diegetically fueled by alcohol, is extradiegetically demonstrative of Choi's technical mastery as a stage-trained actor willing to humiliate himself in the skin of a character for whom inebriation—like hypnosis—provides temporary respite from the problems that plague him. Significantly, in interviews director Park Chan-wook has admitted that Dae-su's rowdy behavior in this scene was Choi's idea, one of many creative contributions that the actor made during the production of *Oldboy* (Kim 100). In Choi's own words, "Words that weren't in the script came out of my mouth without thinking." This "unthinking" approach to *being* (rather than *playing*) Oh Dae-su is further hinted at in Choi's comment, "I don't remember what I said in the film. I went to the extreme."

Many performers relish going "to the extreme," and drunken scenes in particular give them the opportunity to surmount any inhibitions one might have about acting out in socially destructive ways. Choi referred to such uninhibited acting as "going with the flow," a process akin to "surfing." "I was riding the wave," he states in the Tartan DVD interview, suggesting that Park had given him the space (and long takes) to pursue his own moment-to-moment inspiration and ad lib on set during the shooting of key scenes. This includes the agonizing moment in which a desperate Dae-su, seeking to shelter his daughter from the truth of their relationship (which he has just discovered himself), kneels and begs in front of Woo-jin, breaking into their alma mater song and impersonating a dog that licks its master's shoes. This is indeed an "extreme" way of literally staging the actor-director power dynamic, or for that matter *any* asymmetrical relationship between creative personnel on a film set.[1]

Naturalism and expressionism: mixing performative modes

Choi Min-sik's complete immersion and total emotional identification with his role during production is reminiscent of the Stanislavski system practiced by mid-century Method screen actors such as Marlon Brando, Montgomery Clift, and James Dean. However, at first glance *Oldboy* is anything but a naturalistic text privileging the illusion of reality (in the manner, say, of Henrik Ibsen's plays or Classical Hollywood Cinema). Instead, it is representative of Park Chan-wook's self-reflexive style and tendency toward *excess*, characterized by unrealistic plots, larger-than-life characters, flattened depth-of-field, distorted mise-en-scène, *anime*-inspired computer graphics, captions/subtitles, and sound-image mismatches, all of which are on view in the other two films—*Sympathy for Mr. Vengeance* [2002] and *Lady Vengeance* [2005]—which, with *Oldboy*, comprise his "Vengeance Trilogy." Sharon Marie Carnicke divides screen performances and acting techniques into two camps: "Stanislavskian" modes of acting that "create character authentically by merging self with role" and "Brechtian" techniques of estrangement which "stress ambiguity of character" and "maintain [the actor's] objective opinion of the role's behavior" (Baron, Carnicke, and Tomasulo 46). *Oldboy* is a hybrid text—at once an example of East Asian art cinema and a border-crossing genre film—that merges Park Chan-wook's Brechtian aesthetics and Choi Min-sik's Stanislavskian acting techniques.

The film's opening scene is worth examining given this convergence of seemingly opposing directorial and performative strategies. *Oldboy* begins *in medias res* atop a tall building in an urban core. The first shot is an extreme close-up of a man's hand, strong yet shaking as it grasps another man's necktie. The camera tilts up to reveal the main character, framed in silhouette, with the sun behind him contributing to the shot's black-and-white visual design. The audience is unclear as to what is happening, but the second shot provides a clue, showing that the man whom we will come to know as Dae-su is holding another man at the ledge of a high-rise. Clutching a white puppy, the suicidal man is less frightened than baffled, and screams, "Who the fuck are you?" By this point, the colors of surrounding buildings and foliage as well as fleshtones have crept into the mise-en-scène, but a strong contrast between dark and light continues to predominate, contributing to the tension of this scene. Following the urgent question, the image zooms in on the main character's face, but it remains too dark to make out any of his distinctive features. Likewise, his voice is as aloof as his visage is expressionless, as he intones slowly, in syllabic stutter-steps, the following: "To talk . . . I would like . . . I said." What is untranslatable to Western audiences (i.e. not fully conveyed through subtitles) is the artificiality of Choi's speech and the distinctiveness of its delivery. His is a drawn-out, theatrical speech with unnecessary pauses, which creates a kind of "alienation effect" and calls attention to the constructedness of the film's opening scene and central character. In the real world, to save another life, a speaker would more likely say, "Don't jump," "Calm down," or "Everything is okay. Let's talk." Moreover, in the Korean cultural context, one would address another adult (especially a stranger) using the "honorific" form of speech, which Choi's loner character rudely neglects (making his dialogue sound even more unrealistic to native speakers' ears).

A similar example of expressionistic speech can be found in a scene set at Mi-do's sushi restaurant, where Dae-su first meets the young woman who will eventually become his co-investigator and lover. When he orders raw seafood, rather than confirming his order politely the protagonist confuses the young woman by telling her, "Something alive . . . I would like to eat . . . I said" (injecting unnatural pauses in the manner of his earlier rooftop scene). In his Tartan DVD interview, Choi provides a rationale for his character's strange (and estranging) style of speech, stating that, after fifteen years of solitary confinement, a person's linguistic skills would deteriorate from lack of use. In the narrative context of *Oldboy*, he found the seemingly odd-sounding dialogue "realistic." However, he still "had to say it with [his] voice and using [his] feelings" to make it believable to audiences. As written on the page, the dialogue was "vague" and, thus, he had to use his own interpretative skills in trying out different methods to deliver it persuasively.

This interview provides clues to Park and Choi's collaboration, suggesting that a combination of their skills and contrasting yet complementary visions was instrumental in the construction of Oh Dae-su's character. As Choi points out, it was *his* performative acts which materialized Park's abstract written words, *his* vocality which brought the densely packed script to "life." It was *his* emotions, facial gestures, and nonverbal tics which made a fictional character that began as a *manga* hero believable despite excessively artificial speech patterns. Park acknowledges the strength of Choi's vocal performance, which lent verisimilitude to his unrealistic dialogue: "If an unskilled actor did it, I wouldn't have been able to watch. Choi Min-sik is a classically trained [stage-to-screen] actor, so he can convince the audience that if he expresses himself awkwardly in words it's awkward because the *character* is awkward, not because he's not a good actor" (Kim 102, emphasis added). Having built up a reputation as an "actor's director" despite his predilection for baroque visuals and an overdetermined mise-en-scène that sometimes dwarfs the importance of performers (Kim 137), Park allowed Choi to unleash his creative impulses and tap into any acting techniques (including the broad, exaggerated gestures upon which he sometimes relied during days as a stage actor) that might help him personify a psychologically complex, three-dimensional action hero who defies the genre expectations associated with comic book (or *manga*) adaptations.

The actor's face and performed labor

What perhaps lingers longest in the memories of those who have seen *Oldboy*, besides Choi Min-sik's husky voice, which utters syllables in short bursts, is his chameleon-like, soulful face, which registers a plethora of emotions ranging from rage, anguish, and sadism to apathy, frivolity, and protective love. In a matter of seconds, Choi's face transitions from seriousness to silliness, from hardboiled resolution to drunken stupor, from godlike superiority to earthy humiliation. In *Oldboy*'s time-collapsing opening, two matching close-ups of Choi's face effectively take us back from the rooftop scene set in 2013 to a police station scene set in 1988. The film's ambiguous final shot fades out on Choi's emotive yet enigmatic face, which is caught between smiling and sobbing, external-izing the tormented character's inner turmoil. Speaking about Choi, Park once observed, "His face is a sight to see in close-up, because of those deep-set eyes and because his expression has curving lines and changes completely depending on the lighting . . . Choi Min-sik is an actor suited to close-ups" (Kim 102–3). With those words in mind, one can rightly claim that *Oldboy* is as much an "auteur" text for Choi as it is for Park, insofar as it inscribes, through close-ups and extreme close-ups, images of his hands and face as well as the actor's own handwriting in prison diaries. Simply put, Choi's corporeal and vocal traits are ideal conduits for Park's boundless imagination.

Of course, no discussion of *Oldboy* would be complete without mentioning the famous two-and-a-half minute, horizontally scrolling long-take shot in the prison corridor with the outnumbered protagonist, a hammer in his hand, single-handedly fighting and defeating his foes. The shot is indeed an example of Park's bravura as a filmmaker. But it is also testament to how Choi, playing a man who successfully fends off a gang of twenty thugs armed with baseball bats and knives, gave himself wholly to a part that might (literally) have broken other actors of his age (he had just turned forty before shooting began on *Oldboy*). Dae-su is a lonely warrior of vengeance who simply does not give up, despite repeated jabs, kicks, and blows to every inch of his body (and having a knife plunged into his back). Just as the comparatively youthful prison gang members think they have knocked the middle-aged intruder down for good, Dae-su rises up and resumes his fight, now with bare fists. In a panning long shot, Park's camera follows Choi's physical movements, from left to right and back again. It stops when the actor/character stops. Despite a lack of close-ups, through non-diegetic music and camera pans the audience is invited to identify with the protagonist's physical and psychological struggles against seemingly unsurmountable odds.

This shot is representative of Choi Min-sik's excessive performative labor during the film's production. For this one continuous take lasting just under three minutes, he had to undergo four months of physical training and boxing practice while memorizing sixty different action moves along with stuntmen. Three days of shooting exhausted and consumed the actor so thoroughly that he often missed the director's action cues while dozing on set. Park originally intended to break down this action scene and cut it into multiple shots (as Spike Lee does in his 2013 remake of the same title, starring Josh Brolin as the pugilistic protagonist Joe Doucett), but when he saw the master shot dailies he changed his mind. The director explains:

> Choi Min-sik ... stood up against the young stunt actors of the action school and literally fought alone ... capturing that feeling [of struggle] intact was the right thing ... Oh starts fighting heroically, but gradually begins to look exhausted. The actor really was exhausted. That wasn't acting. So you could say that the action was realistic. (Kim 105)

It is difficult to imagine a better way to praise Choi's acting than by citing Park's decision to maintain the temporal, spatial integrity of this moment and show the amateur fighter's performance in a long shot without editorial interventions. Reminiscent of the stunt-filled motion pictures of silent cinema stars Harold Lloyd and Buster Keaton, the scene is a demonstration of performative labor. But it is also a labor of love and a testament to the kind of spontaneous, actor-driven (rather than director-controlled and visual effects-laden) creativity that today's action films, which are so heavily dependent on CGI, sadly lack. The proverbial "blood, sweat, and tears" that were literally shed by Choi Min-sik during the making of *Oldboy* suggest that, beyond simply sharing "authorship" on the film, he has earned a place among the ranks of contemporary world cinema's acting masters.

Note

1. This shoe-licking scene in *Oldboy*, which Choi Min-sik improvised, brings to mind the perhaps apocryphal story of American actor Warren Beatty falling to his knees in Jack Warner's office, where he proceeded to lick the studio mogul's shoes in the hope that he would finance the long-delayed *Bonnie and Clyde* project that Arthur Penn would eventually direct in 1967 (Wrathall and Molloy 106).

Works cited

Carnicke, Sharon Marie. "Screen Performance and Directors' Visions," in Cynthia Baron, Diane Carson, and Frank P. Tomasulo, eds., *More Than a Method: Trends and Traditions in Contemporary Film Performance*, Detroit: Wayne State University Press, 2004, 42–67.

Crawford, Joan. "The Player: A Profile of an Art," in Bert Cardullo, Harry Geduld, Ronald Gottesman, and Leigh Woods, eds., *Playing to the Camera: Film Actors Discuss Their Craft*, New Haven: Yale University Press, 1998, 189–92.

Kim, Young-jin. *Park Chan-wook*. Seoul: Korean Film Council, 2007.

Wrathall, John, and Mick Molloy. *Movie Idols*. Pittstown, NJ: Main Street Press, 2006.

Yu, Sabrina Qiong. *Jet Li: Chinese Masculinity and Transnational Film Stardom*. Edinburgh: Edinburgh University Press, 2012.

Chapter 24

Maggie Cheung in *In the Mood for Love*

Gina Marchetti

Maggie Cheung's portrayal of Su Lizhen in Wong Kar-wai's *In the Mood for Love* (2000) serves as a defining moment in the actress's career. A culmination of her considerable achievements in world cinema, it stands as her penultimate major screen performance, with her career essentially ending in 2004, just as she became the first Asian actress to win top honors at Cannes for her role as a drug-addicted mother and aspiring singer in *Clean*, directed by her ex-husband Olivier Assayas. Although she began acting in kung-fu comedies starring Jackie Chan (*Police Story* and *Project A* series, 1985–92) after winning a local beauty contest, Cheung emerged in the years leading up to and immediately following the 1997 Handover, when the colony of Hong Kong changed sovereignty and became a Special Administrative Region (SAR) of the People's Republic of China, as the face of a ballooning transnational New Wave connecting Europe and Asia through the global success of new Chinese-language cinema (see Marchetti, "New Wave"). Cheung's sense of humor buoyed her in cartoon-like roles such as "Thief Catcher" in Johnnie To's *The Heroic Trio* (1993), but her weightier dramatic performances with key New Wave and Second Wave Hong Kong directors really put her on the map of world cinema and paved the way for her stellar performance in *In the Mood for Love*.

Maggie Cheung worked with many outstanding filmmakers, but her collaborations with Wong Kar-wai take pride of place in the illustrious careers of both director and star. Cheung credits Wong's *As Tears Go By* (1988), the director's first feature, with effectively starting her acting career, and she appears in many of Wong's classics including *Days of Being Wild* (1990), in which she also plays a woman named Su Lizhen, who may or may not be the same character featured in *In the Mood for Love*. Another Su Lizhen, portrayed by mainland actress Gong Li, turns up in Wong's *2046* (2004), and Cheung has a cameo reprising her Su Lizhen in flashback, filtered through Chow Mo-wan (Tony Leung)'s memory, in that film as well. The three films form a loose trilogy set in 1960s Hong Kong with *In the Mood for Love* occupying the heart of the triptych. However, the confusion over the identity of Su Lizhen in *In the Mood for Love* and the nature of her character exasperated Cheung, and, at the film's Cannes premiere, she voiced her discontent with Wong in no uncertain terms:

> Finding my character was the most difficult time, I was confused and frustrated … I thought I was doing something right and then Wong would say we'll do it all different. I hadn't been with him for a long time, not really ten years. I forgot that he works with the actors forever to develop characters, that we all have to write the film together. (Quoted in "In the Mood for Love," in *Gerald Peary: Film Reviews, Interviews, Essays, & Sundry Miscellany* (March 2000), online at www.geraldpeary.com/interviews/ghi/in_the_mood_for_love_.html.)

Although Wong started in the film industry as a scriptwriter, his working method as a director involves considerable improvisation, lengthy shoots with multiple takes, and contradictory instructions to his actors, who may be asked to portray characters in stunningly inconsistent ways. Cheung faced enormous difficulties that forced her to draw from her considerable creative and emotional reservoir to stay afloat in the film. In addition to the challenge of working without a script, she spent hours daily in makeup and wardrobe to be sewn into her form-fitting *qipao* (in Cantonese, *cheung sam*) and coiffed with period bouffant hairstyles and precisely drawn eye-liner (see further "In The Mood For Love: 21

Dresses," *Foam of Days*, 2 June 2013, online at foamofdays.wordpress. com/2013/06/02/in-the-mood-for-love-21-dresses/).

The "adaptation" of Liu Yichang's 1972 novella *Intersection* provided little help in the development of her character, since Wong used only a few quotations from Liu to set the "mood" for the film (see Luk; Deppman). A song by Shanghai chanteuse and actress Zhou Xuan, from which Wong took the film's Chinese title, "In Full Bloom" (*Hua Yang Nian Hua*), gave Cheung, whose parents also came from Shanghai, a little more information. As the song sets the mood, Maggie Cheung draws on her own understanding of what it means to be a Shanghai expatriate in the 1960s in order to supplement Shanghai-born Wong Kar-wai's reminiscences of the sights, sounds, smells, and tastes associated with these displaced people in 1960s Hong Kong (see Marchetti, "Ladies from Shanghai").

Maggie Cheung plays a woman whose life has been upended by the 1949 establishment of the People's Republic of China (PRC) in a film made in 2000, three years after Hong Kong's own reversion to mainland Chinese sovereignty. However, her performance expands beyond its Cold War historical context or even the tropes Wong uses to mark Hong Kong's "borrowed" time (Hughes 1968), such as the oversized clocks and the hotel room number 2046 set for the final full year of the "one country, two system" that shields the Special Administrative Region from full integration into the PRC's political, economic, and judicial systems. Although inhabiting an insular expatriate community, Su Lizhen also lives a cosmopolitan existence as a working woman in a shipping office, and globes, telephones, and model airplanes dot the mise-en-scène as reminders of the ways in which technology shrinks the world and brings local Hong Kong lives into conversation with global trends (for more on the global references in the film, see Cameron).

I argue that Cheung's performance provides the key to bringing coherence to the narrative by concretizing the contradictions between the Shanghai-Hong Kong society of the 1960s and the fin-de-siècle sensibilities associated with global arthouse cinema at the turn of the millennium. Cheung teeters vertiginously between the promise of twentieth-century modernity and the postmodern uncertainty of the twenty-first century by performing a role in a story that only took on its ultimate shape in the cutting room. The craft that was needed for her to make choices available to the director and still provide a convincing character for viewers in the final iteration of the film testifies to Cheung's considerable skills as a screen actress and creative talent.

Hemmed in

Duidao, the Chinese title of Liu's *Intersections*, refers to the *tête-bêche* style by which postage stamps are printed as inverted images. The intersecting characters in *In the Mood for Love* do, indeed, mirror others who appear only in profile or as shadows onscreen. A considerable portion of the plot, in fact, follows Chow Mo-wan (Tony Leung) and Su Lizhen playing the double roles of their adulterous spouses' lovers. While vicariously acting out their partners' love affair, the two appear to fall in love themselves. However, whether or not they consummate their own affair remains a mystery. As Gary Bettinson notes, the film "exploits ground-shifting tactics to render the veracity of character action uncertain" (120). Maggie Cheung, then, plays a character who performs this uncertain role leaving viewers to piece together whether any given snippet of dialogue or gesture provides access to Su Lizhen or her interpretation of her rival, Chow's wife. Added to this, Su Lizhen spends much of her free time at the movies or helping Chow write martial arts fantasies, and it becomes clear that Cheung must allow for these various layers of her performance to coexist as a palimpsest so that Su's own inability to distinguish between fantasy and reality serves as a defining element of the character.

In his analysis of *In the Mood for Love*, Stephen Teo underscores the variable play of surface and depth that Cheung brings to her portrayal of Su Lizhen as "sweet and reticent, cool and hot at the same time, intimating desire but forever repressing it" (123). Given the distanced, layered, often detached nature of Cheung's performance, the physicality of the role of Su Lizhen anchors the character, and her sensuality offsets her emotional reserve. In her examination of the film, Olivia Khoo speaks of the "spectral bodies" onscreen (235–52), and, in fact, Su Lizhen does eventually fade from Chow's life and the continuation of his story. Before she disappears, however, Maggie Cheung manages to give Su Lizhen a very concrete embodiment through gait, posture, mannerisms (facial expressions and hand gestures), and tone of voice. Cheung may have had little control over camera placement, lighting, the design of the sets, and use of locations; however, she has considerable physical control over the way she inhabits costumes, uses props, and responds to the rhythms of her fellow actors.

The actress's own roots in beauty contests and physical comedies serve her well as she taps into a global screen tradition in line with a conception of femininity that Joan Riviere calls "masquerade," John Berger terms a "sight," Laura Mulvey analyzes as "spectacle," and Judith Butler sees as gender "performativity." Simone de Beauvoir succinctly states that "one is not born a woman but rather becomes one" (301), and in this light Maggie Cheung constructs Su Lizhen as having become who she is within the social and cultural strictures characteristic of the Shanghai expatriate community of 1960s Hong Kong.

Conscious of the artifice needed to maintain her role in this precarious environment, Su Lizhen lives under the scrutiny of her neighbors. In her cramped residential quarters, small gestures take on monumental significance. Building up *"guan xi"* connections through the exchange of gifts, meals, and small favors (see Yang) binds landlords and landladies to their tenants, but also opens doors to unexpected intrusions and illicit intimacies. Declining an invitation for dinner, which Su does repeatedly, challenges these connections and arouses suspicions that she must have more pressing engagements. Her acceptance of an invitation later in the film signals her capitulation to propriety by proving she has no illicit rendezvous planned. Behind her back, her neighbors comment on the way she overdresses to go out to see a movie or buy a container of noodles. They prefer to see her as a seductress, bored with her own often-absent husband, hoping to break the monotony with an adulterous affair with her dapper neighbor.

From an older generation, Su's landlady Mrs. Suen (Shanghai-born actress and singer Rebecca Pan) and her *amah* or traditional servant (kung-fu film star Sammo Hung's grandmother and martial arts film pioneer Chin Tsi-Ang) have brought with them a specific style and set of social mores from their lives in Shanghai that run deeper than the local Wu dialect or the regional cuisine transplanted to the domestic Hong Kong setting in the film. They represent the lost possibilities of Republican China, its cosmopolitan charms (e.g., European dance halls, swank jazz clubs, and Hollywood movie palaces) as well as colonial corruption (extraterritorial privileges routinely abused by the sizeable expatriate community), its material splendor (conspicuous consumption of its wealthy elite, spectacular skyscrapers) as well as legendary depravity and decadence (triad gangsters, prostitutes, and con artists). Somewhere between the worship of money and a Christian-Confucian puritanical repressiveness about sexuality, Hong Kong's displaced Shanghai society condenses the excesses of its past into the pressure-cooker of its expatriate present with a considerable degree of disingenuousness.

Keeping up appearances and maintaining the hypocrisy that surrounds her, Su Lizhen performs the role of the perfect wife of a successful businessman for the benefit of her Shanghai landlady, while helping her boss cover up his affairs at work and exploring ways to confront her own errant husband with her handsome next-door neighbor, Chow. Su lives in an environment in which characters notice sartorial details, such as men's neckties, women's handbags, and shoes. When Mrs. Suen's *amah* catches Su in the hallway hobbling back to her own room wearing ill-fitting shoes she has surreptitiously borrowed from Chow's wife, Su is sure she has been found out. Later, after Chow takes a job in Singapore to escape his romantic woes in Hong Kong, Su visits his room unannounced and finds a pair of women's slippers under the bed. She calls him at the Singapore office but does not speak to him or have further contact with him in the narrative, assuming another woman has usurped her place in his life. At another point in the disjointed narrative, a close-up of Su's hand grasping Chow's highlights her wedding ring and wristwatch, as the power of time and the social ties of matrimony pull against mutual desire. Objects define relationships and Cheung's gestures accentuate their significance.

Perhaps more than any other element in the film, however, the *qipao* and the way Maggie Cheung wears that garment define Su Lizhen as a creature of her time and culture as well as an icon of world cinema (for more on the iconic quality of the role, see Yue). Form-fitting with restrictive high Mandarin collars and thigh-high slits to allow leg movement for walking, the *qipao* originally imitated male attire and provided physical freedom for women who gained mobility in the late-Qing/early Republican era when foot-binding vanished. However, by 1962, the garment seemed somewhat old-fashioned.[1] No stranger to wearing the garment onscreen, Cheung played silent-screen star Ruan Lingyu in Stanley Kwan's *Centre Stage* (1992), and the characterization of Su Lizhen in *In the Mood for Love* owes a debt to the *qipao* from that earlier performance. The silent screen diva came from Guangdong and moved between linguistic communities in Shanghai as Su does in Hong Kong. Ruan Lingyu lived as a partial outsider as a result, and was the subject of vicious gossip about her love life, which drove her to suicide. While carefully imitating the distinctive gestures and acting style associated with Ruan Lingyu, Cheung also mastered maneuvering in the *qipao*.

Several scenes in *In the Mood for Love* illustrate the way the *qipao* defines Cheung's performance. For example, in one instance Mrs. Suen scolds

Su—we see this from the back, in close-up—for neglecting her husband. Her rigid collar seems to strangle her and the way Cheung holds her head up in the scene speaks eloquently to the character's dignity as well as to her sensitivity to social opprobrium. The stiff high collar supports Cheung's interpretation of Su as upright as well as uptight. The *qipao* also links Su to Mrs. Suen and the older generation, since her doppelgänger rival Mrs. Chow wears dresses with a distinctively different cut. Earlier in the film, Chow passes Su on a stairway in an alley. He turns to observe her back as she glides up the stairs in her *qipao*, and, even without showing her face Cheung perfectly performs the tension expressed by her character as hemmed in by the materialistic values and constraints of the expatriate community in Hong Kong as well as being a proud Shanghai icon of eroticism, elegance, and style.

Su cleaves to the dress, reflecting her moods through its floral patterns, geometric shapes, and extravagant color palette, and Cheung deliberately exploits the limitations the garment places on her movements as well as the way it provocatively exposes her legs, accentuates her bust, hips, and buttocks, and flatters each contour of her figure. To look elegant, she must keep her head erect, her back straight, and her legs close together to avoid gaps around the "frog" fastenings used to button the flaps over the chest and unsightly slippage of the side panels around the lower limbs. Even when Su reappears in the apartment building a few years later in 1966, with a new hairdo in the company of a young boy (who may or may not be either Chow's lover's or her husband's son), she clings to her *qipao*, which serves Maggie Cheung well in her incarnation as a twentieth-century character and her presence as a twenty-first-century arthouse icon.

Performing a character in quotations

Wong Kar-wai elides the portion of the plot in which Chow Mo-wan and Su Lizhen begin to act out their spouses' illicit affair. This adds considerable confusion to a scene, early in their role playing, when Su has difficulty playing the role of Mrs. Chow. Unable to see herself as a temptress, Su cannot say the seductive words she imagines Mrs. Chow used to seduce her husband Mr. Chan (Su Lizhen's husband). Exasperated, she exclaims, "I can't bring myself to say the line." Of course, the actress Maggie Cheung may be talking about her own inability to say a line fed to her by Wong.

Later, however, Su admits that the performance process has enlightened her: "I wanted to know how it started and now I do. Feelings can creep up just like that." In addition to these self-reflexive moments when the mechanics of acting become entangled with the fiction onscreen, the film also convincingly recreates the performance styles associated with various screen and theatrical traditions.

Performing in what Rey Chow calls an "already-read text" (646) forces the actors to consider the glamour associated with Hollywood, Shanghai, and Hong Kong classical realism (see Bordwell, Staiger, and Thompson) or what Miriam Hansen sees as a style closer to "vernacular modernism" ("Mass Production"; "Fallen Women"; see also Zhang). In his book on Wong Kar-wai, Peter Brunette calls *In the Mood for Love* "Brechtian." Speaking of the characters, he states: "They live within quotation marks and prewritten lines of dialogue" (98). Awareness of performance certainly defines the characters; however, the self-conscious nature of the acting techniques owes more to a postmodern penchant for clichés rather than to the political bite associated with Brecht's epic theater. In fact, Wong claims another New Wave favorite as inspiration for the film, namely Alfred Hitchcock, and, specifically, his 1958 classic suspense-thriller *Vertigo*, also about an enigmatic woman actually playing the part of someone else in which the characters re-enact past events to unravel the mystery (noted in Teo). However, unlike *Vertigo*, which has only a single scene in which the female protagonist does not appear through the perspective of the male lead, *In the Mood for Love* allows Su Lizhen greater autonomy as a character. Maggie Cheung's acting style takes full advantage of this freedom by defining the character's inconsistencies, vulnerabilities, limitations, mysteries, and often surprising reserves of strength, flexibility, and resilience through her performance.

These self-reflexive acting techniques can be witnessed in parallel scenes in which Chow Mo-wan and Su Lizhen Su analyze their spouses' behavior. The pair re-enact the affair in one scene and plan a possible confrontation over the infidelity in another. Tony Leung and Maggie Cheung take on roles in which their characters have an enormous emotional investment, but the scenes also highlight the distance between the performers and the fiction onscreen. The positioning of the camera gives the impression of eavesdropping, underscoring the themes of surveillance, voyeurism, and alienation that run throughout the film.

Chow and Su sit opposite each other in a warm, wooden booth in a quiet, intimate restaurant serving Western-style beef and chicken steaks, which they eat with a knife and fork. As this is the second time they have been shown in the same booth eating similar food, the film sets up this dinner date as part of a routine the two repeat to commiserate about their spouses' infidelities. Chow pretends Su is his wife and puts a large dab of mustard on her plate. She dips her meat and quips that Chow's wife likes her food "hot." Cheung wears a *qipao* with an oversized daffodil in this scene, and she certainly appears to be "in full bloom" as an actress as well as a character able to shift apparently effortlessly from playing the lover to commenting bitterly on her character's circumstances. Later, the location remains the same, but the occasion has changed, noted only through the fact that Su wears a different *qipao*. They have switched roles again, and Su praises Chow's ability to imitate her spouse, saying, "You've got my husband down pat—he's a real sweet talker." Cheung's critical eye as an actress lurks beneath the surface of the remark. Under the beautiful façade and the carefully maintained appearance that dazzles onscreen, the actress creates a character with the ability to step outside herself, note the irony of her own situation in the inflection of her voice, and open her character up to the complexities of her evolving relationship with Chow, running the gamut from an angry desire for revenge to the awakening of an erotic desire for her companion in misery.

As Chow and Su pretend to be their spouses sneaking around to avoid the opprobrium of their watchful neighbors, they really do become a furtive couple trying desperately to avoid being outed and ostracized. Finding it difficult to elude the ever-present *amah* in the hallway between their apartments, Chow and Su decide to meet in a hotel room, ostensibly so that Su can help Chow edit his martial arts novel. However, they continue to re-enact the love affair of "Mr. Chan" and "Mrs. Chow" (as Wong persists in naming them, never giving us more information: we never see their faces, and hear the woman's voice only offscreen; nor are the actors even credited), vowing not to "be like them." In a scene paralleling the earlier one in the restaurant, Su sits in profile on a chair rather than in a booth. Dressed in a white and blue floral-trimmed *qipao*, she eats with chopsticks from a bowl with a similar color pattern (often associated with export porcelain, adding to a sense of Su's fragility as well as connecting her to the commercial world beyond Hong Kong's shores). Side lighting keeps her profile in partial shadow as she picks at her rice. Even though Su has a job, any decision to confront her husband about his affair may have an impact on her ability to keep rice in her bowl.[2] A man's back facing the camera appears out of focus in the next shot, and it is difficult to tell if this figure is Chow or Su's husband, who is almost indistinguishable from Chow from the rear. Su asks if he has a mistress, and the man's voice answers, "Yes." Su swipes at the air as if to slap his face, and the reverse shot shows that the man is, indeed, Chow. She complains that Chow, acting as her husband, admitted the affair too easily, and at Chow's suggestion they agree to go through the scene again.

Chow's idea of starting over serves as a reminder that Wong Kar-wai directs the scene through his surrogate Tony Leung. Wong's authorial signature of having his characters (and asking his actors to) "start over" in his previous Cannes success *Happy Together* adds another dimension to Chow's coaching. Su gives the scene a novel "reading" the second time around for Chow, so he can provide a different reaction—just as an actress might do and just as Cheung, indeed, does. The second iteration leads to a different emotional response, and Su bursts into tears, saying she did not know "it would hurt so much." Later, the mechanics of acting again come to the surface of the film when Chow comforts Su by saying, "Don't be upset ... It's only a rehearsal ... Don't cry ... This isn't real."

Given the difficulties Cheung endured making the film, her tears and the pain she expresses may have as much to do with her own working conditions as an actress as with the character's sudden pain reenacting this confrontation with an errant husband. The layers involved in this performance and the ambiguity surrounding this slippage between character and performer help to balance the film's heated emotional intensity and cool stylish detachment. Just as Maggie Cheung's Su provides a version of a woman wholly modern and cosmopolitan as well as conservative and sensitive to the small-minded gossip that surrounds her, *In the Mood for Love* creates a world that appears to be a nostalgic reflection on Hong Kong's colonial past when, in fact, it speaks to the global festival audiences of the postmodern present through elaborate intertextual citations and self-reflexive performances (for an analysis of *In the Mood for Love* as a "festival" film, see Marchetti, "*Mood*"). Playing a character hemmed in by convention but in full flower as a woman gives Maggie Cheung the opportunity to show her considerable range as a screen performer, and adds a dimension to *In the Mood for Love* that contributes to its unique allure and critical acclaim.

Notes

1. Cheung also plays a modern actress recreating a silent screen star in Olivier Assayas' *Irma Vep* (1996), where she is similarly stitched up into a form-fitting latex body suit, and again uses the costume to help define a character through clothing that dictates posture and restricts movement.
2. In much of the Asian region, "filling the rice bowl" stands in for providing for general material needs. In Mao's China, for instance, the "iron rice bowl" was a phrase used to describe the role the Communist Party played in distributing adequate resources to all.

Works cited

De Beauvoir, Simone. *The Second Sex*. Trans. Constance Borde and Sheila Malovany-Chevallier. New York: Vintage, 2011 © 1949.

Berger, John. *Ways of Seeing*. London: British Broadcasting Corporation, 1977.

Bettinson, Gary. *The Sensuous Cinema of Wong Kar-Wai: Film Poetics and the Aesthetic of Disturbance*, Hong Kong: Hong Kong University Press, 2015.

Bordwell, David, Janet Staiger, and Kristin Thompson. *The Classical Hollywood Cinema: Film Style and Mode of Production to 1960*. New York: Columbia University Pres, 1985.

Butler, Judith. *Gender Trouble: Feminism and the Subversion of Identity*. New York: Routledge, 1990.

Brunette, Peter. *Wong Kar-wai*. Urbana: University of Illinois Press, 2005.

Cameron, Allan. "Trajectories of Identification: Travel and Global Culture in the Films of Wong Kar-Wai," *Jump Cut: A Review of Contemporary Media* 49 (Spring 2007), online at www.ejumpcut.org/archive/jc49.2007/wongKarWai/index.html.

Chow, Rey. "Sentimental Returns: On the Uses of the Everyday in the Recent Films of Zhang Yimou and Wong Kar-Wai," *New Literary History*, 33: 4 (2002), 639–54.

Deppman, Hsiu-Chuang. *Adapted for the Screen: The Cultural Politics of Modern Chinese Fiction and Film*. Honolulu: University of Hawaii Press, 2010.

Hansen, Miriam Bratu. "The Mass Production of the Senses: Classical Cinema as Vernacular Modernism," *Modernism/Modernity* 6: 2 (1999), 59–77.

Hansen, Miriam Bratu. "Fallen Women, Rising Stars, New Horizons," *Film Quarterly* 54: 1 (2000), 10–22.

Hughes, Richard. *Hong Kong: Borrowed Place, Borrowed Time*. London: André Deutsch, 1968.

Khoo, Olivia. "Love in Ruins: Spectral Bodies in Wong Kar-wai's *In the Mood for Love*," in Fran Martin and Larissa Heinrich, eds., *Embodied Modernities: Corporeality, Representation, and Chinese Cultures*, Honolulu: University of Hawaii Press, 2006, 235–52.

Luk, Thomas Y. T. "Novels into Film: Liu Yichang's Tête-bêche and Wong Kar-wai's *In the Mood for Love*," in Sheldon H. Lu and Emilie Yueh-yu Yeh, eds., *Chinese-Language Film: Historiography, Poetics, Politics*, Honolulu: University of Hawaii Press, 2005, 210–19.

Marchetti, Gina. "In the Mood for Love (2000), Wong Kar-wai', in Jeffrey Geiger and R. L. Rutsky, eds., *Film Analysis: A Norton Reader*, New York: W. W. Norton, 2013, 966–89.

Marchetti, Gina. "The Hong Kong New Wave," in Yingjin Zhang, ed., *A Companion to Chinese Cinema*, Malden: Wiley-Blackwell, 2012, 95–117.

Marchetti, Gina. "Wong's Ladies from Shanghai," in Martha P. Nochimson, ed., *A Companion to Wong Kar-wai*, Malden, MA: Wiley-Blackwell, 2016, 207–31.

Mulvey, Laura. "Visual Pleasure and Narrative Cinema," in Leo Braudy and Marshall Cohen, eds., *Film Theory and Criticism: Introductory Readings*, Oxford: Oxford University Press, 2004, 837–48.

Riviere, Joan. "Womanliness as a Masquerade," *International Journal of Psychoanalysis* 10 (1929), 303–13.

Teo, Stephen. *Wong Kar-Wai*. London: British Film Institute, 2005.

Yang, Mayfair Mei-hui. *Gifts, Favors, and Banquets: The Art of Social Relationships in China*. Ithaca, NY: Cornell University Press, 1994.

Yue, Audrey. "In the Mood for Love: Intersections of Hong Kong Modernity," in Chris Berry, ed., *Chinese Films in Focus: 25 New Takes*, London: British Film Institute, 2003, 128–36.

Zhang, Zhen. *An Amorous History of the Silver Screen: Shanghai Cinema, 1896–1937*. Chicago: University of Chicago Press, 2005.

Chapter 25

Omotola Jalade-Ekeinde in *Mortal Inheritance*

Noah Tsika

"Considering how common illness is," writes Virginia Woolf, "it becomes strange indeed that illness has not taken its place with love and battle and jealousy among the prime themes of literature" (101). The same, perhaps, may be said of cinema, and particularly of Nollywood, the commercial film industry of southern Nigeria. Only a handful of well-known Nollywood films deal in any substantial way with illness: Chico Ejiro's *Onome* (1996), which concerns an unnamed, sexually transmitted disease; Ejiro's *Flesh and Blood* (1995) and Tunde Kelani's *Ayo Ni Mo Fe* (1994), which feature mental illness; Kelani's AIDS allegory *Thunderbolt* (1995); and Muhydeen S. Ayinde's *Jenifa* (2008) and *The Return of Jenifa* (2012), which deal with HIV. Occupying an influential position among these films is Andy Amenechi's 1996 melodrama *Mortal Inheritance*, which stars Omotola Jalade (now Omotola Jalade-Ekeinde, and so globally famous that she often goes by her first name only) as a young Nigerian woman suffering from sickle-cell anemia.[1] In *Mortal Inheritance*, Omotola must enact—often simultaneously—the physical pain of serious illness, the emotional pain and profound happiness of young love, the sheer tedium of an extended stay in a treatment facility, the tempestuous melodrama of a much-maligned interethnic romance, and the mixture of hope and terror that accompanies a high-risk pregnancy. Omotola's prodigious performance in *Mortal Inheritance* is thus both a classic of film acting and an index of Nollywood's understudied formal and thematic diversity, of the industry's complex combinations of minimalism and melodrama.

Mortal Inheritance opens with a series of images of Lagos at sunset, culminating in an establishing shot of Motayo Hospital, where much of the action takes place, and where parts of the film were shot. Located in Ikeja, a Lagos neighborhood, Motayo Hospital is not far from Murtala Muhammed Airport, and the screaming of jet engines contributes to a soundtrack of city life, the acoustical counterpart to obligatory images of improbably fluid traffic (rather than a more typical Lagosian "go-slow"), bustling marketplaces, and jam-packed cafés. This is the city of Jonathan Haynes's essay "Nollywood in Lagos, Lagos in Nollywood Films" (2007): "crowded, frenetic, and noisy" (139), yet carefully stage-managed to suggest glamour and mobility rather than squalor and stasis (the latter being, in reality, far more conspicuous in this place of crushing poverty and notorious traffic jams). The inescapable tensions between the "real" Lagos and that of the star-driven *Mortal Inheritance*—a function, in part, of location shooting—serve the film's theme, which involves the search for beauty and romance amid illness and suffering.

Such juxtapositions, moreover, structure the film's star-making presentation of Omotola Jalade. When we first see her, she is resting in a hospital bed, where she remains for the next several scenes. Clad in a red-and-white striped hospital gown, her hair frayed and tangled, Kemi is nonetheless strikingly beautiful, her courageous smiles obscuring the antiseptic blandness of the hospital suite. Visited by her friend Uchenna (Ifeoma Nevoh), Kemi quickly tires of having to comfort those inclined to "dance around" the topic of sickle-cell anemia, saying, "Oh, come on, Uchenna—you mean after all these years, you are still uncomfortable discussing sickle-cell anemia around me?" The poised, confident Kemi simply cannot abide her friend's efforts to employ indirection, wincing whenever Uchenna euphemistically refers to sickle-cell anemia as "this thing," and impatiently shaking her head whenever the other woman is unable to complete her sentences for fear of causing offence. "Look, Uchenna," Kemi continues, "I was born a sickler. My genotype is SS [homozygous]. And because I cannot change that fact, I have learned to live with it and accept it. Simple. I expect my family and friends not to have pity, but to show understanding."[2] Kemi is thus in the awkward position of having to educate others about her condition, but she does so with a plain-speaking aplomb that puts the stuttering Uchenna to shame. "But, you know, not many people talk about sickle-cell anemia like you do," Uchenna protests, further defining Kemi's exceptionality. Not only ravishingly beautiful despite her condition, Kemi is also unafraid of speaking the truth about sickle-cell anemia, even going so far as to refuse pity and to critique those "sicklers" who do not share her candor but who "should—and confidently, too." No mere killjoy, Kemi is willing to punctuate her prescriptive disquisition with a few humorous, self-deprecating asides that complicate her character while showing Omotola's range. Asked when she will be discharged from the hospital, she blurts, "Girl, if I had my way, right now!" Reverting to a long shot for this particular exchange, Amenechi reveals Omotola's expert body language, especially her expressive use of her left arm to indicate Kemi's deliberately comic eagerness to escape the confines of her hospital bed.

Intercut with this opening exchange between Kemi and Uchenna are shots of a handsome young man waiting impatiently outside the hospital. Wearing fancy sunglasses and a bright yellow blazer over a black T-shirt, the man finally leaves his car and enters the facility in search of Uchenna, his sister. He enters Kemi's room in an exasperated state that only subsides when he catches sight of the patient herself. Though running late for an appointment and clearly irritated with his sister, the young man, Chike Morah (Fred Amata), is struck—almost immobilized—by Kemi's face, and says, "You have the most beautiful smile I have ever seen!" Encountering the ravishing Kemi, Chike can well understand why his sister has spent forty-five minutes in an otherwise dreary hospital room, and his departure is marked by a sense of wonder. Kemi, for her part, shares Chike's sense that their introduction is a special experience, one that seems to portend romance: this, the film suggests, is love at first sight.

Following a brief scene establishing the relative wealth of Kemi's parents, Chief and Mrs. Johnson (Kunle Bamtefa and Abiola Atanda), *Mortal Inheritance* reunites the star-crossed lovers in the site of their first encounter. This time, Chike elects to remain in Kemi's hospital room for longer than a few minutes, and the two casually get to know one another before Chike, a stockbroker, is forced to race to yet another business meeting. "I'm obviously detrimental to your timing!" Kemi jokes, in a line that underscores the film's status as a melodrama, one especially attuned to temporal tensions as well as to the power of romantic love to eclipse ethnic and class prejudice. While melodrama has long been at home in a Nollywood committed to the mode as a vehicle of social critique, it is, somewhat paradoxically, precisely as a melodrama that *Mortal Inheritance* manages to demonstrate its productive deviation from Nigerian films in which religion (typically some form of Christianity) holds sway. Rooted in earthly romance and immune to divine intervention (which is absent from the film, in any case), this deviation pays considerable dividends for Omotola Jalade, marking her emergent star persona as a key determinant of Kemi's narrative magnetism.

For her first proper date with Chike, Kemi, now just released from hospital, sheds her drab gown and dons a striking leopard-print shirt and matching hat, a fashion statement that seems to signal her ferocious confidence and lust for life. Meeting Chike for lunch at a popular Lagos café, Kemi fills him (and us) in on her job in advertising. Befitting her stated commitment to telling the painful truth, she immediately confesses that nepotism has played a considerable part in her career success: her father is the chairman of the company for which she works. But Kemi is quick to emphasize her professional talents, telling Chike that she has a "knack for turning out good copy." Asked to elaborate, Kemi rattles off a colorless summary of the advertising industry, Omotola here telegraphing Kemi's disinterest by looking down at her food and letting her voice trail off. Regaining her spark, Kemi begins to tease Chike, calling him a gambler ("Isn't that what you stockbrokers do?") and using her fork as a prop with which to point at him. Nervously insisting that his job is a bit more respectable than Kemi suggests, Chike decides to change the subject by offering a particularly tone-deaf compliment. "You don't look like a sickler," says he, "I mean, if you hadn't told me, I would never have known." "It's not written on our foreheads," Kemi replies, her acidulous tone highlighting Chike's faux pas. Proceeding to speak with her mouth full of food, Kemi lightens the mood with the self-deprecating claim that she eats "for two." "And I also take my medications very seriously," she adds, shaking her knife at Chike as if to underscore the gravity of this remark. Shifting from solemnity to silliness in the space of a single sentence, Omotola makes Kemi the mercurial object of Chike's romantic obsession, a strong-willed young woman who keeps him on his toes.

When Chike says that he wishes that they could "do this more often," Kemi's sarcastic response ("Do *what* more often—sit around some crowded restaurant holding hands?") not only confirms her acerbic tendencies but also serves to temper the sappy montage that follows, a romantic interlude set to Maya Atta's original song "Until I Met You," in which Kemi and Chike are seen shopping together, dining together, meeting on the beach for an afternoon kiss (with Omotola wearing outsized sunglasses and looking very much the major movie star that she would soon become), and finally enjoying a horseback ride at dusk. Like the film's title song (by Nigerian gospel singer Onos Brisibi, who sings in a slow, mournful style), Atta's "Until I Met You" suggests the influence of the Nigerian-born Sade, an immensely popular artist in Nigeria, a conspicuous source of national pride, and a favorite of the character Omotola plays in the later Nollywood film *Last Flight to Abuja* (Obi Emelonye, 2012). Evoking Sade's brand of smooth jazz and neo-soul, the song helps to position *Mortal Inheritance* as a particular kind of modern romance, one rooted (like many of Sade's own songs) in a woman's strength and agency.

It turns out Kemi will need every bit of her built-in fortitude to cope not merely with sickle-cell anemia but also with family pressures that threaten to overwhelm her. When Mrs. Johnson, who wants to set her only daughter up with a wealthy, well-connected young man, discovers that Kemi is dating someone she met at the hospital, she declines to hide her disappointment, eventually warning Kemi against "going out too much" and "getting worn down." "I just want you to slow down a little," Mrs. Johnson adds, to which the headstrong Kemi replies, "Being a sickler doesn't mean I can't go out!" Before offering a complementary scene of Chike with his own parents, *Mortal Inheritance* shows him sitting down with a male friend his own age, boasting about his "new love," to whom he refers as "the one." When he hears that Kemi is the daughter of a wealthy executive, the friend cries, "You just hit the gold mine!"—to which Chike responds with a testy reminder that he is not interested in Kemi's pedigree, much less in her money.[3] Affirming that her father "could have been a truck driver, for all I care," Chike reverts to citing Kemi's exceptional qualities, which seem to transcend language. "I want the whole world to meet her," says he. "When you see her, you will understand."

Forced to confront the biases of his anxious, controlling Igbo mother (Obiageli Molebe), Chike turns to his Igbo father (Ted Mukoro) for support. While Mrs. Morah blindly capitulates to tribalism, rejecting the Yoruba Kemi out of hand (and thus embodying the historical tensions between these two major ethnic groups, so often pitted against one another in Nollywood melodramas), the more even-tempered, self-consciously "modern" Mr. Morah, still subject to tribalism, is at first worried only about his son being "burdened" by a "sickler," chiding his wife for her "provincialism." "Woman, this is the nineties!" he shouts, comically. Then, addressing no one in particular, he observes, "With all her education, she's still *so* tribalistic!" Commenting, in an aside, on tribalism and its negative effects on social life in Nigeria, Mr. Morah introduces the theme of interfamilial conflict that connects *Mortal Inheritance* to an obvious urtext like *Romeo and Juliet* (a not uncommon source of thematic inspiration in African cinema, as films as diverse as Mohamed Camara's *Dakan* (1997) and Boubacar Diallo's *Julie et Roméo* (2011) attest). An act of recycling of the sort that Mattias Krings examines in his book *African Appropriations*, this perceptible connection to *Romeo and Juliet* is also interesting for reasons that have little to do with cross-cultural translation. Watching the allusive *Mortal Inheritance* unfold, one cannot help but recognize one of the film's most striking departures from its Shakespearean source. For unlike the pubescent Juliet, Kemi is, as she herself avers, "a grown woman" (with a thriving career, to boot) whose self-sufficiency is signaled through every narrative development.

But while Kemi is very much an adult, the woman playing her is not. Just sixteen when she auditioned for the role, Omotola Jalade exhibits a preternatural self-possession as the twenty-four-year-old Kemi. Indeed, rarely has a performer so much younger than her role managed to rise to the occasion with such assertiveness, cauterizing any hint of inexperience while communicating a longstanding familiarity with physical pain. It is precisely this familiarity that, in fact, makes Kemi seem considerably older than her twenty-four years—a further indication of Omotola's achievement as a mere teenager.

On another date with Chike, Kemi displays her maturity by pre-empting his flirtatious talk with a few comments about sickle-cell anemia and its implications for reproduction. Insisting that Chike determine his genotype, Kemi indicates her investment in their romantic relationship, in her interest in possibly having children with this man (provided, she implies, he is not a carrier of the sickle-cell gene himself). Chike, who is four years Kemi's senior, doesn't seem to understand her point, asking, "Are you afraid of infecting me?" Kemi calmly considers this facetious question for a moment, then answers, "In a way, yes." She explains her fear not merely of "passing on" sickle-cell anemia but also of experiencing the emotional pain of parenting a child affected by the condition. "When I was a kid," she says, "every crisis that I had was a nightmare—not for me, I could handle the pain, but for my parents." As Kemi, Omotola's singular challenge is thus to believably embody an extreme strength capable of seeing the character through the considerable aches, pains, and blood transfusions associated with sickle-cell anemia, and to calmly articulate this strength through dialogue designed to cement the woman's exceptionality. Cannily reserving displays of hubris for Kemi's more boldly flirtatious moments, during which the character taunts Chike with her astonishing sexual confidence, Omotola delivers lines like "I could handle the pain" and "I've had to learn to be tough" in a matter-of-fact manner, refusing to embellish them with any intimations of arrogance. After all, as Kemi claims, the chronicity of sickle-cell anemia has taught her simply to "plow on," unencumbered by a dangerous investment in the possibility of remission. Habituated to her condition, Kemi cannot describe it in self-aggrandizing or even self-pitying terms, and she tires of having to justify her pragmatic approach to those who want to weep for her (and to congratulate themselves for their sentimentality). But however much she may recoil at the sight of such "sappiness," Kemi is well aware of the strain that her condition has placed on her parents in particular: "Our loved ones—they suffer the most." Reminding Chike that sickle-cell anemia "can be managed" (particularly with access to the sort of treatment that the affluent Kemi enjoys), still, "it's not the best inheritance to give one's kids." Finally comprehending Kemi's point—or, perhaps, willfully ignoring it—Chike simply says, "I love you too much to let a small thing like sickle-cell come between us."

The subject of sickle-cell anemia allows *Mortal Inheritance* to exceed some of the familiar frameworks of Nollywood melodrama. In typical tales of intergenerational conflict, the Nigerian mother is presented as a source of intense procreative pressure (particularly on her daughter-in-law), hounding her children to make babies of their own and even intervening with elaborate fertility rituals. Here, however, both sets of parents fear the reproduction of sickle-cell anemia and exhort the young couple to refrain from procreating. At first, Kemi's father elects to shame his daughter, accusing her of acting "like a slut." "I assumed that at your age, you would have more sense than you are showing!" he shouts, "Have you ever heard of the word 'accountability'?" It is that very word that will acquire a powerful meaning later in the film, guiding Kemi to "do the right thing," as she says. At this point, however, Kemi must meekly listen to her domineering father as he denounces Chike, chiding the young man for dropping his daughter off at the gate "like a common tart," rather than formally introducing himself to her parents and requesting entrance into their lavish home. If Chief Johnson is by far the more abusive of Kemi's parents, Mrs. Morah, Chike's mother, is the one member of the young man's family who most openly objects to his budding relationship. Visiting the Morah home for dinner one night, Kemi compliments Mrs. Morah's soup and asks for the recipe, to which the older woman snaps, "That is the problem with you girls of nowadays—everything has to come out of a book!" At first, Kemi's own mother is scarcely more supportive, prompting Kemi to complain about her "nagging" ways, her incessant questioning of her daughter's taste in men: "It's always 'Who is his father?' 'What is his job?' 'What is his tribe?'" Chike's mother proves no less likely to pose offensive questions about ethnicity, and at one point tells her son, "I don't want you to marry a Yoruba girl!" Firmly believing that "there's nothing that prayer cannot do," Mrs. Morah hopes to "pray away" Chike's attachment to Kemi—another indication of Kemi's almost otherworldly power, at least as viewed by those who fear her. Explaining to Chike that "sickle-cell is an inheritance with no hope of a cure in the near future—a *mortal inheritance*," Mrs. Morah provides not only the film's title (with an accompanying surge of dramatic music on the soundtrack) but also another reason for Chike to reject her exhortations by dismissing both tribalism and fatalism. Arguing that if his relationship with Kemi fails "it will not be because she's a sickler, or because she's Yoruba," Chike underscores his lover's potential to transcend illness, ethnic prejudice, and the odious interventions of family.

Among the challenges for Omotola as a performer was mitigating not just the exceptionalism but also the didacticism written into the role of Kemi and rooted in the character's efforts to clarify the medical as well as social contours of sickle-cell anemia. Not only does Kemi frequently recapitulate the condition's complex symptomatology—episodes of intense pain, bone degeneration, and severe anemia—but she is also made to model ways of living with it, of thriving in spite of it. Co-written by Amenechi and Bond Emeruwa, who spent months researching sickle-cell anemia, the script for *Mortal Inheritance* evinces their commitment to raising awareness about the condition at a time when an estimated 25 per cent of Nigeria's adult population carried the sickle-cell trait. With sickle-cell anemia appearing to disproportionately affect Yoruba populations in southwestern Nigeria, Amenechi and Emeruwa gave Kemi an ethnic identity that served the broader function of signaling the condition's historical impact on the Yoruba. While Omotola herself, who was born in Lagos State, is of Ondo descent (the Ondo people represent one of the largest Yoruba subgroups), she has frequently been called upon to portray ethnically different Igbo characters (as in Chineze Anyaene's 2010 film *Ijé*). She was cast in *Mortal Inheritance* on the basis not of a particularly pronounced ethnic persona but of her debut performance in Reginald Ebere's *Venom of Justice* (1995). Belonging to the first generation of Nollywood performers to bypass Nigerian television in pursuit of film stardom, Omotola learned the craft of acting while working on Ebere's set, making her follow-up performance in *Mortal Inheritance*—only her second film—all the more impressive.

Produced alongside a spate of partly foreign-financed Nigerian television programs about public health education (such as the long-running *I Need to Know* (1997–2002), sponsored by the United Nations Population Fund), *Mortal Inheritance* was one of the first Nollywood films to follow the pedagogical formula, which may explain its modest commercial success. Lacking the more saleable elements of witchcraft, cultism, urban crime, and professional intrigue, *Mortal Inheritance* may well have seemed too close in tone to topical programs being aired on Nigerian television in the mid-1990s. And yet its influence can be felt on other star-making vehicles, such as Ayinde's *Jenifa*, a melodrama about HIV/AIDS that made Funke Akindele a household name, and Desmond Elliot's *Holding Hope* (2010), which introduced audiences to Abiola Segun Williams, who plays a cancer patient. Like these later films, *Mortal Inheritance* ends with a title card that, for readers of English, reiterates the melodrama's subject: "This film is dedicated to the families of the millions of individuals who have died or are afflicted with sickle-cell anemia. We share your fears, your pains, your tears and your trauma. By a twist of fate, destiny has thrust upon you a *Mortal Inheritance*."

While undeniably being part of an emerging cycle of Nollywood films that, with their bourgeois characters, ignore or deny the contemporaneous reality of Nigeria's disappearing middle class (a disappearance bluntly described in the opening title card of Tade Ogidan's multi-part political drama *Owo Blow* (1995–8)), *Mortal Inheritance* occasionally alludes to Nigeria's economic crises, as when Chief Johnson quizzes Chike on current events and the nervous young man blurts that he believes that the "country's political problems are economically related." But more than class issues, the film is invested in addressing sickle-cell anemia and its effects on Kemi. Contentedly cleaning Chike's apartment while the young man is out playing tennis with colleagues, Kemi suddenly becomes exceedingly fatigued. Lying down on the couch to await his return, Kemi is soon writhing in agony. When Chike enters, tennis racket in hand, Kemi breathlessly describes the intensity of her joint pain, saying that she cannot move her legs. In perhaps her most impressive moment in the film, Omotola communicates Kemi's torment with a startling, even terrifying intensity that seems to blur, if not obliterate, the line between performer and role. (As a prodigious display of the physical suffering of serious illness, Omotola's work here ranks with Harriet Andersson's performance as the cancer-ravaged Agnes in Ingmar Bergman's *Cries and Whispers* (1972)). Later, her pain having subsided somewhat, Kemi breaks up with Chike. "I love you too much to drag you through all of this," she says, "My mind is made up. I've thought about this a lot." The tranquility with which she delivers these lines belies her inner turmoil, which leads her to attempt suicide in her childhood bedroom. Just as Kemi is about to swallow a bottle of pills, however, there is a loud knock on her door, causing her to spill the pills on the floor. "You want to kill yourself over an Igbo!" Mrs. Johnson cries, her tribalism knowing no bounds.

After developing nausea and dizziness, Kemi goes to see her doctor, who informs her that she is three months pregnant, and that an abortion—what Kemi wants, given her struggles with sickle-cell anemia—would be more dangerous than carrying the baby to term (a dubious assertion, one that perhaps reflects the filmmakers' concerns regarding Nigerian federal censorship). There follows a sequence that suggests the influence of American romantic comedy: a montage of images of Kemi and Chike, all culled from happier times, leads to a ludicrously bad date that Kemi's parents have set up, with a wealthy young man who bloviates about traveling the world (he's "just back from Switzerland" and on his way to South Korea). It is while she is out with this fool that Kemi re-encounters Chike (apparently on his own bad date). The two quickly get back together, with Chike proposing marriage during a moment of post-coital bliss. Kemi tells him that she is pregnant, news that quickly travels to Mrs. Morah, who accuses Kemi of having "trapped" her son, just like a "typical," manipulative Yoruba woman. The rest of the film is devoted to the couple's efforts to evade the renewed pressures of their parents. Chief Johnson evicts Kemi, whom he calls an "unrepentant slut" because she refuses to travel to England for an abortion, while Mrs. Morah remains vigorously opposed to interethnic marriage. Their loving task now is to figure out how to prepare for the birth of their child. Kemi's doctor reminds her to take folic acid and warns her about the dangers of stress.

But Kemi cannot resist staging a confrontation with her cruel father, hoping that he has had a change of heart. Discovering that he has not, Kemi collapses in her mother's arms, and starts bleeding shortly thereafter. Rushed to the hospital, Kemi undergoes an emergency C-section, giving birth to what her doctor calls a "bouncing baby boy," before lapsing into a coma. The film ends with Chike by her side, restating the qualities that make Kemi so exceptional, and that serve as reminders of Omotola's signal brilliance in the role. Whispering, "You changed my whole world," Chike watches as Kemi gradually awakens from her coma. Her first words—"Please don't cry"—encapsulate the character's uncommon equanimity and capacity to soothe her high-strung lover, even as they speak to the viewer's helpless emotionality in the face of Omotola's poignant achievement.

Notes

1. The image of Omotola appearing with this chapter is in some respects different in format from other images in this book. Like most Nollywood films made in the 1990s—a time when the Nigerian film industry relied exclusively upon consumer-grade camcorders and VHS cassettes—*Mortal Inheritance* betrays what Brian Larkin calls "an aesthetic of piracy." It is important to keep in mind that the film has never "looked good"—or even traditionally "filmic"—owing to an analog mode of production that according to conventional Western metrics appears "illicit" or otherwise substandard, its grainy images (and complete absence from the DVD market) making it impossible to provide a "pristine" digital frame enlargement.—Eds.

2. Kemi is referring here to hemoglobin SS, the most common type of sickle-cell disease. She has two sickle-cell hemoglobin genes, and no normal hemoglobin genes. Thus, her blood cells can clump together, causing a blockage of blood flow and many other symptoms.

3. Chike's ostensible naïveté about class helps the film emphasize the exceptionality of Kemi/Omotola: she's so "special" that she effectively distracts from class, as does every reputable movie star.

Works cited

Haynes, Jonathan. "Nollywood in Lagos, Lagos in Nollywood Films," *Africa Today* 54: 2 (Winter 2007), 131–50.

Krings, Matthias. *African Appropriations: Cultural Difference, Mimesis, and Media.* Bloomington: Indiana University Press, 2015.

Larkin, Brian. *Signal and Noise: Media, Infrastructure, and Urban Culture in Nigeria.* Durham, NC: Duke University Press, 2008.

Woolf, Virginia. "On Being Ill," in David Bradshaw, ed., *Virginia Woolf: Selected Essays,* New York: Oxford University Press, 2008 © 1926, 101–10.

Chapter 26

Gael García Bernal in *The Motorcycle Diaries*

Dolores Tierney

The Mexican actor Gael García Bernal has most recently been in evidence as a young migrant hunted by a murderous anti-immigration vigilante in Jonas Cuarón's *Desierto* (*Desert*, 2015), as a love sick husband, trying to win his wife back in Roberto Schneider's *Me estas matando Susana* (*You're Killing Me Susana*, 2016) and as Rodrigo de Souza, the conductor of the fictional New York Symphony in the Amazon Prime series *Mozart in the Jungle* for which he won a Golden Globe in 2016. Rodrigo is Bernal's most mainstream role to date in a career that has otherwise been characterized by high-profile parts in a newly reinvigorated Latin American and global art cinema. From his film debut in Alejandro González Iñárritu's critically and commercially successful *Amores perros* (*Love's a Bitch*, 2000) followed by major roles in three of the region's other highest grossing films—Alfonso Cuarón's *Y tu mamá también* (*And Your Mother Too*, 2001), Carlos Carrera's *El crimen del padre Amaro* (*The Crime of Father Amaro*, 2002) and Walter

Salles's *Diarios de motocicleta* (*The Motorcycle Diaries*, 2004)—Bernal has become a Hollywood and global star despite working in mostly in Latin American and European art and mainstream projects.

A key factor in Bernal's Latin-American stardom, as it has evolved over time, is the connection to political and cultural activism which is evident both in the roles he chooses to play—Zahara, a transsexual woman abused and silenced by the Catholic Church in *Bad Education* (2004), Maziar Bahari, the *Newsweek* journalist imprisoned as a spy in Iran in *Rosewater* (2014), a mythical Kai fighting developers who seek to destroy the jungle in Northern Argentina in *El Ardor* (*The Burning*, 2014) and a young Ernesto "Che" Guevara in the moment of his awakening to radical consciousness in *Motorcycle Diaries* (for which he was nominated for a BAFTA)—and also in his dedication to particular political causes, most notably highlighting the fate of Central American and Mexican migrants crossing into the US.[1] Another key factor in his stardom, as it has been constructed in his transnational, global, and Latin American star text, is his sex appeal which, determined by a fusing of his Latin Americanness with an imagined post-1960s political radicalism particular to the continent's history of revolution, reflects a more classical version of Latin stardom: the sensual *Latin lover* (see Tierney et al.).

In the role of Guevara, "the foremost icon of a virile Latin American revolutionary tradition" the activism and sex appeal associated with Bernal's stardom come together (De La Mora 164). However, because of the coincidence in some aspects between the actor and the historical figure he is called on to perform—Bernal is, like Guevara a "transnational social act[or/ivist]" (165)—we might be tempted to read Bernal's performance of Guevara according to Stanislavskian expressive-realist assumptions in which "good acting" is "true to life" and at the same time expressive of the actor's authentic "'organic' self" (Naremore 2). These assumptions, and the line between Bernal and Guevara that they imply, limit the consideration of Bernal as a "crafts[person]" shaping his performance for a varied audience and figure him instead as an activist "personalit[y]" acting out a part that embodies his own public self (1).[2] What further complicates the analysis of Bernal's performance in *The Motorcycle Diaries* is the consideration of the auteurist strategies of its director, Walter Salles. Trained as a documentary filmmaker, Salles makes use, throughout his films, of a realist filmmaking style and improvised scenes with non-professional actors. Particularly in *The Motorcycle Diaries* this is as a means of offering a critical realist perspective.

Although, as this chapter will explore, the improvised scenes in *Diaries* might bear the trace of Bernal's personal investment in contemporary social issues in Latin America, his performative moments can also be mined to pin down the discursive strategies of a *Mexican* actor playing Guevara the *Argentine* proto-revolutionary.[3] A final complication to deconstructing Bernal's performance (rather than analyzing it via the expressive-realist route) comes from its institutional position and the stylistic implications of that position. A multinational co-production between Chile, Peru, Argentina, the United Kingdom, France, Germany, and the United States, including funding and support from the American independent sector (Focus Features, and Robert Redford, founder of the Sundance Institute, who commissioned the project), the film is simultaneously embedded in a number of different contexts that again encourage an expressive-realist reading proper to the confrontational aesthetics shared by Latin American art cinema and American independent cinema. Bearing in mind these different challenges to the task of deconstructing Bernal's performance into a set of "culturally and historically specific codes" (Dyer 135), rather than reading them as a reflection of his "personality" (Naremore 3), this chapter will explore how his acting and personal discursive strategies come together in the film with the twin aspects of his stardom (Latin sensuality and politics), elements of Salles's realist filmmaking style, and the film's mise-en-scène to create Guevara as a "ravishing revolutionary."

The Motorcycle Diaries presents a twenty-three-year-old Ernesto Guevara De La Serna, still in medical school and prior to his transformation into continental revolutionary. In January of 1952, together with his friend Alberto Granado (Rodrigo De la Serna),[4] a biochemist, he leaves from his native Buenos Aires with the plan to travel 8000 kilometers through Argentina, Chile, Peru, and Colombia to the Guajira Peninsula in Venezuela, all on Granado's Norton 500cc motorcycle *La Poderosa* (The Mighty One). Playing the young Guevara traveling through Latin America on a trip that is often credited with "politicizing the future revolutionary" (Ryan Gilbey, "The Truth Behind a Revolutionary Road Movie," *The Sunday Times*, 18 October 2009, 10), Bernal is called on to perform as a proto-Che, to act out an anticipation of who his character will become: the charismatic Marxist revolutionary who will fight in the Cuban Revolution (1956–9), become a member of its Revolutionary government, and subsequently take part in anti-colonialist insurgencies first in the Congo and then Bolivia, where he will be executed by

CIA-backed forces in 1967. In addition to foreshadowing the known qualities of the historical figure of whom he is playing a younger version, his acting must also register the part that the journey played in his becoming "El Che." It must effectively exteriorize a process of gradual political awakening.

One of the ways the film figures middle-class Guevara's in-process radicalization and future continental and global struggle on behalf of subaltern subjects, as well as his legendary charisma (Niess 58) is shown in Bernal's variety of encounters on the road with contemporary working-class and indigenous individuals. These encounters, which dramatize Guevara's growing consciousness about class and race, are often unscripted and improvised between Bernal, De la Serna, and characters played by local, non-professional actors (who, met by the filmmaking crew during the filmmaking process, were spontaneously incorporated into the shoot (Geoff Andrew, "Walter Salles," Interviewed at the National Film Theatre, *The Guardian*, 26 August 2004, online at theguardian.com; Williams 13). One such encounter takes place when Guevara and Granado are a quarter of the way into their journey at a market in Temuco, Chile. The scene begins with a shot of a woman ladling food onto a plate. We pan as she hands it to Granado who is sitting at her stall eating. Then we cut to a woman handing a cup of *mate* (a tea drunk in the Southern Cone) to someone who is revealed by the panning camera to be Guevara. He says thank you and asks her name, then introduces himself as Ernesto, shaking her hand. He soon afterward asks a male stall holder to hold up a fish and eagerly takes a photograph, and responds to the stall holder's question, "Are you traveling?" with a casual, "Yes, we are. We're the ones with that beat-up bike over there," as he gestures out of frame. He asks the female owner of a seafood stall the name of different kinds of seafood. Bernal's low-level acting here (in opposition to more ostentatious acting at other points) and the naturalistic acting of some of the stall owners who appear slightly stiff but interested (the man) and giggly (the woman) as they speak to Ernesto, emphasize Guevara's being one of the people. Bernal simultaneously enacts Guevara's personal charm while underlining that this is a largely improvised encounter (albeit based around a dramatic premise). Location and camera work also re-enforce the sense that this is a spontaneous interaction: the scene is filmed mostly in a master shot with occasional whipping between Ernesto and the stall holders as they exchange conversation rather than following a more classical organization of the scene via a shot/reverse shot sequence. Bernal's acting includes plenty of smiling and blocking, which has him turn away deliberately from the camera but towards the individuals with whom he is interacting. Emphasized is Guevara's burgeoning interest in the lived experience of his fellow Latin Americans.[5]

More improvised encounters involving non-professional actors take place in Cuzco, Peru, former capital of the Incan Empire. Guevara and Granado meet Don Néstor, an indigenous boy, whom Guevara describes in a letter to his mother (that we hear in voiceover) as "a very wise man, and our official guide." Néstor gives Guevara and Granado a tour around the ancient city. They ask him about the walls, and he points out the ones made by the Incas and those made by "los *incapazes*" ("the in-cables," that is, the Spaniards). They laugh in response to his joke. Their broad smiles registering delight in this witty child. Emphasizing how they are deferring to Néstor and his greater knowledge, Guevara and Granado are seen initially walking behind him, but then Bernal is seen beside him as he takes them around the city. That Guevara is listening to Néstor represents a shift in his previous somewhat callous behavior towards "ordinary individuals" (which had shown him quick to tell a Mapuche man that his cow was going blind) and consequently indicates how he is learning from and growing in his journey.

In another improvised encounter in Cuzco, Guevara listens to two Quechua women talk about their lives (the younger translating for the older, who, we learn, does not speak Spanish, having been unable to get an education because she had to work as a child), then engages in ritual sharing and consumption of coca leaves. Bernal sits on the road in front of the women, while they sit on the curb. Consequently he has to look up at them slightly as he listens to them and they hand him the coca leaves. As with his position behind Néstor in the previous scene, his physical position and the way he holds his body (leaning slightly, shoulders down) both facilitate our sense of him listening and learning. He is respectful of those he interacts with and also physically places himself at the level of, or below, those who have been subordinated in society. The position and movement of the 16mm hand-held camera also reinforces the sense that this is an improvised encounter (hovering alternately over the shoulders of one speaker and then the other). A sense of improvisation is further supported by the awkwardness of the non-professional actors, the boredom of a child who lolls at his mother's side whilst she talks, and the intrusion of ambient sound (a child crying or a dog yawning). That Bernal is paying strict attention is indicated by his furrowed brows as he listens to the testimony of these two women (and later to that of a tenant farmer who has been evicted from his farm by the landowner). The fact that his lines sometimes accidentally overlap with those of the non-professional actors constructs a sense of Guevara's eagerness to learn from these people about social exclusion and injustice in Latin America, but also adds to the sense of spontaneity of the moment (inasmuch as his is an unpolished performance). That Bernal is a transnational social actor, committed to social causes and political action, gives his role as Guevara an even greater resonance, and in moments like these a sense that as a person he, too, is invested in what ordinary people are telling him about their lives.

After meeting with real people, and other moments of significance to the broader project of showing Guevara's education and externalizing his gradual political awakening, Bernal engages in lots of what Naremore calls "affective thinking" (71). He makes Guevara's thoughts "visible to the camera" by showing the character staring into space, writing in his journal, or writing letters to his mother (72). These moments are often accompanied by Guevara's thoughts rendered through voiceover. For instance, at Machu Picchu in Peru, site of one of the last Inca strongholds to withstand the invasion by the Spanish conquistadores, he ponders the vastness of Incan knowledge yet how they were still powerless in the face of the invaders who had gunpowder. This foreshadows Guevara's own taking up arms in the struggle against (global) imperialism, as does a comment he makes to Granado, who has jokingly presented the idea of starting an Indo-American revolution: "A revolution with no gunshots? You're mad."

These moments of Bernal listening to ordinary people and engaging in affective thinking are juxtaposed significantly with much more overt reactions to "episodes of exploitation of the poor by the powerful" (Williams 17). One of these moments takes place during a visit to the American-owned Chilean copper mine at Chuquicamata. Initially, in a series of shots/reverse shots, the camera registers Guevara watching as the foreman chooses the workers for the day. His folded arms and his narrowed gaze as he witnesses the manhandling of the mixed-race or indigenous workers attest to his increasing disapproval and anger at their rough treatment. Direct sunlight casting Bernal's eyes in shadow further underlines a sense of Guevara's growing anger. When the foreman orders Guevara and Granado away, Bernal walks quickly towards him pointing his finger and saying, "Don't you see those people are thirsty? Why don't you give them something to drink?" His aggressive gestures at this point suggest he is ready to enter into a physical confrontation with the foreman, and Granado has to pull him away. But as the truck carrying the workers and foreman pulls off, Bernal expresses Guevara's frustration and outrage by reaching down and throwing a stone at it, shouting, "¡*Hijo de puta!*" ("Son of a bitch").

Guevara's outburst at the mine significantly takes place the day after he and Granado have met a Chilean man and his wife in the Atacama Desert. Like the evicted farmer, the miner and his wife are also displaced in their own country, thrown off their land because they are communists. Sitting around the fire and interacting with them, Bernal is again mostly listening, his face set in a grim expression as they recount that they are being pursued by the police. In response to the question about why he and Granado are traveling, Bernal shrugs his shoulders apologetically as he explains that they are traveling not for work but for the sake of traveling. It is a key moment of awareness of his own class and racial privilege, and also of the structural inequalities and lack of freedoms experienced by working-class individuals across Latin America. After making this admission, Bernal takes off his blanket and hands it to the miner and his wife. He inhales sharply after doing this to register how cold it is in the desert at night. Giving his blanket away when it is so cold is figured as a gesture of solidarity but also as an act that foreshadows Guevara's future willingness to sacrifice his own comfort for others. The night scene in the desert also cements his emergence as a future leader. The sense of that change was prefigured by Ernesto and Granado's walk into the Atacama Desert, which emphasized the struggle of his quest (shots of Bernal's feet trudging over the dusty ground and of De la Serna stumbling along behind him) also showed Guevara striding in the lead.

The period detail of costume, hairstyle, and artifacts contributes to a sense that encounters like the one in the Atacama Desert, and the ones in Cuzco and Temuco, are realistic and "authentic" representations of Guevara's experiences during his travels in 1952 (Williams 13). Bernal wears his hair short, in a typical 1950s style, and also often wears a tight white T-shirt and battered leather coat. But Bernal's acting also gives Guevara's encounters an immediacy and a sense that the film is casting forward into the present and examining the past in the context of contemporary (ongoing) struggles. In addition to presenting Bernal as a proto-Che, the film's improvised encounters with contemporary individuals highlight how the places Guevara and Granado visited, the lives of the people they met and spoke with, and "the structural problems of poor distribution of land and wealth" have not changed significantly since the 1950s (Andrew; Williams 16).[6]

Ultimately, Guevara reaches an end point both in his attempt to "explore the continent of Latin America" (as expressed in the opening scene) and in his journey to political awakening. This end point is marked at the Leprosarium at San Pablo where he and Granado go to work as interns. At the goodbye/birthday party given by the hospital staff, Bernal gives a speech which, taken verbatim from *Notes on a Latin American Journey*, the published versions of Guevara's diaries, ends with a toast:

> We believe, and after this journey more firmly than ever, that the division of America into unstable and illusory nations is a complete fiction. We are one *mestizo* race from Mexico to the Magellan Straits. And so, in an attempt- to free ourselves from narrow minded provincialism, I propose a toast to Peru and to a united America.

Bernal's speech to the hospital workers (doctors, nurses, and nuns, again played mostly by non-professionals) voices some of the conclusions that ultimately led Guevara to take up arms in a revolution he envisaged spreading across the region. Underlining the portentousness of Bernal/Guevara's speech are frequent cuts to De la Serna/Granado who is watching gravely, as if coming to the realization that his friend will be pursuing radical politics rather than a medical career. Bernal's manner during the speech is sometimes playful (he jokes about his recently showcased inability to dance)[7] but becomes increasingly serious and political. He uses his glass as what Naremore calls an "expressive object," to give thanks (raising it as if in a toast) but also, at the climax of the speech, to emphasize his key points: that Latin America is a single entity (raising it to indicate Mexico at the northernmost tip and lowering it to indicate the Magellan Straits) (83).

After the speech, Guevara takes on the arduous and dangerous task of swimming at night across the Amazon, which separates the two halves of the Leprosarium: medical staff on one side and patients on the other. The film presents Guevara's swim as symbolic of his newfound knowledge that his place is now with "the people." Bernal's performance during the swim, fighting for breath, stopping and slowly slipping under the water, emphasizes the physical struggle the asthmatic Guevara goes through in undertaking such a long swim, and prefigures the future physical struggles he will experience during the different conflicts in which he fights, in Cuba, the Congo, and Bolivia.[8]

Bernal's performance as Guevara actually includes very few moments that explicitly exploit his personal sensuality, limiting it almost exclusively to moments early on when he visits his upper-class girlfriend Chichina (Mia Maestro) and looks longingly and desirously towards her. Instead, the film invests highly political moments with sensuality, folding Bernal's sex appeal into a desire for social justice and revolutionary change. These include his tremulous political intensity during speeches about Pan Latin American Unity, his quivering rage at the mistreatment of the day workers at the mine, and his casual flirting with the women in the market at Temuco and the nurses at the Leprosarium. What is most significant about these moments is how he exaggerates and exploits what in part are his personal qualities (star status/fame) to perform Guevara as a "ravishing revolutionary."

Notes

1. As evidenced by his 2017 Oscars protest against President Trump's planned US/Mexico border wall while he was presenting the award for best documentary short. He has forwarded his dual political and cultural activist interests through founding, with fellow Mexican star Diego Luna and producer Pablo Cruz, CANANA, a Mexican production company whose numerous social issue films have included projects dealing with immigration.
2. Another problem of the expressive-realist paradigm is the suggestion that it is possible to ever portray a "real" Che Guevara, given that, as Eva Bueno points out, "the 'Real Che' is as unrecoverable as all legendary myths" (108).
3. The Argentine accent Bernal adopts is also a key part of the realistic representation of Guevara. Bernal has often been called on to use a range of Hispanic accents: Spanish in *Bad Education* and Chilean in *No!* (2012) and *Neruda* (2016). His Argentine accent in *Motorcycle Diaries* has been read as competent but flat. This flattening in cultural terms relates in part to the geocultural position of the intended spectator of *Motorcycle Diaries* in an international art-cinema audience that may or may not be Spanish speaking.
4. The actor is in fact a distant cousin of Che Guevara.
5. These moments of interaction with real individuals also bear the trace of Bernal, the international actor, trying to act like a normal person traveling in Latin America. The awkwardness of the people he meets at the market points to his "stardom": they know they are meeting a "real" movie star.
6. In a 2004 interview, Salles recounts: "I didn't go ahead on *Motorcycle Diaries* before realizing that the reality of South America in 2002/03 is very similar to that described by Ernesto Guevara in his book. The structural problems are pretty much the same,

of bad distribution of land and wealth. I realized that our own adventure within the continent could somehow mirror what happened to them on a very small scale, and that improvisation was possible" (Andrew).

7. Bernal can actually dance (unlike Guevara)!

8. The diaries themselves make very little of the swim, which is figured more as a physical challenge that Guevara wanted to attempt than as a symbolic crossing to the "other side." The swim also took place in the daytime and there was no welcoming party to receive him at the patients' camp as in the film. Guevara actually arrived several miles down river.

Works cited

Bueno, Eva. "'Motorcycle Diaries': The Myth of Che Guevara in the Twenty-First Century," *Confluencia* 23: 1 (2007), 107–14.

De la Mora, Sergio. *Cinemachismo: Masculinities and Sexuality in Mexican Film*. Austin: University of Texas Press, 2006.

Dyer, Richard. *Stars*. London: Routledge, 1998.

Guevara, Ernesto. *Motorcycle Diaries: Notes on a Latin American Journey*. Minneapolis: Ocean Press, 2003.

Naremore, James. *Acting in the Cinema*. Berkeley: University of California Press, 1988.

Niess, Frank. *Che Guevara*. London: Haus Publishing, 2003.

Tierney, Dolores, Victoria Ruétalo, and Roberto Carlos Ortiz. "New Latin-American Stardom, the Local/Global Stars of Latin American Cinema's New 'Golden Age': Sônia Braga, Gael García Bernal, and Ricardo Darín," in Marvin D'Lugo, Ana Lopez, and Laura Podalsky, eds., *Routledge Guide to Latin American Cinemas*, New York: Routledge, forthcoming 2017.

Williams, Claire. "*Los diarios de motocicleta* as Pan-American Travelogue," in Deborah Shaw, ed., *Contemporary Latin American Cinema: Breaking into the Global Market* Lanham, MD: Rowman & Littlefield, 2007, 11–27.

The cast

Victor Sjöström [Victor David Sjöström] (Arjäng, Sweden, 20 September 1879–3 January 1960, Stockholm). *Wild Strawberries (Smultronstället)* was released in Sweden, 26 December 1957.

Emil Jannings (Rorschach, Switzerland, 23 July 1884–2 January 1950, Strobl, Austria). *The Blue Angel (Der Blaue Engel)* was released 1 April 1930 in Berlin and 5 December 1930 in the United States.

Charles Laughton (Scarborough, Yorkshire, 1 July 1899–15 December 1962, Los Angeles, California). *Hobson's Choice* was released in the United Kingdom, 19 April 1954.

Nikolai Cherkasov [Nikolai Konstantinovich Cherkasov] (Saint Petersburg, 27 July 1903–14 September 1966, Leningrad, Russia). *Ivan the Terrible Part I* was released 30 December 1944; completed in 1946, *Part II* was held back for political reasons until 1958.

Peter Lorre [László Löwenstein] (Rózsahegy, Austria-Hungary, 26 June 1904–23 March 1964, Los Angeles). *M* was released in Germany, 11 May 1931.

Anna Magnani (Rome, 7 March 1908–28 September 1973, Rome). *The Golden Coach (Le Carrosse d'or)* was released 3 December 1952 in Italy and 27 February 1953 in France.

Alec Guinness (Paddington, London, 2 April 1914–5 August 2000, Midhurst, West Sussex, England). *Last Holiday* was released 3 May 1950. Sir Alec Guinness held the Order of the Companions of Honour and was a Knight Commander of the Most Excellent Order of the British Empire.

Ingrid Bergman (Stockholm, 29 August 1915–29 August 1982, London). *Stromboli* was released in the United States, 15 February 1950 and in Italy, 8 October 1950.

Toshirô Mifune [Mifune Toshirô] (Qingdao, Shandong, China, 1 April 1920–24 December 1997, Mitaka, Tokyo, Japan). *Throne of Blood (Kumonosu-jô)* was released in Japan, 15 January 1957.

Setsuko Hara [Hara Setsuko] (Yokohama, Kanagawa, Japan, 17 June 1920–5 September 2015, Kanagawa, Japan). *Tokyo Story (Tôkyô Monogatari)* was released 3 November 1953.

Marcello Mastroianni [Marcello Vincenzo Domenico Mastroianni] (Fontana Liri, Lazio, Italy, 28 September 1924–19 December 1996, Paris). *8½* was released 14 February 1963. Marcello Mastroianni was a Knight Grand Cross.

Jeanne Moreau (Paris, 23 January 1928–31 July 2017, Paris). *The Bride Wore Black (La mariée était en noir)* was released 17 April 1968.

Michel Serrault [Michel Lucien Serrault] (Brunoy, France, 24 January 1928–29 July 2007, Équemauville, Calvados, France). *La cage aux folles* was released in France, 25 October 1978.

Madhubala [Mumtaz Jehan Dehlavi] (Delhi, 14 February 1933–23 February 1969, Bombay). *Mughal-e-Azam (The Emperor of the Mughals)* was released 5 August 1960.

Michael Caine [Maurice Joseph Micklewhite] (b. Rotherhithe, London, 14 March 1933). *Alfie* was released in the UK, 24 March 1966 and in the US, 24 August 1966. Sir Michael Caine is a Commander of the Most Excellent Order of the British Empire.

Amitabh Bachchan [Amitabh Harivansh Rai Shrivastava Bachchan] (b. Allahabad, India, 11 October 1942). *Deewaar (The Wall)* was released 24 January 1975.

Catherine Deneuve [Catherine Fabienne Dorléac] (b. Paris, 22 October 1943). *The Umbrellas of Cherbourg (Les parapluies de Cherbourg)* was released 19 February 1964.

Jean-Pierre Léaud (b. Paris, 28 May 1944). *Stolen Kisses (Baisers volés)* premiered 14 August 1968 in Avignon and was released in France, 4 September 1968.

Isabelle Huppert [Isabelle Anne Madeleine Huppert] (b. Paris, 16 March 1953). *The Piano Teacher (La pianiste)* premiered at Cannes, 14 May 2001 and was released 5 September 2001 in France and 11 October 2001 in Germany.

Emma Thompson (b. Paddington, London, 15 April 1959). *The Remains of the Day* was released 5 November 1993.

Tilda Swinton [Katherine Matilda "Tilda" Swinton] (b. London, 5 November 1960). *I Am Love (Io sono l'amore)* premiered 5 September 2009 at the Venice Film Festival.

Denis Lavant (b. Neuilly-sur-Seine, 17 July 1961). *Holy Motors* premiered at the Cannes Film Festival, 23 May 2012, and was released in France, 4 July 2012 and in Germany, 30 August 2012.

Choi Min-sik (b. Seoul, 22 January 1962). *Oldboy (Oldeuboi)* was released 21 November 2003 in South Korea and screened at the Cannes Film Festival, 15 May 2004.

Maggie Cheung [Maggie Cheung Man-yuk] (b. British Hong Kong, 20 September 1964). *In the Mood for Love (Faa yeung nin wa)* was released 29 September 2000.

Omotola Jalade-Ekeinde [Omotola Jalade] (b. Lagos, Nigeria, 7 February 1978). *Mortal Inheritance* was released in 1996. Omotola Jalade Ekeinde is a Member of the Order of the Federal Republic of Nigeria.

Gael García Bernal (b. Guadalajara, Jalisco, Mexico, 30 November 1978). *The Motorcycle Diaries (Diarios de motocicleta)* premiered at the Sundance Film Festival, 15 January 2004, was screened at Cannes, 19 May 2004, and released 24 September 2004.

The contributors

Ulka Anjaria is Associate Professor of English at Brandeis University. She is the author of *Realism in the Twentieth-Century Indian Novel: Colonial Difference and Literary Form*, and editor of *A History of the Indian Novel in English*. She has published in scholarly journals as well as *Economic and Political Weekly*, *Scroll.in*, and *The Boston Review*. She received an ACLS/Charles A. Ryskamp Fellowship in 2014 for her current book project on representations of the contemporary in Indian literature, film, and television.

Janet Bergstrom, Research Professor of Cinema & Media Studies, UCLA, specializes in archivally-based, cross-national studies of émigré directors such as F. W. Murnau, Jean Renoir, Josef von Sternberg, Alfred Hitchcock, and Fritz Lang as well as French/Francophone directors Chantal Akerman and Claire Denis. She has published five film historical documentaries on DVD, most recently *Josef von Sternberg—Salvation Hunter* (Edition Filmmuseum, Austrian Film Museum, Vienna) with Sternberg's *The Salvation Hunters* (1924).

Hye Seung Chung is Assistant Professor of Film and Media Studies at Colorado State University. She is the author of *Hollywood Asian: Philip Ahn and the Politics of Cross-Ethnic Performance* (2006) and *Kim Ki-duk* (2012). Her latest book, *Movie Migrations: Transnational Genre Flows and South Korean Cinema*, is co-authored with David Scott Diffrient.

Corey K. Creekmur is an Associate Professor of Cinematic Arts, English, and Gender, Women's & Sexuality Studies at the University of Iowa. His research and teaching interests include American and Indian cinema and comics. He is the general editor of the "Comics Culture" series for Rutgers University Press.

Adrian Danks is Acting Deputy Dean in the School of Media and Communication, RMIT University, Melbourne. He is also co-curator of the Melbourne Cinémathèque and was an editor of *Senses of Cinema* from 2000 to 2014. He is the editor of *A Companion to Robert Altman* and is currently writing several books including a monograph devoted to *3-D Cinema*, a co-edited collection on the nexus between Australian and US cinema, and a volume examining "international" feature film production in Australia during the postwar era.

Nick Davis is Associate Professor of English and Gender and Sexuality Studies at Northwestern University, where he teaches and researches in the areas of narrative film, queer theory, feminist and gender studies, and American literature. His book *The Desiring-Image: Gilles Deleuze and Contemporary Queer Cinema* theorizes a new model of queer cinema based more on formal principles than identity politics, drawing heavily on Deleuzian philosophies of film, desire, and unpredictable production. He has published essays on Julie Dash's *Illusions*, Alfonso Cuarón's *Y tu mamá también*, John Cameron Mitchell's *Shortbus*, William Friedkin's *The Boys in the Band*, and James Baldwin's *Blues for Mister Charlie*, among other texts. Since 1998, he has published film reviews and essays at www. NicksFlickPicks.com and is now a contributing editor at *Film Comment*.

David Desser is Emeritus Professor of Cinema Studies, University of Illinois. He has authored and edited eleven books, most recently *Small Cinemas in Global Markets*. His best-known works include *The Samurai Films of Akira Kurosawa; Eros plus Massacre: An Introduction to the Japanese New Wave Cinema; Reframing Japanese Cinema: Authorship, Genre, History; American Jewish Filmmakers; The Cinema of Hong Kong: History, Arts, Identity;* and *Ozu's Tokyo Story*. He is a former editor of *Cinema Journal* and founding co-editor of the *Journal of Japanese and Korean Cinema*. He provided commentary on Criterion DVD editions of *Tokyo Story* and *Seven Samurai*. He also did the program notes along with audio introductions and extensive commentary on the films of Kiju Yoshida from Arrow Films in the UK.

David Scott Diffrient is Professor of Film and Media Studies and William E. Morgan Chair of Liberal Arts (2013–16) at Colorado State University. He is the author of *M*A*S*H* (2008) and *Omnibus Films: Theorizing Transauthorial Cinema* (2014) as well as the editor of *Screwball Television: Critical Perspectives on Gilmore Girls* (2010). His latest book, *Movie Migrations: Transnational Genre Flows and South Korean Cinema*, is co-authored with Hye Seung Chung.

Victoria Duckett is a lecturer in Screen and the Director of Entertainment Production at Deakin University, Melbourne. She has published extensively in the areas of European film and performance. She is on the editorial board of *Nineteenth Century Theatre and Film* and *Feminist Media Histories.* Her book, *Seeing Sarah Bernhardt: Performance and Silent Film* made the list of Choice Outstanding Academic Titles for 2016.

Jason Jacobs is Professor of Film and Television Studies and Head of the School of Communication and Arts at the University of Queensland. He was a lecturer in the Department of Film and Television Studies at the University of Warwick (1994–2000), and Griffith University (2000–8). His books are *The Intimate Screen*; *Body Trauma TV*; and *Deadwood.* He co-edited the collection *Television: Aesthetics and Style,* and has published essays on issues of judgment and value in television studies.

Alexia Kannas teaches Cinema Studies at RMIT University, Melbourne. Her research explores cult and alternative cinemas, cinematic modernism, cross-cultural reception, and music and sound in film and television. She is the author of *Deep Red* and is currently completing a monograph on the Italian giallo film.

Marcia Landy is Distinguished Professor Emeritus in English/Film Studies with a secondary appointment in the French and Italian Department at the University of Pittsburgh. Her books include *Fascism in Film: The Italian Commercial Cinema 1931–1943* (1986); *British Genres: Cinema and Society, 1930–1960*); *Imitations of Life: A Reader on Film and Television Melodrama*; *Film, Politics, and Gramsci*; *Queen Christina* (with Amy Villarejo); *Cinematic Uses of the Past* ; *The Folklore of Consensus: Theatricality in the Italian Cinema 1930–1943*; *Italian Film*; *The Historical Film: History and Memory in Media*; *Stars: The Film Reader* (with Lucy Fischer); *Monty Python's Flying Circus*; *Stardom Italian Style: Screen Performance and Personality in Italian Cinema*; and *Cinema and Counter-History.* Her essays have appeared in *Screen, Journal of Film and Television, Quarterly Review of Film and Television, Historical Journal of Film, Radio, and Television, KinoKultura,* and *boundary 2.*

Gina Marchetti is the author of *Romance and the "Yellow Peril": Race, Sex and Discursive Strategies in Hollywood Fiction*; *From Tian'anmen to Times Square: Transnational China and the Chinese Diaspora on Global Screens*; *The Chinese Diaspora on American Screens: Race, Sex, and Cinema*; and *Andrew Lau and Alan Mak's INFERNAL AFFAIRS—The Trilogy.*

Douglas McFarland is retired Professor of English and Classical Studies at Flagler College, Saint Augustine, Florida where he taught Renaissance literature, Latin, and Greek. He has published on sixteenth-century English and French literature, as well as numerous articles and chapters on film. He is the co-editor (with Wesley King) of *John Huston as Adaptor*.

Adrienne L. McLean is Professor of Film Studies at the University of Texas at Dallas, and the author of *Being Rita Hayworth: Labor, Identity, and Hollywood Stardom*; and *Dying Swans and Madmen: Ballet, the Body, and Narrative Cinema*. She is the editor of *Behind the Silver Screen: Costume, Makeup, and Hair*; and *Cinematic Canines: Dogs and Their Work in the Fiction Film*, and co-editor of *Headline Hollywood: A Century of Film Scandal* as well as a ten-volume book series, "Star Decades: American Culture/American Cinema", with Murray Pomerance. Her own entry in the series is *Glamour in a Golden Age: Movie Stars of the 1930s*. She has published numerous essays in film journals and anthologies, and is working on a monograph on makeup and hair in the studio era.

Jerry Mosher is Chair and Associate Professor in the Department of Film and Electronic Arts at California State University, Long Beach. He has published numerous essays on actors and screen performance, and is completing a book manuscript titled *Bigger Than Life: Fat Actors in Classical Hollywood Cinema*.

Karla Oeler teaches in the Film and Media Studies Program in the Department of Art & Art History at Stanford University. Her research and teaching interests include film history, theory, and criticism. She is the author of *A Grammar of Murder: Violent Scenes and Film Form*. Her work has appeared in *Cinema Journal, The Journal of Visual Culture*, and *Slavic Review*.

R. Barton Palmer is Calhoun Lemon Professor of Literature at Clemson University, where he also directs the World Cinema program. Palmer is the author or editor of more than forty volumes devoted to various film and literary subjects, and he serves as the general editor of book series at six academic publishers. He is also the editor of the *South Atlantic Review* and the *Tennessee Williams Annual Review*.

Homer B. Pettey is Professor of Film and Comparative Literature at the University of Arizona. He serves as Founding and General Editor for three scholarly book series on global film studies. He is co-editor (with R. Barton Palmer and Steven M. Sanders of *Hitchcock's Moral Gaze*, and has co-edited a forthcoming volume on biopics and British national identity. He has two other collections in progress: *French Literature on Screen* and *Emerging Cold War Film Genres*.

Murray Pomerance is Professor in the Department of Sociology at Ryerson University and the author, editor, or co-editor of numerous volumes. His most recent books are *The Man Who Knew Too Much*; *A King of Infinite Space*; and *Moment of Action: Riddles of Cinematic Performance*. He edits the "Horizons of Cinema" series at SUNY Press and "Techniques of the Moving Image" series at Rutgers University Press.

Sergio Rigoletto is Associate Professor of Italian and Cinema Studies at the University of Oregon. He has published on comedy, European television, and contemporary queer cinema. He has co-edited (with Louis Bayman) *Popular Italian Cinema*, and is the author of *Masculinity and Italian Cinema: Sexual Politics, Social Conflict and Male Crisis in the 1970s*.

Kyle Stevens is Assistant Professor of Film Studies at Appalachian State University. He is the author of *Mike Nichols: Sex, Language, and the Reinvention of Psychological Realism*, and his essays have appeared in *Cinema Journal, Critical Quarterly, Film Criticism*, and *World Picture*, as well as several edited collections. He is also editor-in-chief of *New Review of Film and Television Studies*.

Aaron Taylor is Associate Professor of New Media at the University of Lethbridge. He is the editor of *Theorizing Film Acting*, and his essays on performance, film authorship, and comics have been published in numerous journals, including *Cinema Journal, The Journal of Popular Culture, Velvet Light Trap, [in]Transition, Journal of Adaptation and Performance, Quarterly Review of Film and Video, Studies in Documentary Film*, and *The Journal of Film and Video*. His work also appears in several anthologies, including *Make Ours Marvel; The Works of Tim Burton; Millennial Masculinity; Acting and Performance in Moving Image Culture; Stages of Reality; Great Canadian Film Directors*; and *Rethinking Disney*.

Alison Taylor is a Senior Teaching Fellow at Bond University, Queensland and author of *Troubled Everyday: The Aesthetics of Violence and the Everyday in European Art Cinema*.

Dolores Tierney is Senior Lecturer in Film Studies at the University of Sussex. She has published widely on Latin(o/a) American film including articles in *Screen, Quarterly Review of Film and Video, New Cinemas, Studies in Hispanic Cinemas* and *Film, Fashion and Consumption*; the monograph

Emilio Fernandez; and two co-edited anthologies, *Latsploitation, Exploitation Cinema and Latin America*; and *The Transnational Fantasies of Guillermo del Toro*. She is currently completing a monograph on Latin America's transnational cinemas.

Noah Tsika is Assistant Professor of Media Studies at Queens College, City University of New York. His books include *Nollywood Stars: Media and Migration in West Africa and the Diaspora*; and *Pink 2.0: Encoding Queer Cinema on the Internet*. His book *Traumatic Imprints: Cinema, Military Psychiatry, and the Aftermath of War* is forthcoming.

Timotheus Vermeulen is Associate Professor in Media, Culture and Society at the University of Oslo. His current research interests are metamodernism, contemporary film and television aesthetics (in particular, space) and the philosophy of the "as-if". He is joint editor with Alison Gibbons and Robin van den Akker of *Metamodernism: History, Affect and Depth after Postmodernism*; and together with Martin Dines edited *New Suburban Stories*. In 2014 he published the monograph *Scenes from the Suburbs*.

Index